EVERYDAY
INequaLities

Critical Inquiries

Books are †

B

EVERYDAY
INEQUALITIES

Critical Inquiries

Edited by
Jodi O'Brien
and Judith A. Howard

Foreword by Mary Romero

Library of Congress Cataloging-in-Publication Data

Everyday inequalities : critical inquiries/edited
   by Jodi O'Brien and Judith A. Howard.
      p.   cm.
      Includes bibliographical references and index.
      ISBN 1-57718-121-2 (acid-free paper). – ISBN 1-57718-122-0 (pbk.
   : acid-free paper)
      1. Equality–Case studies.   2. Marginality, Social–Case studies.
   3. Prejudices–Case studies.   4. Dominance (Psychology)
   5. Difference (Psychology)   I. O'Brien, Jodi.   II. Howard, Judith
   A.
   HM146.P74   1998
   305–dc21   97-47398
                                                            CIP

British Library Cataloguing in Publication Data

A CIP catalogue record for this book is available from the
British Library.

Typeset in 10½ on 12½ pt Palatino by Newgen Imaging Systems (P) Ltd, Chennai.

Printed in Great Britain by MPG Books Ltd, Bodmin, Cornwall

This book is printed on acid-free paper

Contents

Contributors

Jennifer Eichstedt is an Assistant Professor at Mary Washington College. Her primary research and teaching interests are racism, whiteness, identity, and popular culture. In addition to analyzing multiculturalism and the maintenance of white privilege she is involved in two research projects. The first analyzes the involvement of Euro-Americans in anti-racism activism. The second explores museum-plantations in the South and their relation to racialized ideologies.

Anthony J. Freitas is a doctoral student in communication at the University of California, San Diego. His current research addresses issues of membership and representation in political, economic, and cultural arenas with a focus on sexuality, race, and gender. In particular he is interested in the use of biological and marketing discourses in discussions of economic, political, and social rights.

Tom Gerschick is currently an Assistant Professor of Sociology at Illinois State University. Tom's research and publications focus on how men with physical disabilities create and maintain self-satisfactory gender identities in a culture that does not recognize them as men. A second research agenda involves undergraduate education, especially the role of multiculturalism in education. His future research will compare the gender formation and maintenance processes of women and men with physical disabilities. He is active in the Disability Rights Movement and is temporarily able bodied.

Douglas Hartmann is an Assistant Professor of Sociology at the University of Minnesota. He received his BA and MA degrees from the University of Chicago and his PhD in Sociology from the University of California, San Diego. Most of his work involves the intersections of politics and culture. The piece that appears in this volume is drawn from a larger project tentatively titled: "Golden

Ghettos: The Cultural Politics of Race, Sport, and Civil Rights in the United States Since 1968." Hartmann is also the co-author (with Stephen Cornell) of *Ethnicity and Race: Making Identities in a Changing World* (Pine Forge Press, 1997).

Frances S. Hasso recently (1997) received her PhD in Sociology from the University of Michigan, Ann Arbor, where she is currently teaching. Her dissertation examines the relationship between nationalism, gender, and feminist discourses in twentieth-century Palestine.

Melissa S. Herbert received her PhD in Sociology from the University of Arizona in 1995. She is Assistant Professor of Sociology at Hamline University in Saint Paul, Minnesota where she teaches courses in gender, sexuality, and social psychology, as well as a first year seminar on HIV/AIDS. She is completing a book with New York University Press, *Camouflage Isn't Only for Combat: Gender, Sexuality, and Women in the Military*. Other research interests include lesbian friendships and issues of gender and sexuality in sport.

Jocelyn Hollander is Assistant Professor of Sociology at the University of Oregon. Her research focuses on how gender, race, class, and sexuality are constructed through everyday interaction, and on the consequences of these constructions for both individuals and social structures. Her current project explores the gendered construction of vulnerability and dangerousness in conversation. She is the co-author, with Judith A. Howard, of *Gendered Situations, Gendered Selves: A Gender Lens on Social Psychology* (Sage, 1997).

Judith A. Howard is Professor of Sociology at the University of Washington. She teaches and does research on the micro-level underpinnings of social inequalities, emphasizing cognitions – stereotypes, attitudes, expectations – and how they shape and are shaped by social interactions and macro-level social institutions. She is currently co-editing *SIGNS: Journal of Women in Culture and Society*, and is one of four co-editors of the *Gender Lens* book series. Both positions ensure her acute awareness of the complexity of social inequalities.

Lori Kendall is a doctoral candidate in Sociology at the University of California, Davis. Her research explores the performance of race, class, and gender identities online. She is currently writing her dissertation, an ethnography of the mud BlueSky, focusing on the intersections of masculinities and computer technology.

Shelley Kowalski is a doctoral candidate at the University of Oregon. Her areas of interest include gender, visual sociology and culture, and inequality. Her dissertation is on the formation of the photographic world and the gendering of photographic styles.

Laura M. Lopez is a doctoral candidate in the Department of Sociology at the University of Michigan, Ann Arbor, where she also received her MA degree. She is a native of San Antonio, Texas, where she received a BA in English and Sociology from Incarnate Word College in 1991. She left to do graduate work in 1992. For the past year, she has been living in both Austin and San Antonio doing dissertation research on the Texas farm worker movement (1996–83).

Jodi O'Brien is an Associate Professor of Sociology at Seattle University where she teaches courses in theory, methodology, inequalities, social psychology, and sexual politics. Her research focuses on the cultural politics of marginal identities and communities. She is interested in fostering sociology as a transgressive practice for students and the public. She is co-author of *The Production of Reality: Essays and Readings in Social Interaction* (Pine Forge Press, 1997).

Carl Edward Pate is a PhD candidate in the Department of Sociology at the University of Washington. His substantive areas of study are race and ethnic relations, stratification, and social psychology. His specific interests are affirmative action, segregation, the black community, how racism and discrimination play out on both a societal level, and in everyday life, and the necessity for complicating and problematizing understandings of and approaches to studying race, ethnicity, oppression, and equity.

Martha L. Shockey is an Assistant Professor of Sociology at St Ambrose University. Her courses reflect her interest in the study of deviant behavior, social inequality, social problems, and social psychology. She is particularly interested in the lived experiences of women as they relate to gender issues in the conventional and unconventional labor markets of US society. Her previous research on women's part-time employment has appeared in the *Journal of Business and Psychology* (1944) and *Women and Work: A Handbook* (1996). She remains actively involved in her research with Quad City prostitutes and has future plans to examine childhood prostitution in the Quad Cities.

France Winddance Twine is an Associate Professor of Women Studies at the University of Washington in Seattle and an Assistant Professor of Sociology at the University of California at Santa Barbara. She teaches feminist theory, critical race theory, and feminist media studies. Her research is concerned with intersection of racial, gender, and class inequalities across and within several national contexts including Brazil, Britain, and the United States. Her recent work includes co-editorship of a special issue of *Signs*, "Feminisms and Youth Cultures" (forthcoming, March 1998). She is the author of *Racism in a Racial Democracy: The Maintenance of White Supremacy in Brazil* (Rutgers University Press 1997) and co-produced an award winning documentary entitled "Just Black?: Multiracial Identity in the U.S." (Filmmakers Library, New York).

Linda Van Leuven is a graduate student in sociology at the University of California at Los Angeles, and a former seller and dispenser of fine eyewear. In the meantime, she studies sexualized interactions, and how people manage relational boundaries in body/image-oriented service occupations. Her dissertation is titled: "When Frames Collide: Personal Work and the Negotiation of Relational Boundaries."

Foreword

Mary Romero

Several years ago I was asked to write a report evaluating an existing academic program on the study of diversity. The study was in response to both student and faculty dissatisfaction with the implementation of "diversity requirements" and other efforts made in developing a multicultural curriculum – or what many have defined as the study of "difference." After interviewing interested members of the campus community, it was clear that the controversy was most heated around what category of people identified as "different" should be included. What racial ethnic groups should be taken into account? Should these groups be introduced as pan-ethnic groups or as individual communities as they exist in the local community? Where will persons from multiracial backgrounds appear in this diverse curriculum? Should the focus be solely on domestic "difference" or include the difference/diversity that we Americans find in international groups? Should Jews and Muslims be included? And if so, should other religious groups? Should gays and bi-sexuals be included? How about the groups who are differently abled? The proliferation of groups and topics was clearly a challenge to any committee attempting to establish a "diversity" requirement.

In addition to the discussions about who should be included, who was most competent to teach courses, and what department should house the study of difference, there was also a strong criticism about the politics of "diversity" courses. The mostly widely accepted position is the liberal stance that declares "love sees no color." To many, diversity has come to mean a smorgasbord of culture, preferences, and abilities – all coming together to celebrate "difference." However, several groups speaking from the voice of "difference" have indicated that while the emphasis on difference and diversity may be inclusive, the outcome has not always resulted in equality or justice. Rather than experiencing the multicultural curriculum as "inclusive," students of color described a new form of "othering" in the classroom. Many reported that the consequence of this new attention to issues of difference and diversity was either celebrating "differences," which more often than not functioned to establish forced dichotomies and over-generalizations between "whites and persons of color," "gays and straights," "women and men"; or identifying commonalities between groups and erasing "differences" as insignificant or nonexistent, such as color-blindness – "love sees no color." Many students of color described the courses as voyeuristic journeys through their communities and histories in which they were expected to serve as cultural ambassadors.

Multicultural training and special sensitivity programs in universities and the corporate world would have clearly not eliminated racial tensions. Nor have they drastically reshaped the racial ethnic or gender composition of persons holding the top positions in corporate America or administrative posts in public institutions. The revelation of the tape-recorded meeting of Texaco executives demonstrated that diversity training has done little to eliminate racism from the "hearts and minds" but has provided new metaphors (i.e., colors of jellybeans) to "do discrimination." Well-meaning affirmative action officers and diversity trainers have reinforced notions of cultural deterministic models of "difference" by sensitizing new corporate and university employees to be "tolerant" of different cultural definitions of time, space, and familial relations. It is not surprising that many college students, their parents, and workers view the end of affirmative action as a release from tolerating differences that were always considered as inferior and special privileges.[1]

I see sociological theories as going through similar debates and controversies as those experienced in establishing an inclusive working and learning environment. However, the focus on "difference" is certainly not a new theorizing venture but has a long tradition in American sociology. Theorizing about marginalized individuals frequently began from the context of a social problem. Rather than setting out to study the social, political, and economic circumstances defined as a problem, and identifying ways that other groups may or may not be affected, attention was immediately drawn towards identifying ways that the group most affected was different from the group(s) defined as the "mainstream." This was much like the process that William Ryan outlined as "blaming the victim" or that C. Wright Mills described as "the professional ideology of social pathologists." Much of the early (and not so early) sociological studies conducted on immigrants and racial ethnic groups highlighted their cultural (and sometimes biological) differences and attributed these differences as the source of the problem. Establishing the differences as the cause of inequality was accomplished by ignoring the link between society's norms and the structure of power. Many ethnographic studies focused on how the poor, immigrants, and other groups marked as "different" were engaged in "doing difference" and thus creating and maintaining the circumstances resulting in poverty and crime.

Currently, the sociological theorizing of difference is aimed at being inclusive of race, class, and gender (and to some degree of other "differences") as well as moving the experience of marginalized groups to the center of our analysis. The call for inclusion has served to point out the weaknesses in attempts to compare sexism with racism or classism (and other "isms"). Additive approaches to incorporating race, class, and gender fail to comprehend how experiences are qualitatively different from others rather than being simply an additional component. Theorizing race, class and gender as linkages and intersections highlights the "other" but does not really capture how individuals experience each in the everyday world. Recent challenges have been to capture lived experiences in our conceptualization of the world, recognizing that everyone has a gender, class, and race; and furthermore, that none of these exist exclusively from the other. Issues of manhood are meaningless unless we include race and class. The lived experience of African Americans is not disembodied from gender and class.[2]

Detailed ethnographic descriptions of social relations in everyday life frequently encounter difficulty in linking the individual level of analysis with the institutional and structural level. Theorizing about everyday experiences of racism, sexism, classism, privilege and domination often run the risk of characterizing each as merely individual characteristics rather than making the connection to the structural level. An example is Candace West and Sarah Fenstermaker's notion of "doing difference" which attempted to "map the dynamics of gender, race, and class as they unfold in social relations." They argued "since difference is 'done,' there is both activity (including resistance) and agency at its foundation." However, the most severe criticism of their work was that the attention on "doing difference" obscured institutional and structural power relations.

As I thought about the notion of "doing difference" in reference to a class-based, gendered racial ethnic experience, I recalled a discussion I had with a white middle class woman in my class who expressed her mission to shape a positive racial ethnic identity for her daughter, while at the same time shielding her from racism. She described her daughter as inheriting her father's Guatemalan Indian phenotype. She was taking every available opportunity to expose her daughter to Guatemalan culture. However, she did not want her child to experience the same discrimination she had witnessed the child's father have in the United States. Her strategies involved giving the child her last name rather than the father's Spanish surname and having the child pass for "white" when her ethnic status was socially stigmatized rather than celebrated. I found it very curious that she thought about her daughter's ethnicity as "doing difference" which she wanted to celebrate and perceived the performance as outside the racist, sexist, and class-based social structure. I could not help but ask her if she really believed that her daughter could develop a Guatemalan identity in the US without an awareness of racism and inequality. The more I reflected on this conversation, I realized that "difference/diversity" is assumed to be a performance and can be celebrated, thus eliminating racism, sexism, or classism. Maybe this is why "cultural" activities celebrating diversity on university campuses are much better attended by students and faculty than cultural events addressing issues of social injustice.

However, theorizing everyday life from the perspective of "difference" shares many of the pitfalls identified by Mills' critique of social pathologists; namely, we can too easily lose sight of how norms and values relate to the distribution of power and we "slip past structure to focus on isolated situations" (Mills: 170). However, without understanding everyday racism, sexism, and classism, the link between the individual and the structure remains obscure. Theorizing about opposition, resistance, and collective action requires us to understand everyday life.

Professors O'Brien and Howard's edited collection is a welcome and timely contribution. They do not shy away from the controversies arising from the call for diversity and theorizing about social inequality in everyday life but rather place their volume right smack at the center. Incorporating social science and cultural studies perspectives, O'Brien and Howard have assembled a fresh and exciting list of contributors who explore how dominance and resistance are performed within the hierarchies confronted in everyday situations and the institutional dynamics that shape individual performances. Rather than limiting analysis of performance within the framework of race, class and gendered systems of domination, they have shaken the mix to include sexuality, citizenship, and disabled. The wide range of experiences explored in these studies will no doubt provide the basis for continuing the discussion about diversity and difference as well as advancing our understanding of privilege and power and constraints on life chances, options and opportunity. These systematic observations of how hierarchies are negotiated promise to point to the dynamics of power relations in the micro and macro structures of oppression. Students and researchers will find the collection challenging and may find new directions or questions in our quest for theorizing about social inequality in everyday life.

NOTES

1 Philomena Essed's work on how Dutch racism operates through the discourse of tolerance is applicable to many of the experiences described on college campuses in the US.
2 James Geschwender's use of the concept "ethgender" is an attempt to analyze ethnicity and gender as an entity shaped and reshaped by historical experiences.

REFERENCE

Mills, C. Wright. 1943. "The Professional Ideology of Social Pathologists." *American Journal of Sociology*, XLIX(2): 165–80.

Preface

The conceptualization of this book grew out of several paper sessions held at the Pacific Sociological Association meetings and the American Sociological Association meetings. Convened under the rubric, "Doing Dominance," the sessions showcased a wide range of empirical case studies, all of which dealt in some way with processes of socio-cultural domination and strategies of resistance. In organizing these sessions, we were struck by some related themes that emerged from the papers as a set. Many of the authors indicated that they had been trained in the use of "standard" positivist (quantitative) research techniques, but that they had turned to qualitative case studies when they felt that they were missing the dynamics of the phenomena in which they were interested. As one author put it, "large scale descriptive studies are great for providing the demographic picture of certain inequalities, but you just can't explain how the dominance works using the reductionist concepts of deductive logical positivism, you've got to get a picture of what people are really doing to/with one another."

I (Jodi) had noticed a similar occurrence while serving as a judge for the graduate student paper competition of the Midwestern Sociological Society in 1994. Thirty of the 33 papers nominated for consideration were based on qualitative methodologies. I was struck by the almost militant reclaiming of these methodologies among the authors, all of whom seemed aware that the burden of proof regarding the utility of the approaches was on them. With one or two exceptions, these papers were remarkable. They shed light on heretofore unexamined and/or undertheorized social realms, such as space, the body, faith, and sexuality. They also offered creative, relevant, compelling conceptual bases for continued elaboration of the cultural political dynamics of entrenched social institutions. The winning paper, which was elected by unanimous vote, incorporated a fictive first person narrative into a theoretical reflection on the constitution of identity in liminal spaces. Reading it called to mind Geertz's wonderfully insightful use of story telling in his endeavors to encourage his colleagues to develop methodologies. Geertz's work changed the focus and tone of anthropology. It made it a methodological challenge rather than a failure to admit that social life is messy, complex and quite often unpredictable. It is a common dictum that sociology needs a similar jolt. As I read these papers I wondered who was directing all this promising work, and why we weren't hearing more of it in conference sessions and seeing more of it in our journals and publications.

A second theme voiced by the authors of the studies in this book answered this question. Each of these authors, all of whom are senior graduate students or junior faculty, noted that their work is generally marginalized, often in their home departments, and certainly in the discipline at large. Their case studies are often dismissed as trivial considerations of special interest topics and their methodologies are treated with the suspicion indicative of the relatively low status of qualitative methodologies in the hierarchy of social research. The compilation of these studies has the rich potential to provide new concepts and alternative ways of theorizing the dynamics of social institutions, particularly the prevalence of discriminatory hierarchies that seem to lag stubbornly behind cultural and political shifts. With very few exceptions, the studies that have turned the page of sociological research and ushered in new ways of seeing, fresh ways of tweaking our sociological imaginations, have been focused case studies. Howard Becker's "Becoming a Marijuana User," Rosabeth Moss Kanter's *Men and Women of the Corporation* (preceded by Dalton's similarly jolting, *Men Who Manage*), Elijah Anderson's *StreetWise*, Carol Gilligan's *In a Different Voice* have given us a comprehension of social dynamics, a new set of emergent concepts that have changed the direction of sociology. These studies are in many ways our conceptual canon. Yet we have shunted them to the side as methodological and theoretical models and continue to dismiss as "unscientific" the very work that promises to best prepare us for a future which is even now being written.

Thus we decided to bring together the work of these scholars in a single volume with a general, time honored sociological theme. We hope that readers will find in these studies signposts for the articulation of methodologies and concepts that portray the dynamics of cultural political economy. We are working toward theories and forging methodologies that portray social institutions as dynamic cultural, political, and economic webs which are realized (and thus altered or perpetuated) through interactional processes. Such an enterprise is complex; it requires a comprehension of the mutual constitution of everyday processes among socialized beings and the obdurate social institutions that we collectively acknowledge. The theoretical and methodological writings on how to conceptualize the social, the group, and the self are ubiquitous. In this book, we are interested in providing some case studies that hint at emergent, inductive conceptualizations. In its own way, we view this as transgressive of the general hierarchies that currently guard the boundaries of sociological research. Our intellectual debts and influences lie largely outside traditional disciplinary boundaries and at the same time reflect some of the richest work available within the discipline. We hope this volume will be a significant contribution, both outside and within sociology.

We are grateful to Mary Romero for encouraging us to pursue this book and offering valuable advice on the production process. Our editor, Susan Rabinowitz and production assistant, Katie Byrne, have provided excellent professional support. We also want to note special thanks to Helen Rappaport for her keen editorial advice; this volume was much improved by her work. We extend special thanks to the contributors to this volume for their enthusiasm and persistence throughout the editorial process.

This book is dedicated to those whose work in the academy has been undervalued because of normative practices that dismiss some research enterprises and/or differences among faculty and students as unbefitting of the traditional academic vestments. Certainly not all research projects are relevant, feasible and compelling. Not all pedagogical practices are effective. However, in keeping with the methodological spirit with which this book was conceived, our case observations of our own backyard indicate that the practice of prejudicially based inequalities is thriving in the academy. We systematically discriminate against women, people of color, faculty with parental responsibilities, and faculty who express priorities for teaching and the inclusion of civic responsibility in our curricula and research agendas. We perpetuate a hierarchy of institutional elitism and actively resist attempts to redefine the academy as a multi-faceted enterprise which is supported by a complex division of labor. We participate in the devaluation of our own worth and the significance of knowledge by enabling market forces to narrowly define and determine who "fits" and which institutional affiliations and research agendas "matter." We are, in the battle to maintain a traditional hierarchy, killing our own spirit. May we wake up to these processes and enter into the more honorable battle of wrestling for our cultural soul.

Acknowledgments

The authors and publishers gratefully acknowledge the following for permission to reproduce copyright material:

Routledge, for Douglas Hartmann's "The Politics of Race and Sport: Resistance and Domination in the 1968 African American Olympic Protest Movement," first published in *Ethnic and Racial Studies* vol. 19, no. 3: 548–65.

Harold Ober Associates Incorporated, for the extract from "Let America Be America Again," by Langston Hughes quoted in the Introduction; from *Collected Poems* by Langston Hughes. Copyright (c) 1994 by the Estate of Langston Hughes, reprinted by permission of Alfred A. Knopf, Inc.

Patricia Cornwell Enterprises for quotation from Patricia Cornwell's novel *Hornet's Nest* in Chapter 7.

The Publishers also wish to acknowledge the use of non-copyright photographs from the Civilian Conservations Corps, held at the National Archives, included in Chapter 10 of this volume.

The publishers apologize for any errors or omissions in the above list and would also be grateful if notified of any corrections that should be incorporated in the next edition or reprint of this book.

Introduction: Differences and Inequalities

Jodi O'Brien

"How many of you get nervous when cops are around?" We've been discussing Constance Perrin's hard-hitting, acerbic ethnography of the suburbs, *Belonging in America*. The only black man in the class, a student leader and an athlete, is describing his anxiety about driving in his girlfriend's mostly white, very affluent neighborhood. He is routinely stopped and questioned by police officers whenever he visits this area. "I schedule an extra 20 minutes whenever I'm driving over for a date, just so I won't be late because some cop needs to shake me down first," he jokes. His mostly white, mostly affluent classmates laugh, relieved. They've been squirming at the details of this popular guy's description of his own experiences of racism. The laughter is short-lived. In an uncharacteristic outburst of pique he stammers, "What are all those cops doing there, anyway? You can't find a cop around for miles when you need one in my part of town." "People in my neighborhood complain if the police *don't* drive by their houses at least twice a day," a middle-aged white woman from the same suburb as the girlfriend offers in response. "Having the police around makes us feel safe."

"Not me!" exclaims a young very dark brown Filipino student. "My friends think I'm a wimp because I won't jay walk, but everytime I do you can bet there's some cop just waiting to give me a ticket." "Shopping is the worst," remarks an older black woman. "I'm so used to being followed by store detectives that I've started turning around and asking for their opinions on my purchases. The other day I pointed out a real shoplifter to the gentleman tagging me. You should've seen the look on his face when he caught this pretty young white girl stuffing fingernail polish down her pants." The class howls with laughter. "As far as cops are concerned, if you're dark, you're marked," mutters a Chicano student. "Try being white in Hawaii," another student retorts. "You get called names like *Haole* all the time." This comment stirs murmurs from several mixed race, brown skinned students, all from Hawaii. "It's not the same thing," one of them argues. "Oh yeah?" the white student responds. "I can say that I feel pretty marked when I'm home on the island." "Yeah, but it's different," a young woman who describes her ethnicity as Chinese Korean Norwegian Hawaiian American continues, "we're talking about harassment here." "And I'm saying that when I'm in Hawaii I get harassed for being white," her fellow Islander insists with finality. The woman looks pleadingly at me to help her out, "We're talking about different things. I just don't have the words for it ..." she trails off.

My mind is racing. How did we get from the topic of privileges such as police presence in the suburbs to whiteness in Hawaii? Should I intervene or let them continue? They seem to be on a roll. I'm encouraged by the complexity of the discussion. I worry sometimes that my students, like Americans in general, tend to oversimplify discussions of difference into black/white, rich/poor dichotomies. The perspectives of the Hawaiian, Samoan and Chamorro students, who make up about 25 percent of my class (and about 20 percent of the university at which I teach), add considerable multivocality. In written assignments as well as class discussions these students repeatedly insist that there is no racism in Hawaii. In terms of representation, I can see their point; when these students look around at home they see Chinese American mayors, Japanese American CEOs, brown and yellow skinned civic, cultural and political leaders everywhere. Yet they also tell stories that reveal differences in economic and cultural access based on an ethnic/racial hierarchy. As one student explained matter-of-factly in response to my probing, entitlement is based on who arrived first on the islands as planters: the Japanese, the Chinese, and more recently, and with the lowest status, the Filipinos. From what I have been able to piece together, Anglo, Chinese and Japanese Hawaiians appear to be equally represented across economic and educational levels. Filipinas/os are a distance lower and Samoans are considered the invisible savages. This racial complexity was expressed poignantly in a paper by a Japanese Filipina Hawaiian student who wrote about being ostracized by her paternal Japanese grandparents because of her Filipina mother. She then contrasted this with her mother's own virulent racism toward Black Americans.

I tune back in to the class discussion. They are still wrestling with the issue of whether the white guy from Hawaii has a rightful claim to harassment when he is singled out as a *Haole*. The student in question looks regretful at having raised the topic. He is a conscientious young man with comfortably starched shirts, creased chinos and a well-tended ponytail. I know from the "position biographies" that I require students to write that he is the youngest in a family of successful doctors and attorneys. His goal is medical school. A Latina who describes her fashion preferences as "retro nomad" and has a tendency to roll her eyes in exasperation at her classmates – she is one of a handful of presidential scholars at the university – turns her gaze on him from across the room. "No one's saying that it's comfortable to be called derogatory names because you're different from the majority, but you're missing the point of the discussion." I'm intrigued, I've been wondering myself what the point is. "Remember this course is called 'Differences and Inequalities'," she continues in reference to the class, which is part of the university's interdisciplinary core program. "The emphasis here is on *inequality*. In Hawaii you may get called names because you're white, but I'll bet you get treated like royalty every time you set foot in a store to do some shopping." Well put, I think to myself. I couldn't have said it better. And in this case, nothing I could have said would have had the same impact as this summary comment from a peer.

Whose Liberty? Whose Justice? Whose Equality?

Why do Americans have such a difficult time acknowledging inequalities? Certainly the myth of equal opportunity has something to do with our collective reluctance to establish the connection between culturally inscribed differences, such as race and gender, and access to power and privilege. The slogan "Celebrating Difference" despite its promise of a mosiac of equality, masks the hierarchical scaffold upon which we mount the expression of these differences. The invitation to celebrate detracts from the difficult enterprise of uncovering the more mundane, yet insidious practices of everyday discrimination based on these differences. Like the proverbial party-pooper, those who fail to celebrate and, instead, attempt to draw attention to the injustices we experience as a result of these differences, are shouted down as ungrateful malcontents.

Cherished cultural fables teach us that we can expose the emperor as having no clothes; in other words, in a culture of (meritorious) equality, one's character is revealed not through outward displays of pomposity and grandeur, rather it is an expression of the man (or woman?) underneath. A similar attempt at cultural leveling is revealed in the modern practice of allowing the Ace to occasionally best the King in various card games. Such imagery perpetuates the notion that, to the extent that we wish it so, institutionalized forms of hierarchy can be and have been smashed by the rise of individual character. This myth is rooted in the historical politics of one group of relatively privileged Anglo and Franco men usurping power from the landed aristocracy by denouncing them as a useless drain on resources; these eighteenth-century revolutionaries traded pomp and fiefdom alliances for private property and the right to do what they wanted with it. John Locke and his contemporaries heralded the otherwise pedestrian coup of 1689 that had resulted in the overthrow of James II as a Glorious Revolution. The overthrowing of kings by disgruntled men of means was not particularly unusual during this period; what was new was the idea that government, in the form of the king, should *serve* the people. In framing the King James II coup as a revolution Locke concocted one of the philosophical benchmarks of the "enlightenment" – the idea that the ruler should be the servant of men of means rather than their sovereign lord. Theirs is a story about power brokering between relative equals, about leveraging and limiting the extent of the state. What we now study as philosophies of individual merit (e.g., Locke) were penned largely as an ideological lance used in a jousting match intended to knock the traditional monarchies out of the saddle. It is an ironic cultural legacy that we recall this history as having been done in the name of the "people." And more ironic still that we believe that the mere invocation of this (historically misunderstood) legacy will secure the *practice* of equality.

The modern legacy of the "people" consists of draconian policies for the poor, continuous struggles for civil rights waged by women, blacks, immigrants and homosexuals, wars to reclaim lands and resources among indigenous groups, even the right to speak one's native language. As many, frequently overlooked writers of the modern era observed, there has been very little place in the "enlightenment" story for those whose differences mark them as "other" or "auxiliary" to the main event (e.g., Du Bois 1903; Gilman 1898; Wollstonecraft 1791). It is a schizophrenic cultural political legacy that entreats us to strive to achieve our naked individual potential while simultaneously cloaking many individuals in heavy historical fabrics that mark us as less than "the people."

The ideals of meritocracy and the celebration of diversity entreat us to pay homage to the individual rights of the people, while simultaneously disavowing the patterns of prejudice that shape the lives of women, people of color, the poor, the queer, the disabled, and so many others who constitute the supposed fabric of the American mosaic. Countless numbers of Americans are entreated daily to wear masks of deference, submission, silence and self-betrayal. The insidious reality is that we are entreated to do so in order to perpetuate the belief that these differences don't really matter, it's the character underneath that counts.

Langston Hughes' (1938) sardonic poem of American potential, "Let America Be America Again," portrays the sharp distinction between the celebration of these ideals and the inconvenient realities that distract from the main theme:

> O, let my land be a land where Liberty
> Is crowned with no false patriotic wreath,
> But opportunity is real, and life is free,
> Equality is in the air we breathe
>
> (There's never been equality for me,
> Nor freedom in this "homeland of the free.")
>
> I am the people, humble, hungry, mean –
> Hungry yet today despite the dream…

Marking Differences

Differences bind us and differences set us apart. For an exercise entitled, "Which Box Do You Check?" I have asked each student in my class to write out the term they use to describe their ethnicity. I then write the US Census categories for "race/origin" on the board – American Indian, Asian, Black, White, Non-White Hispanic and Other. I ask students to tell us what they have written down and I then ask them to tell us which box they would check when filling out an official form. I make a list of their preferred ethnic designation on the board as we go. Invariably, the list consists of a dozen or more ethnicities than those on the census list. The disparities are revealing. Students who identify variously as Chinese, Filipina/o, Laotian, Japanese, Samoan, Thai, or Vietnamese describe their dissatisfaction at being grouped collectively under the generic term, "Asian." Native American students who hold strong tribal associations express a similar frustration, as do those who have a geographical and cultural understanding of the differences between Chicana/o and Latina/o. What seems to unsettle many class members is the discovery that several of their peers, who are from mixed race families, must choose to drop an ethnic association with one or another parent whenever they pick a box. They literally leave out a parent every time they fill out a form – unless they want to finagle the form – which can lead to additionally frustrating circumstances. As one woman noted, "I check Native American for my mother, Black for my father, Other for me – I don't much like being an "other" but what choice do I have? Anyway, what always happens with institutions like the university is that they choose whichever part of me best fits their quota needs and ignore the rest. So right now, I'm Native American because that's what they need more of." Is the lack of a box that represents one's complete ethnic identity an injustice? Or would the addition of a multicultural box weaken cultural, economic, and political representation of systematically underprivileged groups? Presumably the answers to this complex issue depend on the purposes of the boxes. How articulate are we as a nation in interrogating the reasons for these boxes of self-identification?

I am intrigued by the number of Euro-American students who further qualify their ethnicity for the exercise – German American, Norwegian American, Irish American, and so forth. When I first heard a student make such a claim during the exercise, I was taken aback. Following several expressions of "white," "Caucasian," and "Anglo" a young woman spoke up in turn confidently stating, "Swedish American." I hesitated before writing this on the board. "Do you really think of yourself this way?" I demanded. "Yes," she confirmed. Reluctantly, I wrote Swedish American on the board. "Well, what do you check on official forms?" I persisted. "Caucasian." "Do you have any second thoughts or hesitations when you check that box?" I asked. "No," she stated without any apparent irony or affect. Was I over-reacting or was she making a mockery of the exercise? Subsequently, several students noted that they had written "white" but that their family heritage consisted of British, Swiss, Italian, and other Western European extractions. "Well what do you want me to write down?" I asked each of them, somewhat dismayed. I noted that in each case, before answering, these white students invariably look around the room at their multi-ethnic, brown skinned classmates, many of whom had identities such as Black Latina/o or Chinese Filipina/o. In some cases, following this scrutiny, the student would shrug and say, "Just put white." Others insist on my writing down the discrete Euro category. I found myself wondering about what appears to be a look of smugness among some of them. Does it reflect a feeling of having trumped me and the students of color in the class?

Later I find myself wrestling with the distinction between differences we use to locate ourselves as members of groups with shared history and meaning, and the marked differences that set some apart as targets of injustice, prejudice and discrimination. There is a joke among Seattleites, of which I am one, that the only real ethnicity in our multiracial, Pacific rim city is Scandinavian. Highly visible ghetto populations such as grungers, Microsoft employees, and coffee baristas notwithstanding, there is a distinctive Scandinavian population that is set apart by their geographical dominance of an area called Ballard and their occupational prevalence in fishing and shipping along the Ballard waterfront. Ballard is home to not one, but several Scandinavian heritage museums. Each year the neighborhood hosts a festival complete with a rousing parade during which one can spot any number of Scandinavians wearing hats fashioned as Viking longships. I suspect that even Garrison Keillor would be bemused by this display of ethnic solidarity and pride.

People are groupish by nature, according to social psychologist Gordon Allport (1956). *Seattle Times* columnist Jerry Large (1997), who writes from "one black man's point of view," echoes this theme in his response to an article written by Harvard Law

Professor, Randall Kennedy. Kennedy has argued that the "sentiments and conduct of racial kinship are morally dubious." Large agrees. "He's right. Racial pride is illogical, racial solidarity is discriminatory and racial loyalty is potentially divisive." Nonetheless, he continues, "Most of us belong to lots of groups – by religion, profession, economic status, neighborhood, gender, age and a whole host of other categorizations, some of which affect our lives more than others. Around here, race is the Grand Canyon of divisions." Large is leading up to his main point, which is that as long as race continues to set Americans apart, *unequally*, there will be a need to find others who share a history of oppression and the everyday experience of discrimination. Large concludes, "I need the little lift I get when someone says with a look, 'I can see the weight on your back, and the strength that allows you to carry it unbowed.' I can smile at a black face and still have some smile left over for my other brothers and sisters."

I appreciate his point. It urges me on toward understanding just what is the distinction between Black Pride and Scandinavian Pride. Certainly being a Black man in America is not the same thing as being a Norwegian man. But how do I explain this to my students and my colleagues in the context of a cultural milieu in which we preach "separate but equal," "celebrate diversity," and "everyman for himself"? In *Ethnic Options*, Mary Waters (1990) writes insightfully of the way in which ethnicity has become yet another form of accessorizing for many Americans. Dusting off the family ethnic heritage and trotting it out enables one to achieve that peculiarly American duality of individual distinction manifest through unique intersections of group attachments, what some scholars these days are calling crossings, such as Catholic Jews, working class academics, religious queers, and conservative cross-dressers, to name a few possibilities. This fluidity of group boundaries is fascinating and portends perhaps the sort of cultural pastiche that the celebration of diversity implies. Still, this insouciance of difference with its promise of hybridity glosses a more intractable reality; all differences are not treated equally.

I find it instructive to return to the writings of earlier observers of difference, such as Simone de Beauvoir (1952) or W. E. B. Du Bois (1903). They write clearly and evocatively of a phenomenon that seems to have been forgotten in the paradoxical contemporary commodification of identity politics; some differences are a marked basis of institutionalized inequality and oppression.

Du Bois was not celebrating his blackness when his offering of a friendship card was refused by a (white) girl in his (relatively privileged neighborhood) elementary school class. He had not chosen to express black solidarity when he first became aware of a "veil" separating him from the rest of his classmates. Beauvoir is, at times, downright scornful of her fellow women when she notes that women are the "objects" of a male history, rather than the subjects of their own history. This is so, in part, she suggests, because women have been relegated to being different through their auxiliary status to men, satisfied to enact their history through their men, men who are actors in their own life stories, men whose differences are possibly a source of individual selection and distinction, men who, due to various circumstances of geography, religion, and profession, may be "separate but equal."

I was pondering this while walking through a turn of the century cemetery in the coal mining town of Roslyn, Washington. I was struck by the layout of the cemetery which was organized according to lodges – Elk, Moose, Odd Fellows. Apparently the choice to be buried under the sign of one's lodge indicates that the coal miners formed primary attachments through these totemic groups. One of the paradoxes of a secular government in which the primary task is to ensure individual liberties and guard against the excesses of centralized interests is that it leaves humans on their own to forge communities. In the absence of extended families and organized religions, these frontier laborers attempted to create some degree of economic security, trust and companionship through their lodges. Undoubtedly, differences of opinion in politics, religion, and labor specialties set the different lodges apart from one another. Points of distinction between say, the Moose and the Elks, probably resulted in more than a few minor skirmishes, even as these disputes helped to strengthen individual commitments to their particular lodge. What caught my attention were the graves of the wives. I found myself wondering if these women might not have preferred to be buried with family – say sisters or parents, rather than under the sign of their husbands' lodges. Or whether such fancies occurred to them at all. Regardless, it didn't appear that they had any say in the matter. Simply by being marked as female, their course in life was set – distinction, if any, came to these women vicariously through the men they wed and bred.

Another feature of the cemetery that has stayed with me was a separate area called Mt Olivet. Recently, a group of black church historians took note of the fact that more than 200 black coal miners lived and worked in Roslyn during the height of its coal mining days. These miners did not belong to lodges. They were given burial by the local black ministers. Unlike the elaborate headstones and gravesites erected by the lodge members to commemorate their dead, the graves of the black miners were originally unmarked, save for simple pine crosses. Differentiated by the totemic symbol of a chosen lodge membership, the dead white miners of Roslyn lay with their individual names etched in stone. Their wives and unmarried daughters lay next to them bearing the same name etched in stone. The black miners lay as one group distinguished only by a common cultural and economic history that has marked them as "other." Their graves bear no names.

A useful conceptual distinction, one that reflects contemporary circumstances but that is frequently glossed in our enthusiasm for cultural fluidity, is whether one is the subject of one's difference or the object. I risk being pedantic in this reminder, but I think it bears repeating. Note that even Large (1997) conflates this highly significant distinction: he begins his remarks with the observation that "most of us belong to lots of *groups* – religion, profession, economic status, neighborhood, gender, age" and concludes his listing with the summary phrase, "a whole host of other *categorizations*" [emphasis mine]. At least three of the classifications on his list are arguably socially imposed categories of objectification (economic status, gender, age) while the others reflect self consciously chosen affiliations that reflect individual subjectivity. Although there is some utility in describing the key distinction as a matter of "choice" (subjective differences are chosen differences, objective differences are imposed), it strikes me that the relevant factors occur in the alchemy of culturally marked differences and relative opportunity – the relative salience of cultural categories in relation to power and privilege. One does not choose one's nose shape for instance, but nose shape, per se, isn't a feature that sets one apart as someone worthy (or not) of everyday basic liberties. Similarly, one doesn't necessarily choose to be Norwegian American. On the other hand, this status is a relatively invisible distinction that tends to go unnoticed as a character trait unless one draws attention to it. And certainly it is not a feature that sets one apart as someone whom cabbies would prefer to pass up or whom bank tellers might frown upon. Compared with the combustive potential of certain marked differences in the chemistry of rights and differences, Norwegian American is a relatively benign ingredient.

Default Assumptions

While the class is listing ethnicities, one student asks plaintively, "Why can't we all just be Americans?" "Whose America would that be?" another queries. "My family has been in the United States for three generations," she continues, "but everytime I date a white guy and I meet his friends or family, the first thing they always say to him is 'you didn't mention she was Japanese.'" "Yeah, I know that scene," another woman chimes in. "And these guys don't get it either. I ask my boyfriend, 'you tell your mother you're dating a Chicana?' and he says what does it matter? Of course it doesn't matter to him. He's white, he's what everybody expects to see, but you can be sure that when he takes me home the only thing about me that his mother is going to see is some brown Mexican touching her white son. Nothing else about me is going to matter in that moment."

Hyphens and qualifiers, such as *African*-American, *Asian*-American, the *women's* basketball team, *black* coal miners, not only indicate a particular feature or social status, they reflect the taken-for-granted, or default assumptions about who or what people are in the absence of such qualifiers. Unless marked otherwise, references to "the college basketball team" call to mind the *men's* basketball team. This is the default assumption. The qualifier "women's team" not only deters us from the default assumption by providing additional information, it designates the persons who are the object of this classification as auxiliary to the main group, the "real" basketball players. I'm reminded of the scene from *Year of the Dragon*, the biographical film of Bruce Lee, where Lee's white girlfriend introduces him to her mother. The mother protests her daughter's planned marriage to Lee by asking about the children. "What will they be?" she demands. "They'll be Americans," Lee answers confidently. "But they can't be!" she exclaims. "You're not American. You're Chinese." In her eyes the designation Chinese American not only marks Lee's ethnic heritage, it disqualifies him from full American status.

Scholars such as de Beauvoir (1952) and Du Bois (1903), Foucault (1977, 1979) to Gloria Anzaldua (1987), Douglas Hofstadter (1985), bell hooks (1994), Patricia Williams (1991) and Cornel West (1995), to name a few, have written about the hierarchies of belonging and entitlement that these language asymmetries reveal. There is a tendency to assume that because the differences are marked through language they are easily transformed through the use of new terminology – we're all just Americans, or just athletes, or just coal miners. This is the hopeful assumption, that justice will be achieved by claiming that we are simply a "just-us" society (Twine and Warren 1991). The practice of prejudicially based injustices is not so easily erased, however. Americanism is a philosophy that competes with individual democracy for doctrinal status in the United States (Rogers M. Smith 1988). According to this philosophy, this land and its endowments belong to a select group of individuals who are ethnically and culturally descended from the original Anglo-European colonizers, WASPs. Promoters of this doctrine maintain that Americanism is a distinct cultural heritage that must be protected in its own right. Americanism supports the idea of a "melting pot" to the extent that this means assimilating persons of different ethnic, linguistic, economic, and religious traditions. Here assimilation means the willingness to throw off these different traditions and completely embrace Americanism. In practice, this philosophy means that anyone who is white, Christian and middle-class has a birthright to the liberties of this nation. Those who do not fit the above categories must continually prove their worthiness. The difference between the ease of entitlement and the strain of proof is indeed a chasm as wide as the Grand Canyon. A lifetime of proving oneself worthy of privileges that others enjoy without reflection is the everyday grand canyon that divides us, the canyon that keeps us separate and not equal.

Carte Blanche

My class is giving group presentations. The assignment is to give a compelling depiction of ways in which various social statuses (race, gender, age, class, and so forth) affect access to privilege.

The room is abuzz. One group has just finished showing a video-tape of a shopping expedition to a well-known department store. The group includes two Filipinas, one Chicano, and one white man. All are in their early twenties. Each group member wore clean, fashionable, casual clothing and appeared well groomed for the outing. The video shows the students moving from department to department and waiting to be served. This upscale department store has a reputation for keenly attentive service. My own experience as a shopper there is that I can expect to be asked, "May I help you?" by a minimum of three salespeople within a matter of minutes. In each department the students browse alone or in various combinations and record the length of time it takes to receive service. In the first scenario, the Filipinas approach the cosmetic counter and one remarks to the other within hearing distance of the clerk that she's eager to try a new line of facial cleansing. The clerk glances in their direction and continues stocking a cabinet. They wait about a minute during which time the clerk, a 40-something white woman, never looks at them again. One of the students continues on to women's shoes. She picks up a pair of loafers and studies them intently. The older, white male clerk walks back and forth behind her twice without speaking. When she looks up and glances around he is gone. As the class views these scenes, the student remarks that when she was ignored twice in a row she thought perhaps it was about age.

The video continues with the two men who have left the department store and moved into the mall. The white man enters a small camera store. "May I help you with something today sir?" A clerk, the only one in the store front, looks up immediately from the counter. He appears to be in his mid-twenties. The student approaches the counter and asks about a particular battery. As he does, the Chicano student enters the store and begins to browse a rack of camera cases and belts. The clerk watches him while trying to maintain his conversation with the first student. A few seconds later, apparently distracted, he says, "Excuse me," and picks up a phone and speaks into it briefly. Immediately another clerk appears from a back room and steps into the store front. He moves toward the brown man but doesn't speak to him. Instead he begins to straighten items on a nearby shelf. "How much is this shoulder strap?" the student asks to the room in general. Both clerks are obviously in hearing range. The clerks look at each other and shrug. Neither offers any help. The student continues to browse for a minute and then leaves the store, followed soon after by the white student who has purchased a battery.

Back in the store the women move to the hosiery department and begin to finger packages of nylons. "Can I help you?" A young brown skinned woman, who appears Asian, steps out seemingly from nowhere. "Don't tell me this is one-color-fits-all?" jokes one of the students as she holds up a pantyhose package marked "nude." All three of the women laugh. During the subsequent debriefing, the students tell the class that they found this clerk to be "really cool" and ended up telling her what they were doing.

They show several more scenarios, including one at the jewelry counter which depicts the white man and one of the women talking to an older white female clerk who addresses all of her remarks to the man.

For this group of students, the final scene is the most revealing. Keeping the camera unobtrusive had been a chore. The white student noticed some lounging chairs under the escalator and across from the men's clothing department and suggested that if he sat in a chair with the camera on his knee he could film the others without it looking too obvious. He took up his position and one of the women and the other man walked over to a nearby display and began looking at men's sport shirts. "I need to get a birthday present for my father," the male student announced to his companion. A clerk standing one aisle over took no notice. The students studied the shirts a bit longer and when no one appeared to offer service they moved on to ties. "Maybe he'd like a tie?" the student said loud enough that the camera picked him up. Deciding to spare the class the tedium, the students fast forward through nine minutes of tape during which the two wandered haplessly in the men's department without ever being approached by a clerk. The tape concludes with another student, the white male, the one with the well-tended pony-tail and well-pressed chinos striding into the men's department. Within ten seconds two clerks drop their tasks and approach him asking if they can help.

The class is amazed at what appears to be very blatant differential treatment on the part of the clerks. They ask many questions and offer related experiences. In interpreting the experience for the class, the group is quick to point out that this was only a handful of situations and that many things could have been going on in each case. Still, in the dozen or so situations that they recorded, the only service proffered to the Filipinas came from young Asian female clerks. The Chicano student was never offered help, though a clerk always seemed to be aware of his presence. The white man was greeted with immediate courtesy in every department that he entered. He seemed quite startled by the apparent differential treatment that his peers encountered. During the debriefing he commented several times that he was accustomed to attentive service, that when he experienced any hesitation from clerks he attributed it to his age; he had no idea that other people were ignored so obviously. As the class discussion progressed, I also noticed that he was doing all the talking for his group.

René Magritte made a painting that he titled *Blank Cheque* (*Carte Blanche* in French). In the foreground of the painting is a woman wearing elegant riding gear sitting tall astride a magnificent horse. Her gaze is aloof and she appears comfortably confident on the horse which seems to be moving at a smooth canter. The theme point of the painting's title appears in the woman's response to the trees which comprise the forested background for her canter. She is unaware of them. Her horse strides directly through a tree as if it were a mere optical illusion, a mirage on the landscape. This lack of obstacles is carte blanche and the woman represents privilege, which Magritte depicts as a lack of interference in one's plans. Whenever I view this painting, I'm inclined to see several additional riders behind the woman. These riders are leaning low and fast in the saddle. They appear sweaty and disheveled and look as if they are riding with grave concentration. The focus of their concentration is the trees which for them are very real obstacles that must be dodged or overcome if they are to maintain their pace and get anywhere. Such a ride strikes me as exhausting, especially in juxtaposition to the serene countenance of the woman who is privilege.

In a culture that cherishes achievement over ascribed privilege and preaches the concept of separate but equal, it is difficult for many to acknowledge that much of what they take for granted as everyday entitlements are not available to others. In fact, many people spend a great deal of energy and resources just trying to skirt obstacles that others don't even see. In addition, because we lack a cultural discourse of class and inequality it can be extremely difficult for persons to describe the obstacles that they must surmount in order to even moderately "level" the playing field. Such discourse, to the extent that it is articulated, is often resisted because it compromises the cherished notions that there is a level playing field, that our differences are matters of horizontal rather than hierarchical distinction and that our achievements are just that, achievements, rather than fate of position.

Taming/Fetishizing Differences

Recently, the citizens of Roslyn crafted a wall of ornate stone masonry set with commemorative plaques around the otherwise unmarked graves that comprise Mt Olivet. This recognition of the final resting place of unnamed black coal miners is one in a series of civic projects undertaken in Roslyn to celebrate the working men who comprise the town's history. Other such projects include a small scale reflection wall in tribute to soldiers. Funding for these commemorative projects was made possible by the lucrative tourist industry that was generated when Roslyn became site to the popular television show, *Northern Exposure*.

I find the Mt Olivet retrospective commemoration suggestive of a peculiar contemporary American paradox; in the rush to reaffirm the ideals of achieving individual distinction, we are collectively willing to recognize those who were not given such a chance due to historical prejudices that imposed categorical limits on individual achievement – retrospectively, we can't give them individual names, but we can acknowledge these black miners as a group. At the same time we are increasingly, resolutely, unwilling as a collective body to acknowledge the continuation of these categorical limitations into the present day. The ideal that people should be valued for individual achievements and neither limited, nor facilitated, based on ascribed, categorical groupings is as American as Chevrolet. This is a very seductive philosophy. It enables us to decree it an historical crime that the individual potential of these miners was overshadowed by their skin color; we chisel plaques in remembrance of individual names sacrificed to group-based discrimination.

Then we extend the same logic to the rescinding of economic programs, such as affirmative action: in a meritocracy it is unfair to mediate individual potential through categorical ascriptions such as race or gender. Certainly. In an ideal world in which additional historical, cultural and political economic factors would not differentially mediate access to the basic means of individual achievement – education, upper level professional employment and lucrative contracts – this logic makes sense. However, despite the collective desire to believe otherwise, as indicated by recent repeals of Affirmative Action legislation in California and Texas, we are a long way from the ideal of a "level playing field." The corollary argument that socially engineered programs such as Affirmative Action have outlived their usefulness is misguided. The logic of such arguments is predicated on faulty statistical reasoning and ignorance of the intent and application of Affirmative Action. Detractors of Affirmative Action make much of supposed claims that women and people of color are making strides in intergenerational (and even intragenerational) mobility. The reality of this progress may be so. But it must be read in terms of the relatively miserly base positions and the mediating effects of socially engineered programs.

The untold story is that these gains are relatively insignificant compared with general rates of mobility, shifts in employment sectors and additional economic indicators that give a fuller account of just who gets which pieces of the pie. For instance, in the state of Washington, those who have benefitted most from Affirmative Action policies in employment are white women and, following at a close second, white men over 40 (Washington State Commission on African American Affairs, June 1995). This rather surprising outcome makes sense when one understands exactly which groups are targeted as "affected groups" in a state, and the ratio of persons in each group considered to already have the skill levels necessary for the job sector in question. Company hiring policies are based on this ratio, not, as is commonly misunderstood, on the general population of the minority. Thus, for the state of Washington, which recognizes Vietnam Veterans as an affected group, it is statistically more likely that the pool of veterans who have the training to meet the Affirmative Action ratio most underrepresented in a particular professional or engineering sector will be white men. This is so simply because white men have more access to the higher levels of education that provide them with this training. Thus, as a group, they have a comparatively higher ratio of trained men who meet an Affirmative Action category. Pause and work out what this means numerically. Because of systematic cultural discrimination and disproportionate lack of financial means, Black men and Chicanos are significantly underrepresented in professional and scientific education. Thus the Affirmative Action ratios for these men in high level professional employment are relatively low, even non-existent in some sectors. What this means in real numbers is that there is no such thing as an "underqualified minority taking a job from someone who is more qualified." In fact, depending on which groups are affected according to a state's policy, it is highly likely that the competition between people of color who meet the qualifications will be stiffer than among white men in similar sectors because the hiring ratios are likely to be higher for the latter group, thus granting them more positions.

My own scrutiny of the complexities of Affirmative Action policies indicates that it is a very necessary plan if we wish to level the grade in our steeply stratified access to education and employment. The increased numbers and wider dispersion of white women across employment sectors suggests that these policies can be very effective for individuals who have traditionally been denied access to certain highly rewarded sectors. The comparative controversies over the success or failure of these policies for people of color suggests just how deeply racist we are as a nation. The policies have gone awry because of a lack of acknowledgement of the connection between marked differences and privilege in this country. This derailing has been fostered by the perpetuation of prejudices that continue to mark some groups as less deserving. An additional poison is in the rhetoric of critics of Affirmative Action who acknowledge the fact that we are a long way from "equal opportunity," but insist nonetheless that the individual doubt and distress experienced by recipients of Affirmative Action constitutes a sort of backlash prejudice that is more harmful than good. They use the logic that no individual should have to be judged solely on ascribed group characteristics. The assumption is that as long as we desire it so, these differences no longer matter. Why have we not taught our young people the politics and economies of discrimination? Why do we nurture the notion that the inequalities they experience are their own fault?

Why don't we teach high school civic courses that detail how Affirmative Action can work and herald it as the achievement of a truly civil country that is uniformly engaged in the pursuit of liberty and justice for all the people? Thus educated, these youth might forge a sense of pride in their potential and their country's concern that they attain it. The mythical notion that we can simply forget years of cultural, economic, and political oppression, wipe the slate clean, pat ourselves on the back and move on, is a collective dystopia. Despite overwhelming evidence to the contrary, we are under the spell of an ideological and political sleight of hand in which individualism has been inverted to mean that anyone who claims categorically based injustices is somehow betraying their individual potential or getting something they don't deserve. What are we to make of this cultural schizophrenia? It is a madness which is neither benign nor inspired, but rather, in the words of Stephen Jay Gould (1995: 11), "reflects the depressing temper of our time – a historical moment of unprecedented ungenerosity."

The sociological picture is straightforward; economically, we are steeply stratified. Demographics of the composition of various economic levels and related employment sectors consistently reveal systematic patterns of difference based on gender and race (Rose 1992). Race and gender are so tightly braided with economic class that it is simply not possible to determine whether the relative lack of access to power and privilege is based on economic or categorical differences. Given our current economic and social patterns, the fact is that both are accurate indices of inequities in access to opportunity for education and employment. Women and people of color do not enjoy the taken for granted privileges suggested by the American Dream of individual liberties and the pursuit of happiness, because we do not have the same social status. This is so because of how we are marked and because of the historical ramifications this has had for access to the economic freedom that enables one to "belong" in America. The way in which these differences are braided together with economic standing provides a relatively definitive equation for one's standing. This is not new information. In the past two decades it has been consistently documented and cogently discussed (e.g., Collins 1991; Howard and Hollander 1997; Reskin and Padavic 1994; Thornton Dill and Baca Zinn 1994). Why then do we have such a difficult time wrapping our heads around the persistence of these systematic differences?

Prejudice and Cultural Cognition

I have suggested that our collective myopia rests in part on the prevalence of the myth of individual achievement. We are culturally blinded to ways in which various differences are connected to social statuses that result in differential treatment, power, and experiences. We also lack a class discourse, a cultural language that reflects the relationship between economics and status. This hinders us in our attempts to make realistic assessments about achievement, merit and the distribution of resources. Our myopia is not benign. As a country we invest enormous amounts of active attention and resources in maligning and maintaining the invisibility of the poor and underprivileged. We want to believe that those less privileged deserve their fate and simultaneously absolve ourselves of any categorically based biases or prejudices, despite overwhelming evidence to the contrary. In its most benign form, this denial reveals ignorance manifest as "good intentions."

For instance, a nationally syndicated columnist reported that black dentists have a difficult time attracting white clients. His explanation for this phenomenon, one offered by the dentists themselves, was that white people are hesitant to have a black hand in their mouths. A white journalist wrote a reponse to this column insisting that the opinions and experiences of the dentists were inauthentic. In support of his position, he noted that he had reflected on 40 to 50 (white) people that he could think of and was convinced that none of them would mind going to a black dentist. He did not suggest that any of these people actually sought the services of black dentists, he simply maintained that he was convinced of their good intentions. In other words, they couldn't be squeamish about black dentists because it wouldn't be desirable for them to be so, and they were people who did the desirable thing. Or, presumably, they would if confronted with the situation. But as none of them apparently had black dentists, we have to be content with the writer's thought experiment as the basis for his glib dismissal of the actual experiences of the black dentists.

I do a real experiment in my social psychology class in which I ask for a volunteer to come to the front of the room, spit into a glass and then drink it back up. Inevitably the volunteer balks and the students in the class grimace and squeal, "gross!" I got this idea from a provocative gem of a book, *This Book Is Not Required*, written by Inge Bell (1985). Bell points out that we are predisposed, through cultural conditioning, to attribute different qualities to the idea of "spit" than we are to the idea of "saliva." Physically they are exactly the same substance, yet we have a deep-seated aversion to one and a relatively unaware or benign feeling about the other. Cognitive-emotive scripts (rather than mindfully reflective responses) are the basis of most of our reactions to circumstances and encounters. According to this logic, we make sense of persons, events and phenomena by imposing culturally learned schemas on the experience. These schemas are not only a way to name, or map our environments, they also involve an emotive reaction as well as a pre-coded recipe for response. Thus, all else being equal, we have a relatively immediate, unreflective "ick" response to "spit."

In recent decades, scholars in the social sciences and humanities have elaborated on this process in attempts to demonstrate the way in which culturally generated linguistic expressions are inscribed with and reveal the cognitive and emotional status of a person or object. The significance of these studies is in the implication that we respond to the "name," not the thing itself. The significance of salient linguistic distinctions as being highly nuanced, deeply embedded in the collective consciousness and emotionally wrought, is indicated in the realization that these distinctions are highly resistant to "renaming" or redefinition. Even those who adopt culturally pejorative terms, such as "nigger" or "queer" as a form of self-referent in the attempt to reframe usage, can find that the words sting a bit on the tongue. Lesbian writers and activists have often remarked in regard to attempts to reclaim the word queer, that they find it a hard word to de-pollute (Warren 1997).

Social psychologist Gordon Allport was one of the first to extend this logic to a study of the deeply entrenched basis of prejudice. In his 1956 classic, *The Nature of Prejudice*, he asks why it is that group differences shade into prejudice and categorically based discrimination. Explanations for the emergence of various forms of prejudice are found in the specific political economic and cultural context of the inscription of differences. Explanations for the *persistence* of such categorically based prejudices can be found in the study of everyday practices and encounters. These studies reveal the nonrational, often mindless, emotionally laden, deeply entrenched processes by which we, often unknowingly, practice categorically based prejudices. These practices have very real discriminatory consequences. The link between everyday interactional processes and the perpetuation of systematic inequalities is strongly evident when it is demonstrated that the structural conditions that originally fueled the discrimination no longer exist.

In a recent groundbreaking article that pioneers a merger of structural analyses and interactional processes, Cecilia Ridgeway (1997) explains the persistence of gender hierarchies in employment, despite shifts in the socio-economic structure that should, in theory, favor women and lead to a decline in such hierarchies. Ridgeway explains the persistence of gender-based discrimination in terms of taken-for-granted interactional processes that "rewrite inequality into new institutional arrangements." As Ridgeway notes, gender is one of the primary ways by which we identify ourselves and make sense of others. In a background way, we are always aware of the gender of those with whom we are interacting (gender awareness enters the foreground in circumstances where gender is ambiguous; we then work consciously to "figure it out."). In this culture, gender is a hierarchical distinction, not simply a matter of difference. In Ridgeway's words, "Gender *status beliefs* are one form of inequality" (221). Part of the package of these beliefs is lower expectations for women in most employment settings (note that these status expectations are general cultural beliefs held by women as well as men). The pivotal explanatory point, according to Ridgeway, is the "extent to which occupational arrangements and wage outcomes are *interactionally mediated*" (my italics). In other words, despite institutional arrangements to the contrary, in this case in the forms of anti-discrimination laws and even a preponderance of female applicants in certain employment sectors, everyday interactional practices mediate who gets jobs and what they get paid. In this case, the everyday practices are based on taken-for-granted expectations about relative differences between men and women as employees. The result is the persistence of various forms of discriminatory practices, chief among which is a continued preference for male employees in what continue to be categorized as male-specific employment sectors.

A relevant case of interactionally mediated gender discrimination is reported in the prestigious science journal, *Nature*

(Wenneras and Wold 1997). In the first study of its kind, two medical researchers investigate the gender disparity in the peer review ratings received by applicants to the Swedish Medical Research Council (MRC). The study was prompted by the fact that although women hold 44 percent of the biomedical degrees in Sweden, they hold only 25 percent of the postdoctoral positions and a mere seven percent of the professorial positions. It has been assumed that once the number of entry level women increased in the field, male domination of the upper echelons would diminish. However, this has not been the case despite the significant number of women who have entered the field since 1970. Authors Wenneras and Wold note that the prevailing stereotypical explanations for the relatively low success rate of female scientists include the idea that women are less career oriented, less productive and/or less assiduous in applying for funding. Wenneras and Wold investigated the MRC, which is the primary funding agency in Sweden for biomedical research.

MRC reviewers rate applicants on three dimensions: scientific competence, quality of the proposed methodology and relevance of the proposal. In general, women applicants are given substantially lower scores than their male counterparts, particularly in scientific competence. Scientific competence is measured in terms of productivity and impact: number of articles published and the prestige of the journal. One interpretation of the lower scores is that women are indeed less productive. Wenneras and Wold investigated this hypothesis. The authors developed a composite index of "productivity variables" based on number and type of publications. When applicants are compared on this alone a clear pattern emerges. Peer reviewers routinely give women lower scores than men who have the same productivity score on Wenneras and Wold's scale.

One of the most shocking results of this investigation is the level of disparity. Women and men with the same high productivity scores on the Wenneras and Wold scale are separated by an average of 64 impact points in terms of peer review assessments of their scientific competency. In other words, a woman applicant would have to have published approximately three more papers in the most prestigious journals in order to get the same score as her male counterpart. In the second tier, still a highly productive arena measured by publication in well-respected specialty journals, women would have to publish nearly 20 more papers to get the same competency score as men published in the same journals! This study, based on 114 applications submitted in 1995 (62 men, 52 women), provides empirical evidence for something that many professional women and minorities have long felt in their bones to be true; we have to work more than twice as hard to demonstrate our competency. Wenneras and Wold conclude that "our study strongly suggests that peer reviewers cannot judge scientific merit independent of gender. The peer reviewers over-estimated male achievements and/or underestimated female performance" (341). In the cognitive-emotive terms of a misogy-nist culture, reviewers have a bit of a "spit" response to the appli-cations of women. It is difficult to pin down this elusive interior reaction, but the generalized impact of such a cultural cognitive prejudice is clearly expressed in the notion that somehow the ideas of woman and scientific competency just don't compute. Thus putting an additional burden of proof on the woman as scientist.

Wenneras and Wold note that this is the first study of its kind to be conducted on a scientific research community in Sweden. They suggest that the lack of previous systematic investigation into gender disparity is due to the prevalent belief that such discrimi-nation is at odds with the intent of equal opportunity. Explaining away cases of blatantly obvious discrimination with the idea that the individuals in question really are somehow less deserving enables us to uphold the myth of equal opportunity.

A recent plethora of research in the United States documents ongoing, systematic discrimination based on gender, race and class in education and employment (e.g., Reskin and Padavic 1994). Bonnie Thornton Dill and Maxine Baca Zinn (1994) launched a call for women of color to study and empirically demonstrate the injustices they experience. The result has been some of the most sociologically relevant and methodologically accessible work produced in the past decade. There is no lack of evidence to support the claims that there remain huge chasms in opportunity for women and people of color in the United States. If we do believe in the justice of a broad based equality, why are we so unwilling to wrestle this discrimination directly? Believing in the desirability of the goal is not enough to make it so.

Ridgeway concludes her analysis with this observation:

> The process [of sex categorization] is insidious because gender is
> usually an implicit, background identity whose salience varies

situationally, acting in combination with more salient work identities... changes in gender beliefs lag behind changes in the distri-
butional inequalities that support them; thus the degree of equality
achieved is likely to be substantially undermined by interactional
processes mediating the decision making through which compara-
ble worth policies would be adopted and implemented... If this
inequality is to be reduced, it is vital to understand the multilevel
nature of gender processes and the role of interactional processes in
maintaining gender inequality. (232)

Constructed Structures

Ridgeway's work is instructive as both theory and methodology.
For decades there has been a battle in sociological inquiry between
the so called "structuralists" and "social constructionists." The former insist on the primacy of institutional arrangements in shaping
who gets what and how; they are critical of social constructionists
for implying that change is within the power of actors to perceive
alternative arrangements. This bifurcation of theory and method
reflects (false) dichotomous debates that seem to concern US social
researchers more so than our European counterparts. Some of these
debates include battles over the primacy of individual vs social
determinism; agency vs institutional structure; micro vs macro
analyses and so forth. Recently, US sociology seems to be coming of age and moving into the more complex recognition that
we are socially constituted subjects who navigate webs of opportunities and obstacles not necessarily of our own chosing. *The
manner in which we envision and respond to these structures is reflected
in discursive strategies carried out through interactional processes.*
This means that a complex, informative sociological reading of
inequalities requires apt descriptions of structural (or institutional) arrangements, but with the understanding that these
arrangements are always shifting, that they are neither necessary
nor natural, but rather obdurate circumstances that reflect the
interaction of cultural beliefs with the realities of existing political
economic practices (cf. Dorothy Smith 1990). At the same time,
explanations of the perpetuation of these practices are likely to
be situated in ongoing, everyday, taken-for-granted practices
that are rooted in cultural habit (Bourdieu 1977) and reflected
in discursive practices (e.g., Foucault 1977). The perpetuation of

these hierarchies of difference is mediated through interactional processes (Garfinkel 1963; Goffman 1967; O'Brien and Kollock 1997).

Though it may sound complex to those who prefer the concision of standard multivariate analyses, this approach is key to understanding the extent and implications of the backlash between cultural beliefs and political economic institutions. Such an approach calls for us to describe situational structures with a particular emphasis on structures of power and privilege, and then to focus inquiry on the ways in which interactional processes perpetuate, inhibit and/or alter the existing structural arrangements. These inquiries enable us to place under a microscope, as it were, processes whereby long held cultural beliefs which are rooted in cognitive-emotive stereotypes and practices of injustice are reproduced. Like particularly adaptive strains of a virus, these practices carry over into new structural contexts. In our collective desire to believe that we have wiped them out, we relax our guard, desist in treating the problem and are then surprised to find that the same old prejudices are alive and active in strikingly insidious new forms.

Consider as a case in point the discursive strategies of backlash and "PCism" that mark the adaptive perpetuation of group-based prejudice and discrimination. I have in mind a recent cartoon I saw in the *New Yorker*. In the cartoon, a middle-aged white woman sits on her middle-class couch addressing her middle-aged, white husband who is reading the newspaper. "Do you think we should try to integrate more gender and ethnic diversity into our marriage?" she asks. Similar in tone is a report made in jest on the local NPR affiliate station. According to the report, a group of hounds at the Humane Society expressed outrage that the Society's literature referred to them as "dogs" rather than "American Canines." I like to think that I have a sense of humor, that I can laugh at myself when I get too serious. Yet I found myself feeling extremely emotionally distant when the close friend who related the NPR jest to me did not seem to comprehend why I found the report clever, but in poor taste. The form of both the cartoon and the report is funny. They compel a chuckle first and consideration of the ideological significance a beat later, if at all. Such forms of joking have become ubiquitous, meant as a slice of Americana offered up in many of the nation's presumably "liberal" venues. I'm not sure whether to cast the rhetoric of

anti-PCism as an instance of extreme cultural absurdity or a dia-
bolical brilliance in maintaining the status quo. This discourse,
which is manifest in countless expressions of eye-rolling, snicker-
ing mimicry of any claim for equality, enables the speaker to
simultaneously acknowledge the inappropriateness of categorical
discrimination – by highlighting and making fun of it – and yet
dismiss it as something that has become a tiresome, overblown
topic of concern. In a sort of "I'm okay, in fact I'm fabulous, what's
the matter with you, crybaby?" manner, anti-PC rhetoric sweeps
aside the gut wrenching circumstances that comprise the reality
for many Americans with a laugh and a wink.

I was thinking about this the other day when I pulled up next
to a blue van at a stop light. The hand painted, counter-culture
markings of the van caught my attention. I was surprised when
I noticed the hand lettered sign posted on the side of the van celebrating the day as "Heterosexual Pride Day." My initial urge was
to roll down the window and explain to this creatively down-
wardly mobile, prominently heterosexual doofus that *every* day is
heterosexual pride day in America. Instead I sat in my own car,
a standard issue, lesbian four-wheel drive with the requisite taste-
fully subtle gay pride bumpersticker and contemplated the sneer
this guy would probably give me as he hollered back something
about "You people have your day, you have a problem with us
having the same thing?"

I thought about the recent arguments I'd been having with the
Vice President of Student Affairs over the inclusion of the term
"bisexual" in the title of the student gay and lesbian organization.
Apparently bisexual implies choice. As a Catholic university, we
want to encourage tolerance of sexual minorities – those of
us who, according to the Catechism are afflicted with a social
disease that we can't help and must bear with dignity – but
not a "lifestyle" choice. I thought about my close friend who is
a transgendered male to female. Although she is a nationally
renowned author and performance artist she rarely leaves her
home because even in this predominantly gay neighborhood she
is subjected to constant heckling. "It just wears me out," she sighs
whenever I try to entice her out for a drink. I worried about
whether I needed to make time later that day to write a letter to
the editor of the newspaper in response to a national advice
columnist, Dr Laura Schlesinger, whose advice in the morning
edition included the pronouncement that gays and lesbians cannot

have "normal" relationships because we are a "social faux pas."
I pondered the recent spate of "white men's clubs" springing up
on college campuses. I recalled the irritating conversations on
"reverse discrimination" that I suffer at family dinners with my
brothers-in-law, all of whom hold advanced professional degrees
and who are practicing in their chosen fields. I thought about the
women in my classes who tell me earnestly that feminism makes
a lot of sense for other women, especially in earlier times, but not
for them. They can't figure out how to love their fathers and their
brothers and their boyfriends and still claim a voice of their own.
I thought about my students who want Norwegian American to
be on a par with American Indian. I think now about the final
papers they write linking privilege to gender, race, and class. In
the end, after ten grueling weeks of serving up every trick I can
conjure to drive into their guts the relationship between social
status and privilege, some of them tell me they get it.

They begin to "get it" they say, when they start to piece together
the statistics and demographics of who has what with everyday
situations, particularly the taken-for-granted aspects of how we
oppress one another. A photo essay of the single welfare mother
who cannot purchase bulk grocery items because she can only buy
what she can carry home on the bus, while minding her two small
children, causes them to rethink the stereotype statement "poor
people spend money poorly." They become quietly silent when
contemplating the invisibility described by the maids in ethnogra-
phies done by Mary Romero (1992) and Judith Rollins (1985).
They are troubled by the ongoing ruminations and frustrations
expressed by "Stephen Cruz" in his interview with Studs Terkel
(1980) about his successes as a Chicano – does he owe it to the
assistance of his fellow Chicana/os and the sacrifices they have
made? or to Affirmative Action? His ongoing dilemma of self-
worth, desire for individual attainment and obligation to his
minority community strikes a chord among students who take it
as second nature, as well as those who have never experienced the
"tyranny of solidarity" in a nation of oppression. Finally, they are
impressed with writers such as Gloria Anzaldua, who speaks
forcefully and eloquently of the advantages, as well as the dilemmas, of a complex, multiple consciousness. It is no accident that
Black Feminist theory is so closely tied with pedagogy as the site
of praxis. As bell hooks insists, education is not only an occasion
to foster awareness of the viruses that lurk beneath our collective

skin, but an opportunity to practice the transgressive acts that upset the status quo.

What can I say to the guy in the blue van that will have more impact than the clever sloganistic lines he can acquire so easily from television shows such as "Politically Uncorrect"? There is no simple innoculation for the virulent denial of categorically based inequality that plagues us. I am not hopeful about a sudden cure. There is no such thing as the "quick fix" multicultural workshop; two decades of Affirmative Action have not resulted in a substantial closing of the gap; the differences don't disappear even with a rhetoric intended to tame and diminish their significance. I am, however, optimistic about the potential of sociology to contribute significantly to the understanding of the connection between these differences and inequality.

Cultural pluralism, in its various forms, has established the legitimacy of a rich array of participants at the collective table. One of the purposes of social research is to give voice. The humanities and social sciences have made considerable strides in this direction in recent years. A task that strikes me as highly suitable to sociology is the enterprise of ascertaining prevalent patterns of categorical distinction that result in continuing inequalities based on gender, race, class, sexuality, immigration status, and various other culturally ascribed statuses. The documentation and analysis of these patterns requires us to develop better theories of obdurate structures (theories not rooted in ontological assumptions of "naturalness" or "functionalism," theories that can incorporate cognitive-emotive level structures as well as institutional ones) and richer methodologies for studying the interactional processes whereby cultural myths, stereotypes, and default cognitive-emotive schema mediate the practice of power and privilege. Through this enterprise perhaps sociology can contribute to the development of discursive strategies that will enable me to swiftly toss a neat little package of cultural awareness into the window of the guy in the blue van so that he will "get" why heterosexual pride day does not mean the same thing as gay pride day; a little explosion of ideas that shakes him into an instant awareness that the issue is categorically based institutional oppression, not simply identity parades. We need new metaphors; a sociological language that reflects the way in which we are all implicated in what might be called the "hoxing" of significant numbers of our population based on socially marked differences. I came upon the reference to hoxing in an essay by the novelist, Jeanette Winterson (1995):

> Hox is a racing word: it means to hamstring a horse not so brutally that she can't walk but cleverly so that she can't run. Society hoxes women [and other marked categories of people] and pretends that God, Nature or the genepool designed them lame. (p. 68)

Outline of the Book

This book is about the ways in which we hox one another; ways in which we practice forms of inequality in our everyday encounters; ways in which we wear masks of difference and entreat others to do the same in a manner that perpetuates categorically based discrimination. Paradoxically, like the unintended transmission of a virus, these inequalities are often perpetuated among those who are consciously opposed to such practices.

Everyday Interaction

The first section of the book demonstrates the way in which social differences and cultural patterns are manifest and reinforced through everyday interactions. These forms are revealed in the way in which persons signal status and expectations in various social settings. Hollander's analysis of the popular television game show, *Studs*, illustrates taken for granted interactional dynamics through which gender hierarchies are performed and reinforced in the realm of flirting and dating. These hierarchical patterns circumscribe who and what persons think they can be in the setting. Through repeated, often unconscious enactment the patterns are reinforced. Hollander describes the subtle but prevalent ways in which women on the show must navigate the tricky line between sexy and slutty. The men, on the other hand, simply enjoy a status of stud. Hollander's study is suggestive of a general asymmetry in men's and women's sexuality; in common renderings women *are* sexuality, whereas men *do* sexuality (Thompson 1995). The extent to which a woman's sexuality still determines her reputation is indicative of a pattern of deeply entrenched cultural inequality.

An eyeglasses shop may seem an unlikely site for studying sexuality, but in her observations of interactions between clients and clerks Van Leuven is able to demonstrate the ways in which sexual expression is an interactional achievement. The interactional scripts employed in professional settings differ from those in settings that are understood to be overtly sexual. Nonetheless, these scripts are not preprogrammed and people must therefore signal intentions to one another. The double entendres, smirks and blushes that accompany conversations in professional settings indicate the extent to which sexuality is a forbidden but desirable topic and further illustrate that people do make attempts to sexualize these settings. Who can say what, how they say it, and whether or not they can redefine what they have said reveals normative practices of sexuality. These conversational dynamics are suggestive of general cultural forms which become manifest when persons try to figure out how and whether a setting is being sexualized. Explaining sexuality as an accomplishment, rather than assuming it to be an expression of personality or a precondition for a setting, is a novel contribution. Understanding it as such opens up new lines of inquiry regarding the dynamics of sexual harassment and the relationship between racial, gendered, and class-based expressions of sexuality.

Kendall takes up the intriguing question of whether and how gender is expressed in online interactions. Cyberspace hype promotes electronic interaction as a site in which physical differences, such as race, gender, ablebodiedness, age, and so forth, won't matter because they can't be seen. Through participant observation Kendall gathers insights into the ways in which gender is a social phenomenon rather than an embodied state of being. Online interactions cannot take place unless participants signal minimal expectations to one another. A basic organizing feature of this signaling is gender; the potential for sustained interaction grinds to a halt if one does not give a gender identity. Even more intriguing is Kendall's observation that because gender is so uncertain online, individuals go out of their way to "sleuth" for gender – "who is he/she really?" This observation supports the interpretation that gender is a primary way through which interactions are organized; embodied or not, we develop an impression of and formulate responses to others based on our presumptions of their gender. The insistence on gendering interactants in online communications results in similar reenactments of gender-based differences, including the dismissal and/or harassment of women by men and the tendency for men to try to help women and downplay their potential skills. Far from erasing gender as a significant form of differentiation, Kendall concludes that, at least for the time being, online communication may actually lead to a reentrenchment of some of the most insidious forms of gender stereotyping and gender inequality.

Pate's focus on a seemingly mundane form of interaction reveals the minute ways in which we recognize our own differences within status hierarchies. Following in the footsteps of Goffman and other ethnographers of public ritual, Pate turns his gaze upon greetings of acknowledgement between strangers. He freeze frames these fleeting interactional moments in order to scrutinize the forms of cultural knowledge that are passed between strangers. The cultural expectation among white, middle-class Americans is the non-greeting. Acknowledgement is minimal unless something out of the ordinary prompts awareness of the other; even then, such people generally ignore one another in public walkbys. Given this, Pate is intrigued with the relatively effusive greetings that black men give to one another when they pass as strangers in public. Through pondering his own participation in this greeting ritual and talking with others, Pate offers the concept of mutual recognition of marginality as an explanation for these greetings. He also speculates about variations in the exchange of symbolic information based on race, gender, and sexuality.

Internalized Contradictions/Revealed Inequalities

In the second section of the book we pursue the theme of the internalization of social hierarchies. These dynamics are revealed through ways in which persons attempt to reconcile personal characteristics and circumstances with desirable social images and expectations. The uniformity of these cultural hierarchies is indicated in the awareness with which persons wrestle their own differences. The authors in this section explore the intra and interpersonal strategies whereby persons attempt to manage stigmatized or problematic identities. These management strategies highlight hierarchical patterns of dominance and exclusion and reveal the extent to which people creatively manage and resist such circumstances.

Lopez and Hasso chronicle the ways in which exclusion and opposition foster ethnic consciousness among Latinas and Arab American women. Based on their own self reflections and interviews with university students, the authors illustrate the ways in which racial-ethnic identities are "constructed and redefined in social interaction and through social practices." The authors debunk the notion that ethnic identities are "natural and fixed", by focusing on the ways in which the women they interviewed "tailor" their ethnic identities in accordance with various sites, occasions, and assumptions about the dominant culture. The range of identity strategies practiced by these women reflects "an oppositional consciousness governed by 'structural' location," as well as subjective experiences and responses to rigid, racist identity categories.

Herbert's reflections on her experiences in the military and her surveys of the experiences of military women focus on the dilemmas that these women face in what is still considered a "man's world." The various strategies that military women use to prove their competence are indicative of unequal gender expectations. This is intriguing in its own right, but equally remarkable is the paradox whereby women must not only prove their competence, but maintain their femininity in the process. In a sort of damned if you do, damned if you don't clinch, women are expected to prove their competence, but when they do so, their status as women is tainted. The choice it seems is between being considered incompetent but feminine or competent but too masculine (manifest through the stigmatizing accusation of being called a lesbian). Herbert's observations and analysis indicate pervasive patterns of gender inequality manifest through the gender-specific expectations for work and sexuality. Some of the strategies that women use to exert femininity while also being capable military workers are reminiscent of "Hot Lips," in *M*A*S*H*. Sexy underwear, flirtatious behavior and dating practices all serve to enhance femininity. But, as Herbert points out, these strategies reinforce gender stereotypes about work, they reinscribe women as objects of sexuality rather than as agents of their own work and their own sexuality, and they reinforce homophobia.

Gerschick takes on a similar paradox in his discussion of men with disabilities. The stigma that these men encounter takes a form of gender exclusion which reveals the extent to which masculinity is associated with strong, able-bodies. In Gershick's account, the men struggle deeply with their tarnished masculinity. The extent to which personhood for these men is akin to possessing a fully functioning male body reveals a hierarchy framed not only through wholeness, but also on gender. The image many of these men have had of themselves is entirely defined through a general concept of themselves as "male." For many of them, this status would seem to have been enough to mark their rightful spot in the cultural hierarchy. The struggle for visibility and acceptance as a disabled person is secondary in many cases to the struggle to regain a sense of maleness. Gershick concludes with the paradoxical statement that it is only through letting go of an attempt to regain superiority through gender that these men find effective strategies for coping with the inequities of disability.

Prostitution has become a fashionable topic of study. In part, this can be interpreted as a result of women claiming agency for their own sexuality, including the right to commodify it and to determine their own terms for doing so. Indeed, several "sex positive" activists currently writing on the cultural politics of prostitution are engaged in the business themselves. The transgressive potential of women who are pursuing PhDs and simultaneously turning tricks (e.g., Carol Queen 1997) is fascinating and, in our colonialist capitalist commodity culture, exotic as well. Long before the subject became glamorous, Shockey began studying prostitution in an attempt to "give voice" to women who, within the academy, have either been lumped in with the study of deviance or treated as practitioners in just another labor market. One of her most compelling (and potentially controversial) findings is the class distinctions within the enterprise of prostitution itself. Despite the existence of feminist oriented activist organizations such as COYOTE, many women who engage in prostitution do so with little or no control over their own working conditions. These women's stories reveal class differences in terms of the opinions they hold of themselves, their work, and the desirability of *the life*. Strategies for coping with the stigmas of prostitution reflect everyday attachments and concerns as well as class-based differences in the experience of and adjustment to cultural expectations.

In a world in which love supposedly conquers all, Twine documents the stigma experienced by transracial mothers, particularly white birth mothers of nonwhite children. The literature on motherhood (with the exception of black feminist theorists) has assumed a white mother in a white family. Thus it has contributed little to our understanding of the *contingent* nature of white privilege. As "race traitors," these women are, to some extent "unwhitened" by their own families while being "hyper-whitened" by their black family members. Their whiteness comes into relief in the context of their extended black family members. This is a paradoxical and painful situation; they come to embody and signify both whiteness and nonwhiteness because of their relationship to their birth children. Twine's focus on multiracial families highlights some of the "limits" of white privilege and exposes sites where transgressive mothers challenge white supremacy.

(Contesting) Institutional Practices

The third section of the book deals with institutional dynamics – normative practices in cultural settings and formal organizations that reflect entrenched forms of dominance and inequality. Again, paradoxically, because these patterns are the result of inequities which are mediated through interaction, they are often perpetuated in forums which have as an explicit goal the erasure of categorical inequities. The authors in this section write about specific interactions among members of particular organizations or movements which both reinforce and challenge practices of inequality.

In a fascinating pictorial analysis of government sanctioned photography produced during the New Deal Era for the specific purpose of enhancing the image of the working man, Kowalski demonstrates that there is no intrinsically moral/immoral rendering of art. Responding to claims such as those made by Jesse Helms and other detractors of the NEA, Kowalski argues that cultural interpretations of art are embedded in concurrent cultural and political circumstances which shift over time and across the gaze of various constituencies. In short, art is what we make it. In a sort of checkmate manuever, Kowalski demonstrates that the New Deal photographs are easily rerendered as homoerotic in the current cultural milieu. These culturally constructed readings of art imply that agendas to advance or inhibit the production of any type of art are politically motivated and reflect attempts to contain the expressions of certain segments of the population imagined to be represented through the art.

Eichstedt also focuses on the production of art, particularly the processes whereby funding agencies determine whose work is a "legitimate" representation of multiculturalism. In a study based on participant observation, she analyzes the activities of a predominantly white board responsible for funding "ethnic" art. Her observations detail a disturbing perpetuation of "othering" accomplished through practices of benevolent interest and a failure to relinquish creative control to anything deemed too "marginal." Her conclusion is that artists who are able to create work that reflects the colonizer's gaze are rewarded; those who are unable to assimilate are considered problematic and troublesome.

Hartmann looks at the relationship between institutionalized sports, racial ideals, and inequalities. Through an historical case analysis of the 1968 African American Olympic protest movement in Mexico City he provides a "window onto the possibilities and ultimate limitations of sport's relationship to racial change." Hartmann notes that because of its cultural visibility and significance, sport can provide a powerful platform for racial-ethnic concerns. At the same time, because sport is rooted in a deep ideological commitment to the individual-meritocratic ideals that dominate American conceptions of political legitimacy, this platform may have a tendency to shape change toward individual-integrationist visions of racial justice and civil rights. Hartmann concludes with an insightful analysis of why cultural forums such as sport, and practices such as identity politics have become more prevalent than traditional materialist forms of resistance.

One of the paradoxes of social movements is that in the attempt to gain recognition and acceptance from the mainstream, marginal groups engage in assimilative practices that may eventually result in the demise of the distinctive edge that defines them as a group. Anticipating a trend that has recently become manifest, Freitas began an inquiry into the cultural political implications of "queer markets" several years ago. His thesis, which has become increasingly apparent in the writings of others, is that the political gains in the gay and lesbian movement have been substantially buttressed by the economics of a queer market. In attempts to distinguish ourselves, to signal our status to others and to claim pride for our existence, queers constitute a market niche for products such as symbols, clothing, travel to gay ghettos, etc. The successful establishment of such markets has also established gays and lesbians as a desirable "target market." Political acceptance in this capitalist culture is mediated through economic viability. Thus, through the approving nod of market capitalism, gays and lesbians have achieved citizenship. This process reflects a political economy in which *all* modes of self and community expression are shaped through market structures. It also indicates that the fear and loathing which are the hallmark of homophobia have not necessarily been stamped out, rather, queerness has become a commodity fetish. The implications for and the price of acceptance in such an environment reflect a deep ambivalence about cultural diversity and assimilation.

REFERENCES

Allport, Gordon. 1956/1980. *The Nature of Prejudice*. Reading, MA: Addison-Wesley.

Anzaldua, Gloria. 1987. *Borderland = La Frontera: The New Mestiza*. San Francisco, CA: Aunt Lute Books.

Bell, Inge. 1985. *This Book is Not Required*. Fort Bragg, CA: The Small Press.

de Beauvoir, Simone. 1952. *The Second Sex*. New York, NY: Vintage.

Bourdieu, Pierre. 1977. *Outline of a Theory of Practice*. New York, NY: Cambridge University Press.

Collins, Patricia Hill. 1991. *Black Feminist Thought: Knowledge, Consciousness and the Politics of Empowerment*. New York, NY: Routledge.

Dill, Bonnie Thornton and Maxine Baca Zinn (eds). 1994. *Women of Color in U.S. Society*. Philadelphia, PA: Temple University Press.

Du Bois, W. E. B. 1903. "Double-Consciousness and the Veil", in *Souls of Black Folk*. New York, NY: Bantam.

Foucault, Michel. 1977. *The Archaeology of Knowledge*. London: Tavistock.

———. 1979. *The History of Sexuality* Vol. 1: *An Introduction*. London: Allen Lane, Penguin Press.

Garfinkel, Harold. 1963. "A Conception of and Experiments with 'Trust' as a Condition of Concerted Stable Actions," in *Motivation and Social Interaction, Cognitive Determinants*, O. J. Harvey (ed.). New York, NY: Ronald Press Co.

Gilman, Charlotte Perkins. 1898/1970. *Women and Economics*. New York, NY: Source Book Press.

Goffman, Erving. 1967. *Interaction Ritual*. New York, NY: Doubleday.

Gould, Stephen Jay. 1995. "Curveball," in *The Bell Curve Wars*, Stephen Fraser (ed.). New York, NY: Basic Books, 11–22.

Hofstadter, Douglas. 1985. "Changes in Default Words and Images Engendered by Rising Consciousness," in *Metamagical Themas*. New York, NY: Basic Books.

hooks, bell. 1994. *Teaching to Transgress*. New York, NY: Routledge.

Howard, Judith A. and Jocelyn A. Hollander. 1997. *Gendered Situations, Gendered Selves: A Gender Lens on Social Psychology*. Thousand Oaks, CA: Sage.

Hughes, Langston. [1938]/1994. *Collected Poems by Langston Hughes*. New York, NY: Alfred A. Knopf, Inc, 4.

Large, Jerry. 1997. "Reaching Beyond the Group" *Seattle Times*, July 6, L1.

O'Brien, Jodi and Peter Kollock. 1997. *The Production of Reality*, 2nd edn. Thousand Oaks, CA: Pine Forge Press.

Queen, Carol. 1997. *Real Live Nude Girl*. Pittsburgh, PA: Cleis.

Reskin, Barbara and Irene Padavic. 1994. *Women and Men at Work*. Thousand Oaks, CA: Pine Forge Press.

Ridgeway, Cecilia. 1997. "Interaction and the Conservation of Gender Inequity." *American Sociological Review*, 62: 218–35.

Rollins, Judith. 1985. *Between Women: Domestics and Their Employers*. Philadelphia, PA: Temple University Press.

Romero, Mary. 1992. *Maid in the USA*. New York, NY: Routledge.

Rose, Stephen. 1992. *Social Stratification in the United States: The American Profile Poster*. New York, NY: New Press.

Smith, Dorothy. 1990. *The Conceptual Practices of Power: A Feminist Sociology of Knowledge*. Boston, MA: Northeastern University Press.

Smith, Rogers M. 1988. "One United People: Second Class Female Citizenship and the American Quest for Community." *Yale Journal of Law and the Humanities*, 1: 229–93.

Terkel, Studs. 1980. "Stephen Cruz", in *American Dreams*. New York, NY: Pantheon.

Thompson, Sharon. 1995. *Going All the Way*. New York, NY: Hill and Wang.

Twine, France Winddance and Jonathan Warren. 1991. "Just Black? Multi-Racial Identity." New York, NY: Filmakers Library.

Washington State Commission on African American Affairs. 1995. "Affirmative Action: Who's Really Benefiting?" *Part 1: State Employment Report*. Olympia, WA.

Waters, Mary. 1990. *Ethnic Options*. Cambridge, MA: Harvard University Press.

Wenneras, Christine and Agnes Wold. 1997. "Nepotism and Sexism in Peer-Review." *Nature*, 387: 341–43.

West, Cornel. 1993. *Race Matters*. Boston, MA: Beacon Press.

Williams, Patricia. 1991. *Alchemy of Race and Rights.* Cambridge, MA: Harvard University Press.

Winterson, Jeanette. 1995. *Art Objects: Essays on Ecstasy and Effrontery.* New York, NY: Vintage Books.

Wollstonecraft, Mary. 1791/1982. *A Vindication of the Rights of Woman.* Harmondsworth: Penguin.

Part I

Everyday Interaction

1

Doing *Studs*: The Performance of Gender and Sexuality on Late-Night Television

Jocelyn A. Hollander

"We always start out watching Nightline, but we just can't help taking a peek. Then we're hooked. Why? Is it putty-faced Mark DeCarlo's smarmy repartée? Is it the lewd double-entendres written for the contestants by the show's uncredited geniuses? Is it the slow-witted mooks who punch each other's shoulders when they answer correctly? Or is it the user-friendly babes? Yes! Yes, it's all that."

Rolling Stone (May 14, 1992)

"Gender, not religion, is the opiate of the masses."

Erving Goffman, "The Arrangement Between the Sexes" (1977)

Popular conceptions of gender center around the seemingly huge differences between women and men – in behavior, talk, and even feelings – and the "war of the sexes" that results. Books, magazines, and film share with most traditional scholarly work on gender the assumption that gender is a dichotomous attribute possessed by individuals. Whether they believe that gender is biologically innate or socioculturally determined, these authors imply that gender – the social expression of maleness or femaleness – is something that individuals *have*.

In contrast to these approaches, an increasing number of scholars have begun to theorize gender as something that is enacted rather than possessed, something that must be constantly achieved rather than simply expressed. For example, West and her colleagues (West and Zimmerman 1987; West and Fenstermaker 1993, 1995) define gender not as a characteristic of individuals, but as "the activity of managing situated conduct in light of normative conceptions of attitudes and activities appropriate for one's sex category." (West and Zimmerman 1987: 127) They contend that gender is "not simply an aspect of what one is, but, more fundamentally, it is something that one *does*, and does recurrently, in interaction with others." (140) When we interact with others, we manage our behavior in order to confirm our gender. According to Fox, "a woman (or man) must earn the label of "feminine" (or "masculine") through traditional sex-appropriate behavior, and one must act feminine (or masculine) continually in order to retain this label." (1977: 809–10; see also Goffman 1976, 1977; Kessler and McKenna 1978; Connell 1987, 1995; Bem 1993; Thorne 1994; Bornstein 1994; Lorber 1994).

The performative nature of gender is rarely salient; because we perform gender (and see others perform gender) continually from the time we are children, gender performances tend to be invisible unless they are inadequate or interrupted. Nonetheless, individuals are constantly performing gender, and these performances are not only a means of claiming membership in a gender category but a strategy for constructing identity and image. My goal in this paper is to demonstrate *how* gender is performed, and identity is constructed, through interaction. It is important to recognize, however, that these actions do not take place in a vacuum; they are constrained by, and simultaneously reinforce, social structures (Lorber 1994).

The performance of gender can be seen clearly on television, where actors tend to play stereotypical roles and where, even in non-dramatic media, the pressures for successful self-presentation are high because of the public nature of the performance. In this analysis, I focus on a television performance that purports to be realistic and in which gender is central: the late-night dating game show *Studs*.[1]

Studs premiered on the Fox television network in mid-1991, and from the beginning, its popularity was enormous. Although the show finally ended production in 1994, it sparked a series of similar "kiss and tell" shows, both in the US and internationally. *Studs* is clearly a caricature of real-life dating. However, I suggest that it mirrors – and indeed, provides a stark view of – some of the gendered elements of everyday interaction. In addition, shows such as this help create the cultural context in which this interaction takes place.

The basic premise of *Studs* is the same as that of most dating shows: the contestants – in this case, two men – each go on blind dates with three women (for a total of six dates), and then return to the show to answer questions about their dates. The sequence of events in the half-hour program is as follows: host Mark DeCarlo introduces "the ladies" (whom I will call the "dates"), who are seated on a couch to stage right. He presents their names, ages, and professions, and then asks them, "So what are you looking for in a guy?" After each woman has answered, DeCarlo introduces the two "studs," who literally bound onto the set and sit on a couch to stage left. Once this introductory sequence is complete, the contest begins. The body of the show consists of three guessing sequences separated by advertisement breaks. In the first, DeCarlo asks the first "stud" contestant a preliminary question (for example, "What's the first thing you notice when you look at a woman?") and, after the contestant has answered, says "Well, we asked them what they thought when they first saw you, and here's what they said." Then, three quotes attributed[2] to the "dates" are flashed onto the screen. The contestant selects a quote, and guesses which woman has said it. If he is correct, DeCarlo tosses him a decorated fabric heart, which the contestant affixes to his clothing. DeCarlo questions the "date" and/or the "stud" about the quote, and then the process is repeated for a second turn. If the contestant answers incorrectly, he receives no heart (and no second turn), but DeCarlo still questions the women about the quotes. This guessing process is repeated for the second contestant.

In the second sequence, this guessing process is repeated, but with different questions. Typically, the preliminary question is about dating behavior (e.g., "How do you make the first move on a date?") and the quotes similarly address romantic dating behavior (e.g., "We asked them about your romantic moves, and here's what they told us.").

The third sequence follows a different format. DeCarlo alternately asks the two men questions beginning with, "According to the ladies, who's most likely to...?" Common endings include "kiss a woman's hand," "wear makeup," "fall asleep during sex," "be a peeping tom," or "sell his sperm for rent money"; in all cases, the questions reflect on the contestant's gender, sexuality, or both. After the contestant guesses, the women say the correct name in unison. Correct answers earn the contestant a heart, and both correct and incorrect answers are followed by an explanation from one of the women.

Winning the game is a complicated process. First, a contestant must earn more hearts than his "co-stud" by answering questions correctly. Second, he must choose which woman he would like to date again, *and* that woman must also choose him. The men present their choices verbally at the end of the show, after explaining why they did not choose the other women; the women reveal their choices by uncovering a written name, but do not have the opportunity to describe the reasons behind their choices. If all of these conditions are met, the winning contestants go on an all-expenses-paid "fantasy date" to the destination of the stud's choice; in the case of a tie, both winning couples receive a fantasy date.

Two variations on this general sequence should be noted. First, there is another, more ambiguous way to be a successful "stud": a contestant who answers all questions correctly is crowned "King Stud" and decorated with a shiny gold necklace with "STUD" in large gold letters. However, being King Stud does not entitle a contestant to further dates or prize money. Second, occasional episodes are "reversal shows," in which two women play the "stud" roles (they are described as "studettes" and are eligible to become "Queen Stud") and three men play the "date" roles. Interestingly, these reversal shows are always "theme shows," featuring some unusual type of women (e.g., hot mud oil wrestlers or construction workers), and are often part of some larger theme week such as "Fantasy Week" or "Wild Women Week." Apparently some justification is necessary for women to play the typically masculine role.

To examine the performance of gender on *Studs*, I videotaped 18 episodes between October 29 and December 9, 1992. I transcribed these episodes, also noting the contestants' nonverbal behaviors and the audience members' responses. The basic unit of analysis is the communication turn; I define this unit to include not only conversational turns, but also gestures and other non-verbal actions.[3] I examine these communication turns within several contexts. First, I analyze a particular communication turn in relation to the speaker's other turns: how does the turn interact with what the contestant has said or done previously? In other words, is the contestant's performance internally consistent? Similarly, I analyze turns in relation to the other contestants' turns. Often, both the stud and his date will describe a particular date: are their separate accounts mutually supportive or contradictory? When there is inconsistency in a speaker's own turns, or between the accounts of the stud and the date, I analyze the circumstances of the contradiction: do contradictions occur on some topics more than others? How are the contradictions resolved, and what are the consequences for the speakers?

The third type of context is that of role, or the particular part being performed. In fact, there are two types of roles performed by each person on *Studs*. First, each contestant plays a specific role on the show – i.e., that of "stud/studette" or "date." This role is symbolized by the couch on which a contestant is seated – studs sit to stage left, dates to stage right – and the contestants' performance of these roles presumably ends when their participation in the show ends. However, each contestant also performs a second, more permanent role: that of being a woman or man in everyday life. These roles are signalled by the performers' appearance and behavior; as Kessler and McKenna (1978) note, although people generally believe they assign gender based on physical features such as genitals or genes, they rarely see these features and it is in fact social behavior that triggers gender assignment in everyday life. West and Zimmerman call these two types of roles "situated identities" and "master identities," respectively: the first type is "assumed and relinquished as the situation demands," while the second is constant across diverse situations (1987: 128). The reversal nights on *Studs*, during which women play the "studette" roles and men play the "date" roles, highlight the differences between these two types of roles or identities.

Finally, I examined the contestants' communication turns in the context of the *Studs*-like genre (or frame, in the Goffmanian sense) of performances – what Bauman (1986) has termed "burlesque performance." The game show is ultimately a source of entertainment for viewers, and the contestants' job is to provide an entertaining performance. In this genre, sexual innuendo, hyperbole, and outrageous double entendre are legitimized and expected; in fact, skillful performance requires that contestants imply as much risqué behavior as possible. In this context, a good story can be personally beneficial to the performer, even if the story does not present the self in a favorable light. The expectations of this genre enable the situated "stud" and "date" roles to be played; nonetheless, the normative expectations of the contestants' master (gender) identities still exist, and it is in the management of these often conflicting demands that the contestants show their most skillful gender performances.

Performing Gender: Studs, Studettes, and their Dates

According to West and Zimmerman, "doing gender means creating differences between girls and boys and women and men,
differences that are not natural, essential, or biological. Once the
differences have been constructed, they are used to reinforce
the 'essentialness' of gender." (1987: 137) Bem calls this process
"gender polarization": the organization of social life around
perceived differences between women and men. Gender polarization "defines mutually exclusive scripts for being male and
female," and also "defines any person or behavior that deviates
from those scripts as problematic." (1993: 81) On *Studs*, differences
are created and maintained in myriad ways. The initial structure
of the set and the show, the nonverbal gestures and positions of
the contestants, the stories they tell about the dates, and the statements they make about men and women – all of these serve to
construct and emphasize gendered differences between the
"studs" and their "dates."

Setting the Scene

From the first moment of *Studs*, the male and female contestants
are separated and treated as different. Men and women are always
seated on opposites sides of the stage, and their numbers are
always unequal. The fact that there are always more "studs" than
"dates" means that at least one "date" is never chosen. Because
the "dates" are nearly always women, at least one woman is
always left out of the final pairings.

As the show begins, the "dates" sit demurely to stage right,
while the "studs" run onstage soon after and often engage in some
sort of clowning as they sit down to stage left. The host always
rises and shakes hands with the "studs," but never with the dates;
at the end of the show he congratulates only the winning "stud."[4]
The physical separation of the sexes results from the show's focus
on heterosexual dating – mixing the participants might suggest a
less orthodox bisexual pairing of contestants. This separation,
together with the contrasting entrances of the contestants onto the
stage and their differential treatment by the host, serves to emphasize the differences, rather than the similarities, between the men
and women.

The contestants' clothing is perhaps the most salient marker of difference and gender.[5] With very few exceptions, the female contestants wear some sort of revealing clothing: short, tight miniskirts, low-cut shirts or blouses, skin-tight bodysuits, or some variation on these. High heels are *de rigueur*. Even when the episode is a "theme show" that would demand some other sort of dress from the women (female construction workers, for example), the women's outfits conform to these guidelines as much as possible (for example, both construction workers wore tight jeans shorts and low-cut, midriff-baring tops along with their work boots). Occasionally, a female contestant does not conform to this implicit dress code (for example, wearing a calf-length rather than thigh-length skirt); in my sample of episodes, these women are less likely to be chosen as desired future dates.

The men's clothing, in contrast, serves to emphasize masculine strength rather than feminine curves. Their clothing is seldom revealing; the only exception to this rule is that highly muscular men occasionally wear shorts or sleeveless shirts that emphasize their muscled arms and legs. Form-fitting jeans and cowboy boots are the most common dress for men. This stereotypical attire is, of course, indicated by the stud and date roles the contestants are playing, as well as by the burlesque genre: the task of the contestants is to be as sexually suggestive as possible. In a heterosexual context, this task requires a polarization of the sexes, which is precisely the effect produced by the contestants' clothing. Interestingly, however, even when the stud/date roles are reversed – i.e., the women are seated to stage left – the contestants' clothing remains the same, suggesting that it is not only the situated roles that produce these differences, but the gendered "master identities" of the actors.

Bodies in Motion

Another indicator of gendered performance is the nonverbal communication acts performed by the contestants. This category includes the positioning of the contestants' bodies and the gestures they make in reaction to others' communication turns. Although sitting and moving need not be gender-specific activities, these behaviors are markedly different for the "studs" and their "dates."

The most subtle of the nonverbal expressions, and the most constant across the duration of the show, is body positioning. Without exception, the women in this sample of shows sit in a "feminine" way: legs together or tightly crossed, arms held close to their bodies. Some of this positioning might be accounted for by the mode of dress adopted by the women: miniskirts do not lend themselves to sitting with legs apart on national television. Nonetheless, even when the female contestants wear longer skirts, pants, or shorts, their body positioning is the same.

The mens' body positioning contrasts sharply with that of the women. From the moment they sit down on the couch, the men sit widely, legs apart or crossed knee-to-ankle, arms often extended from their bodies along the back or on the arm of the couch. The men's bodies seem to take up all the space allotted – they often appear to be crowded on their couch – whereas the women seem to be trying to take up as little space as possible. This difference between the men's and women's body positions persists even in reversal episodes.

The contestants' gestures mirror their body positions. In general, the men make big, expansive gestures. When they are introduced, they clap with their arms spread widely; they punch each other playfully, slap each other on the back, raise or pump their fists in the air, and so on. These gestures are most obvious when the men win a heart or are the subject of some particularly bawdy comment. When they receive a heart, they slap it forcefully onto their bodies; in both situations, they clap vehemently and are congratulated by their "co-stud" through mock punching, elbowing, high fives, and the like.

The women, in contrast, use small, contained gestures. When they are introduced, they nearly always give small, cute waves, smile at the camera, and then clap for themselves with their arms close to their sides. In contrast to the friendly camaraderie evident between the male contestants, the women never interact physically with each other, and rarely interact verbally. In the reversal shows, they press rather than slap the hearts they win onto their bodies. When they are the subject of some highly sexual comment, the women may laugh, clap quietly, or hide their faces in embarrassment; other than these gestures, running their fingers through their hair or adjusting their clothes are their only motions. Again, these nonverbal behaviors do not change when the stud/date roles are reversed; here too, master identity seems to override situated identity when the two are in conflict.

Overall, the men's body language is expansive and active: they run onstage, take up all the available space when seated and move freely and frequently. The women's body language is dramatically different: they fold themselves into a minimum amount of space, make small, infrequent gestures, and generally sit passively for the duration of the show. This active/passive distinction is further emphasized by the separation of the women and men onstage and by the host's behavior: he interacts frequently with the men but rarely with the women. Thus, men's gender performances entail activity and interaction; women's center around display. This differentiation heightens the perceived polarization of men and women.

Gender Prescriptions

The first time the "dates" speak on *Studs* is during the introductory sequence when host DeCarlo asks them each, "What are you looking for in a guy?" (or, in the case of a reversal show, "What are you looking for in a woman?"). A selection of these responses follows:

Q: What kind of guy are you looking for?

A: A big, strong *man.*
A guy I could get along with, a good personality, and dresses nice.
Tall, lean, mean rock-and-rollers.
A guy who's sexy, casual, clean-cut, and conservative.

Q: What are you looking for in a woman?

A: Someone who's going to put up a big challenge – make me work for what I want.
A woman with a nice firm athletic body, a woman who looks conservative, but likes to get wild.
A woman who knows what she wants, and knows how to use what she's got.
I like a woman who has a nice body, long legs, nice breasts, and a little bit of, you know, an airhead. [Mark: You like an airheaded girl.] Yeah. [Mark: Why's that?] You don't have to worry about what they're going to say, you don't have to go into complications, you can just let things happen.

These responses constitute both gender performances on the part of the speaker and gender prescriptions for the "studs" or "studettes." Most obviously, these statements tell the other contestants (and, indirectly, the audience members) what is expected of them: what gendered characteristics or behaviors are necessary in order to be desirable. To be successfully masculine, one should be big, strong, and sexy; to be successfully feminine, one should have a nice body, be an airhead, like to get wild, and so on. These kinds of demands are predictable from the genre of the show; yet once again they serve to highlight differences between women and men. Unfortunately, it is difficult to determine how the two types of roles – the situated stud/date roles and the master gender identities – affect these comments, because only those playing the "date" roles are asked what kind of person they are looking for.

In terms of performance, these prescriptive statements situate the speakers as masculine or feminine, emphasizing their sexuality – and, perhaps more important, their *hetero*sexuality – and defining the speaker as the type of man or woman who values the qualities desired in the other sex. For example, the man who said he liked "airheaded women" can now be categorized as the kind of man who values airheads; the man who asked for "someone who's going to put up a big challenge – make me work for what I want" can now be categorized as a very different type of man.

These prescriptive statements also serve as a reference point for the speaker's other communication turns. Having made this kind of prescription, the speaker later can be judged as behaving consistently or inconsistently ("Aha! She said she likes tall, lean, mean rock-n-rollers, and yet she chose a man who is a short, sweet, classical violinist!") and thus as putting on a credible or less-than-credible performance. In addition, the other performers can also be judged with respect to these prescriptions: the statements define "stud success" and thus, implicitly, "stud failure." Host DeCarlo often uses the prescriptions as an opportunity to joke about the kind of man who would *not* fit the requirements for "stud." For example, on one episode featuring "pirate Harley girls," DeCarlo made the following jokes:

MARK:　　　What kind of guy do you like, Stephanya?
STEPHANYA: A big, strong, *man*.
MARK:　　　Someone who would ride maybe like a 150 moped, perhaps?

MARK:　　　And Martine, I'm sure Alastair Cook is your type, right?
MARTINE:　 [laughs] Alastair Cook??? Well, I don't know about him. I like men that are strong, rough, and ready.

DeCarlo's jokes make it clear that "real studs" are not Alastair Cook kinds of men – quiet, intelligent, reserved – and that they ride big, powerful motorcycles, not small mopeds. These types of exchanges demonstrate that gender is negotiated through inter-action – and imposed by some on others – rather than simply expressed or spontaneously performed. Through interaction with each other and with the host, the contestants on *Studs* enact gendered behaviors and collaboratively define what kind of quali-ties are necessary in order to be attractive to others.

Telling Stories

A final way in which gender is constructed and performed is through the use of stories. There has been growing attention in recent years to the phenomenon of storytelling as a means of describing and understanding social life (for example, see Bauman 1986; Read 1987; Plummer 1995). Narratives about the contestants' dates are the core of *Studs*. It is through the stories that the audi-ence is told what "really" happened on the dates and that the quality of the contestants' performances – both as dating partners and as bawdy storytellers – can be assessed. These stories not only describe the events that occurred on the dates, but also make sense of them by giving the events order and meaning, and evalu-ate them by defining the events and the actors as good or bad, proper or improper. At the same time, they serve to construct a social, gendered identity for the storyteller and his or her date.

Stories on *Studs* are generally prompted by the quotes from the dates, which are flashed onto the screen and which are almost uni-formly sexually suggestive.[6] A sampling of these quotes:

> "He bucked around the room with the force of a lovesick bronco."
> "A couple of warm splashes and his boxers were bubbling over."
> "A few short grunts and I was ready to worship the king."
> "I started to giggle when he kissed that rear end."
> "You gotta love a woman who can handle a really big crankshaft."
> "For a little girl, she can sure gulp a whole lot of foam."

The sexual implications of these comments are clear. After the contestant has guessed which of the dates is responsible for one of the quotes, DeCarlo asks the date to explain the quote, thereby prompting storytelling. One of the most interesting facets of these stories is that when the date is female, the story is often a repair sequence of sorts: although she has purportedly made the bawdy comment herself, her explanation of it is generally a denial or minimization of the sexual behavior it implies. Some examples:

QUOTE: "One mighty shove from behind and I was seeing stars."

EXPLANATION: 'Well, it was night, it was late and we were at the park and ... and it was starlit night and he was pushing me on the swing, from behind.'

QUOTE: "A few quick slurps and he was spilling his seeds all over the table."

EXPLANATION: 'He had some melon, some watermelon, and he had some juice, and the seeds, it's from the seeds, from the watermelon, that fell on the plate.'

QUOTE: "One mighty plunge and the log was soaking wet."

EXPLANATION: 'We went to Disneyland, so we went on Splash Mountain, and so all the way down he held my hands up so I could get wet in front, in front of him, blocking him.'

Thus, although the burlesque genre of the show and the roles the women play within that genre demand sexually suggestive comments, the women also seem to be expected to deny the very sexuality they profess. These contradictory demands do not appear to apply to men: in my sample of shows, no male contestant ever denied a sexual encounter. In fact, one man insinuated that a sexual encounter had occurred, but later apologized to the woman for making this suggestion, assuring the audience that nothing had happened. When men's sexuality or sexual behavior is described, men react very differently than women: they applaud enthusiastically, and they generally engage in some congratulatory behavior with the other male contestant – back-slapping, high fives, or pumping raised fists. In contrast, when it is implied that the women have engaged in sexual behavior beyond simply kissing, they often appear embarrassed (for example, covering their faces with their hands) and attempt to deny or minimize the occurrence. Moreover, the other women never acknowledge that the sexual behavior has occurred, let alone congratulate the others on their conquest. The implications of this kind of sexuality for women and men are very different: men tend to be seen as studs, women as sluts (Kimmel 1993; Orenstein 1994).

From these differences, I suggest that the participants in *Studs* are performing and constructing identity along two linked dimensions: gender (masculinity/feminity) and sexuality. For men these dimensions are congruent: for both masculinity and sexuality, more is always better. Using the tools described above – positions, gestures, statements, and stories – men emphasize their masculinity and the differences between themselves and women. They also emphasize their sexuality, implying that sexual encounters took place and congratulating each other when sexually suggestive comments are made. Thus for men, sexuality reinforces masculinity, and vice versa. A man who is highly sexual is seen as more masculine; a man who is more masculine is assumed to be more sexual.

For women, however, the dimensions of femininity and sexuality are at least partially opposed. Like the "studs," the female contestants use verbal and nonverbal communication to emphasize their femininity and their differences from men. In terms of sexuality, however, the women's task is more complicated. On the one hand, the women must appear sexually provocative, both in their appearance and in their comments about the dates. On the other hand, however, there seems to be strong pressure to mask or minimize this sexuality. The racy quotes, although appropriate to the burlesque frame of the show, constitute gender transgressions for the women. In order to repair these transgressions, and maintain a credible gender performance, the women must dispel the implication of sexual behavior created by the quotes. This dichotomy between gender and sexuality is reminiscent of the good girl/bad girl distinction of past decades (Fox 1977), when men would be attracted to "bad girls," whose sexuality was evident, but desire to marry "good girls," whose sexuality was hidden. The performance of gender on *Studs* suggests that in the 1990s, this distinction has shifted from one between women to one *within* women: to be considered attractive, women must be both sexually provocative *and* sexually restrained – both a "bad girl" *and* a "good girl." Performing both of these roles requires a subtle, skillful balancing act between conflicting demands.

But are these demands made by the situated "date" role that women usually play on the show, or by their master identity as women? These two identities can be teased apart by examining the role-reversal episodes in which women play the "stud" roles and men play the "date" roles. In these episodes, several interesting changes in gender performance occur. First, sexuality seems to become more acceptable for women. There is even greater use of sexual innuendo (by both women and men), and the women are not as quick to deny sexual events, as in this example:

> QUOTE: "A rip here, a tear there, and lips and clothes were everywhere."
>
> MARK: What does that mean, Milton?
>
> MILTON: What that means is we were having a pretty good time when we left the bar, and we pretty much did the streets of San Diego.
>
> MARK: So how'd your date with Miltie end up, Tracy? After you're driving around the city streets for a while...
>
> TRACY: It ended up the next morning.
>
> MARK: Fun evening?
>
> TRACY: Yeah, kinda sticky. [Audience: "Wooo..."] He poured a can, he poured Dr Pepper on me.

In this narrative, there is an acknowledgement of female sexual behavior that is rarely found in the stories of women playing the "date" role. Interestingly, this type of acknowledgement was also more frequent during "theme" episodes that legitimated unconventional female behavior. For example, the following story was told on an episode featuring "pirate Harley girls" during "Wild Women Week":

> QUOTE: "A couple of warm splashes and his boxers were bubbling over."
>
> STEPHANYA: We went jacuzzi-hopping at a couple condos, different condos actually...
>
> MARK: How do you jacuzzi-hop?
>
> STEPHANYA: Well you get half-naked and you jump from jacuzzi to different jacuzzi.
>
> MARK: So you weren't wearing a bathing suit.
>
> STEPHANYA: Um, no, I was wearing his boxers actually.
>
> ACE: I helped her get into them...
>
> MARK: And?
>
> ACE: I did. It was fun. It took a while before we got in the jacuzzi, but it was fun, it was a very fun date.
>
> MARK: So you just crash these places when you go?
>
> STEPHANYA: Yeah. That's the fun part, getting in, and then, well actually that's not the real fun part, but yeah. [laughs]

OTHER WOMEN: Oh yeah?? Oh yeah??
STEPHANYA: Stop it! [pointing to other women]

In both of these situations – when women play the "stud" role and when they are characterized as "Wild Women" – gender transgression is legitimated, and open acknowledgement of sexuality becomes more acceptable. On the other hand, both women still perform a modified repair sequence: Tracy attributes the stickiness of the evening to having had soda poured on her, while Stephanya cuts short the other women's sexual innuendo.

Thus even on the reversal and theme shows, sexuality that is too overt must be repaired. For example, both of these exchanges took place on reversal shows:

QUOTE: "Her savage growl made me feel like king of the jungle."
MARK: Why, what'd you talk about?
MILTON: We talked about wet things, oceans, and you know, fun things we don't want to talk about here.
MARK: What'd you talk about with Milt? Fill me in, Trace. [Tracy covers her face, looking embarrassed]
TRACY: Well, we just basically talked about getting together and going somewhere because everything was just so spur-of-the-moment, but we like that.

QUOTE: "One night of wild passion, and I was a mass of throbbing flesh."
MARK: Yeah? Want to explain that, Darryl?
DARRYL: I don't think my couch will ever be the same again.
MARK: What were you doing on the couch?
DARRYL: Um, major kissing, caressing, and then loving.
MARK: How long was she over there?
DARRYL: Come on! Uh, it was a while.
MARK: It was a while. How long was it, Sherry?
SHERRY: I left at like 1, 1:30, somewhere around that. He had to work, so ...
MARK: What were you doing on the couch?
SHERRY: Watching TV.
MARK: What were you watching?
SHERRY: *Home Improvements.*
MARK: *Home Improvements?* That's on at one in the morning now? Pretty romantic, Darryl?
DARRYL: I think it was working into that, but she had to leave.
MARK: Would you have wanted it to go on longer?
DARRYL: Of course.

MARK: Sure. How about you, Sherry?
SHERRY: [unenthusiastically] Yeah.

Because of the reversal show setup, the male "dates" give the first
descriptions of the events. Host DeCarlo then asks the women about
the dates, and, as is obvious in the stories above, the women often
give very different accounts than the men, even when asked exactly
the same questions as the men. In the first story, when asked
about the phone conversation, Milton says they discussed "wet
things, oceans, and you know, fun things we don't want to talk
about here." DeCarlo immediately turns to the female "studette"
and asks her precisely the same question, to which she answers,
"Well we just basically talked about getting together and going
somewhere." The contestants are describing the same conversation in response to the same question, but his response implies
sexuality while hers denies it.

The same difference occurs in the second story: DeCarlo asks
Darryl what he and his date were doing on the couch, and he
answers, "Major kissing, caressing, and then loving," implying
extensive sexual behavior. However, when DeCarlo asks Sherry
the same question, she responds, "Watching TV." Not only does
she deny that sexual behavior occurred, she also flatly contradicts
her date. Female contestants, despite their role as "studettes," still
both imply and deny sexuality, although there is a tendency to
acknowledge more sexual behavior when the women are in the
"studette" role than in the "date" role. Male contestants, on the
other hand, seem to become even more overtly sexual in their
quotes and stories when they are in the "date" role – perhaps
needing to display masculinity and sexuality even more clearly in
order to overcome the feminine implications of the role – although
this apparent difference may also be due to the fact that those in
the "date" role generally have more opportunities to tell stories.

Thus, women and men experience different demands for sexuality and gender on *Studs*. While men are expected to be both
highly masculine and highly sexual, women must balance the
conflicting demands of femininity and sexuality. Although this
conflict appears to be exacerbated by the "date" role they usually
play, it is not eliminated by switching roles. Some other set of
expectations, constant across roles, appears to be responsible.
There are two possible explanations: the burlesque genre of the
show, or the master gender identities that the participants hold

despite their varying roles. I hypothesize that it is identity, not genre, that produces these differences between men and women. Because the burlesque genre thrives on bawdy performances, if the genre were the more pressing source of expectations I would expect the women to be more, rather than less, sexually suggestive. The master identity of "woman," however, prescribes restrained sexuality. It is this force, then, that I suggest is ultimately responsible for the different performances of men and women on *Studs*. West and Zimmerman suggest that "to be successful, marking or displaying gender must be finely fitted to situations and modified or transformed as the occasion demands. Doing gender consists of managing such occasions so that, whatever the particulars, the outcome is seen and seeable in context as gender-appropriate" (1987: 135). The reversal episodes on *Studs* illustrate how gender can be negotiated even when performing gender-atypical roles.

Multiple Performances

Although I have focused here on the performance of gender on *Studs*, it is clear that gender is not the only identity being constructed in this context. A number of scholars (e.g., Spelman 1988; Hill Collins 1990; hooks 1984) have criticized studies that attempt to analyze gender separately from other statuses such as race and class, arguing that this approach tends to privilege white, middle-class experiences and ignore the experiences of poor people and people of color. In their recent paper, "Doing Difference" (1995), West and Fenstermaker take up this challenge, and argue that individuals "do race" and "do class" at the same time that they "do gender." All interactions, they write, "regardless of the participants or the outcome, are simultaneously 'gendered,' 'raced,' and 'classed'" (1995: 13). Although their attempts to provide a model for understanding these intersections was only partially successful (see critiques in Hill Collins et al. 1995, for example), their argument that race, class, and gender affect individuals and interaction simultaneously is important. I would add that sexual orientation and age are also implicated in most interactions. These performances are interwoven with the gender performances of the *Studs* contestants.

Most salient, perhaps, is the construction of sexuality. The burlesque nature of *Studs* induces both men and women to display sexuality – but, although never stated explicitly, this sexuality is always *hetero*sexuality. The link between gender and heterosexual orientation is absolute and unquestioned on *Studs*: to be a successful "stud" or "studette," one must be both attracted to and desired by the opposite sex. Alternative sexualities – homosexuality or bisexuality, for example, or even heterosexual women being assertively sexual – are never mentioned directly. Because traditional heterosexuality is assumed, other sexual possibilities need not even be mentioned; this silence both reflects and reinforces the hegemony of heterosexuality. Despite the invisibility of homosexuality or bisexuality, sexuality on *Studs* is constructed via implicit contrast with these other possibilities. In examples discussed earlier in this paper, judgments about the type of masculinity desirable in a "stud" (strength, roughness, and so on) were conveyed through contrast with less valued masculinities: Alastair Cook types and men who ride mopeds rather than powerful motorcycles. A similar type of contrastive process occurs during the third guessing sequence in each episode, in which the host asks the "studs" to guess which man is more likely to perform a number of behaviors, such as kissing a woman's hand or wearing makeup. In each case, differences within gender categories are constructed and evaluated. Connell describes this process as "the construction of hierarchies of authority and centrality within the major gender categories" (1987: 109). In the hierarchy of masculinities constructed on *Studs*, heterosexuality is valued over homosexuality and other less stereotypically "masculine" or "feminine" sexualities.

The construction of race is more subtle, but equally powerful. There is almost complete racial segregation on *Studs*. There is never any mixing of African American and white contestants; there are only all-black and all- or mostly-white episodes. Occasionally, one Asian American or Latina woman is included in an otherwise all-white episode; in contrast, there were no Asian American or Latino men among the male "studs" in my sample. As with gender, "the accomplishment of race consists of creating differences among members of different race categories – differences that are neither natural nor biological" (West and Fenstermaker 1995: 25). On *Studs*, this creation of difference is accomplished in part by assigning participants of different racial and ethnic categories to separate episodes. This separation of racial groups both mirrors and reproduces existing segregation in the wider world. The message about race here is clear: interracial contact, especially sexual contact, is unthinkable. It is taken for granted that whites and blacks will not be interested in each other as dating partners. The only racial mixing possible involves white men and Asian or Latina women; men of color do not date white women in the world constructed by *Studs*.

Race is also accomplished *within* racially homogeneous episodes. As West and Fenstermaker note, "the accomplishment of race, class, and gender does not require categorical diversity among the participants" (1995: 31). On the all-white (or mostly-white) episodes, race is never discussed. There is no questioning of the racial segregation of participants, and no references to race ever occurred in the verbal interactions among contestants. These silences are telling: one of the hallmarks of privileged status is that privilege is taken for granted and not even noted unless it disappears (Frankenberg 1993). To these white participants, race does not seem to be a salient feature of interaction.[7]

Race is mentioned much more frequently (although obliquely) on the all-black episodes.[8] The most frequent comments refer to skin tone. For example, when asked what she was "looking for in a guy," one African American contestant said she wanted a "nice chocolate guy"; another stated that her ideal man would be a "tall, dark guy with smooth skin." Skin color is discussed later in this same episode, when a female "date" comments that "I thought he was going to be light skinned, but he was dark." Other race-related comments referred to hair texture and style and clothing choices. Through these comments, the participants evaluate others' appearance and behavior in terms of racialized categories, and make it clear which of these categories are more highly valued. These evaluations also serve as performances of race for the speakers, locating them as the type of people who prefer certain characteristics. It is also important to note that these statements simultaneously enact other statuses as well as race: by saying that she wants "a tall, dark guy with smooth skin," the speaker accomplishes gender, sexuality, and race.

The construction of age and class is more subtle, but also important, in these episodes. Virtually all the episodes of *Studs* focus on young adults in their twenties. Although the age of the typical contestant undoubtedly mirrors that of the target audience, it nonetheless suggests that only young adults are sexual and desirable. One episode in my sample did involve middle-aged adults, and demonstrated clearly that people in their late 30s, 40s, and 50s can be as sexually provocative as young adults. However, this was the only episode with contestants over age 35 in both the formal sample of 18 shows used for this analysis and the much larger informal sample of episodes I watched; on *Studs*, as in much of the media, the sexuality of middle-aged and older adults is invisible.

Another age-related pattern on *Studs* was that the men were generally older than the women they dated. For example, on one typical episode, the "studs" were age 23 and 27; their "dates" were 20, 21, and 23. The age gap was even more pronounced when the contestants were older; in the episode mentioned above, the "studs" were 49 and 52; their "dates" were 37, 41, and 43. Here again, the patterns illustrated on *Studs* both reflect and reinforce patterns of domination in the wider world. Women are encouraged to pair with older, more powerful men; romances between older women and younger men are invisible, or are met with derision and even disgust. These patterns, while not necessarily harmful in individual cases, reinforce men's power over women in the aggregate.

Messages about social class were similarly embedded in these episodes. In the opening sequence, contestants are introduced by their name, age, and occupation, thereby providing hints about their class position. It was not clear from this sample of episodes whether contestants were deliberately matched on class position as they were with respect to age and race, although there were some indications that this might be the case. For example, in one episode, women who were described as a nutritionist, a secretary, and a community college student – all white-collar occupations – were matched with an economics student and a hotel "guest services rep." The youth of many of the participants, however, made a more conclusive analysis difficult.

What was clear from these episodes, however, was that financial generosity, and the class status it implies, was important – but only for men. On several occasions in these episodes, men's willingness to spend money on a date was assessed. For example, one woman reported that her date had "stiff[ed] the waiter at Red Lobster." The host probed for more details:

MARK: Did you give the waiter at Red Lobster a tip?
MICHAEL: Oh yeah.

MARK: How much?

MICHAEL: Five...

MARK: Five dollars.

MARION: Because I made you give it to him.

MARK: Why weren't you going to give him a tip? Was it bad service? If the service is crappy, I don't tip people either.

MARION: No, the service was great, it's just that...I don't know what happened, he just really embarrassed me, actually.

Indeed, one of the few things male contestants are criticized for is appearing stingy, either by not spending enough money on the date or by failing to leave a generous tip in restaurants. These kinds of assessments were never made of women. Thus it is the interaction of gender and class that is important here; these statuses cannot be considered individually.

Conclusions

Recipes for Success

Becker (1991) suggests that one way to understand a social phenomenon is to devise a "recipe" for its creation. This analogy is particularly appropriate when discussing performance, because the recipes can be understood as a sort of script for actors. In this spirit, then, I offer the following recipes for studhood and studettehood. Although my comments below refer to the social context of *Studs*, I suggest that these recipes apply to everyday interaction as well:

Recipe for Studhood	**Recipe for Studettehood**
1 Be big.	1 Be small.
2 Be strong.	2 Be beautiful.
3 Be (hetero)sexual.	3 Be (hetero)sexually provocative...
4 Be young.	4 but not too sexual.
5 Be generous.	5 Be young.
6 Desire a studette of the same race and similar (or younger) age as yourself.	6 Desire a stud of the same race and similar (or older) age as yourself.

To be a successful stud, a man should be big and strong (qualities many of the women say they are looking for at the beginning of the show). He should dress in "manly" clothes – jeans and boots are ideal, unless of course the man is particularly muscular, in which case he may wear clothes that reveal and emphasize his strength. He should also be big in terms of body position and gestures: he should move in a masculine fashion, sitting so as to take up the maximum space, gesturing widely and engaging in playful, ritualistic aggression with other men when introduced or when sexual comments are made. On dates, the man should engage in sexual behavior if possible (although being overly boorish or overly hesitant may lead to criticism from his dates). He should be young and, as discussed above, he should be generous with his money. A stud should look for and ultimately select a woman who embodies the qualities of a studette; heterosexuality and masculinity are tightly linked. Finally, a stud should focus only on women of the same race and similar (or younger) age as himself as possible sexual partners.

Women who aspire to studettehood have very different requirements. As with men, they should be young. However, they should be small, not big, and beautiful, not strong: the most consistently admired women are thin (although buxom) and conventionally pretty. The way the women sit and move emphasizes their smallness: they sit in a way that minimizes the amount of space they take up, and their gestures are small and contained. Like men, women should also be sexually attractive and provocative: on *Studs*, their official quotes about the dates should be as racy and sexually suggestive as possible. In particular circumstances – if they are playing the "studette" role, or if they are "wild women," women may admit to some sexual activity. However, they should not be *too* sexual. After making suggestive comments, they should deny that sexual activity has occurred, although this denial may be less robust if they are playing the "studette" role. Thus their job is to be sexually provocative but still maintain the appearance of virtue. And finally, women should desire, and ultimately select, a man who is also a stud – but one of the same race and similar (or older) age as herself. Each of these requirements serves to maximize the differences between women and men, constructing gender as dichotomous.

Gender as Performance

The main argument of this paper is that gender is not something we have, but something we do in interaction with others. Although the performance of gender may be habitual and therefore taken for granted, we are constantly, skillfully, enacting what it means to be masculine or feminine in both our situational and cultural contexts. The behavior of the contestants on *Studs* provides a glimpse of precisely how gender is performed. Because gender is so salient in this context, its performance is obvious.

I want to emphasize three additional points. First, I contend in this paper that the enactments of gendered behavior exemplified by *Studs* are skillful performances rather than the expression of innate qualities. However, an important feature of these performances is that they are perceived to be natural expressions of underlying masculinity and femininity. Bem (1993) calls this "biological essentialism": the belief that gender polarization is "the natural and inevitable consequence of the intrinsic biological natures of women and men" (1993: 2). Although great skill is required to juggle the conflicting demands of gender and situational roles, there is never any acknowledgement of these talents, nor any hint that gender might be enacted differently. Thus this view of gender is consistent with Goffman's contention that gender "is not instinctive but is socially learned and socially patterned; it is a socially defined category which employs a particular expression, and a socially established schedule which determines when these expressions will occur. And this is so even though individuals come to employ expressions in what is sensed to be a spontaneous and unselfconscious way, that is, uncalculated, unfaked, natural" (1976: 7).

The second point is that although gender is a constructed performance, rather than an innate characteristic, it does not follow that gender performance is voluntary or consequence-free. Although the men and women on *Studs* clearly choose to participate in the show, the details of their roles, as well as their everyday behaviors as men and women, are constrained and subject to evaluation and sanction. Properly performing gendered behavior elicits social approval (e.g., applause and whistles from the audience), "stud success," being chosen for future dates, and so on. Improper performance, on the other hand, is socially punished by disapproval (e.g., booing, groaning, or lack of applause from the audience), "stud failure," and being passed over for future dates.

Examples of gender transgression – and the consequences it entails – were visible, although infrequent, in these episodes of *Studs*.[9] For instance, one male participant admitted using self-tanning lotion – a practice associated with femininity. This participant, who worked as a bouncer at a bar, commented, "I work during the day, I don't get out into the sun. So when I get back to the bar, I put some tanning stuff on my face, everyone was ragging on me, 'Aw, you're putting on makeup.'" The derision with which such transgressive behavior is met is evidenced both in the comments he reports and in the response of the studio audience, who groaned "Ohhhhh…" when he admitted using this product.

Women also suffer consequences for gender transgression. For example, one woman was particularly open in her admission of sexual behavior, as is evident in the following exchange:

LARRY: "He blazed a trail across my belly like 1,000 horny homesteaders" has got to be Cheryl.

CHERYL: Yep.

MARK: There you go! All right Cheryl, when last we left Larry's loveboat…

CHERYL: Well, we came back from dinner, and we're on the balcony, and he's still determined on that bikini.

MARK: How did he do?

CHERYL: Very well.

MARK: Uh huh. How did…

LARRY: I told her I like tall girls, and she said, well, it might be nice to have a tall girl with legs wrapped around you, but she said it's a lot more fun to have a short girl tryin'.

Although it was clear from Cheryl's comments – and from her selection of Larry at the end of the show as her preferred future date – that she had enjoyed her date with him, Larry did not choose her for future dates. Why? As he put it, "because I've already seen everything she's got." Gender transgression, such as admitting sexuality in women, is punished.

Finally, I want to emphasize that individuals' enactments of gender and other statuses are not solo performances. Individuals do perform gendered behaviors, but they do so in interaction with other people and in specific contexts that provide opportunities to perform gender, set expectations for gendered behavior, and then evaluate this behavior. On *Studs*, there are several types of interaction that work together to construct gender. First, the performers evaluate each other's comments and behaviors, both on and off the set. For example, consider this set of conversations reported by a "date":

QUOTE: "One quick shake and he was finally satisfied."

MARK: What kind of shake are you talking about?

NICOLE: I mean a handshake. Um, him and Patrick had talked, and said I don't kiss on the first date, which I don't. And he analyzed me for like two hours asking me why I don't kiss on the first date.

MARK: Why don't you?

NICOLE: I just don't, that's something that I, I'm not interested in doing, so I don't –

MARK: Okay. So in your whole life, you've never kissed on the first date.

NICOLE: No. I didn't say all that, I didn't say that, I just said –

MARK: You did! You said "I don't kiss on the first – "

NICOLE: I, I said I don't! That's, that's, that's now. [Audience: laughter]

MARK: Well, that's about as clear as you can get it.

In this example, Nicole reports that the two "studs" discussed her refusal to kiss on the first date (a behavior which implicates both gender and sexuality) both with her and with each other.[10] Clearly, her choice not to kiss was not evaluated positively. The host then probes for an explanation for this choice – a second type of interaction that elicits comments from the "date" – and then evaluates it (negatively, in this case).

Another type of interaction involves the studio audience's responses to the contestants. In the example above, the audience laughs at Nicole when an apparent inconsistency is found in her performance (i.e., she asserted that she didn't kiss on first dates, but then acknowledged having done so). Laughter is only one kind of audience response; there are a number of other common audience reactions that evaluate the success or failure of the participants' performances. For example, the audience rewards adherence to expectations about gender and sexuality by applauding, whistling, and saying "Wooooo!":

QUOTE: "His skin's as soft as satin panties."
AUDIENCE: "Wooooo!"

The audience also makes it clear when gender transgressions have occurred, by laughing, hissing, booing, or groaning ("Ohhhhh!"), as in these examples:

QUOTE: "I didn't kiss him, but I'm sure the girl he left with did."
AUDIENCE: "Ohhhhh!"

QUOTE: "He's a really big tipper – if you've got change for a quarter."
AUDIENCE: "Ohhhhh!"

Through these interactions, expectations for behavior are set, individual performances are evaluated, and alternative masculinities and femininities are suppressed. The range of performances permissible on *Studs* is highly restricted; individuals may choose to transgress, but they do so at the risk of evaluation and social sanction.

Is Studs just trivial entertainment, or does it have a deeper message? My suspicion is that the situated stud and date roles performed on *Studs* are simply stereotyped exaggerations of everyday gender performances. Nonetheless, my conclusions are limited by the fact that this analysis explores only one context, and, moreover, that this context is clearly unusual: as well as being part of a specialized genre, it is exceptionally public, at least partially scripted, and probably edited. On the other hand, this show was extremely popular; in my informal discussions and presentations of this paper, the overwhelming majority of my colleagues and students had seen the show at least once. Although many viewers criticize the show for its sexism, racism, and a host of other faults, I suspect that its gender prescriptions and performances may influence even critical viewers. Recent studies documenting the effects of viewing attractive models on subjects' perceptions of self and others (for example, see Kenrick and Gutierres 1989) also suggest these effects. I suggest that performance of gender on Studs and in other media serves to both model and reinforce the more subtle gender performances found in everyday behavior and thus to recreate existing differences and hierarchies based on gender, race, age, class, and sexuality. The stylized interactions on *Studs* illustrate how these statuses (and the institutional-level hierarchies they represent) are simultaneously constructed and maintained through everyday interaction. West and Zimmerman argue that "if we do gender appropriately, we simultaneously sustain, reproduce, and render legitimate the institutional arrangements that are based on sex category" (1987: 146). Examining the micro-level processes of interaction shows both how enmeshed these systems of hierarchy are – and how difficult they are to resist.

NOTES

1   Of course, even "spontaneous" television entertainment, such as talk and game shows, is highly scripted. Nonetheless, these shows remain

a good site for studies of gender performance. First, the scripts themselves illustrate popular conceptions of and prescriptions for gender. Second, the gendered behavior of performers that goes beyond these already-gendered roles shows the compulsory nature of gender performance. Participants are still responsible for their individual gender performances, even when playing scripted roles.

2 The credits following the show include this disclaimer: "Contestants' answers which appear on screen are the contestants' own, but may have been paraphrased or edited by the producer."

3 A conversational turn is defined as "a single contribution of a speaker to a conversation" (Crystal 1987: 432); communication turns similarly represent discrete contributions, either verbal or nonverbal, to an interaction.

4 The host's role is clearly intended to be neutral: he wears a suit to distinguish him from the younger, more casually-dressed participants, and although in fact unmarried, he wears a gold wedding band to signify that he is not sexually available. Although this role may be sexually neutral, however, it is not gender neutral. The host is clearly aligned with the male "studs" rather than the female "dates." He stands up to greet the male contestants when they arrive on stage, congratulates them after the show, asks them whether they consider the game's rules to be "fair enough," and engages the men in playful joking. He performs none of these behaviors with the female participants.

5 The amount of choice the contestants have regarding attire is unknown. However, the fact that there is some variation in dress suggests that they have at least some control over their clothing choices.

6 A second type of quote occurs regularly, although considerably less frequently: derisive comments about the "studs'" appearance or behavior. For example, the sample of episodes I use here included comments such as "He's the handsomest man on the planet... if you live on the planet of the apes" and "Food swirled through his mouth like clothes in a dryer."

7 Of course, this may be less true for the Asian American and Latina women who appear on the otherwise all-white episodes.

8 These episodes are infrequent, so I am generalizing here from a sample of only three episodes.

9 The relative lack of gender resistance is probably due in part to processes of self-selection. Those who choose to transgress the normative boundaries of gender and sexuality are unlikely to volunteer to participate in a television show focused around conventional notions of heterosexuality. If such individuals did volunteer to participate, moreover, they are not likely to be chosen as contestants. In this way, resistance becomes invisible: the contradictory goals of resistors and

gatekeepers both result in the marginalization of those who choose
to resist gender expectations.
10 Note women's presumed responsibility for determining and policing
sexual boundaries.

REFERENCES

Bauman, Richard. 1986. *Story, Performance, and Event: Contextual Studies of
Oral Narrative.* Cambridge: Cambridge University Press.
Becker, Howard S. 1991. Personal communication.
Bem, Sandra Lipsitz. 1993. *The Lenses of Gender.* New Haven, CT: Yale
University Press.
Bornstein, Kate. 1994. *Gender Outlaw: On Men, Women, and the Rest of Us.*
New York, NY: Vintage.
Clark, Herbert H. 1985. "Language Use and Language Users," in *The
Handbook of Social Psychology*, G. Lindzey and E. Aronson (eds),
3rd edn. New York, NY: Random House, pp. 179–231.
Connell, Robert W. 1987. *Gender and Power: Society, the Person, and Sexual
Politics.* Stanford, CA: Stanford University Press.
——. 1995. *Masculinities.* Berkeley, CA: University of California Press.
Crystal, David. 1987. *The Cambridge Encyclopedia of Language.* Cambridge:
Cambridge University Press.
Fox, Greer Litton. 1977. "'Nice Girl': Social Control of Women Through
a Value Construct." *Signs* 2(4): 805–17.
Frankenberg, Ruth. 1993. *White Women, Race Matters: The Social
Construction of Whiteness.* Minneapolis, MN: University of Minnesota
Press.
Garfinkel, Harold. 1967. *Studies in Ethnomethodology.* Englewood Cliffs,
NJ: Prentice-Hall.
Goffman, Erving. 1976. *Gender Advertisements.* New York, NY: Harper
and Row.
——. 1977. "The Arrangement Between the Sexes." *Theory and Society* 43:
301–31.
——. 1974. *Frame Analysis: An Essay on the Organization of Experience.*
Cambridge, MA: Harvard University Press.
Henley, Nancy M. 1977. *Body Politics: Power, Sex, and Nonverbal
Communication.* NewYork, NY: Simon and Schuster.
Hill Collins, Patricia. 1990. *Black Feminist Thought.* New York, NY:
Routledge.
——, Lionel A. Maldonado, Dana Y. Takagi, Barrie Thorne, Lynn Weber,
and Howard Winant. 1995. "On West and Fenstermaker's 'Doing
Difference'." *Gender and Society* 9(4): 491–506.
hooks, bell. 1984. *From Margin to Center.* Boston, MA: South End.

Kenrick, Douglas T., Sara E. Gutierres, and Laurie L. Goldberg. 1989. "Influence of popular erotica on judgments of strangers and mates." *Journal of Experimental Social Psychology* 25(2): 159–67.

Kessler, Suzanne J. and Wendy McKenna. 1978. *Gender: An Ethnomethodological Approach*. New York, NY: John Wiley and Sons.

Kimmel, Michael. 1993. "Clarence, William, Iron Mike, Tailhook, Senator Packwood, Spur Posse, Magic … and Us," in *Transforming a Rape Culture*, E. Buchwald, P. R. Fletcher and M. Roth (eds). Minneapolis, MN: Milkweed, pp. 121–38.

Lorber, Judith. 1994. *Paradoxes of Gender*. New Haven, CT: Yale University Press.

Orenstein, Peggy. 1994. *SchoolGirls: Young Women, Self-Esteem, and the Confidence Gap*. New York, NY: Anchor.

Plummer, Ken. 1995. *Telling Sexual Stories: Power, Change and Social Worlds*. London: Routledge.

Read, Stephen J. 1987. "Constructing Causal Scenarios: A Knowledge Structure Approach to Causal Reasoning." *Journal of Personality and Social Psychology* 52(2): 288–302.

Spelman, Elizabeth. 1988. *Inessential Women: Problems of Exclusion in Feminist Thought*. Boston, MA: Beacon Press.

Thorne, Barrie. 1994. *Gender Play: Girls and Boys in School*. New Brunswick, NJ: Rutgers.

"We Always Start Watching …" *Rolling Stone*, 14 May 1992: 89.

West, Candace, and Don H. Zimmerman. 1987. "Doing Gender." *Gender and Society* 1(2): 125–51.

——, and Sarah Fenstermaker. 1993. "Power, Inequality, and the Accomplishment of Gender: An Ethnomethodological View," in *Theory on Gender/Feminism on Theory*, ed. Paula England. New York, NY: Aldine de Gruyter, pp. 151–73.

——. 1995. "Doing Difference." *Gender and Society* 9(1): 8–37.

2

"I Need a Screw": Workplace Sexualization as an Interactional Achievement[1]

Linda Van Leuven

Introduction

That workplaces get sexualized is nothing new. Much current attention has been given to workplace sexualization; however, most studies simply give a causal nod to the role of structures and forces behind any such occurrences. For example, whether seen as the trappings of specific work environments (bars,[2] restaurants[3]), the invention of corporate maneuvering (hiring practices, sexualized ad campaigns[4]), or individuals pursuing intimate relationships (Schneider 1984), the sexual "happens" at work, and often seemingly out of the control of those experiencing it.

Sexualization approached in this way can be seen as natural to workplaces: intrinsic to the business of the setting, or alternatively inherent to it through participants' sexuality. Under both conditions, the sexual is assumed to be always and already there, without regard to what the participants themselves are doing in such moments. This essentialist position relegates sexualization to a mere component of the context.

An essentialist treatment may be due in part to prevailing attitudes regarding sexuality that are used to interpret the sexual at work. For example, one taken-for-granted attitude conflates gender with (hetero)sexuality. Even in the most detailed workplace studies,[5] heterosexualized assumptions of gender make sexualized interactions between males and females appear normal and, therefore, remain relatively unquestioned.

In addition to being subsumed under the category of gender, workplace sexualization has been cast in three other primary ways: as sexual harassment (Barr 1993; Schneider 1982), as sexual relationships (Reinemann 1945; Roy 1974; Schneider 1984), and as desexualization (Emerson 1970a; Henslin and Biggs 1971; cf. Heath 1988).[6] In all three instances, the sexual often has negative consequences – adversely affecting the work, the workers, or both.

Furthermore, workplace sexualization typically gets studied retrospectively. For example, the categories "sexual harassment" and "sexual relationships" represent end-points of some unspecified process and often are based exclusively on survey data.[7] This combination of focus and method has several results. For sexual harassment, this type of analysis does not fully address issues of context (Brewer 1982), thereby missing the complex unfoldings and situational contingencies of unwanted sexualization. Consequently, these studies gloss over the divergent meanings of participants and the specific practices involved. Such an approach leaves harassment as the property of certain personality types, the work of the hyper-sexed, or the insensitive.[8]

Likewise, the category of "sexual relationships" serves to blanket a whole series of interactive steps that go into establishing sexual relations. This treatment ignores the first moves and many moments that might have been ambiguous along the way (i.e., "was she looking at me?"). In addition, while never explicitly defined, it appears that what makes sexual relationships "sexual" is genitalized contact. Such a limited focus on the sexual obscures what might be some other forms or functions of sexualization, and thus it does not represent the universe of consensual sexualized encounters. Moreover, given this definition, it is unclear how "sexual relationships" can represent workplace sexualization in any true sense. Where does such genital contact take place? At work?

In contrast to a retrospective method, some researchers have taken a processual approach to investigate how workplace encounters are "desexualized" (Emerson 1970a; Henslin and Biggs 1971; cf. Heath 1988). For example, studies of doctor–patient interaction depict both parties (and an occasional nurse) collaborating to desexualize the medical encounter which often includes the inspection or touching of private areas (Emerson 1970a). Desexualization takes much on-the-spot coordinated interactional work.

Nevertheless, even in these processual studies, the researchers presuppose a sexualized environment specific to the nature of the work (i.e., gynecological examination) and the opposite-sexed interactants (i.e., heterosexed assumptions of gender). Once again such studies view the sexual as an inherent component of the context. Thus, even when taking an interactional approach, the researcher does not necessarily bring an interactional awareness to interpreting the sexual.

In sum, just how interactions come to be sexualized remains largely unexamined. Whether as a consequence of assuming sexuality, of limited sexual categories, or of end-point methodology, the actual social process by which workplaces become sexualized has not received adequate attention.

Through an analysis of service encounters in a retail optical store, I investigate sexualization as an emergent process of workplace interaction. Specifically, I examine how clients and workers sexualize service encounters. Thus, this project reconceptualizes sexualization as an achievement, rather than accepting it as a given. Even if we assume that all humans "have" sexuality, sexualized expressions must be produced and managed locally in interaction. In a sense then, sexuality, like gender,[9] must be done. Whereas doing sexuality might entail confirming or fabricating one's sexual status (Guiffrey and Williams 1994; Woods 1993), my perspective is not limited to identity work. Rather, my approach suggests that any form of sexualized expression is an achievement of a particular interactive moment. Such an angle on doing the sexual, I refer to as sexualizing.[10] As a verb it reflects the active work involved in producing, managing, or negotiating these moments. Sexualizing thus provides a conceptual framework for understanding the complexity of sexualized encounters that can not be captured by essentialist or identity-based interpretations. Looking directly at how people sexualize in particular moments, in particular encounters, and in particular settings, reveals that sexualization does not just happen; rather it is a creative production reliant upon the same mechanisms of interpretation and practical action that pervade all encounters.

In the course of the research process, I discerned various aspects to the sexual. Therefore, in examining sexualization as an achievement, I conceive of the sexual in the following ways: first, the sexual has many forms of expression beyond genital manifestations. These forms can include talk, commentary, looks, touches, and other displays that reference sexualized content. Second, participants may have discrepant perceptions of what is sexualized in any given situation; such a recognition suggests the fragility of these encounters, and forestalls the temptation to deem unwanted sexualization as the work of "bad" people. Third, people sexualize interactions for reasons often unrelated to expressing desire, interest, or without intentions of moving beyond the current encounter. This means that sexualizing serves many social and inter-/intra-personal functions beyond mating such as: doing gender, bonding, displays of power, being playful, and opportunities to reinvent one's sexual self, however fleetingly.

Setting

The setting is a retail optical store located in an affluent shopping area in a large metropolitan city. Through a large front window, one can see eyeglass frames and sunglasses lining the walls and in display showcases. At two work stations customers can sit down to try on glasses. In the back at a long work counter staff routinely dispense and repair eyewear.

The staff and clients at Valley Vista Optical[11] are a mixed bag. Staff refers to the six females and four males who sell glasses.[12] They range in age from 27 to 47 years old. While all male workers are self-defined heterosexuals, the females include both self-defined lesbians and heterosexuals. About half the staff are single.[13] The clientèle allegedly also includes both gay and straight persons, and those partnered and single.

While folks from all walks of life shop here – a baggage handler, celebrities, students, housewives, gardeners, executives, artists – this store is no one-hour "Frame 'n' Lens." Wherever you come from, whatever you do, you have to be prepared to spend some money. Eyeglass frames alone start at $200, and adding lenses can bring the total anywhere from $350 to nearly $700. In addition, clients spend many hours and possibly several visits to purchase their glasses. They also are encouraged to come in for routine adjustments and when in need of repairs.

Optical shops can be considered both as medical-technical and as fashion-oriented. At this store, a combination of the two exists, and an unstated charter might be: "to see better, and to be seen better." But the technical angle is often overshadowed by an environment that is visibly appearance-based. This emphasis is apparent in the personnel choices and dress code of the store. For example, all female employees are attractive, yet only one of the six women is a licensed optician.[14] In addition, while some optical stores require their employees to wear white smocks, promoting more of a medical definition, the staff at VVO are expected to dress up to reflect the type of clientèle and location of the store.[15] At VVO, dressing-up means dressing hip, trendy, or sophisticated.

The nature of optical work also entails many site-specific practices and conventions. For example, to fit or adjust glasses typically involves a closeness and physical touching between the worker and client. The touching is specific to the head and face: in placing a frame on a client, the worker's own face is about three to 20 inches from the client's as s/he inspects the fit of the glasses. Direct eye contact is routine in this process of adjustment. Looking and commenting on looks is also quite common in this optical store, as how one appears in a pair of glasses is crucial to making the decision to buy the frame. Mirrors around the store invite people to check themselves out. While looking at oneself is routinized at VVO, so is looking at others and commenting on their appearance. Staff often offer appraisals of looks whether or not they are sought out by the client.

Despite an emphasis on appearance, VVO principally may be seen as a place of business. But workers and clients must interact in ways that achieve this definition of the situation. Similarly, participants might shift their attentions to ways that display a more personal orientation.

Methods

I worked at Valley Vista Optical for eight years from 1988 to 1996, gathering participant-observation and interview data for the last six years. Thus, I was an insider in this setting, with both backstage and frontstage access. Because sexualizing is often done in ways that are subtle, specific to an interaction, or keyed only to members, an insider has the immediate and close contact for recognizing those nuances which might escape the outside observer. Relatedly, the outside observer may have a considerable effect on sexualization, perhaps suppressing it. Thus, in the study of sexualizing, not only being an insider, but also a longtime member of the setting is a particularly desirable stance for an ethnographer.

Maintaining dual researcher/member roles gave me great access from which to do participant-observations, informal interviewing of my co-workers, and to listen when they routinely unloaded about their encounters with clients. As a worker I also had frequent reasons to write things down which made doing on-the-sport jottings no problem. When immediate jottings might be awkward, there were many natural breaks in a service encounter where going downstairs to look for a frame, or going to the back of the store to repair a frame, were also opportunities to make notes.

Through writing fieldnotes, I gained insight into some sexual happenings of which I was previously unaware. Though I entered the field thinking I might find something about people's changed self-perception through buying new updated eyeglasses, this idea quickly changed. From rereading and the initial coding of my notes, I discovered a sexual subtext to much of the interactional work at VVO. My researcher role, and the constant writing and analysis of notes, allowed me to see the subtleties of sexualized interactions, and to appreciate the work done to produce, maintain, curtail, or remedy them.[16]

While my member's status afforded me great access to data, it also meant navigating the differing allegiances of being both researcher and member. Each of these roles made certain claims on my attention in the field. Though the competing demands gave me insight into sexualized practices, the tension between these roles often made me feel divided. A sense of splitting was also a part of the data analysis, because as a member I was present in many data fragments. It was awkward, enjoyable, and horrifying to come in contact with myself in this way – revisiting the moments I had laughed, the things I had said – over and over again. The good news is that this positioning grants me license to make some "in the mind" interpretations of at least one participant.

Sexualization as an Emergent Process of Interaction

Sexualizing starts somewhere in interaction. There is an initial movement, a bringing to attention, a series of actions, each reflecting how participants are making sense of the situation. Viewing sexualization as an emergent process thus means it is not a haphazard occurrence. Rather, it is organized by way of formally describable practices. Of course, not every interaction at VVO gets sexualized, but I am concerned with the procedures through which some of them are.

These procedures include beginnings. In any environment there are numerous resources that can be used as vehicles for making sexualizing moves. Some of these include joke formats, providing accounts, noticing jewelry, body comments, etc. For the purposes of this paper, I look exclusively at how tasks and conventions common to this eyeglass store, and the selecting/repairing of eyewear, are used to sexualize. I analyze three: double entendres in repair talk; appraisals of the look; and personalizing the service relationship. Initially, I detail the mechanics of how participants signal a double entendre in repair talk as hearably provocative. Next, I examine how participants use appraisals of "looks" to package their sexualizings. Finally, I show how conventions specific to the service relationship are used to launch the sexual.

Repair Talk/Double Entendres: "I Need a Screw"

So how do people sexualize service encounters? One recurrent way is through the signalling of a double entendre in repair talk. Repair talk is common because people often roll over on, sit and step on, or have their dogs, kids, mates mangle their glasses. Sometimes they have just lost an eyeglass part. The need for one particular missing piece, a screw, can provide the occasion for making a double entendre by playing off two potential meanings, one innocent, one risqué. In this case, the word "screw" might refer to a metal fastener and/or be slang for a sexualized act. While using a double entendre to sexualize may seem a fairly straightforward practice, it is actually quite an accomplishment because using the word "screw" does not necessarily mean that it gets played out as provocative. Consider the following:

> A man walks up to Eva at the counter. He says, "I didn't get these here. But I need a screw for these." Eva says, "OK, let me see." The man adds, "They're my favorite bicycle glasses, can't ride without them." Eva says, "OK" and goes to fix them.

This episode is treated as a simple repair request by both parties. However, in the next four data fragments, workers and clients use a variety of techniques to connote a sexualized nuance.

One way participants signal a double entendre is by adding a gesture to their comments. A playful tone sweeps through the following interaction beginning with one female worker's self-mocking offer to help, which provides a perfect opening for the screw request:

> Terri [a female co-worker] and I are hanging out in the back of the store. A white man about 45 approaches with a ruddy complexion and thinning blonde hair. He is in a maroon polo shirt and brown loafers. Terri cocks her head to the side and in an ironic tone asks, "May we help you sir?" He says, "Is it possible that I may trouble someone for a screw?" He raises his eyebrows up and down and looks at me. Terri extends her arms and says "I'll help you." He hands the glasses to her, announcing that he rolled over on them. Terri says, "How self-effacing of you sir." He says, "I thought I should be up front." Terri leaves with the frames.

Initially, "Is it possible that I may trouble someone for a screw," could be just a repair request. But there are many other ways of doing this same type of asking: "My glasses are broken," "I think I'm missing something here," "I'm missing a screw." While this last one can open itself up to wordplays about having "loose screws," for the most part these requests are not easily sexualizable. "May I trouble someone for a screw," however, is hearable as a potential double entendre, in part because the object to be screwed is left ambiguous, leaving open to interpretation whether or not he is sexualizing. But what tips the scales toward a particular meaning? Here, the speaker signals a risqué angle by adding an eyebrow flash, then looking for collusion. Now, this eyebrow flash has a playful quality which might suggest an implicit understanding at some level that the screw line is only in fun, and not an actual attempt to solicit sex. This interpretation, however, is up for grabs. The staff might or might not pick up the sexualized line or find it funny.[17] Here, Terri does not respond directly to the specifics of the allusion; however, she does address its teasing quality indirectly by her bantering tone, and use of "sirs" to sustain the playfulness.

In addition to gestures, signalling a double entendre can also be done through talk. In the next instance, a female customer adds a personal story fragment to her request for a screw. It appears these women are bonding by finding a common topic of interest.

> Terri and I are at the back counter. A white woman, about 43 approaches with her glasses in hand. Terri asks if she needs help. The woman says, "Well, I need a screw," and then says something about having recently broken up with her boyfriend. We all laugh. Terri commiserates, "Yeah, I can relate, I just broke up with my boyfriend last night." Terri takes the client's glasses and goes to fix them. When she returns she hands them to the woman along with a miniaturized screwdriver on a keychain, instructing the woman, "You can do it yourself from now on." The woman takes the screwdriver and retorts, "Great, another thing I can do better by myself." We all laugh and she leaves.

It is common practice for clients to walk in with their broken glasses. Glasses in the hand, and not on the face, can indicate something is wrong. While it is not clear whether Terri has accessed this visual information, the client's announcement that she needs a screw makes what is going on here seem relatively self-evident. Before Terri can respond, however, the client adds something about recently having broken up with her boyfriend. This not only serves to overtly expand the universe of interpretations about what she needs (a repair? or to get laid?), but also reframes which object it is that needs the screw, as both she and her glasses are broken-up. In addition, the client's reference to a boyfriend, though absent, invokes a heterosexual framework that could keep her request for a "screw" from being seen as her flirting with Terri. Here, the sexual is introduced perhaps only as a topic, and not as possible action between the parties. After the laughter, Terri picks up on the least overtly sexual part of the message, and uses it to identify with the client: "Yeah, I can relate. I just broke up with my boyfriend last night." But what is it that Terri is relating to? That she too has broken up with her boyfriend? Or the implications this has about her also needing a screw? What is clear, however, is that one innuendo can lead to another; all of which gets worked up by the participants, creating a sense of sustained sexualizing.

In contrast, offering personal information, such as age, to signal a double entendre can have a limited interactional lifetime when delivered to someone who might be a potential partner and hear it as a come-on. In one instance, Terri adds a tag line indicating her well-seasoned expertise, thus casting her offer to help in a sexual light.

> Terri is helping Ben, a thirty-something artist who has been coming in for the last few years. They are talking about Ben's frames that he

wants repaired. Terri explains, "Can't do it now, you'll have to leave it." Ben says, "Oh really." Terri continues, "This is a vintage screw, babe." Ben says, "Oh." Terri bursts in, "I specialize in vintage screws, I'm 43" and starts a cackling laugh. Ben gives a low and limited laugh. Terri continues, "No, this is a vintage screw, [it's] got to go downstairs." They then start talking about Christmas presents, and Ben volunteers that he's getting his girlfriend some Williams-Sonoma [a specialty kitchen store]. "She needs mixing bowls," he says.

There is a set-up quality to this sexualized move. "This is a vintage screw" refers to the client's antique glasses needing a specific type of fastener. But Terri tags on a "babe" at the end of her statement that can signal either playfulness, familiarity, or a swinger attitude. Ben's "Oh" is perhaps merely an acknowledgement that he has received the information related to the glasses – however, he does not take up or pursue the familiarity she is offering. But he just gets this out before Terri rushes in saying, "I specialize in vintage screws." Now, the fact that she specializes in vintage screws could, or could not, be heard as sexualizing. But Terri plants her sexualized intent with the tag line, "I'm 43," claiming a level of expertise beyond the repair of old eyeglass frames. Whether this is to be taken seriously or in fun is open to interpretation. At this point, Ben gives a limited laugh but does not take up the sexualizing. As a result, Terri moves to distance herself from the allusion by saying "No, this is a vintage screw." A "no" in the turn-initial position marks the transition from a joking stance to one that is serious (Schegloff 1996). Terri indeed says "no" to intimate she was only kidding, returning the "vintage screw" to its original eyewear context. Ben's unwillingness to play with their relational boundaries or engage any suggestive innuendos is made perfectly clear when he starts talking about his girlfriend and her rather expensive domestic present. He uses this talk to reflect exactly how he is already taken.

In the previous three episodes, the person who introduced the "screw" comment also worked to signal it as hearably sexualized, with varying results. In many instances, however, it might be less clear who, or what, signals the sexualized angle. In such moments the sexualizing becomes a truly collaborative endeavor.

How the person responds to a request for a screw might be the opening for signalling a double entendre; such responses might include verbal exclamations (oh really?), laughter, or outbreaths.

In the following example, the respondent's silence creates that shift.

> A woman is walking quickly towards me with glasses in her hand. She is about 60, with lots of foundation and eye make-up, wearing what looks to be an expensive floral print outfit. I say "Hi," she says, "This is desperation time. I need a screw." I think to myself that this is one of those negative cases where someone doesn't sexualize, and that I'll have to make a note of this. As I finish this thought the woman says, "I mean in my glasses." As she says this she throws her head and torso backwards while letting out a large and loud laugh. I am in a small state of shock and I laugh a little as this is such a weird moment. I go to write a note of what she said, pretending to be repairing the frame.

This client introduces what initially can be heard as an urgent repair request: "This is desperation time. I need a screw." It appears to be a repair request because the customer does not immediately signal any other possible interpretation. There is no gesture or tag line, there is only silence. My silence. When I should be responding, I am instead preoccupied with an analytically interesting moment where someone has not sexualized. It is, however, at this point that the client offers "I mean in my glasses," both clarifing and calling attention to what could have been heard as ambiguous. The client works to acknowledge the sexualized potential of her utterance, while disaffiliating from any sexualized intent. That she clarifies her meaning at this particular point can be understood by the turn-taking structure of conversation (Sacks, Schegloff, and Jefferson 1974). Specifically, a recipient's silence can signal disagreement with, or some problem in understanding what the speaker has said (Pomerantz 1984: 152–64). Thus, my silence is heard as a response. It now makes more sense why the client chose that particular moment to call attention to the screw comment.

What can be heard as repair talk might also be double entendres and signaled as sexualized. Signalling can be done by either the person who initiated the screw comment, a hearer of this comment, or perhaps attributed to the recipient and disclosed specifically by the speaker. Once introduced, however, sexualizing become interactional property and subject to the rules of conversation. While some participants appear to set-up, or rush into double entendres, others gave the impression that they stumbled into them. At some point, however, at least one person produced a response that was heard as disambiguating the double entendre; however, it may be unclear just who made this move.

But what kinds of sexualizing moves are these? Are they jokes and easily keyed as play (Goffman 1974: 40–1)? What might suggest a joke or play is using a classic double entendre, or the particular way it is signaled (an eyebrow flash), or the rush and pacing of the delivery ("I'm 43"), or that it is accompanied by laughs. But finding its humorous qualities does not mean that it was only a joke (Jefferson, Sacks, and Schegloff 1987), for there can be serious implications and undertones to humor (Emerson 1969). Additionally, these incidents suggest that much social and relational work gets done through sexualizing: having fun and connecting, flirting, gender bonding, and making intimacy claims. That adults would play through double entendres displays not only their clever wordsmith talents, but also the degree of their cultural competence with sexualizable talk.

Appraising the Look: 'What Do You Think of These?'

Requesting a screw is situationally appropriate when one brings broken glasses into an eyeglass store. But how do sexualizings get introduced at Valley Vista Optical beyond a relatively accessible double entendre? Appraisals are one other way. Appraisals are the verbal or gestural responses to how one looks in a particular pair of glasses. These can be initiated by staff and offered to the clients as assessments of the look. They can also be the self-assessments done by the client when looking at her/himself in a mirror.

Sometimes customers initiate sexualized self-appraisals on their own appearance in eyewear. In the following, Paula, a female customer, reveals the erotic power of a frame:

> Paula has found another frame. Returning to the table she sits down and tries on the rectangular, black plastic frame. "Oh I love it!," she says. I don't. I tell her I think it's a little hard. Her friend Amy agrees [with me]. "This is so sexy," coos Paula. Amy and I look at each other. "This frame makes me want to make love," says Paula. I laugh, and say, "Whatever makes you want to make love is a good thing." Paula's face drops a little as she turns to Amy and says, "It's been three weeks since he's called." ... Later, Paula

reiterates that this frame makes her want to make love, and again mentions that "Bob" has not called.

Paula sexualizes through a form of adult dress-up, playing with her image in the mirror. This is not an uncommon practice. Nor are the two verbal self-appraisals she adds: "Oh, I love it" and "This is so sexy." What is interesting is that each pronouncement Paula makes is met with either a negative response, or no uptake and a collusive look between Amy and myself. Given this, Paula increases the sexualized magnitude of each successive turn: "Oh, I love it" becomes "This is so sexy," becomes "This frame makes me want to make love." In this final spin, Paula escalates her sexualizing by attributing certain powers to the frame.[18] But what is going on here? For one, Paula is sharing intimate information about herself fairly quickly with a relative stranger of the same sex (Gershun 1994). Whereas "wanting to make love" is personal, it is not directed to anyone specific. Unfortunately, my response that "Whatever makes you want to make love is a good thing" reminds Paula that the other thing that inspires her is Bob, who has not called in three weeks.

Customers can also request appraisals from staff that are more clearly directed to the worker. In the following, Peter, in a conversation with me, recalls how one female celebrity uses a frame and her actress friend to pose a sexual query:

> Peter says that he thought of something funny and asks if I remember when Pia and Michelle came in. I say yes, ask if it was before Pia got a crush on him. Peter says, "Yeah it was the first time they came in." He continues, "Pia points to Michelle who is trying on frames and says to me, 'Which one of these would make you want to sleep with her?'" Peter continues, "So I say OK, let me see this one [referring to one of the frames], and now let me see the other one." He laughs, "I mean I didn't say either one of them, but I just considered each frame seriously."

"Which one of these would make you want to sleep with her" represents the eyeglass frame as the erotic selling point, and situates the sexualizing within the legitimate practice of asking for an appraisal. While clients often ask "which one do you like better," this particular formulation does many things beyond asking for an opinion of the look. It simultaneously makes assumptions and inquiries into Peter's sexual identity, partnered status and sensibilities: is he heterosexual, available, and open to this topic? This question is fishing for any number of responses; however, Peter does not bite and instead treats it as a serious request for an appraisal.

At other times, directed requests for appraisals might be a gratuitous flaunting of self and a call for attention. Terri remembers helping one male client:

> then he puts it [the frame] on and he stands back in the middle of the store, and in the loudest voice [says], "Well would you go out with me if I wore these?" and looking around not even directly at me; its [a] general question for any woman who happens to be near him as he's looking at himself in the mirror. Ok, then he turns around and he goes, "WOW, look at that BA:BE," and he's talking about some woman that's walking in front of the store.

Clients often make various statements of the "What do you think of these?" type. "Would you go out with me if I wore these," however, turns a request for an appraisal into a quasi pick-up line. The "if I wore these" part suggests that the eyewear is the pivotal point in the equation making the customer more appealing. But is he asking for an appraisal or asking Terri out? Maybe neither. While this is a directed question, the phrase "Would you go out with me if I wore these?" is said out loud to a general audience of women. He follows the allusion with commentary about some "babe," taking the seriousness out of it as a clear pick-up attempt. Both utterances trade upon his use of the "looking" and "commenting on looks" conventions in this store.

Having command of conventions means that clients can then put their own creative spins on them. Clients doing self-assessments routinely strike provocative poses in mirrors. Sometimes even these are refashioned to yield a more unexpected, and ambiguous erotic element:

> Later, Paula [who said "These frames make me want to make love"], is still deciding between two frames. I tell her they are very different looks for her. She gets up to go look in the big mirror. I follow and am standing to the side. She turns to me, sucks in her cheeks, pooches out her lips and tilts her head to the side, doing the eyeglass face in an exaggerated and intense way. She says, "See, I'm flirting with you …" I am caught off guard by this, and try to figure out what she is doing here. Wasn't she just talking about missing Bob?

The "eyeglass face" is a pose that customers do when looking at themselves in a mirror to appear more glamorous or sexy. Here, however, Paula makes the pose more distinctly sexual and consequential by doing it to me and not into a mirror. Additionally, Paula escalates this pose by adding her own formulation for doing it, "See, I'm flirting with you." Now, this is a loaded interactional moment. Because "See, I'm flirting with you" is said between two people of the same sex, it might require different interpretive work to make sense of what is occurring, than if said to someone of the opposite sex. For example, "See, I'm flirting with you" may indeed be a come-on. Alternatively, it may be specific to the pose as something that is recognizable by this client as sexy and flirtatious. Paula could also be banking on heterosexual assumptions of gender such that she feels safe to play with me without it meaning anything beyond this. Determining the intent of such a comment is just one aspect of the work entailed in responding to it. At this point, background information about Paula's alleged heterosexual relationship with Bob does little to relieve the ambiguity.

By using the appraisal format to sexualize, clients display an awareness of being in an eyeglass store. In some instances, however, it is unclear what they are shopping for: an invigorated sense of self? some attention? a date? Perhaps just an assessment of the look. Whatever they are doing, they do it by fashioning eyeglasses as compelling erotic objects. Sometimes this is brazen: "Which frame would make you want to sleep with her?" But even something this direct still offers up the eyeglass talk, and the glasses, as a way out. Like double entendres, using appraisals to sexualize has built-in retreatability making it safer. But unlike double entendres, appraisals are not as easily cast or maintained as jokes. While participants may just be playing, the directness of the requests could leave recipients without much room to maneuver.

Personalizing the Service Encounter: Does this Come With the Service?

Up to this point, participants have used conventions and practices specific to eyewear to completely package their sexualizing. At other times, however, sexualizing references the service encounter, the service, or the staff/client relationship.

Remarks praising the quality of the optical service are common, and typically refer to the workmanship, the speed of delivery, or a worker's willingness to help. Sometimes customers use these routine comments to springboard into more personal territory:

> Tom is helping a woman, mid-forties, in dark clothes with dark wild hair. He is adjusting her glasses. Sam is in the adjustment room and I am off to the side. I hear the woman say that her glasses are fitting better, "You're the King. You're the king" she says to Tom. She then leans forward and in a lowered voice asks, "Are you single?" Tom is holding her eyeglasses and says, "Used to be. But I'm still the king." The woman says, "No, you're the prince," then says, "You're the king." Sam chimes in, "Peter is single. Peter is the prince," referring to one of the owners. The woman says, "We tried that with Peter." The woman then asks Tom, "Know any nice single guys?" and then relates that "Guys can't even commit to dinner, they'll say, 'well let's just do coffee'." Tom says, "Don't know any good enough for you." The woman says, "I just want to get laid." Tom shrugs and says, "Sorry, can't help you." The woman comments on how nicely her glasses fit now, and as she leaves says to Tom, "I'll tell Peter you're the king."

"Are you single?" is a direct personal question, and follows what appears to be the client's announcement of having received good service, and of Tom as the "king" of eyeglass adjustments. While "Are you single?" can be heard as continued flattering of Tom, she could have simply said: "Gee, you are really great at this"; "How long have you been doing this?"; "You must love what you do." "Are you single?" is a clear and blunt move away from being strictly business. Tom hears this as more than flattery, and asserts that although not single, he is still the king. But what is he the king of? eyeglasses? and is he attempting to move back to that understanding? or is he aligning with the sexualized sidebar and alluding to something else he is still the king of? The more personalized talk about dating gets taken up and bounced around by the participants. While Tom is not a single guy, he is now, however, treated by the client as an expert on their whereabouts: "Know any nice single guys?" Her continued and disappointed search has Tom letting her down easy, "Don't know any good enough for you." The client follows this flattery by escalating her approach: "I just want to get laid." "Sorry, can't help you" is Tom's bottom line response which shuts down any further playfulness or involvement with the sexualized topic. At this point the woman orients back to the good service she has received and the original understanding of what makes Tom the king.

Sexualizing can also be introduced in relation to a service "prop." In what follows, Eva, a female co-worker, tells me how one male customer uses the information on her business card to pursue a distinctly personal agenda:

> Eva is helping a tall tan-complected and attractive man in his mid-thirties. I look over and see them both leaning back in their chairs, as if resting. After the customer leaves, Eva comes over and says, "This guy just tried to pick me up." I ask what happened, and she says, "He was going to ask me out, it was weird, I could feel it." She continues, "I offer him my card and he sees my Dutch name, then he says, 'So do you know any Dutch people?' I say, 'Yes, there's a lot of Dutch people here.' Then he says, 'Do you know that makes you so much more sexy.'" As she says this to me, Eva opens her eyes wide, raises one brow in a mocking way and says, 'Oh OK, so do you want the reflection-free coating [on your lenses]?' Where do you go from there?"

Business cards are used to personalize a service encounter such that it is not an anonymous adventure. In most cases, giving a business card typically signals the end of an encounter, which for participants could spell the last chance for them to have a legitimate occasion to engage in face-to-face contact. People often make moves at this point. In Eva's account, the client makes use of her printed name to shift to personal talk and ground his sexualized move: "Do you know that makes you so much more sexy?" Interestingly, the client uses a question format to convey his attraction. The personal question directed to Eva makes an awkward moment. Eva alludes to this difficulty when she does a mock version of that moment, wondering aloud, "Where do you go from there?" Not easily back to a work interaction, particularly when the encounter is over.

Service encounters can also be personalized through a greeting or a leave-taking token. For example, while handshakes are the most common form of gesture to mark the beginning or end of a service transaction, hugs and kisses can point to a level of familiarity between the parties. At these moments, sexualizing makes real claims on the nature of the relationship. A female co-worker experiences a shock when helping one of her longtime male clients:

> Carla runs to the back, looks freaked, starts downstairs, then comes back and reaches into the cupboard, grabs the bottle of mouthwash

and continues back downstairs. When she returns she says that her client, the married father of a young woman Carla also helps, has just attempted to french kiss her. She says that when she went to kiss him goodbye on the lips, like she normally does, he tried to stick his tongue in her mouth. She says she pulled back quickly, ended their contact and left the scene.

This ending provides a vehicle for a sexualized beginning. In this instance, the male client unexpectedly exploits a lip-to-lip kiss these two had previously routinized as symbolic closure of their in-store contact. The french kiss is a sexual upgrade that was not agreed upon by Carla. Here, the participants clearly have divergent understandings of their relational boundaries. Additionally, though the kiss is done in public, the sexualizing is introduced in a private or hidden way: sticking his tongue in her mouth. To call attention to this transgression would publicize it and perhaps create a scene. Instead, Carla mutes the drama, making it appear as if nothing unusual is happening (Emerson 1970b), then runs for the mouthwash.

Sexualizing is built on routine aspects of personalizing the service encounter: commenting on good service, giving business cards, and friendly goodbyes. In these instances, sexualizing takes on a serious tone; because it is directed to the worker, rather than couched in eyeglass talk, s/he becomes the undisputed erotic object. While it is unclear whether the clients are trying to get dates, or just to expand the boundaries of what is included in the service, they are making claims on the nature of the encounter. Two clients attempt this by introducing talk, while one client makes a unilateral decision and forces his way there through a gesture. But even something as extreme as a french kiss is still deniable and retreatable, because it is introduced in a hidden way and upon exit.

Conclusion

Sexualization is a complex phenomenon, and its production, interpretation, and response takes effort. Staff and clients work to sexualize their interactions using resources such as double entendres in repair talk, appraisals of the look, and conventions common to personalizing the service encounter. In this process, participants are continuously making sense. While making sense is pertinent to all encounters, it is particularly important in cases of sexualizing because of the interactional and personal implications of this practice. For example, because the sexual can be considered taboo, or out of place, sexualizing is often packaged in ways that intimate that it was either all in fun, or that leave escape hatches so claims can be made that while one was doing something, one was not really doing anything (Sacks 1992).

Furthermore, sexualizing is an emergent process, unfolding in a specific interactional moment. Even sexualizings that appear out of the blue must start somewhere. For example, "Do you know that makes you so much more sexy?" follows Eva giving out her business card. While certain environments can seem to set the sexual stage, it is people who sexualize. They choose to introduce and sustain sexualized interpretations. Thus, sexualizing does not just happen: someone makes a move, whether or not anyone is willing to take responsibility for it.

Sexualizing also has clear situational properties and what is appropriate in one encounter is not necessarily so in another. In other words, while many sexualizings are similar in appearance, they are not alike. Specifically, their interactional consequentiality differs. Is the move taken up? ignored? shut down? One key factor is the way the sexualizing is "framed" which presents different interactive opportunities for participants.[19] For example, that a sexualizing move is introduced vis-à-vis eyeglasses provides a type of legitmized cover for the person introducing it, and also more latitude for the recipient to negotiate a response. On the other hand, less eyeglass-related or direct sexualizing is more distinctly personal and may be difficult to respond to.

In addition, while sexualizing takes many forms (double entendres, gestures, stares, comments), it also has many social and relational functions. Some of these include having fun, playing, connecting, doing gender, gender bonding, doing power, flirting, and come-ons. Sexualizing may also be a way of killing time, obtaining sneaky thrills, feeling alive(ness), or reinventing one's sexual self. The point here is that sexualizing exceeds simplistic connections to a linearly defined and genitally understood sense of the sexual: it is not always about mating or intentions to move beyond the current encounter. Instead it is about the moments. I suggest our conceptions of sexuality might need to be examined and redefined to include such an interactional perspective.

Additionally, sexualizing makes certain claims about the nature of the relationship between participants, such that "I can say this sort of thing to you." This is power at a micro level. Attempts to transform or impose a definition of the situation is no small feat and may be agreed upon or not. In this process, participants often make claims about sexual selves, one's own and others', that might include sexual presumptions of gender. For example, consider the man who said out loud to Terri and surrounding women, "Would you go out with me if I wore these?" What sense is he making about Terri, and displaying about himself? Or the woman who says to Tom, "You're the king. You're the king... Are you single?" Or that Eva suspects her male client has certain intentions, "He was going to ask me out." To what extent is "gender" a relevant factor in making, or making sense of, sexualized moves? Does it affect how participants read the move, or just how the analyst interprets it? Though participants are always making sense of sexual moves, the interaction often remains ambiguous. For instance, a reliance upon heterosexualized assumptions, or claims, can create uncertainties in encounters between same-sexed persons, such that one may never know if one is being hit on, or whether one is just the safe pal that provocative things can be said to. While it is arguably difficult to make claims about the relevance of gender in many interactions (Schegloff 1992), sexualizing provides a strong case in which participants can be seen orienting to gendered assumptions.

Finally, while it might be difficult, or artificial, to make analytic distinctions between sexualizings, such as those that are more playful/serious or those that appear consensual/imposed, I think it is useful. Constructing workplace sexualization as a continuum of interactional practices and experiences has potential implications for research on sexual harassment: locating the broader context of workplace sexualization might give us better ways of assessing just what it is, and what it is not. Conversely, perhaps what this study points to are the limitations of pursuing surveyed perceptions of harassment. The intricacies of the sexualized interactions in this paper would be lost in a survey format. This project thus illuminates the benefits that can be gained by research agendas that include detailed descriptions of sexualization as an emergent process. Ultimately, however, the issue for sociologists is not whether sexualizing is doing something "bad" or "good"; rather, it is always doing something: what this is, how this is done, and its consequences for interaction are ripe for investigation.

NOTES

1　This paper has had many incarnations. A version of it was presented at the Annual Meeting of the Pacific Sociological Association (1995). Since then, it has benefited from comments and conversations with Bob Emerson, Jodi O'Brien, Steve Clayman, Rachel Fretz, Carol Brooks Gardner, John Heritage, Judith Howard, Jack Katz, Maggie Kusenbach, Kari Lerum, Manny Schegloff, Elyse Schiller, and Tamara Sniezek.

2　See Spradley and Mann 1975 and Cavan 1966.

3　See Guiffre and Williams 1994.

4　See Hochschild 1983.

5　Included are many pioneering studies of gender at work, such as Spradley and Mann 1975; Kanter 1977; Hochschild 1983; Westwood 1984; and Kingsolver 1989.

6　Beth Schneider (1985) who is responsible for much current research on workplace sexualization, offers her own characterization: "The sexualization of the workplace is conceptualized as all consensual and coerced sexual interactions at work, that is, sexual harassment and sexual relationships" (p. 93).

7　Many of the most recent studies use survey methods. For example, a call for a shifting of attentions and research strategies away from descriptions of harassment, to surveyed perceptions of it was made by Schneider (1982) and echoed by Barr (1993). For alternative treatments of harassment that include accounts of unwanted sexualization, see Farley 1978.

8　Jodi O'Brien offered this characterization and connection to a personality model.

9　See Garfinkel (1967), and West and Zimmerman (1987) on doing gender.

10　The term "sexualizing" emerged from early discussions with Mel Pollner.

11　All identifying names are ficticious.

12　One of these males is part-owner of the store, and another is a manager. Because they also work on the floor and sell glasses, they will be included as "staff" in this particular project.

13　The information on self-defined identity and partnered status is meant merely to describe a range of potential experiences, and not as a necessary predictor of behavior. While both sexual identity and marital status are often seen to "bound" sexualized expression or experience, it is not always the case: straight women flirt with lesbians, lesbians flirt with gay men, and some married folks flirt with anyone. In addition, when strangers meet, one's self-definition may not be readily apparent, though there may be much reliance on sexualized assumptions of gender. Being in an environment that is not only "straight," however, can increase one's awareness of sexualized complexities.

14 Also, only one of the males is a licenced optician.

15 Dressing-up is not just a tactic created by management, and imposed on the workers. Staff also recognize that dressing-up can be good for sales. In addition, staff can choose a variety of ways to "dress up," some more sexy than others. Female staff in particular have made comments to me about how they enjoy dressing in a sexy way because it makes them feel good about themselves.

16 I have also used this process of data analysis to distance from troubling field experiences. This idea is developed in my paper "Sexing the Field: Experiencing, Observing, and Reporting the Erotic in Ethnographic Fieldwork," which was presented at the 1995 ASA Annual Meetings in Washington, DC.

17 Because people often deliver this "I need a screw" line as an entendre, it gets old after a while. Clients, however, typically act as if they have just invented this connection.

18 See *Seductions of Crime* (Katz 1988) for a great discussion of how people ascribe magical powers to objects, thereby explaining away their own seduction and subsequent actions. In Katz's work, pieces of jewelry allegedly call out to female shoppers to take and possess them. Katz refers to this as "conjuring the spirit of determinism"; it is also known as shoplifting.

19 Of course another key factor is who these people are to each other.

REFERENCES

Barr, Paula A. 1993. "Perceptions of Sexual Harassment." *Sociological Inquiry*, 63(4): 460–70.

Brewer, Marilynn. 1982. "Further Beyond Nine to Five: An Integration and Future Directions." *Journal of Social Issues*, 38(4): 149–58.

Cavan, Sherri. 1966. *Liquor Licence: An Ethnography of Bar Behavior.* Chicago, IL: Aldine Publishing Company.

Emerson, Joan P. 1969. "Negotiating the Serious Import of Humor." *Sociometry*, 32(2): 169–80.

——. 1970a. "Behavior in Private Places: Sustaining Definitions of Reality in Gynecological Examinations," in *Recent Sociology* no. 2, P. Dreitsel (ed.). New York, NY: Macmillan, 74–97.

——. 1970b. "Nothing Unusual is Happening," in *Human Nature and Collective Behavior*, Tamotsu Shibutani (ed.). Englewood Cliffs, NJ: Prentice-Hall, Inc., 209–22.

Farley, Lin. 1978. *Sexual Shakedown*. New York, NY: McGraw-Hill Book Company.

Garfinkel, Harold. 1967. "Passing and the Managed Achievement of Sexual Status in an Intersexed Person, Part 1," in Garfinkel's *Studies in Ethnomethodology*. Englewood Cliffs, NJ: Prentice-Hall, 116–85.

Gershun, Martha. 1994. "Presumed Intimate." *New York Times Magazine*. June 12.

Goffman, Erving. 1974. *Frame Analysis*. Boston, MA: Northeastern University Press.

Guiffrey, Patti A. and Christine L. Williams. 1994. "Boundary Lines: Labeling Sexual Harassment in Restaurants." *Gender & Society* 8(3): 378–401.

Heath, Christian. 1988 "Embarassment and Interactional Organization," in *Erving Goffman: Exploring the Interaction Order*, P. Drew and A. Wootton (eds). Cambridge: Polity Press, 137–60.

——. 1984. "Talk and Recipiency: sequential organization in speech and body movement," in *Structures of Social Action*, J. M. Atkinson and John Heritage (eds). Cambridge: Cambridge University Press, 247–65.

Henslin, J. M. and M. A. Biggs. 1971. "Dramaturgical Desexualization: The Sociology of the Vaginal Examination," in *Studies in the Sociology of Sex*, James M. Henslin (ed.). New York, NY: Appleton-Century-Crofts, 243–72.

Hochschild, Arlie. 1983. *The Managed Heart*. Berkeley, CA: University of California Press.

Jefferson, G., H. Sacks, and E. A. Schegloff. 1987. "Notes on Laughter in the Pursuit of Intimacy," in *Talk and Social Organization*, G. Button and J. Lee (eds). Intercommunication 1: Multilingual Matters, Ltd., 152–205.

Kanter, Rosabeth Moss. 1977. *Men and Women of the Corporation*. New York, NY: Basic Books, Inc.

Katz, Jack. 1988. *Seductions of Crime*. New York, NY: Basic Books, Inc., ch. 2.

Kingsolver, Barbara. 1989. *Holding the Line*. New York, NY: ILR Press.

Pomerantz, Anita. 1984. "Pursuing a Response," in *Structures of Social Action*, J. M. Atkinson and J. Heritage (eds). Cambridge: Cambridge University Press, 152–63.

Reinemann, J. O. 1945. "Extra-Marital Relations With Fellow Employees in War Industry as a Factor in Disruption of Family Life." *American Sociological Review*, 10(3): 399–402.

Roy, Donald. 1974. "Sex in the Factory: Informal Heterosexual Relations between Supervisors and Work Groups," in *Deviant Behavior: Occupational and Organizational Bases*, Clifton T. Bryant (ed.). Chicago, IL: Rand McNally College Publishing Co., 44–66.

Sacks, Harvey. 1992. "The Dirty Joke as Technical Object," in *Lectures on Conversation*, G. Jefferson (ed.). Oxford: Blackwell Publishers, 470–94.

Sacks H., E. A. Schegloff, and G. Jefferson. 1974. "A Simplest Systematics for the Organization of Turn-Taking for Conversation." *Language* 50(4): 696–735.

Schneider, Beth E. 1982. "Consciousness About Sexual Harassment Among Heterosexual and Lesbian Women Workers," *Journal of Social Issues* 38(4): 75–98.

——. 1984. "The Office Affair: Myth and Reality for Heterosexual and Lesbian Women Workers," *Sociological Perspectives* 27(4): 443–64.

——. 1985. "Approaches, Assaults, Attractions, Affairs: Policy Implications of the Sexualization of the Workplace." Oxford: Elsevier Science Publishers B. V., 93–113.

Schegloff, Emanuel A. 1992. "On talk and its institutional occasions," in *Talk at Work*, P. Drew and J. Heritage (eds). Cambridge: Cambridge University Press, 101–34.

——. 1996. "Getting Serious: Joke → Serious 'No'." Delivered at the Annual Meeting of the American Sociological Association, New York, NY.

Spradley, James P. and Brenda J. Mann. 1975. *The Cocktail Waitress: Women's Work in a Man's World*. New York, NY: John Wiley and Sons.

West, Candace, and Don Zimmerman. 1987. "Doing Gender." *Gender & Society*, 1(2): 125–51.

Westwood, Sallie. 1984. *All Day, Every Day*. Urbana, IL: University of Illinois Press.

Woods, James D. 1993. *The Corporate Closet*. New York, NY: The Free Press.

3

Acknowledgment Rituals: The Greeting Phenomenon Between Strangers[1]

Carl Edward Pate

For years I've noticed and participated in a greeting phenomenon that occurs between African American males who do not know each other. The greeting can take several forms: a head nod only, a head nod accompanied by a verbal recognition, a verbal recognition only, or a nonverbal gesture. Why and how does this phenomenon happen? Does this greeting phenomenon occur out of an expression of a common experience (i.e., a shared definition of the situation which recognizes the oppression felt by people of color in general and African American males specifically)? Does this greeting phenomenon happen because of a perceived in-group or a fictive kinship relationship? Would this phenomenon occur in situations where African American males are in the majority? Do acknowledgments occur in New York or Chicago as often as they do in Seattle or smaller communities or other mostly white communities? What is sociologically significant about Acknowledgment Rituals?

I will attempt to isolate and illuminate a micro level greeting phenomenon which occurs between *strangers*. Elijah Anderson's (1990) work on greetings between African American men provides the reference point for framing my inquiries. I attempt to extend his research across cultures and gender, examining greetings between and among African, Asian, White, Mexican, and Latino Americans, men, women, and gays, bisexuals, and lesbians. I attempt to tie this phenomenon to the importance of daily interaction as a means of group identification and as a means of defining self. I employ social psychological perspectives to establish that an acknowledgment ritual exists between strangers, to identify what situations facilitate these greetings, who participates in greetings between strangers, and what role they play or what importance they have in common everyday interaction. I use participant and non-participant observations, as well as interviewing strategies, both focus group and individual, to illuminate the complexities of this greeting phenomenon.

Interactive Greetings

Anderson (1990) addresses the issue of greetings in a chapter from his book *Street Wise*, titled "The Black Male in Public." In this chapter, he suggests that greetings serve the function of protection or as a way to determine whether someone is a "predator" or member of a "wolfpack." Anderson focused on the stigma black males face in public associated with their skin color, age, gender, appearance, and self presentation. Anderson notes that these black men have to fight this stigma because most residents of Village-Northton ascribe to them (anonymous black males) the characteristics of criminality, incivility, toughness, and street smartness. Anderson also raises the issue of encounters between strangers in urban communities. He indicates that because "public encounters between strangers on the streets of urban America are by nature brief, the participants must draw conclusions about each other quickly, and they generally rely on a small number of cues. This process is universal, and it unavoidably involves some prejudging – prejudice – but its working out is especially prominent in the public spaces of the Village-Northton (163)." Some of the interactive dynamics Anderson describes refer to the etiquette of "strangers in the streets": for example, young black men making extended eye contact as a means of presenting self. According to Anderson, the response of the other person to this extended eye contact is to avert their eyes from the black males, and thus not provoke a potentially threatening response. The subtle averting of the eyes during interaction that Anderson refers to is but one example among many which I frame in terms of the interactive dynamics of greetings between strangers.

Anderson specifically addresses the issue of greetings between non-familiar African American males. Anderson not only establishes the existence of acknowledgment rituals between strangers, but also illuminates the intricate relationships between greetings and categorical characteristics (i.e., race), in terms of in-group/out-group dynamics. He suggests that greetings within the African American community are salient for the development of self as well as a community identity. His focus is mainly black men, but I suggest that greetings are also important for black women, other members of other racial/ethnic groups, and members of the gay community. Anderson's perspectives are captured in this passage:

> Among blacks, the act of greeting is of great cultural importance… Blacks in the Village still spontaneously greet other blacks they are sure they do not [underline added] know. In fact Northton blacks, many of whom have southern roots, seem to be more forthcoming with such greetings to fellow blacks on the streets of the Village than they are on their home turf, reflecting a need to express color-caste solidarity. In contrast, middle-income blacks of the Village are more likely to greet their white counterparts, while remaining somewhat reserved in their overall behavior.
>
> To many blacks, greetings carry an obligation to respond in kind. Not to return a greeting is uncommon, and the person is considered "strange." Blacks are more likely to speak to those they do not know, including whites, than whites are to speak to unfamiliar whites or to blacks in public places. (1990: 168–69)

Using Anderson's work as a starting point, I expand the scope of inquiry beyond African American males, adding a potentially illuminating comparative frame to understanding acknowledgment rituals. My intuitive sense is that other groups might participate in some form of acknowledgment ritual, since, like African Americans, commonalties exist between individuals and groups that may also encourage this greeting phenomenon. A comparative design allows me to address the following questions: Is the acknowledgment ritual an intra-group phenomenon (i.e., between women, or gay, bisexual and lesbians, or between individuals in the Asian community, or between Jewish people, or Anglo American males)? Or is it an inter-group phenomenon that occurs across races or cultural groups, across men and women, across age or generation and/or between homosexuals and heterosexuals? Do some groups participate in acknowledgment rituals more often than other groups? Are the reasons for participating in an acknowledgment ritual the same for all groups? Is the performance of solidarity the focal point of acknowledgment? Do acknowledgments that occur between oppressed individuals reflect their membership in subordinate groups in American society?

Conceptual Framework

Mead (1934) advanced the idea of the self as a social construction.[2] Following the logic of Mead's concept of self as a social construction, I suggest that an acknowledgment ritual may serve the purpose of connecting self, via self-schemas, with the other.[3] Through this process we enact our sense of who we are as well as our identity or association with a particular in-group. A result of this interactional achievement is the reinforcement of community and in-group solidarity.

Self is also created and reinforced through the process of rituals (Goffman, 1967; McCall and Simmons, 1966). Goffman (1967) suggested that a minor, taken-for-granted, everyday ritual, such as a greeting, maintains social order. Acknowledgment rituals likely serve this same function. For example, African American interviewees referred to a situation where an acknowledgment to another African American wasn't reciprocated, and this angered them because of the perceived lack of respect for the solidarity that this greeting phenomenon represents. This response echos Anderson's (1990) reference to African Americans being labeled "strange" when they fail to respond to or participate in this greeting phenomenon.

Charon (1989) illustrates the relationship between self, interaction and identity as follows:

> Identity is an important part of self-concept. It is who the individual thinks he or she is and who is announced to the world in word and action. It arises in interaction, it is reaffirmed in interaction and it is changed in interaction. It is important to what we do. Not all identities matter. However, some may matter almost all the time. (80)

Acknowledgment rituals represent a presentation of self, a statement of membership in a particular group, to another member of that group.

Howard (1994) suggests that social identities (as opposed to personal identities) are more important for dominated groups, not only in interactions with dominant group members, but also within their own self-concepts. Her point is that social power plays a salient role in the process of self and social categorization. This is consistent with my point that some groups use acknowledgment rituals as a show of intra-group solidarity in situations which may be potentially oppressive (i.e., college campuses for most minority groups such as gays, bisexuals, and lesbians or African Americans). This is also consistent with a finding noted below, that members of dominant groups, such as Anglo American males, do not participate in acknowledgment rituals as frequently.

In a section of his book, *Relations in Public*, titled "Supportive Interchanges," Goffman (1971) primarily focused on familiar individuals in terms of the social significance of greetings. He wrote:

> Two individuals upon approaching orient frontally to each other. Their glances lock for a moment in communion, eyes glisten, smiling expressions of social recognition are conveyed, and a note of pleasure is briefly sustained. Hand-waving, hat-tipping, and other "appeasement gestures" may be performed. A verbal salutation is likely to be provided along with a term of address. When possible, embracing, hand-shaking, and other bodily contacting may occur. (74)

He referred to greetings among strangers as a guarantee for safe passage, and suggested that such greetings seldom occur. Even though Goffman wrote primarily about familiar individuals, I suggest that his implicit reference to the significance of social recognition and gestures fits for strangers.

In constructing definitions of the situation, Goffman (1959) suggested that individuals participate in performances in which each participant orchestrates gestures to present oneself in a specific manner.

> When an individual enters the presence of others, they commonly seek to acquire information about him or to bring into play information already possessed. They will be interested in his general conception of self, his attitude toward them, his competence, his trustworthiness, etc. Although some of this information seems to be sought almost as an end in itself, there are usually quite practical reasons for acquiring it. Information about the individual helps to

define the situation, enabling others to know in advance what he will expect of them and what they may expect of him. Informed in these ways, the others will know how best to act in order to call forth a desired response from him. (1)

Goffman's point is that during interaction individuals look for clues as to who each other is, and how each person is bound to react to the other. My research indicates that acknowledgments are outcomes of the presentation of self and an aspect of impression management. People present themselves as a member of a group or show support for the other's presentation of self through the acknowledgment ritual.

Goffman (1971) refers to "tie-signs" as "evidence about relationships, that is, about ties between persons, whether involving objects, acts, expressions, and only excluding the literal aspects of explicit documentary statement" (194). That is, cues (such as gender, race, manner of dress, etc.,) may act as an anchoring mechanism for interacting individuals to quickly assess the other's in-group/out-group status, and thus facilitate greetings that express intra-group solidarity. Tie-signs, in conjunction with people's abilities to schematically categorize and organize information, further explain how meaning-laden acknowledgments pass between one another on the street, at a bus stop or down a hallway.

Methods

Research Sites

I used participant and non-participant observation, focus groups, and individual interviews, to assess the acknowledgment ritual phenomenon. The ubiquitous nature of greetings enabled me to conduct research almost anywhere; research sites varied according to my normal day-to-day travels and included interactions on buses and at bus stops; in restaurants and shopping malls; walking down streets, or on the University of Washington's and Humboldt State University's campuses; and while driving in cars. Observations were made and noted throughout the city of Seattle, as well as in adjacent cities and communities for a period of one year. Observations were also made elsewhere, including various locations in California (i.e., San Diego, San Francisco, and Oakland).

Observed Subjects

Subjects included anyone I encountered in the research sites. The varied locations enabled me to interact with both men and women, and individuals representative of multiple racial groups.[4] I did not specifically select sites where I expected to see individuals from specific racial groups. However, I interacted with individuals from various racial groups, as a participant or non-participant observer, when the opportunity presented itself.

Participant and Non-Participant Observations

Participant and non-participant observations were conducted during the entire study period. Initially, these methods were used to answer several questions: Does this greeting phenomenon occur? Who participates in it? What does it consist of? Participant and non-participant methods were also useful in the later stages of my study to facilitate ongoing, post interview observations.

Participant observations are defined in this study as observations collected while I actively participated in the acknowledgment ritual by being either the initiator of an acknowledgment or the recipient of an initiated acknowledgment.[5] These interactions were noted on tape or in a notepad to be recorded at a later time on an acknowledgment ritual observation form. Non-participant observations were recorded while watching potential and actual interactions from the perspective of an unobtrusive observer.

To a limited degree, I used Goffman's (1974) notion of frame analysis to assist in "picking up" subtle differences between individuals' and groups' avoidance of or participation in this greeting phenomenon between non-familiar individuals. Paying attention to the smallest of details enabled me to distinguish and quickly categorize behaviors or actions.

As I note below, my observations seemed to support the hypothesis that individuals do participate in this greeting phenomenon. Several questions followed: What specific meanings are attached to this greeting phenomenon? Do these acknowledgments symbolize a common experience framed within a shared subordinate status or are they a response to a specific situation? What intra- or inter-group dynamics are occurring, if any? Focus group and individual interviews were conducted to analyze these questions.

Interviews and Interviewees

I conducted nineteen formal interviews, including 13 individual and six focus group interviews, and an unspecified amount of informal interviews.[6] The majority of formal interviews were conducted on a West Coast university campus and primarily involved students. The interviewees ranged in age from early twenties to mid-forties, and included 45 females and 32 males (n=77). The racial composition of the interviewees included African, White, Mexican, and Asian (including Filipino, Korean, Japanese, Chinese, and Vietnamese) Americans. Interviews were conducted to uncover and illuminate the process of acknowledgment rituals, to specify who was involved and to identify patterns in the interviewee's personal accounts of this greeting phenomenon. Informal interviewees included both students and non-students, males and females and had the same racial composition as the formal interviewees. Formal interviewees were contacted prior to the interview, met in a designated interview site and followed standard interview procedures. Informal interviewees were unscheduled but presented spontaneous opportunities to inquire about acknowledgment rituals and greetings. Informal interviews were not taped, because of their spur of the moment nature, however, any useful information was later recorded.

The largest focus group interview was with the Asian Student Commission, and included 25 participants. The remaining focus group interviews were conducted with ten members of the Black Student Union, six members of the Black Student Commission, five members of the Women's Commission, six members of the Women Engineers Association, and 12 members of the Gay, Bisexual, and Lesbian Commission. Focus group interviews were conducted prior to individual interviews as a means of generating multiple perspectives and conceptions that could then be further analyzed during individual interviews. Open ended questions were used to stimulate discussion. These interviews were conducted in a give-and-take conversational manner to minimize my influence on the information given and to not appear authoritarian or intimidating. Each focus group interview was taped and later transcribed.

The individual interview questions were all open ended. An initial set of questions was used to stimulate discussion, and additional questions were formulated to probe any comments that needed clarification or elaboration. The interviewees included both women and men, and people self-identifying as, Japanese, Mexican, white and black. Each interview was taped and later transcribed.

To facilitate understanding and theorizing about acknowledgment rituals, I conceived of three stages in the acknowledgment ritual: (1) The initial acknowledgment; (2) the actual acknowledgment or greeting; and (3) the post acknowledgment. During the *initial acknowledgment* there are three sub-stages. First, an assessment or definition of the situation, including an initial presentation of self; second, a cognitive assessment of who the other is and whether the acknowledgment is likely to occur; and third, a decision to acknowledge the other or not. The *actual acknowledgment* or greeting (when the decision to do so is made) involves five possible forms: (1) Nod only; (2) Nod and Verbal; (3) Verbal Only; (4) Non-Response; and (5) Other Non-Verbal (e.g., raising the eyebrows).[7] The *post acknowledgment* is a period in which one takes the role of the other and attempts to ascribe meaning to the greeting, if warranted. This stage is also salient for continuing the presentation of self, in terms of showing the appropriate "face," as well as enabling the other to present "face" also, until each interactant is sure the greeting is complete. This final stage normally covers the period of time from the actual greeting until the interactants have passed by each other.

Findings

The first question is whether acknowledgments between strangers occurred. My initial participant and non-participant observations indicated that strangers do participate in acknowledgment rituals, and that these greetings occurred intra-group, as well as inter-group.[8, 9] Interview transcripts indicated that, indeed, greetings between strangers occur and that there are shared understandings of the greetings as well as the symbolism of what a greeting means. In other words, individuals are collectively aware of the symbolism of a smile or a head nod as opposed to a quick glance or a verbal communication such as "hello."

The interviewees were very "Goffmanesque" in their descriptions, being able to relay minute detail describing (and at times demonstrating) subtle glances, intentional averting of the eyes to avoid eye contact or body language which made the other appear either open or closed to a greeting. For example, Interviewee C not only indicated, in relaying an experience, examples of what constituted a greeting but also illustrated the second step of the initial acknowledgment stage (described above). Interviewee C stated:

> if you see somebody, like I am walking, getting ready to acknowledge someone and I'm looking up and I'm getting ready to smile at them or nod at them or say good morning or something, and I see that they are not going to acknowledge me, then I'll ignore them. And sometimes you can tell that someone is determinedly looking away from you.

She is also clearly weighing whether to acknowledge the other by participating in a give-and-take interaction with the other where she is presenting self (looking up, getting ready to smile), but defines the situation, based on her perception of the other's body language, such that it is unlikely that a greeting will occur.

There was some disagreement as to precisely what form of nonverbal communication was "enough" to qualify as a greeting. The disagreement focused on whether eye contact alone constitutes a greeting or whether something beyond simple eye contact is necessary for an acknowledgment to have occurred. There also seemed to be a significant difference in the degree and form of eye contact which counted as an acknowledgment or greeting. Interviewee J felt that eye contact was not enough to qualify as an acknowledgment when she stated:

> If I make eye contact, I crack a smile, and that to me, I'm acknowledging that person. And so it's not enough that they make eye contact, but that they acknowledge that they've made eye contact with some emotional or physical manifestation.

However, Interviewee L indicates that eye contact is primary and does qualify as a greeting in and of itself, as well as in conjunction with other gestures. Interviewee L's reference to "meaningful contact" also fits well with my contention that some greetings are purposive and symbolic and are not only perfunctory acts:

> Well, I would have said at least eye contact. I mean I immediately want to qualify it by saying eye contact and then some facial expression that indicates that the person sees you, but I think, if

a person is walking past and you just can tell they noticed that you were there and they're going to steer around you, that's not acknowledgment. But if there's some kind of meaningful contact.

Group Specific Findings

African Americans   The most striking finding was the difference in how often African American males participated in the acknowledgment ritual as compared to any other group. African American males acknowledge one another at a rate exceeding all other groups combined. I noted, in both participant and non-participant observations, hundreds of examples where, in multi-racial situations, African American males were the only ones to participate in acknowledgment rituals. There were literally hundreds of opportunities for individuals of all races and sexes to acknowledge one another; the only consistent acknowledgments were between African American males. (This is not to say that other groups do not participate in acknowledgment rituals; they do, as I comment on below.)

The interviews corroborated my claims that African American males participate repeatedly in this greeting phenomenon; all of the interviewees (across sex, age, and race) perceived that African American males significantly acknowledge one another more often than any other group. One African American woman, during the Black Student Commission focus group interview, illustrated this fact with a humorous statement that initiated agreement and laughter from all of the participants:

> There's that damn nod, most of the guys go like this [she demonstrated an exaggerated head nod], when they're walking.

Anderson (1990) made reference to the 'amazement' White people express in terms of how often Black men greet one another. He also indicated that greetings hold "instrumental" meaning which is shared and understood collectively, including serving as a means of expressing one's tie to a particular "community" (i.e., black or gay community). Anderson wrote:

> When with a black person, a white person may be amazed that so many "unknown" blacks will speak. In this way, unacquainted

blacks can give the appearance of a unified public community on the streets of the Village. Such greeting behavior is not simply an ingrained ritual; it may be viewed as instrumental, as a way for Northton blacks in the Village to come to terms with an environment they see as not always welcoming. (169)

Respondent 4 of the Black Student Union focus group, illustrated Anderson's point when she indicated the salience of greetings for establishing in-group cohesion and tie to one's community. She also implicitly suggests that an acknowledgment can serve as an antidote for the oppression felt by African American males, indicating an interesting nexus of race and gender. Respondent 4 said:

I do believe that the black community is the lowest person on the pyramid. And us acknowledging one another is rising us up. I mean ... the reason why I acknowledge men more than women is cos I believe that the black male has been brought down so low, that he needs to be pumped up. And I think a black sister needs to do that ... And that's why I acknowledge people, cos I know I feel good when people acknowledge me, and I know they're doing it because I'm a black female.

She links self-esteem and social identity with her desire to give as well as receive acknowledgments, corresponding to one of Tajfel and Turner's (1986) main assumptions about social identity: "Individuals strive to maintain or enhance their self-esteem: they strive for a positive self-concept." (16) In doing so, Respondent 4 implicitly refers to the role that acknowledgment rituals play in "rising us up," which is a functional means of fighting against African American subordinate or oppressed status through a relatively simple symbolic gesture of unity. This particular function of acknowledgment rituals was a fairly common theme for some other minority groups as well, especially gay, bisexuals, and lesbians, Mexican and Chicano Americans and to some degree women in their mid-twenties and older. The question then is why are African Americans much more likely to participate in the acknowledgment ritual than other groups?

One explanation is that there is an unwritten law within the African American community that "brothers and sisters" should acknowledge one another. In other words, it is a group-specific norm, a shared understanding that to acknowledge one another is correct and to ignore someone within the community is non-normative (i.e., deviates from social expectations). Recently the cover of a *Newsweek* magazine[10] read, "What Color is Black?: Science, Politics and Racial Identity." The very first article dealing with the issue presented on the cover was written by a journalism student attending the University of Tennessee.[11] Courtney's opening two sentences stressed exactly this point:

> As my friend Denise and I trudged across the University of Tennessee campus to our 9:05 a.m. class, we delivered countless head nods, "Heys" and "How ya' doin's" to other African Americans we passed along the way. We spoke to people we knew as well as people we didn't know because it's an unwritten rule that black people speak to one another when they pass. (*Newsweek*, February, 1995: 16)

Describing a black community in a Midwestern city, Stack (1974) discussed the concept of kinship and its importance to the Black social structure. She used the notion of "fictive kinship" to refer to those people who one can count on as family but are not genetically related. Stack (1974) stated, "The offering of kin terms to "those you count on" is a way people expand their personal networks." (58) Stack further suggested that "fictive kin relations are maintained by consensus between individuals" (59) and that "social relations are conducted within the idiom of kinship." (60) This notion of *fictive kinship* may be one explanation for why African American males, in particular, participate in the acknowledgment ritual, and why African American females feel compelled to prop up their "brothers" through greetings. I argue that fictive kinship is most salient in situations that are potentially oppressive, such as situations of extreme numerical disadvantage (i.e., most college campuses regarding racial groups).

A second explanation focuses on the stigma of being an African American male in American society today. My observation is that acknowledgments or greetings between African Americans serves the purpose of symbolically saying "society doesn't value you as an individual (or a people) but that by acknowledging you I am saying you count." This notion of giving respect is a plausible explanation why African Americans participate in the acknowledgment ritual to a much greater degree than other groups. This particular explanation is consistent with Howard's (1994) notion that dominated groups are more likely to rely on social identities, because I suggest that these identities are bolstered by the collective response to oppression. Finally, it is evident that race is not the only identifiable factor which explains the noted disproportionate participation in acknowledgment rituals; otherwise there would not be such a sharp distinction between African American men and women. Clearly, the unparalleled participation by African American males indicates that sex as well as race (i.e., the nexus of the two) helps to shape the interactive accomplishment framed within this greeting phenomenon.

Mexican Americans The second most frequent rates of acknowledgment were among Mexican American or Latino males. Again, this held true both when I was a participant and an observer. Interview data indicate that many of the same issues prompted greetings between Mexicans or Chicanos who did not know each other. However, there was a notable difference in the meaning of an acknowledgment to Mexican Americans. According to Interviewee M, a Mexican male, acknowledgments by strangers serve as a means of acquiring "respect." He illustrated this frame of reference and also added issues of inter-group interactions and relations to the equation:

> It's just, sometimes I think the ones that acknowledge me, gives me a little bit more respect cos of who I am, just walking by the street. I know that other people sometimes, they give 'em dirty looks or just by their race or by the way they look, they dress or something. It really makes me feel good just walking down the street and someone saying "hi" to me, that I don't even know.

Interviewee M also stated a preference for acknowledging certain racial groups, besides his own, as well as corroborating my earlier point that African Americans are perceived to be the most active acknowledgment ritual participants:

> And it's mostly blacks and Filipinos and other Hispanics that acknowledge, I mean, and say "hi" with a head nod or just by saying, "How you doing?" or things like that. But, yeah, I mostly don't really interact with the Asians and the Chinese or Japanese or Whites, you know. It's mostly black people and then, uhm Filipinos.

African American women The next group among whom acknowledgments were most frequent were African American women. Their acknowledgment rates far exceeded those of other women, Asian males and White males. For African American women, race commonalty is a plausible explanation for their participation in acknowledgment rituals. Heterosexual attraction is also a feasible explanation for explaining the frequency of acknowledgment rituals among African American men and women. The frequency of interaction between African American women and men provides a salient illustration of the nexus of race and gender framed in an acknowledgment ritual context.

White, Mexican/Latina, and Asian women White, Mexican/ Latina, and Asian women, in terms of participant observations, were as a group the next most likely to participate in acknowledgements. White women and Mexican, or Latino women were approximately equal in their receptiveness to initiated acknowledgments. Both far exceeded Asian women in this respect.

Asian and White males Asian males and White males were the least likely to participate in acknowledgment rituals. Asian males, however, were relatively more receptive to an initiated acknowledgment than were White males. Asian or White males often completely ignored my initiated greeting, both verbal and non-verbal, in situations where it was highly unlikely that they were unaware of me (i.e., stairwells, or empty hallways). In those situations, the usual reaction to my greeting was to look away or stare straight ahead without any noticeable physical change. Respondent 1 of the Asian Student Commission focus group interview corroborated this point when he said, in response to my question "what if you are walking down the hall and there is only one other person coming towards you, what do you do?": "I'm looking away." Interviewee H (a White male) said:

> I wouldn't necessarily greet people I don't know unless there's a particular situation ... so, it's just like walking down the street, I tend not to really notice people too much."

I rarely observed either Asian and White males acknowledging someone of their own race or gender. And when Asian or White males initiated an acknowledgment, it was usually with someone outside of their racial group, and in a majority of the cases it was with a Black male. This is consistent with the general perception that Black males are the most receptive to acknowledgments and that they are the most active participants in acknowledgment rituals.

Asian Americans and Asians Asians and Asian Americans may share a cultural aversion to participating in acknowledgment rituals, illustrated during my interview with the Asian Student Commission. Respondent 2, of the Asian Student Commission focus group interview, summed this up in cultural terms:

> In our culture, eye contact is considered rude.

Respondent 7, of the Asian Student Commission focus group interview, said:

> You just don't acknowledge people you don't know.

The aversion is manifest in three ways: first, a perceived lack of unity among different nationality groups; second, as tension between Asian Americans and Asians; and third, an apparent affinity to acknowledge out-group members. Addressing the first point, a participant in the Asian Student commission focus group interview came up to me after concluding the interview to emphasize that there was not as much unity within the Asian community as it appeared during the interview. A number of other Asian students stopped to contribute to our conversation; they expressed consensus that in fact Asian people would rather not acknowledge strangers, or if a greeting did occur it would most likely be with someone who is not Asian. The second point was illustrated well by Respondent 1, of the Asian Student Commission focus group interview, who stated:

> I tend to relate to people who grew up here than that's coming over here, or what we call as FOB, fresh off the boat.

Respondent 4, of the Asian Student Commission focus group interview, not only mentions the lack of intra-group acknowledgments but also indicates that African American people often do acknowledge others. He said:

> I walk like past an Asian person, they won't even look at me. I mean they'll just walk straight ahead. But if I'm like, when a black person or something walking past me, and they'll just like nod at me or something.

White Americans It is obvious from the discussions above that White Americans as a group participate in the acknowledgment ritual less frequently than any other group. However, White women do participate considerably more often than White men. There is also the perception among other groups that White men in particular don't participate in any kind of acknowledgment ritual. The observations bear out this perception. Interestingly, when I asked the interviewees who tends to acknowledge whom and under what circumstances, White men were never mentioned without prompting. Interviewee A left no doubt about her perspective regarding White American participation in the acknowledgment ritual as well as implicitly naming the intersection of gender and race as a salient factor:

> I've never noticed White people acknowledging other White people in the way other Black people do it. Do you know what I'm saying, in the very outward …I mean White people walk by White people all of the time, but I, rarely do I see Black people not have some sort of eye contact and I think that is great. I mean I think it is a sense of comfort. At least I know when I'm a woman in the minority, do you know what I'm saying, it is a feeling of comfort and that's something I want to do.

Respondent 2, of the black student commission, suggested a theory for the lack of acknowledging among White people, while implicitly pointing to the influence of numerical inferiority on greeting behavior:

> And I think maybe it's because they don't have to, because of the fact that they see a ton of white people all day long. They don't feel that it's necessary to say "hi" to whoever that is over there, because they don't know that person. Maybe they don't feel that same kind of need.

Gay males, bisexuals, and lesbians For many observers, gay males and lesbians are not necessarily as easily identifiable as those of racial minority groups or women. I did observe on several occasions lesbian couples holding hands and have seen individuals pass by and acknowledge them. I was not able to determine visually whether the persons who greeted the couples were a part of the gay community, but the interview data indicate that there is a significant commonalty or solidarity in the gay community which would suggest that the greeters were themselves gay.

For individuals in the gay community there appears to be a strong need to acknowledge another gay person to signal in-group support or, in this case, acknowledging the other's sexuality. Implicit in this discussion are issues of identity and self. Respondent 2, who self-identifies as a bisexual Mexican male, said:

> I think also straight people, they might acknowledge you, but they wouldn't necessarily acknowledge your sexuality. Where, in the queer community, an acknowledgment, even if I acknowledge a lesbian, I'm acknowledging her sexuality as well as her person.

This data also indicates the salience of the intersection of race, gender and sexuality during greetings.

Respondent 4, of the gay, bisexual, and lesbian student commission illustrated that greetings for him can simply be the courteous thing to do, but he did indicate that acknowledgments also are tied to in-group cohesion and identity:

> For me, it's mostly out of politeness sake. Like, I'll just like acknowledge someone … gay or straight, but if I do notice it or realize, oh, they are gay, then it's kind of letting them know I know and that they know, just kind of acknowledge who they are.

There is also the perception that gay men do far more cruising than lesbians. (Cruising refers to a gay person who is actively or purposefully trying to "hit on" or get a relationship going (sexually or otherwise) with another gay person.) This is an important distinction, because this subtle difference in greeting patterns between gay men and lesbians shows the importance of considering layered frames (i.e., the nexus of gender and sexuality) when investigating interactional accomplishments. Woman 3, of the Women's Commission focus group interview, (self-identified lesbian) referred to this perception:

> Also that is different among men, between gay men and lesbians. Gay men do far, far more cruising than lesbians. I'm not saying that lesbians don't, but uhm, and that it is more blatant in a different way.

Gendered Patterns in Acknowledgments

Gender differences The difference in acknowledgments as a result of gender provided some of the most fascinating findings.

For women, three themes consistently recurred in discussing when they engage in acknowledgment rituals: (1) a sense of common bond as women; (2) a sense of vulnerability, particularly in potentially dangerous situations; and (3) for very young women only, a sense of competition. Women, of course, also participate in acknowledgment rituals for other reasons, like those noted for men, including normative behavior (i.e., etiquette), mood, physical attraction, etc. The three themes noted above were the most frequently cited, however. I have already discussed above how acknowledgments can affirm a common bond (see commonalty and other sections). The issues of vulnerability and competition require more explanation.

Women and situations of vulnerability When asked, "when do you acknowledge people and what characteristics of the other are important?," women responded consistently by referring to acknowledging women in situations of vulnerability. They said that women felt more secure in potentially dangerous situations when other women were around to provide support and help if necessary. This also indicates a sense of in-group cohesion and cooperation, as well as signaling trust, channeled through an acknowledgment ritual. Interviewee L said:

> at bus stops, late at night, which tends to be the times that I would be out. And you're really kind of checking out your support, in a way. I mean you're standing there and you're thinking, I know I shouldn't be waiting for this bus late at night, I know this is a risky thing to do. God knows when the bus is going to come, cos you can't ever tell in Philadelphia when the bus is going to come. And there's this other person standing there. And it's really common that someone will just sort of ask you for the time or say, "God, I can't believe how long it is between buses," or "I wish they had a shelter at this bus stop because it's raining" or whatever it is that they say … and you want to assess, if you get attacked, is this person going to support me, kind of. Yeah.

Woman 3 of the Women's Commission focus group interview, said:

> I was in a drug store, a while back, and I bought a box of condoms. And I thought to myself I am not going to acknowledge anyone who just saw me buy these condoms, because it might be a guy who thinks I'm a slut. You know stuff like that. You know, where

there is something about you that could create an impression of you that might be dangerous for the other person to have.

This aspect of acknowledgment rituals requires further examination, because the greeting phenomena played out among women speak of larger societal issues. For example, women deal with the increasing potential of being raped or becoming victims of other violent crimes. Women also have to contend with single or multiple minority statuses (i.e., being a white woman or a woman of color), in terms of power.

Women and the issue of competitiveness The theme of competitiveness among women as being relevant to participation in acknowledgments was unexpected. This surfaced repeatedly throughout the interviews with women, regardless of race. Interestingly, there appears to be a transition from a focus in competitiveness with other women to a focus of commonality among women, that occurs approximately in women's mid-twenties. Interviewee K spoke of the connection between age and competition:

> For women, I would say it's, well, it's difficult with women because with younger women, I'm finding I'm finally reaching this age, like mid-twenties, where women aren't so competitive with each other. So I can have friendly acknowledgments with women. But before then, like in my early twenties and teens, there was a lot of competition and I felt [it] in acknowledging women on the streets. Most women, like on campus, because they're primarily undergraduates, might check me over, see what I'm wearing. See if my outfit, you know, meets with their standards. And they they'll either smile, because they know that I've seen, caught them looking at me. Or they'll just like glance away. But recently I've noticed women, like around my age range, mid-twenties or thirty, will acknowledge me.

Heterosexual dynamics Other factors also come into play in cross-sex (and presumably heterosexual) acknowledgments. One theme is a fear of transmitting the wrong message to a member of the opposite sex during an acknowledgment (i.e., "I'm physically attracted to you"). This particular theme was expressed by both men and women, regardless of race, and dictated whether an acknowledgment occured. Interviewee F quite emphatically presented her choice of acknowledging women, because of the potential for an acknowledgment with a male to be seen as a "come on":

> I've worked in a lot of construction or male-dominated jobs, and any form of acknowledgment can be taken as a come-on, and more often than not, it is. So rather than put up with that horseshit I just don't.

Respondent 3, of the Black Student Union focus group interview, said:

> Some women will hold back saying "Hello" to men or acknowledging men cos they're like … he might get the wrong idea, he might follow me, that kind of thing, it's those kinds of things that go through your mind not just, why a person would say "Hello" … I would rather acknowledge a woman knowing I feel comfortable saying "Hello, how you doing?" And she'd be like, "Hello, how you doing?" And there's not a sexuality issue. Rather than with a man, I know if I say, "Hey, how you doing?" I am going like, [going to] ask him out, you know.

In addition, attraction also influenced whether one acknowledged someone of the opposite sex, or of the same sex for members of the gay community. Interviewees mentioned others' physical features, the way they dress or any possibilities that make others seem attractive. The theme of attraction was mentioned by all groups and both sexes as a significant reason for deciding to acknowledge or not acknowledge someone.

Other findings

Presenting self and community solidarity For some groups, acknowledgment rituals are conducted with the explicit intention of presenting self as a legitimate member of an in-group and as a means of expressing a sense of intra-group solidarity. Presenting self to the other and establishing a sense of "community" are two important interrelated aspects of the meaning expressed through acknowledgment rituals. The shared understanding obviously is something that requires cooperative group or cultural frames of reference. According to Mead (1934), cooperation and group life require knowing one's position in terms of a complex set of others. It is also through this process that identities are created and linked to particular communities. As Berger (1963) wrote, identities are "socially bestowed, socially maintained, and socially transformed." (98) In other words, defining self is undertaken via interaction with others, in this case, a greeting. Identity, then, is reaffirmed, and is changed through interaction. Respondent 2, of the Black Student Commission focus group, articulated in-group association in terms of commonality and cohesiveness, while also stressing identity:

> The acknowledgment is the way of showing that there is cohesiveness, that I do care about what happens to my community. I do care about people who are like me. I do care about who I am.

Respondent 2 of the Gay, Bisexual, and Lesbian Commission, also stressed the sense of community and identity, but for him the symbolism of the acknowledgment was important also in dealing with his feelings of oppression:

> even just kind of the need for support, like from within the community, because it, at least, for out gay, lesbian, bisexual people, it can be very exhausting. And so, it's nice to just kind of get that brief eye contact, it's kind of like, oh yeah, we're all here together.

Situational commonality I also observed commonality influencing acknowledgment rituals, both as a participant and nonparticipant observer. A sense of commonality expressed through greetings or acknowledgment rituals permeated all of my interviews. Thus greetings also happen because of very minute, seemingly inconsequential, factors. The diversity of common bonds does not diminish the salience of larger issues, such as oppression or vulnerability-driven acknowledgments, but is simply another aspect of greetings, that may influence who we are, how we perceive and present ourselves, and how we think we are perceived.

Respondent 2 of the Women Engineers Association focus group interview illustrated another example of commonality expressed between two people who overhear a funny comment made by a child and the resulting laugh and smile represented a greeting that might not otherwise have happened:

> I was downtown a long time ago, walking past one of these theaters, the X-rated whatever, triple X theaters, and there was a black gentleman walking the other way with a little girl in tow. And we

probably wouldn't have made eye contact, except the little girl looked up and I don't remember her exact words but she said something like, "Daddy, is that where they make something movies," and we caught each other's eyes and we both burst out laughing, because I overheard it … And so we smiled at each other and, you know, walked past. Otherwise, we probably wouldn't have even acknowledged each other.

Age   Age was also relevant to participation in acknowledgment rituals. Younger, teenage boys and girls hardly even greeted someone older. Except for a very few occasions, I was ignored by teenage boys and girls when I attempted to initiate an acknowledgment. However, on the rare occasion when I was acknowledged by a teenager, it normally was a solo African American male. In groups, the teenagers I observed did not interact with older people unless the situation necessitated an interaction (i.e., overly crowded bus). Interviewee F illustrated the salience of age as well as the process of defining the situation in terms of subtle cues during an interaction, which determine the outcome of that interaction:

> I think the first thing that I consciously do is, yeah, I say I'm walking down the street where there's long visibility. I see someone coming towards me. I try to, and this is actually a conscious process of looking at their body language and their face and are they looking at me or are they looking away, turning away, walking stiffly, whatever. If they look relaxed, if they're looking up, then I'm much, that's like a yes, I'll probably look at them. And whether or not I say "hi" depends on whether or not I get eye contact with them. I usually smile almost automatically. If they smile back warmly, then there's going to be a verbal greeting as well. Age probably has something to do with it … Very elderly people, I'm, I consciously say I'm going to acknowledge them regardless of what they say to me. And I tend not to acknowledge younger people, like elementary, middle school, or high school kids as often.

I also did not see older individuals, who by all appearances were strangers, acknowledge one another, regardless of race or sex. However, during informal interviews, several older interviewees have indicated that it is not uncommon for older people to acknowledge one another while walking (particularly in one's neighborhood). During my interviews most interviewees indicated an affinity for acknowledging older individuals out of respect, regardless of race or sex, but this was not apparent to any extensive degree during observations. This may indicate that "situation" really matters and perhaps my area of study did not include areas where older individuals are more likely to acknowledge one another.

Discussion and Conclusion

Acknowledgment rituals help define who one is in terms of community ties, social identity, and self-esteem; they may in fact be a symbolic statement in response to societal oppression. The development and maintenance of self and social identity were recurring themes given as reasons for participating in this greeting phenomenon. This was particularly evident for all groups except for White and Asian males. Why is this so? Are White males numerically so superior that they have no need for acknowledgment rituals as an explicit means of expressing social identity? Is personal identity their primary frame of reference? Do cultural factors block Asian male participation? Why do not some groups (for example elderly persons) participate in acknowledgment rituals on a regular basis? Or do they, perhaps, but in areas other than those where I conducted observations? Further investigation of acknowledgment rituals would illuminate whether other groups (e.g., the elderly, the obese) participate in this greeting phenomenon in ways similar to the groups discussed here. For instance, do physically challenged individuals or obese persons feel compelled to acknowledge other people like themselves or would this draw too much unwanted attention to their stigmatized personal characteristics?[12]

The Roots of Acknowledgments: an African American Experience

Acknowledgment rituals or greetings are ubiquitous, purposeful, symbolic, and governed by rules and norms. At the same time, rates of acknowledgment vary considerably across social groups. African American males participate in this greeting phenomenon far more often than all the other groups combined. The following example illustrates how powerful the desire is for African American males to acknowledge one another. This occurred in a situation where acknowledgments violate normative behavior for that particular setting.

The example occurs in a restaurant setting, and entails the behavior of buspersons. It is not a part of busperson's job to greet customers who are seated at tables not in need of their service. (As a matter of clarity, buspersons are restaurant employees who remove all dishes and clean the table once the patron(s) has (have) completed dinner, paid the bill and left.) However, African American buspersons do participate in acknowledgment rituals with African American customers seated outside their primary task area. I have been a participant observer in this exact situation; I have been greeted by and have initiated greetings with African American buspersons in many different restaurants. I have not, however, ever observed this greeting phenomenon between other non-African American buspersons and restaurant customers, regardless of race or gender. Nor have I been the recipient of an acknowledgment by a non-African American busperson. This is unusual behavior for a restaurant, but nonetheless is readily observable between African American males.

Dr Henry Louis Gates, Jr, (1994) wrote specifically about this greeting phenomenon in a powerful preface written in personal letter form to his children. He wrote,

> I have written for another reason, as well. I remember that once we were walking in Washington, D.C., heading for the National Zoo, and you asked me if I had known the man to whom I had just spoken. I said no. And, Liza, you volunteered that you found it embarrassing that I would speak to a complete stranger on the street. It called to mind a trip I'd made to Pittsburgh with my father. On the way from his friend Mr. Ozzie Washington's sister's house, I heard Daddy speak to a colored man, then saw him tip his hat to the man's wife. (Daddy liked nice hats: Caterpillar hats for work, Dobbs hats for Sunday). It's just something that you do, he said when I asked him if he had known those people and why had he spoken to them.
>
> Last summer, I sat at a sidewalk café in Italy, and three or four "black" Italians walked casually by, as well as a dozen more blacker Africans. Each spoke to me; rather, each nodded his head slightly or acknowledged me by a glance, ever so subtly. When I was growing up, we always did this with each other, passing boats in a sea of white folk. (xii)

What Dr Gates, Jr, explicitly articulates speaks directly to my impetus for investigating this greeting phenomenon. I've repeatedly asked myself what is the significance of acknowledgment rituals for African Americans? Why do African Americans participate more than other groups? What are the origins of this behavior? I've discussed the first two questions above, but I have yet to address the latter issue. What are the origins of this greeting behavior for African Americans? I speculate that acknowledgment rituals for African Americans start with the institution of chattel slavery.

First, I speculate that a slave's everyday life was so controlled that verbal communication with another slave wasn't always "encouraged,"or allowed; acknowledgment rituals became an alternative way to communicate. In other words, subtle non-verbal communication in the form of extended eye-contact, a head nod or the raising of eyebrows may have been developed to facilitate acknowledgments of one another's plight, without incurring punishment for "stepping out of line."

Second, it is well documented that specific efforts were made to culturally mix slaves on one plantation, so that language and other cultural differences made it difficult for the slaves to communicate, therefore decreasing the potential for organized rebellious activity (Patterson 1982). Language barriers made it necessary for slaves to find alternative communication methods which transcended cultural and linguistic differences. One may further speculate that this behavior spread among slaves from different plantations via incidental contact, and eventually incorporated verbal communication, evolving into what we see today: a greeting phenomenon within the African American community, ritualized and important for communicating or signaling trust, commonality and a shared understanding of community, identity, and fictive kinship. Acknowledgment rituals, for African Americans at least, may have their roots in strategies for surviving the oppressive situation of slavery. Even outside of the African American experience, this logic may partially explain what may have triggered similar behaviors in the gay community or for women in vulnerable situations.

The degree to which African Americans participate in this greeting phenomenon may also reflect southern or rural norms, in conjunction with historically situated experiences such as slavery. Reputed southern hospitality and friendliness may have facilitated the perpetuation of acknowledgment rituals, in that there was some degree of White Southern cultural assimilation that took place in the African American community after emancipation. This type of cultural characteristic is what Anderson referred to when he wrote of it being considered "strange" for African Americans not to speak, regardless of whether the individuals knew one another.

Several other issues related to the African American experience deserve attention. First, are African Americans as likely to participate in acknowledgment rituals in situations where they are numerically a majority (e.g., an inner-city ghetto area or a "black" community)? My research shows that even in situations where African Americans are numerically the majority, they participate in acknowledgment rituals more often than any other single non-African American group. The frequency of greetings does decrease, but nevertheless they are still readily observable. There is not, obviously, the same sense of being "two passing boats in a sea of white folks," but I surmise that the issues of identity, self and commonality among African Americans, in terms of survival strategies for dealing with the oppressive nature of American society, are present regardless of numerical strength. Another question concerns the effect of my multiracial appearance on the acknowledgment ritual process. Racially, I am part Black and part White. Did my biracial appearance (i.e., my light complexion as a result of being both Black and White) cause any confusion, in terms of the perceptions of the other, as to my African American identity or kinship in the African American community at large? There have been times during the initial acknowledgment stage (when cognitive assessments of whom the other is are made) when I have "sensed" that the prolonged eye contact normally present prior to an acknowledgment went beyond deciding whether to greet the approaching stranger. I speculate that on occasion the prolonged eye contact also had to do with deciding whether to classify me as African American. In this situation, I speculate that by initiating the acknowledgment ritual, (i.e., a head nod accompanied by a verbalization of "what's up") I gave an appropriate response which helped clarify or dispel any uncertainty over my identity. I further speculate that when I wasn't acknowledged by another African American male in situations where I expected to be, this may be partially explained by confusion about my biracial appearance and hence my in-group status. This is an empirical question that also requires further study.

Prevailing stereotypes about race or other identity characteristics may also be relevant. I recently spent six weeks at a large mid-western university; I was surprised to find that whites acknowledged me far more often than my previous observations would have predicted. This mid-western university has similar characteristics, in terms of size, racial and ethnic makeup, as other universities in this study. Initially, I attributed this increase in greetings to regional differences (i.e. reputed mid-western friendliness), but I was not satisfied with that conclusion. In situations where greetings were exchanged in more closed or movement limiting settings (e.g., elevators, restaurants, or waiting in lines), an interesting pattern emerged. In almost every situation where a greeting was followed up by any verbal communication, the first question I was asked was "Are you a member of the football team?"

I discussed this observation with several colleagues and they were not at all surprised by this observation, especially considering my size and build, clothing selection (tank-tops and shorts) and race. This particular region is extremely football-oriented and any opportunity to affiliate oneself with a football player was valued. The phenomenon of "basking in reflected glory" (Cialdini and De Nicholas 1989; and Cialdini et al. 1976) may explain those acknowledgments. Cialdini et al. (1976) refer to the tendency of individuals to manage their public images by announcing their association with successful others (e.g., wearing school or team identifying apparel), regardless of whether the one who is basking in the glory of the other has actually contributed to the other's success. "Basking in reflected glory" in this particular situation moved beyond simply wearing school or team identifying apparel. The expression of association with a successful other took on an interactive component via the acknowledgment ritual. I speculate that when I was greeted by white strangers, who in other settings normally ignored me, I was the object of their desire to bask in the reflected glory of someone they perceived as successful (i.e., a member of a championship football team). I did not observe any other interactions that were contrary to my previous findings.

This observation prompts several interesting additional questions. When a community's identity is characterized by some important binding element (e.g., the irrepressible devotion to a sport or championship team), do acknowledgment rituals take on another level of *situational* complexity, in terms of the rules governing who acknowledges whom and under what circumstances? Would those same individuals acknowledge African Americans in other settings that are not associated with their fervor for football? Are stereotypic notions of African American Athletic prowess prompting these greetings? Are African American women viewed in the same stereotypic way and hence acknowledged more often as a result? Or is this a gender-specific or football-specific fervor, therefore limiting the increased participation in acknowledgment rituals to African American males who are athletic looking?[13] What about Athletic looking Anglo American men? Are they acknowledged more often than Anglo American men would otherwise be?

Vulnerability, and the Intersection of Gender and Race: Issues to Reveal

Although the disproportionate participation of African Americans in this greeting phenomenon generates some of the most striking findings, there are other significant patterns. The theme of vulnerability as a catalyst for acknowledgments between women is particularly interesting. Greetings between female strangers that occurred out of a sense of vulnerability crossed all racial boundaries and seemed to be gender-specific. Marking "vulnerability" in gendered terms does not go far enough, however. I would surmise that a relationship between age and vulnerability exists. I speculate that Signaling *trust* is an important part of this aspect of acknowledgment rituals. How does a head nod or a smile signal trust to the other? Is this gender-specific? Is it even possible for a man to signal trust or for women to interpret greetings in this way in situations of vulnerability? Is perceived or potential physical attraction (between heterosexuals or homosexuals) such a salient factor that the signal of trust is often misinterpreted or at least conflated during an interaction where vulnerability would be a factor (i.e., a bus stop late at night)?

Other interesting issues related to women's participation in acknowledgment rituals require more research. For instance, non-African American women more often than not "avoided" acknowledgments by looking away or down as I approached and attempted to initiate a greeting. In comparison, African American women were significantly more likely to respond to, as well as initiate greetings, with me. Why are African American women more likely to participate in this greeting phenomenon compared to other women? There are other issues at play however. To what degree does physical attraction affect one's decision to acknowledge the other? What role do societal norms regarding physical attraction have to do with the amount of participation in acknowledgment rituals? Are taboos against interracial dating or attraction prevalent enough to prevent participation in an everyday behavior such as acknowledgment rituals? What role does an African American woman's multiple subordinate statuses (i.e., being female and a minority) play in how often they participate in acknowledgment rituals compared to other women or African American males who have one subordinate status (i.e., minority)? Because of their multiple subordinate statuses, I expected African American women to acknowledge one another more often than they did. What factors are involved in the decision-making processes for African American women in terms of when and with whom they choose to acknowledge? This indicates that this greeting phenomenon is not solely based on race, but that issues regarding the intersection of race and gender are also salient. This raises a general issue of whether women use public spaces differently than men. That is, are women less likely to be forward in public spaces even considering the subtle nature of acknowledgment rituals?

The Gay Community: Echoing the Black Experience and Regional Complexity

Several interesting findings from gay, lesbian, and bisexual informants also merit final comments. First, gay, lesbian, and bisexual experiences, in terms of the reasons for and experiences with acknowledgment rituals, closely mirror those of African American informants. Wanting to support others "just like me" as a strategy for combating the oppressive nature of society surfaced many times during interviews. Another interesting finding is that the initial acknowledgment stage for homosexuals showed a regional complexity. There are region-specific clues or tie signs which indicate to the other whether one is gay or lesbian; therefore gay migrants new to this area (i.e., from the East Coast), and unfamiliar with local norms, may initially have difficulties properly identifying gay or lesbian others. Until these local norms are learned, there may be some confusion in terms of purposeful, commonality-oriented acknowledgments and hence any benefit derived from these interactions will be delayed. How this affects one's identity, presentation of self, or efforts to assimilate oneself into the local gay culture requires further study.

Acknowledgment Rituals: A Final Word About Complexity and Interactional Achievement

Many other questions and issues regarding acknowledgment rituals deserve attention. Social cognition and symbolic interactionism as theoretical perspectives together provide a useful framework for understanding the intricacies and implications of this greeting phenomenon. Even something as taken-for-granted as an acknowledgment ritual can have profound social implications, and hence is sociologically important. The research shows that what appears to be a subtle, seemingly taken-for-granted behavior, is best characterized as a salient *interactional achievement* that is significantly intertwined in the development and maintenance of identity and self. This research endorses the necessity of understanding the importance of *everyday* interactive behavior, and points to the necessity of "complicating" these issues. Understanding everyday interactive behavior necessitates viewing these phenomena within a frame of complexity built upon the nexus of factors such as race, gender, class, age, region, and sexual orientation.

NOTES

1   This research could not have been completed without the support of the Minority Education Office, a part of the Graduate School Administrative Division at the University of Washington. I am also indebted to Judith A. Howard, Robert Crutchfield, Jodi O'Brien, and Howard Becker for providing guidance throughout this endeavor.
2   See Charon 1989; and Mead 1934 for discussions of the self and its development.
3   A schema is defined as "a cognitive structure that represents knowledge about a concept or type of stimulus, including its attributes and the relations among those attributes" (Fiske and Taylor 1991: 98).

4 I relied upon my perception of an individual's race when doing non-participant and participant observations. If I was unsure of an individual's race, I did not count that interaction in my data.

5 My purpose for not always initiating a particular acknowledgment episode was to ensure variation.

6 Informal interviewees were unscheduled but presented an opportunity for me to inquire about acknowledgment rituals and greetings. Informal interviews were not taped, because of their spur of the moment nature, however, any useful information was later recorded.

7 These five forms represent categories of greetings which I've observed or participated in.

8 I observed Asians, Whites, Blacks, and Mexicans (Latina(o)s). I identified people as members of particular groups based on my individual, accumulated knowledge and interation with different peoples. If I was unsure of a person's race, I did not include that interaction in my data.

9 I also noted observed inconsistencies. That is, according to both participant and non-participant observations, there seems to be a difference in the "actual" amount of acknowledgment ritual participation compared to the stated or implied frequency of participation (noted during interviews) for all groups except African American males. Why this inconsistency exists requires further investigation.

10 *Newsweek*, February 13, 1995 issue.

11 Ibid., p. 16: Brian A. Courtney, "Freedom From Choice: Being biracial has meant denying half of my identity."

12 Several comments were made during one of my interviews regarding "fat oppression" and the stigmas associated with being obese. The obese woman felt she was unduly torn in these directions. Should she acknowledge another obese person and possibly draw attention to their weight "problem?" Should she become active in fat oppression issues and in doing so, acknowledge other obese people in a stand of unity and social identity? This same issue or dilemma could also operate among gays and lesbians.

13 I qualify this question with a reference to "athletic looking" because I surmise that not all African American males are greeted more often in this setting. Only those African American males who have the appropriate build, size, and confident demeanor defining them as an athlete would experience an increase in greetings from strangers.

REFERENCES

Anderson, Elijah. 1990. *StreetWise: Race, Class, and Change in an Urban Community*. Chicago: The University of Chicago Press, 163–89.

Berger, Peter. 1963. *Invitation to Sociology*. New York, NY: Doubleday.

Charon, Joel M. 1989. *Symbolic Interactionism: An Introduction, An Interpretation, An Integration*, 3rd edn. New Jersey, NJ: Prentice Hall.

Cialdini, Robert, Richard J. Borden, Avril Thorne, Marcus Randall Walker, Stephen Freeman, and Lloyd Reynolds Sloan. 1976. "Basking in Reflected Glory: Three (Football) Field Studies." *Journal of Personality and Social Psychology* 34(3): 366–75.

Cialdini, Robert and Maralou E. De Nicholas. 1989. "Self-Presentation by Association." *Journal of Personality and Social Psychology* 57(4): 626–31.

Fiske, S. T. and Taylor, S. E. 1991. *Social Cognition*. 2nd edn. New York, NY: McGraw Hill.

Gates, Henry Louis, Jr. 1994. *Colored People: a memoir*. New York, NY: Vintage Books.

Goffman, Erving. 1959. *The Presentation of Self in Everyday Life*. New York, NY: Doubleday.

——. 1967. *Interaction Ritual: Essays on Face-to-Face Behavior*. New York: Pantheon Books.

——. 1971. *Relations in Public: Microstudies of the Public Order*. New York: Basic Books, Inc.

——. 1974. *Frame Analysis: An Essay on the Organization of Experience*. Cambridge, MA: Harvard University Press.

Howard, Judith A. 1995. "Social Cognition," in *Sociological Perspectives on Social Psychology*, Karen Cook, G. Fine, and J. House (eds) Needham Heights, MA: Allyn & Bacon, 90–117.

McCall, George J. and Simmons, J. L. 1996. *Identities and Interactions: An Examination of Human Associations in Everyday Life*. New York, NY: The Free Press.

Mead, George H. 1934. *Mind, Self and Society*. Chicago, Ill: Chicago University Press.

Patterson, Orlando. 1982. *Slavery and Social Death: A Comparative Study*. Cambridge, MA: Harvard University Press.

Stack, Carol B. 1974. *All Our Kin: Strategies for Survival in a Black Community*. New York: Harper & Row publishers.

Tajfel, Henri and John C. Turner. 1986. "The Social Identity Theory of Intergroup Behavior," in *Psychology of Intergroup Relations*, 2nd edn. Stephen Worchel and William G. Austin. (eds) Chicago: Nelson-Hall Publishers, 7–24.

4

"Are You Male or Female?" Gender Performances on Muds

Lori Kendall

I think that when you get down to it, if people really think about it, gender matters for little ultimately. Like take you for example – your @sex is set to 'female' – but does that mean anything other than the 6 bytes it takes up to store the text? Not really. I treat you the same whether it says female, male, neuter, or whatever – assuming that we're not roleplaying something or the like.

Carets, a male regular on BlueSky

I'd like to think, I don't really know, because I'm not a guy, but I would like to think that when you're online as a woman that the fact that you're a woman is backseat to the personality.

Peg, a female regular on BlueSky

A female newbie will be given more breaks and more attention, even (especially?) by women.

Beryl, a female regular on BlueSky

Women get treated differently from men. It's not that they get more slack or anything, but they get chased out differently. Part of it is that most women tend not to talk immediately, just by normal socialization. Guys are much more likely to mouth off early. But women often get turned off by less nasty hazing than men.

Spontaneity, a male regular on BlueSky

Introduction

Identity concepts such as race, class, and gender, and the hierarchical systems of interaction based on these concepts, form an integral part of the fabric of everyday life. New arenas for social interaction provide potentially fresh perspectives on such systems. Online networks, and the social forums they provide, afford opportunities to examine the construction, reconstruction (and potential deconstructions) of gendered, raced and classed systems of meaning. In particular, text-based interactive forums such as Internet Relay Chat and other types of "chat rooms" such as muds can necessitate more attention from participants towards issues of representation and identity than face-to-face interactions generally require. Therefore, examination of identity performances in these forums can highlight power issues and yield new insights into the performance of identity both on and offline.

However, online forums provide a demographically limited population for study. As many as 87 percent of Internet participants are white, approximately 65 percent are male, and nearly all are middle class.[1] Given these figures, it is not surprising that for many online participants, gender identities appear to be more salient than other facets of identity. Information about gender identities and gender performances are more readily available online than other aspects of identity. However, in separating out gender, as I do in this chapter, I risk reifying the biases of the mostly white, middle-class participants I study (particularly since I, as a white, middle-class woman, also tend to "see" gender more easily than I do race or class). On the other hand, because it is generally more socially acceptable online to take note of gender differences than to note race and class differences, looking at gender performances provides a convenient starting point for the examination of identity and dominance relationships based on identity online. I try to make clear at various points in this chapter that the gendered identities I consider are also raced and classed, but my analyses here should be considered partial and preliminary.

As demonstrated by the four epigraphs to this chapter, online participants, like the researchers who study them, present a range of different views of gender's importance online. Carets believes gender doesn't matter at all, while Peg more ambivalently hopes it doesn't. Beryl, on the other hand, has noticed different patterns of treatment based on people's declared online gender identity. Spontaneity further notes that people bring different behavior patterns to their online interactions, based on their previous gendered (offline) socialization.

In this chapter, I explore these and similar claims. I look at the gendered quality of online spaces, and examine the performance of gendered identities within those social spaces. My examples come from a particular type of online forum known as muds, and I begin by explaining what muds are. After briefly discussing some previous research and commentary regarding gender online, I consider some norms of interaction in muds and the ways in which these norms create a particular gendered environment. Next, I consider the kinds of gender identities which participants perform on muds, looking both at people who perform online gender identities congruent with their offline identity and people who "masquerade," using a gender identity different from their offline identity. I argue that the male bias of many online spaces requires performances of masculinity from both male and female participants. Finally, I consider more specifically the difficulties imposed on participants attempting to perform female identities.

Introduction to Muds

Muds are a form of interactive, online, text-only forum. Mud originally stood for Multi-User Dungeon, based on the original multi-person networked dungeons and dragons-type game called MUD. Muds are also sometimes referred to as Multi-User Domains or Dimensions. As in other online chat programs, people use Internet accounts to connect to mud programs running on various remote computers. They then communicate through typed text with other people currently connected to that mud. Muds also allow participants to create programmed "objects," which facilitate the feel of being in a place, adding richness to the social environment. There are hundreds of muds available on the Internet and through private online services. Many still operate as gaming spaces. Others are used for meetings, pedagogical purposes, and as social spaces. My research has been based primarily on social or chat-oriented muds.

For the past two years, I've been a participant-observer on a mud I call BlueSky.[2] I've also spent many hours on several other social muds and have supplemented my participant-observation by reading various online resources relating to muds, including Usenet newsgroup and email list postings. I began my participation as a newcomer to muds. During my participation, I tried to keep others informed of my status as a researcher. My participation has included both online and offline interactions with other mud participants. I also conducted 30 in-depth face-to-face interviews with BlueSky participants in several US cities.

Gender: Online and Off

A large and growing list of articles suggest that norms of gendered behavior continue to shape online interactions. (Some examples include: Cherny 1994; Herring 1992 and 1993; Kramarae and Taylor 1993; Sutton 1994; We 1994.) In most of the forums discussed in these articles, people portray their online gender identity in congruence with their offline identity, or at least members of these groups presume that other participants will do so. In contrast to these descriptions of online groups in which offline gendered norms and power structures prevail, accounts of participation in forums where people do *not* necessarily portray their online gender identity in congruence with their offline identity have suggested that such "gender-switching" behavior can change people's expectations and understandings of gender. Researchers have suggested, for instance, that "gender-switching" can lead to a greater understanding of gender as constructed, and of the self as mutable. (Bruckman 1994; Deuel 1995; Dickel 1995; Poster 1995; Turkle 1995; Burris and Hoplight 1996.) These accounts have relied predominantly on participants' own assertions regarding the liberatory potential of their online interactions. Most accounts have not contextualized such assertions through consideration of the social norms and expectations within the online groups, or through specific analysis of online gender enactments. Further, insufficient attention to the power differences inherent in gender, class, and racial identities leads these researchers to overestimate the ability of online interactions to displace power hierarchies.

Bruckman (1994), Dickel (1995), and Turkle (1995), for instance, confuse limited gender *exchangeability* (the ability to *represent* oneself, with variable success, as a different gender identity from one's offline identity), with gender *malleability* (an understanding of gender as constructed, fluid, and changeable). As Bornstein (1994) and others have pointed out, changing one's gender identity, even offline, can still perpetuate a rigidly binary understanding of the gender system. Bornstein indicates that "most transsexuals opt for the theory that there are men and women and no in-between ground: the agreed-upon gender system ... [I]n my world view, I saw myself as ... something that needed to be ... placed neatly into one of the categories" (64). Bornstein later came to a more fluid understanding of gender identities. But the experience of changing identities, whether through behavioral change and/or through surgical body modifications, remains for most insufficient in and of itself to bring about this understanding.

Gender identities may be more readily changed at will online than off. However, regardless of their connection or lack of connection to offline identities, online identities can continue to carry rigidly defined expectations. As Cheris Kramarae (1995) states in reference to virtual reality programs, although "as in other kinds of play-acting, women and men can temporarily change their gender, there is little to suggest major overhauls of those so-called sex roles in VR programming" (40). Stone (1992) also finds it "significant that almost without exception a binary gender system is ontologized in virtual space" (618).

The act of "switching" genders online, while it crosses a gender boundary, need not blur that boundary. As Thorne (1993) indicates in her discussion of the concept of "borderwork," crossing gender boundaries can strengthen those boundaries, rather than dissolve them. Differences between these two types of action can be subtle. Offline, the availability of information on a variety of verbal and non-verbal levels allows for more nuance in gender performances. But bodies and the gender identity cues they enact are unavailable in most online interactions. Also, particularly on interactive forums such as chatlines or muds, online interactions often involve short bursts of text. These factors can result in gender identity enactments online which rely to an even greater degree on stereotypical notions of identity than do offline enactments. Under these circumstances, as in Thorne's study of children's play, gender enactments online become "stylized moments [which] evoke recurring themes that are deeply rooted in our cultural conceptions of gender, and they suppress awareness of patterns that contradict and qualify them."

Thus, in evaluating the effects of gender performances, and particularly of gender "masquerades" online, researchers must take account of context, motivation, and salience. People engage in gender masquerade online for different reasons and with different results, both for the social groups online (and off) and for their own understandings of gender identity. In the following sections, I consider the gendered context of muds within which particular performances of gender occur. I then look at specific gender performances.

Conversational Norms and Muds as Masculine Spaces

Many women would find the atmosphere on muds uncomfortable and unfamiliar. While muds vary considerably in terms of social norms and general atmosphere, conversations encountered on muds often resemble those of pre-adolescent males, or of male locker-room discussions. The following exchange occurred in an easily-accessible ("public") area of GammaMOO, a large social mud:

> Blue – Guest says, "I said, 'Are there any EXTREMELY DESPER-
> ATE women in the house?'"
> Titwillow [to Blue – Guest]: and i asked why you wanted to know!
> Blue – Guest says, "For my own info. dude!"
> Green – Guest says, "...Chris Bloyd is gay...he sucks Quinton
> Brockman..."
> Ebony – Guest says, "Fuck all of you muthafuckas"
> Blue – Guest says, "Eat me Blissful, you must be a fag!"

In the above excerpt, participants take advantage of the complete anonymity provided by guest characters. (In order to acquire a named character on this mud, participants must register an email address, providing at least some link to an off-mud identity.) Their obnoxious rowdiness recalls groups of young adolescent or pre-adolescent boys testing each other's tolerance, loyalty and adherence to gender-appropriate behavior. (It emerged later in conversation that the entire group of guests were logged in from a single computer lab located at a large university. Hence, the per-sonally-directed insults no doubt refer to names of others in the group.) As in similar offline male groups, homophobic insults demonstrate the interconnections between male gender identity norms and expectations concerning sexual identity (Connell 1995).

The male-dominated character of these norms and expectations stems in part from the particular history and development of muds. Muds initially drew much of their population from com-puter science, engineering, and related university departments, all of which are also male-dominated (Spertus 1991). Muds became widely available on the Internet in about 1989. At that time, most people on the Internet were white, middle-class, male, and associated with technical work or academic departments, especially in computer-related fields. Since then, the demographics of the Internet have been gradually changing, especially to include more women and white people in non-technical fields. Mud populations have also changed, although they remain largely college-aged.

But muds also draw upon the particular gendered context of various other interconnected subcultures. Despite the expansion of muds and their use for a variety of purposes, a large number are still dungeons and dragons-style gaming muds. Many of the social and role-playing muds also borrow themes and scenarios from science fiction and related genres. Thus, mud subcultures overlap with a variety of other subcultures which have historically been largely white and male (Fine 1983; Jenkins 1992). Even as a more diverse group of people discovers and participates on muds, they enter as newcomers (termed "newbies" on the net) into a cultural context established by the previously more limited demographic group. Despite increasing diversity on muds, then, the mud subculture still tends to valorize values associated with masculinity over those associated with femininity. This creates a hierarchy of activities in which puzzle-solving, programming, and other computer skills-related activities have more value than other uses of muds, with "chat" and socializing falling to the bottom of the list.

The greater participation by males, as well as intersections with other male-dominated subcultures, make muds male-defined spaces in a variety of ways. On BlueSky, one facet of this is the acceptance of obnoxious behavior as a norm of interaction. BlueSky participants' obnoxiousness constructs BlueSky as a male space, regardless of the gender identities of the participants or their characters. In the following excerpt of a conversation on BlueSky, I deviate from my previous relatively quiet comportment on the mud and attempt to respond in kind to a prevalent form of obnoxious bantering. (My character name here is Copperhead; allia is the only other woman present.)

Florin has arrived.
Shub says "Baron Florin of Shamptabarung!"
Copperhead says "hi Florin"

Florin says "shub, copperhead. who the hell is copperhead?"
Shub says "copperhead is your future wife, Florin."
Copperhead WHULPs at the thought of being Florin's wife
Florin says "bah. every woman on this earth bleeds from the crotch at the thought of being my wife."
Florin isn't sure whether it's GOOD or BAD, but that's what they DO.
allia thinks every woman on this earth gets a yeast infection at the thought of being florin's wife.
Florin SILENCE, UNSHORN HUSSY
Shub wondered why they all bleed from the crotch ...
Florin says "because their WOMBS are FERTILE"
Florin must PROCREATE
Copperhead says "uh-oh"
Copperhead hands Florin a Petri dish
Florin says "well, if you're nasty looking, CH, i'll just hand ya sperm in a petri dish. i understand."
Florin won't deny any woman the chance to bear his offspring; he only denies them the chance to touch his Captain Happy, when they're unacceptable.

As with the earlier group of guests, this conversation revolves around sexual references and insults. Acknowledgements of gender identities in this conversation tie directly to assumptions about sexual relationships and demonstrate the connection between gender identities and the normative status of heterosexuality. Shub, knowing that I present myself as female, suggests me as a potential wife for Florin, who presents himself as male online. Florin further boasts of his desirability to women but connects women not so much to sexual activity as to procreation. Given these terms of the interaction, my attempt to give as good as I get gains me little satisfaction.

As a woman newly entering the group, I have a limited set of choices regarding how to deal with this masculine pattern of interaction. I respond to perceived pressure to conform to a particular style of interaction, and while I receive no more nor less attention than anyone else (neither negative nor positive), the end result is not a conversation I enjoy. As Fine (1987) suggests:

Women who wish to be part of a male-dominated group typically must accept patterns of male bonding and must be able to decode male behavior patterns. They must be willing to engage in coarse

> joking, teasing, and accept male-based informal structure of the
> occupation – in other words, become "one of the boys." While some
> women find this behavioral pattern congenial, others do not, and
> they become outcasts or marginal members of the group. (131)

Thus, my performance in the above can be read as an attempt
to perform a masculine identity which partly fails because of
people's previous knowledge of my female identity and their con-
sequent references to my female body. On the other hand, the performance succeeds partly in that the other participants accept my
behavior as normal. My own obnoxiousness, while out of character with my previous demeanor, fits into the conversation without
apparently causing anyone to change their definition of the situation or their understanding of my self-presentation (Goffman
1959).

This incident reveals that even when participants treat male
and female characters identically, different participants in the
interaction will nevertheless have different experiences of that
interaction. As Spontaneity indicates in one of the quotes at the
beginning of this chapter, "women often get turned off by less
nasty hazing than men." This illustrates his understanding that
hazing constitutes normal treatment on muds. As a relative
newcomer being subject to such hazing, I'm treated more or
less like the others in the conversation above, but that treatment
itself remains gendered. The resultant social context still casts
women as outsiders even while I, as a woman, am accepted in
the group.

Both this conversation and the earlier example of guests on
GammaMOO took place in relatively accessible "public" areas of
the muds, with numerous participants, both male and female, present. Certainly not all mud conversations look like these, but similar forms of banter are not unusual. By contrast, I can think of very
few *offline* social contexts in which I, a woman in my thirties,
would find similar jovial insults exchanged around me. This
demonstrates a couple of potential effects on gender (and on other
forms of identity) of the lack of visual cues in online interaction.
First, without the constant visual reminders provided by physical
copresence, the dominant group can ignore or forget the presence
of members of other groups. Because of this, members of
oppressed groups may more easily join in with interactions with
the dominant group *as long as they conform to its norms*. Thus online

forums have the potential to be nominally more inclusive, but in terms which still effectively limit participation.

Even as members of non-dominant groups increase, their impact on the existing social norms may be minimal. For instance, in the following conversation, I comment about the atmosphere on BlueSky, comparing it to a male locker-room.

> Copperhead makes some quick notes about "locker room atmos-phere" and "male bonding."
> henri says "what did we say that was locker room llike"
> Mender exposes himself to Copperhead
> Mike Adams l henri thinks about the cool guys girlfriend "MAN she is a babe"[3]
> henri says "that's not locker room, that's angst"
> henri says "locker room is 'well my date with so and so last night was hot, she was all over me' etc."
> Mender snaps henri with a towel
> henri YEEOOWWW
> Copperhead was referring more to the general repetitiveness of topic than to the flavor of any particular comment.
> henri says "the only things people talk about on muds are (i) tech-nical issues, (ii) sex, (iii) idiots"
> Mike Adams says "lessee, common repetitive topics here: comput-ers, dating, lack of dating, computers, sex, sexual deviance, com-puters, jobs making money, lack of jobs making money, computers..."
> henri says "see I'm right"

The other participants (in this case, all male except for myself) object to my characterization of the space. They also demonstrate their understanding that I may be accusing them of sexism (Menders' joking comment that he is "exposing himself to Copperhead"), and their knowledge of the cultural code I have evoked through their pantomime of locker-room behavior (Mender's snapping of henri with a towel, and henri's yelled response). While more or less agreeing with my identification of repetitive topics, they disagree with my characterization of the space as therefore potentially excluding women. They represent their discourse as just normal topics of conversation, to which anybody can contribute. But henri's and Mike Adams' descrip-tions of these "normal" topics nevertheless reflect the identities of the majority of participants on BlueSky as young, white, male, and middle-class.

"Nerds" and "Babes"

As in the above example of my conversation with Florin and Shub, and as I discussed with fellow BlueSky participants in the conversation about its "locker-room" atmosphere, BlueSky's conversational style and topics reflect its male-dominated character as a social space. This dictates that to a certain extent all BlueSky participants perform male gender identities within that social space. However, they perform a particular type of masculine identity which sometimes resists as well as recreates dominant expectations of masculinity. Masculinity does not constitute a single uniform standard of behavior, but rather comprises a range of gender identities clustered around expectations concerning masculinity which Connell (1995) has termed "hegemonic masculinity." Connell defines hegemonic masculinity as "the configuration of gender practice which embodies the currently accepted answer to the problem of the legitimacy of patriarchy, which guarantees (or is taken to guarantee) the dominant position of men and the subordination of women" (77). While few men actually embody the hegemonic masculine ideal, they nevertheless benefit from the "patriarchal dividend" of dominance over women. However, they must also negotiate their own relationship to that ideal.

Most of the participants on BlueSky are sophisticated long-term computer users. Many have jobs related to computers, whether as programmers or system administrators, and in addition to their socializing on BlueSky, many employ computers for other leisure uses, including playing networked games available on the Internet and buying computer games for their home computers as well. They are well aware that the extent of their computer use places them within the definition of the "nerd" stereotype, and many feel they have other personal or social characteristics which brand them as nerds, as indicated by the following quotes from different conversations on BlueSky.

> Ulysses looks in henri's glasses and sees his reflection, and exclaims "Oh NO! I'm a NERD!"
> Mender says "when you publish please feel free to refer to me as 'nerdy but nice'"

The nerd stereotype includes elements both of congruence with and rejection of hegemonic masculinity. While the term "nerd" still carries negative connotations of failed masculinity, it has become part of a reconfiguration of middle-class male masculinity, centering around changing patterns of work and technology. The nerd identity comprises one type of masculinity which Connell identifies as complicit "with the hegemonic project" (Connell 1995: 79–80).

Conversations on BlueSky particularly demonstrate the nerd identity's ultimate complicity with hegemonic masculinity in terms of relationships to women. Discussions of nerdism and masculinity are conversations with and regarding other males (whether present or absent, real or imagined). In these conversations, women are mainly adjunctive objects which convey or express aspects of masculine status.

For example, the term "babe" is ubiquitous on BlueSky. Usually it denotes a woman outside the mud group. The woman's connection with a mud participant is usually romantic or potentially romantic, although that connection may only be in fantasy. In the following brief excerpt (taken from a much longer conversation), Mender and henri (who live in different areas of the country) discuss possible plans for the evening; people offer joking responses to Mender's request for entertainment ideas; and Tempest waits for a response to a phone call.

> Mender says "What should I do tonight henri"
> henri says "Mender, rent The Quiet Earth"
> Roger Pollack says "find a babe and rent the fisher king"
> Roger Pollack says "okay, okay, forget the first part"
> Mender stares at Roger
> Mender says "I HATE YOU"
> Tempest waits for his party to respond
> Roger Pollack says "is this the babe, tempest"
> Tempest says "babe?"
> Tempest says "not, just some woman"
> Tempest says "i mean, she's a babe, but not any specific babe :)"[4]
> Roger Pollack says "weren't you eyeing some babe? or was that madmonk"
> Tempest "that was madmonk :)"
> Roger Pollack ose
> Mender says "what should I do tonight"
> Mender says "the bar with all the babes isn't serving alcohol tonight"
> Mender says "no point going if there's not even a chance of me getting tipsy enough to talk to them"
> Perry says "so get drunk beforehand"
> Mender ! @ pairy[5]
> Mender says "YOU'RE A GENIUS"

Mender's request for suggestions concerning "what to do tonight" sets a joshing tone, and both his statements and others' suggestions include ironic insinuations regarding their inadequate social lives. (I've only reproduced some of these insinuations in the excerpt above.) Mender in particular implies by his continual requests for suggestions about what to do that he needs to be talked into undertaking social activity. He also indicates that he needs alcohol to talk to women. This conversation demonstrates BlueSky's use as a place in which to share anxiety regarding socializing with women and strategies for decreasing that anxiety. In this context, Mender particularly uses "babe" to denote anonymous women of potential sexual interest.

Roger Pollack and Tempest demonstrate uses of the term "babe" connoting attractiveness and also a specific relationship. (I've excerpted a portion of their conversation again here for ease of reference.)

> Roger Pollack says "is this the babe, tempest"
> Tempest says "babe?"
> Tempest says "not, just some woman"
> Tempest says "i mean, she's a babe, but not any specific babe :)"
> Roger Pollack says "weren't you eyeing some babe? or was that madmonk"

Tempest's correction of Roger Pollack's use of the term babe demonstrates the relational quality of the term and also exposes the element of sexual attractiveness contained in its definition. Tempest refers to the woman he phones as a "babe," in the sense of "attractive woman," but stresses that that she is not a "babe" in the sense of her relationship to Tempest as a potential sexual object, such as the one madmonk was eyeing.

These uses of the slangy, offhand term "babe" fit the casual, clubby atmosphere, while also keeping concerns about sexuality and relationships at a distance. BlueSky participants refer to "the receptionist babe," "the yale babe," "the swim babe," etc. This allows them to designate sexually attractive women by monikers relating to their position vis-à-vis the participant or some outstanding but still relatively generic feature. For instance, "the receptionist babe" designates a sexual interest who serves as the participant's company receptionist. But even with these particularizing classifications, all of these women remain fundamentally undifferentiated in that they are all just "babes." This allows the guys to discuss potential (or unlikely) exploits, and to bemoan the fact that they "can't get babes" without it reflecting too negatively on their masculinity. Further, they can deflect the loss of masculinity connoted by the inability to get dates, through their camaraderie in bemoaning the fact. "Babes" become an abstract, an unattainable; talked about and theoretically longed for, they are always a distant object.

While some versions of this type of "guy talk" likely occur in most male groups, this group enacts a particular style of masculinity relating to their use of computers and the social stereotypes which accompany that use. They reject some aspects of hegemonic masculinity, leading them to reject my attempt to construe their interaction in male-specific sports-related terms (as in the "locker-room" conversation earlier). But for the most part, they conform to dominant masculinity standards. They relate to each other in ways which support heterosexual masculinity (despite the fact that not all identify as heterosexual), and in the process continue to objectify women.

Women in the Men's Club

However, on BlueSky, the distancing and objectifying statements about women generally refer to women "out there" in participants' offline lives, and *not* to women on BlueSky. Several women do actively participate on BlueSky. As suggested in my discussion of obnoxiousness and masculine space on BlueSky, these women often conform to a conversational style congruent with masculine identity. The women who accept these norms and derive benefits from their participation in the group have particular relationships to men and masculinity. They often have histories of participation in male-dominated activities and groups.

During my interview with Beryl, we discussed our different feelings about aspects of BlueSky culture, and our perception of what it meant to be a woman on BlueSky.

> LORI: One of the things you compared it to interests me. You said it was like a men's club. I don't think that's inaccurate, but what does that do then for the women who are participating?
>
> BERYL: Well, I don't know. I've always been around men, groups of men. Because I've been interested in role-playing games, and science fiction, and computers.

LORI: Those are all pretty male-dominated.

BERYL: Yeah. So I feel totally comfortable. Even though it's weird to notice that sometimes I look around and there's ten guys in the room and ... me. But then sometimes there'll be four or five women in the room and just a couple of guys. It swings the other way. Not as far. I feel totally comfortable, do you?

LORI: Yeah, most of the time I do. Sometimes I don't.

BERYL: How come?

LORI: Um. When, I guess sometimes when the guys are talking about babes, or are being very graphic in some ways.

BERYL: I think it's hilarious.

Beryl notices, and finds it "weird," that sometimes she's the only woman among male participants. However, she takes pains to differentiate herself from my stance, and indicates that she is quite comfortable in general with the cultural atmosphere on BlueSky.

Peg similarly notes some differences in men's and women's experiences on BlueSky. But in the following excerpt from my interview with her, she suggests that gender doesn't matter much in terms of how people are treated on BlueSky.

LORI: You've talked a little bit about women getting different treatment on BlueSky. What have your experiences been?

PEG: Really I don't pay attention to that. When I just started mudding, people flirted, but that's when I wasn't thinking about how people were treated. Half the time you couldn't tell what sex somebody was anyway. I think on BlueSky it's the classic geek thing. I still get the feeling sometimes that the guys think of themselves as – they're all sitting around in this guy geekhold and any woman who comes in it's like the things will be ...

LORI: Different

PEG: Yeah.

Here and in her comment at the beginning of this chapter, Peg connects gender to sexuality. In the earlier quote, she assumes that she can't know whether being a woman online really matters, since she isn't a guy, and therefore can't know what they might think. She assumes then, that her status as a woman online means something different to guys than it does to other women. Here, she replies to my question about differential treatment with reference to flirting. In both comments, Peg reveals a degree of uncertainty and ambiguity in her characterization of the mud social space. Although she claims not to pay attention to differential treatment, she nevertheless characterizes BlueSky as a "guy geekhold" which changes when women enter it.

Beryl, Peg, and I all share histories either of interest in science fiction and computers, or of primary friendships with men or boys with those interests. Our previous experiences in male-dominated subcultures prepared us for the tone and character of BlueSky's social atmosphere. While we all have female-designated characters and make no efforts to hide our female status, our familiarity with the dominant topics of conversation, and our ability and willingness to conform to the social norms of the male-dominated space enable us to perform (at least in part) masculine identities and enjoy the enhanced social status attendant on being "one of the guys."

The "masculine" performances of Beryl, Peg, and I remain attached to female identifiers and the group's knowledge of our female identities offline. In contrast, one female participant on BlueSky has a male-designated character and consistently refers to herself using masculine pronouns. Toni has been mudding for several years, but joined the group on BlueSky fairly recently. She interacts with the others using a male character named Phillipe. In a face-to-face interview, she described for me the process of choosing a name for her character.

> When I was sitting there thinking what am I going to name this character, I had heard so much about what a weird place GammaMOO was that I just didn't want to go there as myself. It wasn't like I decided "Oh I'll make a male character because it's safer to be male online or something like that," I didn't really ever feel that. I just liked the notion of not being myself. I wasn't really sure of the environment or anything.... And so I just, I had a cat named Phillipe, and so I just borrowed his name. So then I got in the habit of naming characters Phillipe or Phill, some variation of that whenever I went somewhere that I wasn't sure I was going to be comfortable.

Toni's use of Phillipe highlights the centrality of gender to identity even while she attempts to downplay its effects on social interaction. Toni de-emphasizes differences between male and female character portrayal, as well as the importance of her choice to masquerade as male online. Choosing a male character was for her the easiest way of "not being myself," indicating the degree to which that self is self-understood as gendered.

Although Toni attaches little significance to her online gender-switching, her choice to portray a male character in an unfamiliar environment affords her particular types of treatment. Being male allows Toni to rely on offline gender understandings of that identity in order to negotiate the online social world. Toni's masquerade as Phillipe demonstrates that not all gender masqueraders gain a new sense of gender identity. Toni also demonstrates that many women may be motivated to masquerade as male because males achieve a better fit in the social and cultural environments of most muds.

Acting Female

Mud subcultural and historical ties heavily favor participants with computer skills and interests. Such participants are far more likely to be male and to expect that others in the group will also be male. Since, based on dominant cultural assumptions, participants already associate computer competence and interest with masculinity, femininity can come to be associated with lack of competence and an inability to fit into the dominant social norms. Shelly, a woman who Muds on BlueSky infrequently, said that she wasn't interested in all the "tech talk" that occurred on BlueSky, and that therefore "they all consider me a bimbo here … ;)" Another more frequent participant, Sparkle said:

> In the bar [on BlueSky], I most likely seem more flakey than I am, but that's mostly because they don't talk about things I know anything about. All I can do is crack jokes and laugh when I read something that's funny to me. … For the longest time, I was too scared to talk to anyone on here, I just hung out in the bar and laughed – which is why people think I am a ditz.

Shelly and Sparkle refer to themselves using gendered terms – bimbo and ditz – which denigrate their intelligence and connect that denigration specifically to femininity. They thus connect their lack of technical knowledge to negative female stereotypes. As indicated previously, BlueSky participants take for granted that computers comprise a major topic of conversation on Muds. As long as women participants share an interest in computers, they can fit into this taken-for-granted conversational pattern. However, to some extent, when they can do so, they become "one of the guys," while women like Shelly and Sparkle remain gender outsiders.

These social norms tend therefore to reify connections between technical competence and masculinity. Because the male-dominated nature of the social space combines with an emphasis on technical talk, people who join the technical talk more successfully perform the type of masculine identity dominant in the subculture. As Cockburn (1985) explains, "technology enters into our sexual identity: femininity is incompatible with technological competence; to feel technically competent is to feel manly" (12). To the extent that conforming participants, whether male or female, are defined as "one of the guys," participants perceived as not technically competent are also perceived as *not* "one of the guys." They become, in both cultural and gendered terms, Other.

Muds have been male-dominated, and also can sometimes provide a relatively anonymous forum in which to experiment with identity. Mudders' own awareness of these facets of mud experience leads them to sometimes question the gender performances of others. BlueSky participants treat the question "Are you male or female?" as a joke because it is so frequently asked in large public rooms on muds and other online chat spaces. Mudders also warn newbies that exaggerated femininity probably indicates that the participant behind the female character is male (Deuel 1995). These understandings of mud gender performances mean that participants may read only particular types of gender enactments as "really" female.

Consider for instance a comparison between the female character of a long-term male participant on BlueSky and my own character. Fred for a year portrayed himself as female, using the character name Amnesia and not informing the other BlueSky participants that his offline identity was male. Although Fred revealed his male identity to other BlueSky participants several years ago, ending his masquerade, he retains the character name Amnesia and continues to self-reference using female pronouns. I asked Amnesia about this in a whispered conversation (meaning that other participants could not see the text Amnesia and I exchanged).

> Copperhead whispers "so I'm curious – if everyone knows you're not female, why still the female pronouns? Continuity?"

> Amnesia whispers " 'Amnesia' is a woman, and always has been. Amnesia was (is) my 'ideal woman,' and so is more caricaturial than any real woman can be. I think that means her femininity shows through easier via text."
> Copperhead whispers "your 'ideal woman' is caricaturially female?"
> Amnesia whispers "no, I mean that I have no real experience in being a woman, so can only draw a crude image with a broad brush when I'm acting. Also, my 'ideal woman' has qualities not available in humanity, so there's another thing that doesn't translate into reality well."

Fred considers himself to be acting and does not expect characteristics of his "ideal woman" to translate into reality. This points to his reliance on stereotypical notions of femininity in order to accomplish his masquerade.

As Amnesia and I continued to discuss gender portrayals online, it became clear that, at least with Fred's orientation towards role-playing online and gender portrayal, ideas about gender and appropriate gendered behavior might become even *more* rigidly defined through such online enactments.

> Amnesia whispers " 'Oblivious' was my male persona briefly, but it was less fun"
> Copperhead whispers "less fun? how so?"
> Amnesia whispers "hard to say. Perhaps less attention is paid male characters."
> Copperhead whispers "hmmm. I've heard that from other people as well."
> Amnesia whispers "when I was full-out a woman, the differential was unbelievable and measurable."
> Copperhead whispers "but you know, I haven't really noticed it. 'Course, I haven't been on here as a male, but comparing myself to other people, it doesn't really seem to me that I get more attention. Heh. Maybe if I was male, I'd get *no* attention."
> Amnesia whispers "you don't 'act female' in the traditional sense, as far as I've seen."
> Copperhead whispers "ah. I suppose that's true. So maybe it's not females that get more attention, per se. Am I less a woman than Amnesia? ;)"

Fred interprets my presentation of myself online, in which I make no particular effort to emphasize a gendered identity, as not "acting female." With the limitations inherent in text-based online interactions, and the absence of cues we usually use to assign gender identity to others, Amnesia's caricature of femininity becomes more real – more female – than my character Copperhead's less stereotypical guise.

Conclusion

The text-only environment of muds changes some conditions of gender performances, providing new opportunities for play with gender, but also creating new constraints. Some mud participants may experience greater freedom from gender requirements online. People can experiment with different identities and can choose to hide gender identity information about themselves more easily than is usually possible offline. Women can avoid some types of sexual harassment by representing themselves as male or neutral. Men can play with roles of sexual seduction usually deemed inappropriate for a masculine identity.

However, the history of greater online participation by certain groups of people, and the cultural contexts (both online and off) of mud participants, favor particular styles of interaction, such as the obnoxiousness common on BlueSky. Failure to conform to these styles, while not usually identified by participants as *gender* transgressions, can nevertheless lead to the ostracism of particular gendered Others, as Shelly and Sparkle found. Women who successfully participate in such groups often do so by in some sense performing masculine identities, whether with a male character designation, like Phillipe's, or a nominally female character, like those of Beryl, Peg, and myself. The spaces within which these gender performances occur remain not only profoundly gendered, but specifically biased towards some types of performances and against others.

The performances and interactions I've discussed here demonstrate that predictions concerning the liberating potential of online spaces have been premature. More importantly, these examples illustrate the gendered quality of all our interactions, both online and off. As Toni indicates, our sense of self is gendered. Many of the examples I have used also point to the deep interconnections between sexual identity and gender identity.

Freedom to choose a gender designation has led some mud participants (such as Carets, quoted at the beginning of this chapter) to claim that gender online is nothing more than "the 6 bytes it takes up to store the text." But gender draws its meaning and power from the cultural contexts within which it is performed and by which such performances are constrained. Mudders draw upon both offline and online experiences in order to enact and interpret online identities. Researchers also need to consider both online and offline contexts in their own interpretations of gender performances online.

NOTES

1   Various sources for online demographics can be found at (among other places) http://www.cyberatlas.com/demographics.html and http://www.ora.com/ research/. A caveat about these figures: most of the studies available online are conducted and reported by consulting companies which provide such information for a fee. They post partial results of older studies on a website for free access, but often reserve their most recent information for paying customers. They also do not always reveal information about methodologies used. Therefore, these figures should be viewed as rough estimates only. However. I checked many sites other than those listed in this footnote, and figures on gender and race (where available) were consistent with those I report here.
2   All names of muds, characters, and participant "real life" names have been changed throughout this essay.
3   The | symbol after Mike Adams' name indicates he is quoting something which occurred previously in the conversation.
4   The colons followed by a right parenthesis in this excerpt – :) – are called "smilies," a type of "emoticon." They represent a smiling face, and help introduce emotional nuance into the textual communication. (If you're not familiar with these, it helps to tilt your head to the left.)
5   The exclamation point in this line indicates surprise. The @ symbol is read as "at." Mender also misspells Perry's name. I read this type of name play, particularly when it exaggerates pronunciation, as connoting affection or friendly connection. (Note that I have changed these names and have represented a name mispelling *similar* to the original.)

REFERENCES

Barlow, John Perry. 1996. "A Declaration of the Independence of Cyberspace." Widely available on the World Wide Web. One website is http://www.eff.org/pub/Publications/John_Perry_Barlow/barlow_ 0296.declaration.

Bornstein, Kate. 1994. *Gender Outlaw: On Men, Women, and the Rest of Us.* New York, NY: Vintage Books.

Bruckman, Amy S. 1993. "Identity Workshop." Paper obtained on the World Wide Web at ftp://ftp.media.mit.edu/pub/asb/papers/.

———. 1994. "Gender Swapping on the Internet." Proceedings of INET '93.

Burris, Beverly and Andrea Hoplight. 1996. "Theoretical Perspectives on the Internet and CMC." Paper presented at the annual meetings of the American Sociology Association, August 17, New York.

Cherny, Lynn. 1994. "Gender differences in text-based virtual reality," in *Cultural Performances: Proceedings of the Third Berkeley Women and Language Conference*, April 8–10, 1994, ed. Mary Bucholtz, et al. Berkeley, CA: Berkeley Women and Language Group, University of California.

Cockburn, C. 1985. *Machinery of Dominance: Women, Men and Technical Know-How.* London: Pluto Press.

Connell, R. W. 1995. *Masculinities.* Berkeley, CA: University of California Press.

Curtis, Pavel. 1992. "Mudding: Social Phenomena in Text-Based Virtual Realities. *Intertek* 3(3): 26–34.

Deuel, Nancy. 1995. "Our passionate response to virtual reality," in Computer-Mediated Communication: Linguistic, Social and Cross-Cultural Perspectives, ed. Susan C. Herring. Amsterdam: John Benjamins.

Dickel, M. H. 1995. "Bent Gender: Virtual Disruptions of Gender and Sexual Identity." *Electronic Journal of Communication* 5(4): 95–117.

Fine, Gary Alan. 1983. *Shared Fantasy.* Chicago, IL: University of Chicago Press.

———. 1987. "One of the Boys: Women in Male-Dominated Settings," in M. S. Kimmel, ed. *Changing Men: New Directions in Research on Men and Masculinity.* Newbury Park, CA: Sage Publications.

Frankenberg, Ruth. 1993. *The Social Construcion of Whiteness: White Women, Race Matters.* Minneapolis, MN: University of Minnesota Press.

Goffman, Erving. 1959. *The Presentation of Self in Everyday Life.* New York, NY: Anchor Books.

Herring, Susan. 1992. "Gender and participation in computer-mediated linguistic discourse." Washington, DC: ERIC Clearinghouse on Languages and Linguistics, document no. ED345552.

———. 1993. "Gender and democracy in computer-mediated communica-tion." *Electronic Journal of Communication* 3(2). Special issue on Computer-Mediated Communication, ed. T. Benson. Reprinted in R. Kling, ed., *Computerization and Controversy*, 2nd ed New York: Academic (1996).

Jenkins, Henry. 1992. *Textual Poachers: Television Fans and Participatory Culture*. New York, NY: Routledge.

Kaplan, Nancy and Eva Farrell. 1994. "Weavers of Webs: A Portrait of Young Women on the Net." *The Arachnet Electronic Journal on Virtual Culture*, 2(3), obtained via ftp (file transfer protocol).

Kramarae, Cheris. 1995. "A Backstage Critique of Virtual Reality," in S. G. Jones, ed, *Cybersociety*, Thousand Oaks, CA: Sage Publications.

Kramarae, Cheris and H. Jeanie Taylor. 1993. "Women and men on electronic networks: A conversation or a monologue?", in H. J. Taylor, C. Kramarae and M. Ebben, eds, *Women, Information Technology, and Scholarship*. Urbana, IL: Center for Advanced Study, 52–61.

McRae, Shannon. 1995. "Coming Apart at the Seams: Sex, Text and the Virtual Body," in *Wired Women*, eds, Lynn Cherny and Elizabeth Weise. Seattle, Wash.: Seal Press.

Poster, Mark. 1995. *The Second Media Age*. Cambridge: Polity Press.

Rheingold, Howard. 1993. *The Virtual Community*. Reading, MA: Addison-Wesley Publishing Company.

Smith, Jennifer. "Frequently Asked Questions: Basic Information about MUDs and MUDding," widely available on the World Wide Web. One site is http://www.cs.okstate.edu/~jds/mudfaqs.html.

Spertus, Ellen. 1991. "Why are there so few female computer scientists?" AI lab Technical Report, available on the World Wide Web at http://www.ai.mit.edu/people/ellens/Gender/why.html.

Stone, A. R. 1992. "Virtual Systems," in *Zone 6: Incorporations*, eds Jonathan Crary and Sanford Kwinter. New York, NY: Zone, distributed by The MIT Press.

Sutton, Laurel. 1994. "Using Usenet: Gender, power, and silence in electronic discourse." *The Proceedings of the 20th Annual Meeting of the Berkeley Linguistics Society*. Berkeley, CA: Berkeley Linguistics Society, Inc.

Thorne, Barrie. 1993. *Gender Play: Girls and Boys in School*. New Brunswick, NJ: Rutgers Universtiy Press.

Turkle, Sherry. 1995. *Life on the Screen: Identity in the Age of the Internet*. New York, NY: Simon & Schuster.

We, Gladys. 1994. "Cross-Gender Communication in Cyberspace," *The Arachnet Electronic Journal on Virtual Culture*, 2(3), obtained via ftp.

Part II

Managing Self/Society Conflicts

5

Frederick the Great or Frederick's of Hollywood? The Accomplishment of Gender Among Women in the Military

Melissa S. Herbert

Introduction

In an article on military culture, Karen Dunivin writes, "the combat, masculine-warrior paradigm is the essence of military culture" (1994: 534). For military women, this may pose something of a contradiction. Women are often expected, by virtue of the perceived relationship between sex and gender, to display societal norms of femininity. What is expected when women fill an occupational role whose defining characteristics are inexorably linked with masculinity? While these women, by virtue of being in the military, fill a masculine work-role, it is quite possible that they are also penalized for being "too masculine," or, in essence, violating the societal expectations that they maintain some degree of femininity.

Masculinity in military men is not only rewarded, but is the primary construct around which resocialization as a soldier takes place. It is not surprising that femininity, or characteristics believed to be associated with femininity, would be discouraged. On the other hand, the military, reflecting the broader society, may find that women's femininity serves "to validate male identity and both individual and collective male power" (Lenskyj 1986: 56). This is, I believe, illustrated by the recently abandoned Marine Corps policy of requiring female Marines to undergo make-up and etiquette training and in current regulations that require women's hair to not be cut "so short as to appear masculine." Additionally, the military is a highly traditional, primarily conservative, institution in which we may expect the expression, "men are men and women are women" to be taken seriously. Exactly how are women in the military supposed to "be women?"

In 1942, shortly before the establishment of the Women's Army Auxiliary Corps, civilian and military personnel alike expressed concern over the type of women who might join such an organization. In response, Mrs Oveta Culp Hobby, chief of the women's interests section of the War Department's Bureau of Public Relations, said that the members of the proposed corps would be neither "Amazons rushing into battle" nor "butterflies fluttering free" ("Freedom of Press"). Many believed that women who would be interested in the military would be either fierce, masculine women wishing to act like men or delicate, feminine women who, presumably, were unfit for such service. It seemed impossible for them to imagine that reality might lay somewhere in between. That was over 50 years ago. The notion of gender as a continuum rather than as discrete categories of feminine and masculine continues to elude the social imagination. While some might wonder why "feminine women" would even be imagined to consider the military, it is important to recall that this was an era of fervent patriotism. Women were being recruited for noncombat positions, and recruiting strategies played on women's ability to help in the war effort while not surrendering their femininity. Unlike today, recruitment did not focus on occupations and the acquisition of skills, but on one's patriotic duty. Thus, it was not unlikely that some "feminine" women might apply and while the military did not want women to think they had to give up their femininity, neither did it want women who would not be able to do the job.

Perceptions of women and their "fit" with what is believed to be gender appropriate may be critical to the ability of women to become accepted as members of the military. The integration of women into an institution *defined* by its association with masculinity may pose an interesting dilemma for military women. Can one truly be a soldier[1] and a woman and not be viewed as deviating either from what it means to be a soldier, or from what it means to be a woman? I can recall being asked by a fellow soldier why I, and other women, didn't "dress up" when we were off duty. It struck me then, as it does now, that we were expected to do our jobs "like the men," and transform "into women" once we removed our flak jackets and helmets and turned in our rifles and ammunition. One respondent spoke to these contradictions when, addressing men's perceptions, she wrote, "If you're too feminine, then you're not strong enough to command respect and lead men into battle, but if you're strong and aggressive you're not being a woman."

Those in the military, but particularly women, must "do gender." In their article, "Doing Gender," West and Zimmerman argue that gender is "a routine accomplishment embedded in everyday inter-action" (1987: 125). The ethnomethodological conceptualization of gender maintains that gender is "the local management of conduct in relation to normative conceptions of appropriate attitudes and activities for particular sex categories" (West and Fenstermaker 1993: 156). Although women in the military are clearly recognized as women, that is, as belonging to both the female sex (i.e., physiologically female) and female sex category (i.e., perceived as physiologically female; what others might call gender), given their role as members of the military, these women must constantly create and manage their gendered identities. While all women must do so, it should be noted that men also "do gender," on a daily basis. As Ronnie Steinberg notes, men "actively recreate their dominance every day"(1992: 576).

The military, I believe, is a particularly good site in which to examine the "everyday" ways in which women negotiate a world in which they must simultaneously be recognized and accepted as women, but must perform a job that has been perceived by many as appropriate only for men. Not only has the "soldier" been con-structed, both ideologically and historically, as male, but soldier-ing has been the very means by which men have "become" men. Thus, the masculinity of soldiering is not "just" masculinity, but hypermasculinity. Not only have military men been constructed as "real" men, but questions have recently been raised as to whether we should, in fact, accept a degree of sexism and violence against women by male soldiers if they are to be successfully trained to engage in the conduct of war.[2] Thus, while women and men throughout society must "do gender," the increased salience of gender within the military makes it possible that it may be even more true within that setting, at least with regard to traditional conceptions of gender.

Joan Acker has outlined four institutional processes that create and re-create gender. The first refers to "the overt decisions and procedures that control, segregate, exclude, and construct hierarchies based on gender" (1992: 568). While the focus here is gender, Acker is careful to note that such processes also underlie the construction of class and race. The second process is "the construction of images, symbols, and ideologies that justify, explain, and give legitimacy to institutions" (Ibid.). I will focus on the third and fourth processes: The third process is interaction. "Interaction between individuals and groups is the medium for much institutional functioning, for decision making and image production" (Ibid.). It is through this process that gender is created and re-created. Goffman, addressing the "interactional field" and the interactions themselves, argues that "these scenes do not so much allow for the expression of natural differences between the sexes as for the production of that difference itself" (1977: 324). Gender is not accomplished solely on the basis of specific actions (e.g., wearing a skirt instead of pants), but it requires that interactions occur in which the action is recognized as placing the actor in a particular gendered context. West and Zimmerman write:

> While it is individuals who do gender, the enterprise is fundamentally interactional and institutional in character, for accountability is a feature of social relationships and its idiom is drawn from the institutionalized arena in which those relationships are enacted (1987: 136–7).

The fourth process, as desribed by Acker, is internal. At this level, individuals must "construct personas that are appropriately gendered for the institutional setting" (1992: 568). Gender identity, Acker notes, "is not necessarily an adequate guide" (Ibid.). Institutions, as well as individuals, are accountable to normative conceptions of gender (West and Fenstermaker 1993: 158). The military is no exception.

West and Zimmerman (1987) pose three central questions: "If, for example, individuals strive to achieve gender in encounters with others, how does a culture instill the need to achieve it? What is the relationship between the production of gender at the level of interaction and such institutional arrangements as the division of labor in society? And, perhaps most important, how does doing gender contribute to the subordination of women by men?" (140). In this paper I respond to these questions by examining the place of gender in the lives of women in the United States military. In doing so, I believe that I also respond to the call of West and Fenstermaker "for a renewed rigor in articulating *how* the accomplishment of gender determines gender inequality" (1993: 299).

Methodology

The findings in this paper are based on 256 surveys collected from women who are veterans of, or currently serving in, the United States military. I used a variety of avenues to identify potential respondents including posting notices at women's bookstores, gay and lesbian community centers, on computer bulletin boards, in publications such as *Minerva's Bulletin Board*, *The Register* (the newsletter of the Women in Military Service for America Project), and at college and university veterans' program offices around the nation. The 15-page questionnaire contained seven sections with items in formats varying among yes/no questions, multiple choice questions, open-ended questions, check off items, and Likert-scale items. Each section has a different focus. The sections of the questionnaire assess the following: (1) personal information, (2) military service, (3) education, (4) personal assessment of military service, (5) personal resources, (6) gender, and (7) sexuality. The surveys were used to create a computerized data set as well as text files of the answers to open-ended questions. I should note that my own military service formed the basis for many of these questions. Though my experience is limited to the Army, I was able to formulate questions about uniforms, on-post and off-post activities, chain of command, etc., on the basis of not only familiarity with scholarship on women in the military, but with the aid of 15 years experience in both the active and reserve components of the US Army as both enlisted and officer.

The women who answered the survey came from over 40 states, all branches, all ranks except flag officer (i.e., General/Admiral), and served as early as the 1950s. The major weakness of these data is an inadequate representation of racial and ethnic minority women. Part of this can be attributed to the fact that it was only in the 1980s that these populations started to have significant representation within the military and the respondents' dates of service cover a wide range of time. But, my best guess for further explanation is that the identity of "veteran" is not as salient for these women or, while it might be salient, there is a perception that veteran's organizations, not unlike other organizations, would be predominantly white and possibly not welcoming of their participation. As indicated above I sought out participants through bookstores, women's veterans organizations, and colleges and universities. Since I had to rely on the women and their interest in responding to my call for participants, there was little I could do to increase their participation. Given the fact that minority women, African American women in particular, are actually over-represented in the current military, additional research that oversamples for this population would add significantly to the strength of these findings. As it stands, they are, perhaps, best generalized to white women veterans.

Additionally, one might question representation by class or socio-economic status. I collected information about what type of paid work the respondent was doing at the time she completed the survey as well as what the respondent's parents/guardians did during the time that she left high school. I did not attempt to gather information about income of either the parent or the respondent for the following reasons. First, the standard method of assessing class by income seemed faulty because the women left high school at different times across decades and in many different regions of the country. Second, I was not convinced that many women would know, with any degree of accuracy, what their parents' income had been at that time. It was my conclusion that this information would be very unreliable and thus add little to the analyses.

The other option would have been to consider the class of the respondent herself. This, too, was problematic because of the fact that they were being asked to provide information about times past. Current income seemed largely irrelevant to what a respondent was indicating about attitudes and behaviors that, for some, occurred as many as 16 years prior to the time they were completing the survey. Another option was to consider one's class while in the military, but if this were based on income and occupation the only distinction between respondents would be rank and length of service, information which was already included in the survey.

Members of the military cannot really be seen, at the time they are in the military, as belonging to different classes. In sum, it is not possible to analyze differences between respondents according to class and none of those interviewed brought up class as an issue. In my experience, service members were less aware of class differences than they were of education and rank differences.

The survey asked respondents to indicate whether they believed that penalties exist for women who are perceived as "too feminine." In a separate question, it asked whether they believe that penalties exist for women who are perceived as "too masculine" and to provide examples of what the penalties might be. The results presented here are based on descriptive statistics and analyses of the open-ended responses about types of penalties.

The survey also included a list of 28 behaviors. Respondents were asked to "check any of the following that you believe applied to yourself" (while on active duty). These items consisted of behaviors such as polishing one's fingernails, wearing cologne on duty, keeping one's hair trimmed above the collar, socializing with the men in the unit, and so on. Respondents were then asked, "Do you believe that any of those behaviors checked ... were part of a conscious attempt to insure that others perceived you as feminine?" The survey also asked, "Do you believe that any of those behaviors checked ... were part of a conscious attempt to insure that others perceived you as masculine?"

Respondents were asked the question: "Are there other things that you did that you believe were a conscious attempt to insure that others perceived you as feminine/masculine?" This question was included in the survey because it was impossible to identify a list of all possible strategies. Answers to questions, both closed-ended and open-ended, illuminate how women strategize about gender.

By examining if and/or how military women believe that gender is policed and what they do in response, we can begin to understand how women engage in the accomplishment of gender as opposed to simply "being" feminine or masculine. By "policed," I mean that their behaviors are monitored or censured by other members of the military, female and male and at all levels, to insure that women are not seen as violating norms of gender appropriateness. The strategies that women employ are both interactional and internal and, as such, speak to the processes that Acker highlights. The strategies are interactional in that their existence, and perpetuation, is dependent upon the response that the individual receives from others. And, they are internal in that, to some degree, they become incorporated into the persona of the person deploying them.

Additionally, an important aspect of West and Zimmerman's conceptualization of gender is the notion of accountability. "Gender display" (e.g., wearing make-up) alone is not enough. The observation of gendered behaviors is not enough to distinguish between gender display and "doing gender." In this research I must rely on the accounts of the actors to document that the actions are interactional in nature. That is, the respondents distinguish between those actions that they simply "do," whether because of socialization, internalization, and so on, and those actions in which they engage specifically because of the meaning that a given action holds for the observer, and the possible "end" they seek to either avoid or insure. Some might argue that "conscious intent" is irrelevant. That is, whether it is the result of socialization, or is an act we do with knowledge of it as a means to an end makes little difference. I would agree that in the "big picture" it makes little difference. In this research, however, I wanted to see if women would recognize and acknowledge their consciously engaging in strategies to manage gender.

Perceptions of Femininity

Do women believe that they are penalized for being perceived as "too feminine" or "too masculine?" Findings indicate that there is very little latitude for women when it comes to perceptions of gender. Sixty-four percent believe there are penalties for being perceived as "too feminine," while 60 percent of respondents indicate that they believe there are penalties for being perceived as "too masculine." These two variables are correlated only at 0.44. That is, not everyone who saw penalties in one case saw them in the other. Yet it is instructive that the correlation is positive, not negative. One might have thought, for example, that those who saw penalties for femininity would be less likely to see penalties for masculinity, and vice versa. In fact, many recognize that there are penalties for any perceived extremes in gender presentation.

Those women who believed there are penalties were asked to describe what they believed such penalties to be. One-hundred and sixty-five women described penalties for femininity. One hundred and fifty-seven described penalties for masculinity. Rather than starting with expected categories and coding the answers for whether or not they "fit" a particular category, I conducted a content analysis on the responses to see what categories emerged. Some answers could be coded into more than one category, as some respondents provided numerous examples, sometimes just listing words (e.g., "being perceived as an airhead, bimbo, or slut").

In some cases responses were ambiguous. In these instances I opted for a conservative approach and did not consider a response to fit. For example, one respondent simply wrote, "Talk." Another wrote that "regardless of her behavior, rumors will circulate about her." These statements might be understood, in common parlance, to refer to gossip about sexual behavior. On the other hand, this may not be what the respondents had in mind and, therefore, it seems inappropriate to overinterpret the data.

Though the penalties for femininity were quite varied, six common themes emerged: (1) ostracism or disapproval from other women, (2) being viewed as a slut or sexually available, (3) being perceived as weak, (4) being perceived as incompetent or incapable, (5) not being taken seriously, and (6) career limitations. While some of these categories overlap and might even be perceived as one and the same (e.g., weak vs incompetent), the specific words were used enough, and often within the same response, that it seemed as though they had different meanings for the respondents and should be coded accordingly.

The first five penalties are related to the sixth, and most frequently mentioned penalty: that of career limitations. This is true almost by definition, in that if there were no potentially negative impact on one's performance or career aspirations, one might question the way in which a given situation constituted a penalty. It is difficult to think of a situation in which a woman is penalized that does not carry with it the potential to damage one's work relationships and/or career.

"Career limitations" is actually a catch-all phrase for a number of career penalties. As illustrated by the respondents, they include, but are certainly not limited to, obvious limitations such as not being allowed to perform the job for which one was trained, not being promoted, not sent to a school needed for promotion, not getting choice assignments, etc. One woman wrote, "They are not assigned to 'career building' areas such as pilots, maintenance, security police – the generally thought of 'male jobs.'" Another woman wrote:

> I was a long haired blonde, outstanding figure, long beautiful nails (my own!), etc., etc. I was constantly told I couldn't do my job (working on aircraft) as I was a dumb blonde, I'd get my nails dirty, I was a danger to the guys working on aircraft because I distracted them, etc., etc. My first rating was not a favorable one even though I scored higher on the OJT [on-the-job-training] tests than anyone had ever scored in that shop!

Another indicated that "you don't get the tough jobs you need to be in good shape for promotion, and women who are too feminine usually get ignored or put in office jobs with no troops." Command positions, leading troops, are critical to the promotion of those in the officer ranks. Many women mentioned the penalty of being "removed from position[s] of authority and placed in somebody's office," or being "given more feminine jobs to do." Command positions are definitely not considered "feminine." One woman expressed her opinion on this issue:

> It is a great privilege as an officer to be in a command position. Part of being a commander is having a "command presence." I greatly doubt that women who wear lots of perfume, make-up, speak softly, and/or make strong efforts to appear feminine are considered frequently as serious contenders for command positions.

The categories of penalties clearly overlap. Especially in a military that "has no place for weakness," it is difficult to discuss attributions of weakness without discussing incompetence as well. It is difficult to discuss perceptions of incompetence without noting its relationship to not being taken seriously and suffering career limitations. In sum, while about one-quarter of the respondents mentioned career limitations explicitly ("Not selected for schools, promotion."), virtually all of the penalties discussed are related, whether directly or indirectly, to the ability of women to be treated equally with men and, therefore, to achieve the same degree of success as their male counterparts. While the penalties for being perceived as too feminine are varied, they do share a common theme. Whether at the informal (e.g., perceived as a slut by other members of the unit) or formal level (e.g., not selected to attend leadership training), each of these penalties serves as a mechanism for insuring that women remain "outsiders" to the boys' club of the military.

Perceptions of Masculinity

If women who are perceived as too feminine experience penalties, what happens to those women who are perceived as too masculine? Are they polar opposites on some scale of acceptability? One might argue that the best mechanism for combating penalties for being too feminine is to insure that one is perceived as masculine. Examination of the data reveals that this is not the case.

Of the 157 women who described the penalties for being perceived as too masculine, over half indicated that such women would be labeled as lesbians. There were a number of responses that seemed as though that was what was being inferred, but because it wasn't stated explicitly I opted for a conservative approach and did not code them as such. Consider these examples: "Comments," "Many lewd remarks were made about 'masculine' type women," "I think they may have to prove themselves more especially if not married," and "'Too masculine' tends to be equated with 'man-hating.'" If descriptions of this type were included, about two-thirds of the responses could be considered to address lesbianism.

Although the label "lesbian" emerges as a single category of penalty, it is illustrative to look at the different ways in which the issue is addressed. In many cases women stated very plainly, "Perceived as being a lesbian," "Perceived as lesbians," "Lesbo, dyke, etc. – Need I say more!" In other cases their descriptions were much more colorful or detailed. Consider the following description:

> Being teased by other servicemembers … called "butch," "bitch," "dyke," a lesbian. If a female can't be told apart visually, at first glance, from a male she *will* be subjected to being called sir vs. ma'am and may be kicked out of a few female restrooms, at first glance.[3]

A number of respondents, as was the case when a woman is perceived as too feminine, indicated that penalties also came from other women. One woman wrote:

> If you go past gender neutral (the 'ideal' woman officer), past masculine (conspicuous), to too masculine, you were courting being

labeled a lesbian. Too masculine made men and women nervous.
Me, too.

Another indicated that "they are often avoided by both male and
female soldiers. They are the outcasts of the unit."

One of the most revealing findings regarding the penalty of
being labeled a lesbian is the understanding that this label was
often applied to women regardless of sexual orientation. This fact
serves as a wonderful illustration of the way in which homophobia and perceptions of sexual orientation serve as mechanisms
for the subjugation of all women. "I believe they are labeled as
homosexuals, 'dykes,' whether they are or not." "Of course, they
are tagged or stereotyped as lesbians, whether they are or not."
The impact of such allegations can extend well beyond having to
tolerate "talk." As one woman writes:

> One of the women in the unit who had a masculine appearance was
> accused of being a lesbian even though she wasn't. When her time
> was up she got out because of the accusations she was gay. She was
> a good soldier.

Being labeled a lesbian was the only category that clearly
emerged from a content analysis of these items. Some answers
occurred more frequently than others, but none so much as the
penalty of being labeled a lesbian. Other penalties that respondents described included: (1) ostracism and ridicule and, (2) career
limitations. Though they each constituted only about 10 percent of
the descriptions, in these "non-sexualized" instances women are
receiving social and career penalties for exhibiting behavior that is
highly desirable in male soldiers. It is critical to understand that
women are being penalized for exhibiting gendered behaviors
that are consistent with the work-role of "soldier."

Bearing in mind that I am talking about the military, consider
this description of how, and for what, women are penalized.
"Women who were seen as too aggressive – too much focus on
aggressive or violent activities were not seen as 'normal' or to
be 'trusted.'" Exhibiting interests in activities that many would
agree form the core of military ideology (i.e., aggression and
violence) results in the penalty of not being considered "normal"
or "trustworthy." Another respondent indicated that "women
were discouraged from being aggressive, displaying leadership
skills, being self-assured and independent."

The ostracism that women describe is often, but not always, linked to the subject of lesbianism. While some women offered comments such as, "They are shunned, called names (e.g., dyke)," others were less specific in their remarks. "Rejected by both male and female peers," or "A woman who appears too masculine may be ridiculed for it." One woman wrote, "Yeah, everybody hates them." Whether explicitly related to sexual orientation or not, it seems apparent that women who violate gender norms of femininity are "outsiders" to the same degree, albeit in a different fashion, as are women who violate the masculine work-role of the military by being too feminine.

By understanding that women receive career penalties for being perceived as too masculine, as well as too feminine, we begin to understand the degree to which women are required to walk a fine line. One woman's comments capture this contradiction beautifully:

> [I] knew a female airman [*sic*] who could do her job on the flight line better than most of the guys in her unit. This convinced some people she was a "dyke" – just had to be a lesbian otherwise she wouldn't have been so good at a "man's job."

Although cast in the light of sexual orientation, such a description illustrates the difficulties women face when simply trying to do the job for which they were recruited. Another wrote:

> A female commander who does the exact same discipline as a male commander is probably seen as a bitch on a power trip. You're derided and not respected for playing tough by the rules... You play by their rules but then you lose because they didn't consider you part of their game.

In other instances, the examples described specific career penalties such as "not selected for 'high profile' jobs," "poor evaluations or less than deserved marks," and "overlooked for awards/promotions." As one woman described, "I believe it can affect performance reviews, assignments, and coaching or counseling which is provided for developmental growth." While the cynic might argue that women "just have to tough it out," it is clear that there are plenty of formal mechanisms by which women can be penalized if they are perceived as gender deviant, regardless of the direction of the alleged deviance. What, then, do women do?

Conscious Strategies – Femininity

If a respondent indicated that at least one of the 28 closed-ended
strategies was part of a conscious attempt to be perceived as
feminine or masculine, then that respondent was coded as having
strategized. Forty-one percent, or close to half, of the sample indicated that they engaged in some form of gender management, or
strategizing. When strategizing is examined with regard to femininity *only* or masculinity *only*, I find that 29 percent indicated
strategizing toward femininity only, while five percent strategized
toward masculinity only. Seven percent indicated strategizing in
both directions. Thus, 36 percent engaged in *any* strategizing
toward femininity (i.e., "femininity only" and "femininity and masculinity") and 12 percent engaged in *any* strategizing toward masculinity (i.e., "masculinity only" and "masculinity and femininity").

Of those respondents who indicated employing strategies to be
perceived as feminine, at least one-third chose each of the following strategies: wearing make-up on duty (40 percent), wearing
long hair (38 percent), wearing earrings while in uniform when
permitted (37 percent),[4] wearing cologne or perfume (35 percent),
and wearing make-up off duty (34 percent). Slightly less than one-
third indicated that they wore pumps instead of flat shoes (low
quarters) with the dress uniform (32 percent) and that they wore
skirt uniforms instead of pants uniforms (28 percent) as strategies
to be perceived as feminine. The fact that these items focus on
clothing is primarily a function of the choices that were provided
in the survey.

One of the most interesting aspects of clothing as a strategy for
being perceived as feminine was the *way* in which clothing was
often worn. This is of interest not only because it goes beyond the
issue of clothing *choice*, but because the way in which an item was
worn was often in violation of the regulations. Consider the following examples of strategies that women described: "My uniform
skirt was always too short," "[I] did not wear a t-shirt under
fatigues," and "I wore my BDU cap and Class A cap way back on
my head to look more like a female." Such violations could lead to
formal punishment, such as receiving a counseling statement, or
to informal punishment, such as being the subject of negative
comments. In my military experience, women were frequently
ridiculed for not wearing their uniforms properly. Such women

were viewed as not being serious soldiers and as being more concerned about their appearance than doing their job. Thus, women may highlight femininity as a means of being viewed more favorably, but to do so they may choose a strategy that has negative repercussions as well.

Women not only strategized with props such as clothing, jewelry, and make-up, but they also used their bodies to highlight femininity. One example of this is seen in the closed-ended item regarding hair length. As indicated above, 38 percent of those who indicated strategizing said that they wore their hair long as a strategy for being perceived as feminine. In the open-ended question, others referred to hair styling in general: "I tried to keep my hair in a feminine style that suited me. This involved getting a perm every 3–4 months."

Another strategy was the intentional avoidance of swearing. One woman wrote that she "never used bad language like many other women in [the] military do," while another wrote that she simply, "did not swear much." Other strategies that appeared repeatedly included home and office decor ("Flowers on my desk, my Noritake coffee cup and picture frames on my desk"), and watching one's weight ("I kept a close watch on my weight because I was under the false assumption that 'thinness' and feminine were related"). In sum, conscious manipulation of one's appearance and engaging in behaviors traditionally marked as "female" were common strategies for managing the perceptions others had about one's status as feminine.

All of the strategies discussed thus far focus on appearance, personal space, and personal habits. None of these strategies are particularly surprising, nor can most immediately be labeled as detrimental to one's physical or emotional well-being. The same cannot be said of the last group of strategies.

It is evident from the data that both men and women not only shape ideas of femininity, but also mete out the penalties for gender violations. While men were not surveyed or interviewed, the women gave many examples of how both women and men let women know when they were seen as deviating from accepted norms of gender. Most strategies, while influenced by others, were engaged in on an individual basis. That is, they did not involve the active participation of another individual, but could be accomplished alone (e.g., wearing make-up or a knife). In the last group of strategies addressing femininity, discussed below, men play

a key role. These strategies are those in which women intentionally engaged in social or sexual relations with men.

The closed-ended question revealed that anywhere from 6 to 10
percent of those who strategized either socialized with the men in
their units (seven percent), dated men in their units (11 percent), or
married while on active duty (six percent) as a conscious attempt
to be perceived as feminine. Four percent indicated that, as a strategy for being perceived as feminine, when they had a boyfriend
they "made sure people knew it." These numbers may seem
inconsequential until we realize that this means that people are
intentionally engaging in personal relationships as strategies for
altering or enhancing the perceptions that others have of them.

One woman wrote, "I believe I did a little 'indiscriminate' dating, more than I should have, maybe to feel more feminine."
Another "made up stories re: boyfriends, het[erosexual] sex, dates;
even slept with man/men (when I was drunk) to cover for myself
and the company." One woman said that she "tried to date civilian
men," while another said, "I felt that I *had* to have a boyfriend."
The relationship between femininity and heterosexuality is a key
element to understanding why such social and sexual relations
with men would serve as strategies. As one woman said, "I mostly
made conscious attempts to appear heterosexual v. feminine."
Another woman answered, "Hanging around with nothing but
males and having sex with them to prove I wasn't a lesbian."
Because of the obvious link to displays of heterosexuality, it is
worth noting at this point that there was an entirely separate question, not analyzed here, about strategies to avoid being perceived
as lesbian. The responses provided here are specifically in
response to the question about being perceived as feminine. This
is powerful evidence of the link between the ways gender and sexuality have been constructed.

Conscious Strategies – Masculinity

Although a majority of women who strategized did so toward
femininity, this was not true for everyone. Twelve percent of those
who employed strategies aimed some or all of their efforts at masculinity. Seventy-four percent of the respondents who indicated
employing at least one masculine strategy said they wanted to be
considered "one of the guys." Forty-one percent said that they

"socialized with men" in their unit as a strategy. Thirty-one percent wore pants uniforms rather than skirt uniforms as a strategy and 30 percent indicated that their preference for work uniforms (e.g., camouflage uniforms) to dress uniforms was a strategy for being perceived as more masculine. Thus, clothing was also a strategy for being perceived as masculine, but not nearly as frequently as it was a strategy for being perceived as feminine. Clearly, being seen as "one of the guys" and/or socializing with men were key strategies for women wishing to be perceived as masculine.

Analysis of the open-ended items revealed strategies similar to those above. The four main strategies identified in the qualitative data are: swearing, drinking, working out, and doing other "guy things." In the findings concerning feminine strategies we saw that avoidance of swearing was considered by some to be a strategy for being perceived as feminine. In the results presented here we see the opposite approach. In answer to the open-ended question about strategies, one woman wrote, "My favorite cuss word is 'shit.' I cussed when I wanted to make a point." Other examples include: "Started cursing," "Swearing," "Perhaps a bit cruder, earthier way of talking," "Talk nasty like guys, swear and stuff," "Use foul language to the extent men did," and "Used profanity when around men." Clearly, the expression "the mouth of a sailor" held some meaning for these women, as a number of them put the cliché to work.

A number of women indicated that drinking also served as a strategy. One woman said that she drank more than she should have. Another said, "Drinking with the guys – trying to keep up." One woman, however, did not acknowledge employing strategies, but then wrote, "Maybe – I tried beer because all of the guys were drinking it." Yet another mentioned "the amount of substance abuse" as a strategy for being perceived as masculine. As one woman wrote, "Foul language, smoking, drinking, joking – I am undeniably feminine – but I tried in many ways to 'compensate' (unfortunately)." While not all would agree, many would argue that swearing and drinking are more acceptable in men, relative to women, especially in the military.[5] Thus, it is not surprising that if women wished to emphasize masculinity, they would seize on these "available" behaviors as strategies for doing so.

A third strategy described by respondents was "working out" or concentrating on physical fitness. In the military, especially in recent years, we would expect this to be a "positive" strategy because of the military's emphasis on physical fitness. Additionally, if feminine women are perceived as weak, then it makes sense that some women might try to ensure that they are perceived as physically fit. As one woman described, "I made sure that I was physically fit to avoid being perceived as a weak female." Another wrote, "[I] Thought many other women were weak and pathetic. Made sure I was *very strong* physically." Several made specific mention of training in weight lifting, a stereotypically masculine mode of working out.

In a related vein, a number of women mentioned not allowing co-workers to help them with physical tasks. Typical responses included: "Not asking assistance of others when lifting heavy things" and [I] "lifted heavier things on the job than I should have." Another wrote:

> I did not let others (men) help me, unless a job normally required 2 people, and the guy was *assigned* to work with me. I only asked other women to help me, or went to great lengths to use leverage and improvise.

Demonstration of physical strength, whether through physical development or task accomplishment, is apparently one mechanism by which women try to be perceived as masculine and, as such, to fit in.

Though the last decade has led to significant change in this arena, the strategy of "working out," especially weight lifting, is viewed by some as "doing guy things." Some would say the same of swearing and drinking. If this weren't the case then it is unlikely that these would be identified as strategies for being perceived as masculine. Yet, the frequency with which these behaviors were mentioned warranted their being considered separate categories. The fourth strategy, "doing guy things," is distinct. Women mentioned a variety of behaviors, apart from those discussed above, that they exhibited as a means of being perceived as masculine. In some cases, these were specific behaviors (e.g., "learned to scuba and skydive"); in others they were general statements (e.g., "Go out with the guys and do the types of things they like to do"). The following comments illustrate these findings: "I drove a Pinto station wagon with a tool box in the back. I did my own oil changes." "Talked about stuff I did as a civilian – played in rock band, rode motorcycle, etc." "Auto hobby shop – fixed guys' cars – took flying lessons and mechanics with the guys." Again, certain behaviors, hobbies, etc., are culturally defined as masculine. If participation in these events is readily available then it is understandable that they would be part of the behavioral repertoire of those women who wish to be perceived as masculine.

"Demeanor" is another strategy of "doing guy things." One woman discussed "using the language and mannerisms of men," while another said she "became more assertive/aggressive." One woman said she "learned to be aggressive when necessary," while another said, "High assertiveness; low exhibited emotionality." As one woman described it, "Developed a tougher attitude and tried to hide my softer side at work."

Related to the strategy of "doing guy things" was the strategy of *not* doing "female things." One woman "attempted to downplay feminine 'traits' such as gossiping, flowers on desk, being emotional" while another wrote:

> Whenever I deployed, I reduced my attachment to "feminine" stuff; no contacts, no make-up, no complaints if I couldn't shower/wash hair, no perfume – made fun of women who continued these trappings while deployed.[6]

In some instances, and as would be the case with some weight lifters, such behaviors involved physical change. One woman said, "I didn't wear make-up, I never swayed my hips, I strode along." Another said, "I kept my fingernails short and never polished them!" To some degree, the absence of the feminine may be seen, by default, as an approximation of the masculine. This is akin to Nancy Chodorow's (1978) claim that boys, and men, define what is masculine by virtue of it *not* being feminine.

Results show that the types of strategies employed by women seeking to manage gender are numerous and diverse. Whether one is trying to be perceived as feminine or masculine there is an available repertoire of strategies from which one may choose. As I have shown, close to half of the women in this sample acknowledge the employment of strategies to manage gender. While most opt toward femininity, some do strategize toward masculinity.

The theoretical formulation of "doing gender" does not require that we be conscious of our actions nor that they be deliberate and with intent. It is important to note the difficulty, if not impossibility, of distinguishing between "true" preferences and those that result from socialization. Thus, I chose to operationalize the concept by focusing on those actions which the actor clearly identified as a means to an end: to be perceived in a more gendered fashion, whether feminine or masculine. In the following sections, I discuss how these results serve as evidence for what West and Zimmerman might call the "consequences" of doing gender (1987).

Doing Gender/Doing Sexuality

The first question posed by West and Zimmerman addressed the question of how a culture instills the need to achieve gender by examining the way in which young children "acquire the requisite categorical apparatus and other skills to become gendered human beings" (1987: 140). By examining the process by which young children act to be seen as socially competent, West and Zimmerman conclude that:

> gender differences, or the sociocultural shaping of "essential female and male natures," achieve the status of objective facts. They are rendered normal, natural features of persons and provide the tacit rationale for differing fates of women and men within the social order. (142)

By establishing ideas about what is essentially female or male, what is "normal" or "natural" the culture instills within us a need to maintain these gendered identities. That is, we must continually create and recreate our identities as gendered beings.

I believe that this analysis is accurate, but fails to consider another important mechanism for insuring that we feel compelled to engage in the active accomplishment of gender. I argue that the link between gender and sexuality also serves to reinforce our need to "do gender." There are at least two ways in which sexuality functions to reinforce our need to do gender. First, notions of what types of sexual behavior are appropriate are used to insure that women work to be seen as "good women." For example, a woman who does not want to be viewed as a "whore," or a "tramp," must modify her appearance, and possibly demeanor, so that she fits "acceptable" ideas of how a "good woman" looks or acts. Similarly, men who have a certain "look" are assumed to possess, or not possess, a degree of sexual prowess. And, sexuality is viewed as being composed of the good vs the bad. If all sexuality were viewed positively, there would be no negative connotations to labels such as whore or tramp. Homosexuality would not be viewed as bad; homophobia would not exist. If there were nothing "wrong" with being labeled a whore or a lesbian the labels would not be threatening.

Second, perceptions of gender are used to make assessments of one's sexual orientation. In women, femininity implies heterosexuality, masculinity implies homosexuality. And conversely, a woman known to be a lesbian may be assumed to possess more masculine traits than her heterosexual counterpart. Thus, perceptions about gender are used to make inferences about sexuality, and vice versa. This research provides ample evidence for the way that "masculinity" is used to "determine" that a woman is a lesbian.

Our culture instills the need to achieve gender not only by creating a sense of the "natural" or the "normal," but also by threatening social actors with penalties for violating prescribed notions of acceptable gendered behavior and acceptable sexual behavior. By linking the two together, we insure that violations in either arena result in penalties. Specifically, and because gendered behaviors are the more visible, the threat of being labeled sexually deviant may function to insure that we "do gender" in the appropriate fashion. That is, women enact femininity, and men enact masculinity. West and Fenstermaker make clear that "doing gender does not always mean living up to normative conceptions of femininity or masculinity" (1993: 157). But, they also note that "To the extent that members of society know their actions are accountable, they will design their actions in relation to how they might be seen and described by others" (1993: 157). They write:

> First, and perhaps most important, conceiving of gender as an ongoing accomplishment, accountable to interaction, implies that we must locate its emergence in *social situations*, rather than within the individual or some ill-defined set of role expectations ... What it involves is crafting conduct that can be evaluated in relation to normative conceptions of manly and womanly natures (Fenstermaker and Berk 1985, p. 203), and assessing conduct in light of those conceptions – given the situation at hand (West and Zimmerman 1987, p. 139–140). (157)

Thus, it is not simply that women, for example, seek to enact femininity because it is expected of them, but also that situations call for such enactment. The social situation in which femininity serves as an indicator of heterosexuality can only compel one to enact femininity if there is some reason to want to insure that one is perceived to be heterosexual. Sociocultural attitudes toward homosexuality function to insure that this is the case. But, some situations are especially strongly marked, or call more strongly for gendered behavior. The military is one such situation.

The ban on lesbians, gay men, and bisexuals exacerbates this situation even further. As of this writing, military policy "allows" lesbians, gay men, and bisexuals to serve as long as they "don't tell." This, of course, requires that lesbians in the military do what they can to mask all potential "markers" of homosexuality. While the policymakers claim that they would not "ask" about sexual orientation and servicemembers could "be" homosexual as long as they didn't "tell" the military has not upheld their end of the bargain. People continue to be harassed, investigated, and discharged for being lesbian, gay, or bisexual. While there are many instances outside the military where this is so, there are few, if any, places where federal law supports such discrimination. Federal law may not *protect* civilians, but neither does it compel an employer to fire them if it is discovered that they are lesbian, gay, or bisexual.

As was addressed earlier, to be perceived as masculine may result in one being labeled a lesbian. Not only may women be "shunned," or lose the respect of their peers, but the institutional requirement that lesbians be discharged may result in investigation and, ultimately, discharge. One way of avoiding such charges is to insure that one is perceived as feminine, and thus, heterosexual. While I would not argue that this is the sole explanation for women enacting femininity, I do believe that it is a significant factor. As a number of women indicated, it was more important to be perceived as heterosexual than feminine, but the latter helps insure the former. Remember, one woman wrote, "I mostly made conscious attempts to appear heterosexual v. feminine."

Thus, not only do we feel compelled to do gender because of the way in which we are socialized, but because of the social situations in which we find ourselves. In this instance, the link between gender and sexuality *and* both societal and institutional attitudes toward homosexuality function to insure that most women will choose to enact strategies aimed at highlighting their femininity, thus insuring that they are perceived as heterosexual. In short, this process instills in individuals a need to "achieve gender" in their encounters with others. For women in the military, women must "do femininity" to insure that they are perceived as heterosexual and, as such, are somewhat protected from potential stigma and/or expulsion.

Gender and the Institution

The second question posed by West and Zimmerman (1987) is: "What is the relationship between the production of gender at the level of interaction and such institutional arrangements as the division of labor in society?" In the case of the military, gender is produced at the level of interaction, but the result is the reinforcement of perceptions of women as unfit for military service. These perceptions are not merely micro-level assessments, but perceptions that permeate the broader institution. When the majority of women can be labeled "feminine," and anything feminine is viewed as inappropriate for military service, women, as a group, can become viewed as "inconsistent" with, or less than capable of performing, military service. Thus, by producing gender at the level of interaction (e.g., enacting femininity), a broader ideology, as well as institutional arrangements (e.g., job restrictions) in which women are perceived to be second class soldiers is maintained.

If women were aggressive they were seen as lesbians; if women were not aggressive enough they were seen as incapable of leading troops and could receive poor evaluation reviews. In either case, the ultimate penalty could be discharge. At the least, women as a group are subject to the label of "unfit." Women have to prove themselves the exception to the rule. One interesting example of this is the experience of the male sergeant who, together with a female flight surgeon, was captured by the Iraqis during Desert Storm. After their experience as prisoners of war, he acknowledged that she could go into battle with him anytime, but that he wasn't prepared to say the same for all women. SGT Troy Dunlap stated, "I was really amazed ... I was overwhelmed by the way she handled herself ... She can go to combat with me anytime" (Pauley 1992). He made it clear that she was the exception. One woman had proven herself; women as a group remained questionable. As MAJ Rhonda Cornum said in response, "I don't think I'll ever change his mind that says that women as a category of people shouldn't go to combat, but I think I did change his mind that this one individual person who happens to be female can go" (Pauley 1992).

When women "produce enactments of their 'essential' femininity" (West and Zimmerman 1987: 144), they are not being good soldiers. When they are "good soldiers," they often risk being labeled as lesbians. As Navy Vice Admiral Joseph S. Donnell wrote in 1990, lesbian sailors are "generally hard-working, career-oriented, willing to put in long hours on the job and among the command's top performers" (Gross, 1990: 24). It is not difficult to imagine how women who fit this description, regardless of sexual orientation, may be labelled as lesbian (Shilts 1993). Thus, the enactment of gender at the interactional level has the potential to reinforce perceptions of women as inappropriate for military service for a number of reasons. Such a perception of women then reinforces the belief that men are somehow uniquely suited to serving in the nation's military. Thus, the production of gender at the interactional level reinforces both ideological and institutional arrangements that place women at the margins of military participation.

It should be noted that stereotypical gay men do not fit the model of "soldier," in that they are not seen as masculine "enough." If gay male soldiers, or *any* male soldier for that matter, were not seen as appropriately masculine they would risk censure. The paradox is that the stereotypical lesbian *does* fit the model of "soldier," and, yet, risks censure for being "gender appropriate" to the work role of soldier. While a gay man can "pass" by "doing masculinity" in the appropriate fashion, women are faced with the contradiction that "doing masculinity" results in being perceived as a lesbian.

Gender as a Tool of Male Dominance

The third question posed by West and Zimmerman (1987) is "how does doing gender contribute to the subordination of women by men?" If, as described above, women in the military are perceived as second class soldiers, or as less than capable, it is not farfetched to argue that women are being subordinated by men. It is important to reiterate that clearly not all women, as individuals, are seen as second rate or unsuccessful. There are thousands of women who have served admirably and have earned the respect of their male co-workers, peers and superiors alike.[7] The case I am making here is that military women *as a group* are viewed as second class and are subordinated by the male institution of the military. Whether women are sexually harassed, denied assignments, or prohibited from performing particular jobs, we must realize that it is not simply the case of a poor performing individual that allows such incidents to occur. The social and institutional arrangements (e.g., the prohibition of women from most combat jobs) which permit women to be viewed as poor substitutes for male soldiers subordinate women to men and limit their participation as full members of the military. In some cases, attributions of inadequacy have followed women to their deaths.

LT Kara Hultgreen was one of the first women to qualify to fly a Naval fighter jet, the F-14. LT Hultgreen died on October 25, 1994 when she crashed in the Pacific during a training exercise. The Navy rumor mill immediately spun into action with some going "so far as to send out false information in anonymous phone calls and faxes purporting that Hultgreen was unqualified and received special treatment by a politically correct Navy. In fact, Hultgreen was third out of seven flyers in her class" (*Minerva's Bulletin Board* Fall/Winter, 1994: 3). Subsequent investigation revealed that the aircraft had lost an engine and that even skilled pilots would have had a difficult time landing successfully. CDR Trish Beckman, president of Women Military Aviators, writes:

> A combination of factors and limited time to recognize and correct them, put Kara in a "deep hole" which cost her life (and would have done the same to skilled Test Pilots in the same situation). What is different in this circumstance is that unnamed Navy men have attempted to slander and libel her reputation publicly (something that has never been done to a deceased male aviator, no matter how incompetent he was known to be or how many lives he took with him)." (*Minerva's Bulletin Board* Fall/Winter, 1994: 3–4)

In contrast, when two Navy pilots flew their helicopter past the demilitarized zone into North Korea in December 1994, resulting in the death of one and the capture of the other, no mention was made of blame or incompetence. No one suggested that perhaps permitting men to fly was a mistake.

Does the above question address the issue of the relationship between doing gender in the military and the subordination of women to men? I believe so. When military women enact femininity, they are subject to accusations that they are not capable of performing tasks, etc., that have been labeled as "masculine." When military women enact masculinity, they are subject to accusations of lesbianism. Doing gender results in women being subjected to an endless range of accusations, which together result in the subordination of women as a class of citizens. The question, however, remains, is it possible to avoid doing gender?

West and Zimmerman (1987) write:

> If we do gender appropriately, we simultaneously sustain, reproduce, and render legitimate the institutional arrangements that are based on sex category. If we fail to do gender appropriately, we as individuals – not the institutional arrangements – may be called to account (for our character, motives, and predispositions). (146)

While it is unlikely, given the existing social order, that we can avoid doing gender, we can begin to tackle the resulting inequities in a number of ways. "Social change, then, must be pursued both at the institutional and cultural level of sex category and at the interactional level of gender" (West and Zimmerman 1987: 147). That is, we must challenge the institutional and cultural arrangements that perpetuate distinctions made on the basis of sex, or sex category. In the military, one way to accomplish this would be to eliminate prohibitions of women in combat. Another would be to eliminate the ban on lesbians, gay men, and bisexuals in the military. If we eliminate the importance of sex category in the "politics of sexual-object choice" (Connell 1985: 261) we eliminate the need for compulsory heterosexuality. That is, if whether a potential mate is female or male is irrelevant, heterosexuality loses its hegemonic stranglehold on society and its institutions. Thus, eliminating compulsory heterosexuality would do much to reduce the pressures women feel to be seen as feminine as well as the fear of being seen as too masculine, and not without significance, the fear men have of being seen as too feminine.

Conclusion

This chapter provides empirical evidence for the points raised by West and Zimmerman (1987): (1) gender is something we do as opposed to something we simply possess, and (2) given current social arrangements, "doing gender" disadvantages women, in this case, military women in particular. One could also argue that men, too, are disadvantaged by the way in which they are expected to "do masculinity," a point made in men's studies literature.

A majority of the women in this sample believe that there are penalties for women who are perceived to be "too feminine," or "too masculine." The penalties for femininity include, but are not limited to, attributions of sexual availability and perceptions of weakness and incompetence. Penalties for masculinity are less varied, with the predominant penalty being the label of lesbian. While a majority of women do not acknowledge employing strategies to manage gender, of those who do, most work to be seen as more feminine. There are several important implications of these findings.

I begin with the obvious. There are some very real implications for women's day to day participation in the military. Women are likely to be subjected to a variety of unpleasantries ranging from sexual harassment to being shunned, from being denied access to schooling to being denied promotions. While the penalties are varied, they share one potential outcome. All of the penalties discussed in this research may lead to women being discharged or feeling compelled to leave the service. Thus, the major implication of this research is that the perpetuation of an ideology in which soldiering and masculinity are closely bound results in the perpetuation of a military which is not only ideologically, but numerically, male as well.

There are several mechanisms which function to keep the military "male." In addition to women leaving the service, whether by force or choice, perceptions of the military as male also limit the numbers of women who will consider the military as a career option. As of late 1993, the proportion of enlistees who were women was, in fact, on the rise (*Minerva's Bulletin Board* Spring, 1994: 1–2). As of this writing, the Army had experienced a slight drop in women recruits after widespread sexual harassment was exposed in late 1996. Whether this will have any long term effect on Army recruiting is not yet known. It is impossible, at this point, to determine if women are finding the military more attractive than has been true in the past, or whether smaller numbers of male recruits are inflating the proportion of female recruits.

In addition, the ideology of the "male military" and restrictions on the participation of women function together to limit the number of positions open to women. Thus, fewer women, compared to men, can enter the service. That is, even if huge numbers of women wished to enlist, their numbers would be suppressed by the comparatively fewer numbers of available positions, especially in the Army where large numbers of jobs are classified as combat arms and, as such, are off limits to women.

As long as the military is viewed as the domain of men, women will be outsiders and their participation will be challenged. Thus, a cycle of male dominance is perpetuated. The military is defined as male, a small proportion of women are allowed to participate, the participation of these women is challenged and penalized, the military remains ideologically and numerically male dominated, the numbers of women remain small. How can this cycle be broken? First, we can challenge cultural constructions of sex/gender. Second, we can challenge institutional arrangements which allow the perpetuation of distinctions on the basis of sex/sex category. That is, reduce the importance of being feminine or masculine and female or male.

The first of these institutional arrangements is the classification of military job eligibility by sex. That is, one is eligible for a particular job only if one is male. In the military this is the case for jobs coded as having a high likelihood of engaging the enemy. Women, as a group, are thus excluded from some specific occupations and some specific assignments. Barriers are being broken, but many remain. As long as women are eligible only for some jobs, they will be viewed as second class soldiers (or sailors, "airmen," etc.). If we eliminate such barriers and assign individuals on the basis of their performance, ability, etc., it is highly likely that we will see a corresponding increase in the acceptance of women as participants in the military.

The second arrangement which will improve the ability of women to participate on equal terms with men is the repeal of the law prohibiting the participation of lesbians, gay men, and bisexuals in the United States military. It is painfully apparent that this ban hurts many lesbians, gay men, and bisexuals. Many wish to serve in the military, but know that to do so is not without risk. Many do join the military only to have their careers ended prematurely. But, as I have indicated, the ban on lesbians, gay men, and bisexuals also impacts negatively on all women and men, regardless of sexual orientation. If the confirmation of heterosexuality were not imperative, women would be free to engage in a much wider range of behaviors, particularly those labeled as masculine. If women did not feel compelled to ensure that they are seen as heterosexual, there would be less pressure to enact femininity, a marker of heterosexuality.

By having to confirm heterosexuality, women enact femininity, thereby ensuring that they will be perceived as less capable than their male counterparts. The link between gender and sexuality, situated in an organization which has an institutional mandate for heterosexuality, ensures the subordination of women. To eliminate compulsory heterosexuality would greatly enhance the more equal participation of women. To be sure, eliminating the degree to and manner in which women deploy gender at the interactional level would also enhance equal participation. But, without corresponding changes at the institutional level such changes are unlikely to occur. By understanding: (1) how gender is produced at the interactional level, (2) how the interactional level is related to existing institutional arrangements, and (3) how the link between gender and sexuality empowers this relationship, we can offer a new vision for the equal participation of women and men in the military and, more importantly, throughout society.

NOTES

1 Members of the military are also referred to as airmen [*sic*], sailors, Marines, etc., depending upon their branch. For ease of discussion I use the term soldiers, as the Army is the largest branch and in common parlance many often refer to all members of the military as soldiers, regardless of branch.

2 In the wake of various incidents of sexual assault, sexual harassment, and other sexual activities by military personnel, questions have been raised about the role of the military with regard to sexuality. One question that has been posed is whether men who are being trained to engage in combat are even capable of "normal" interactions with military women and whether sexual "bantering," "conquests," etc. are, in fact, legitimate mechanisms for male bonding; bonding that some argue is essential for successful teamwork, etc. Such debates, I argue, mask the real issue: that men are looking for any way to maintain control over what many believe is the last "bastion" of masculinity. Nonetheless, these arguments illustrate the degree to which traditional conceptions of masculinity not only define soldiering, but are used expressly to legitimate male dominance over women.

3 For an interesting, non-military, account of the experiences of androgynous women see Holly Devor's *Gender Blending: Confronting the Limits of Duality*, Bloomington, IN: Indiana University Press, 1989.

4 This figure may have been even higher if women had always been permitted to wear earrings. It was only in the 1980s that women were granted permission to wear earrings with certain dress uniforms.
5 In the past swearing was not viewed as inappropriate or unprofessional and drinking was not only tolerated, but encouraged. New policies on sexual harassment and alcohol abuse have led to significant changes in recent years.
6 I attended basic training with a woman who brought a battery-operated, lighted, make-up mirror on field exercises.
7 Of course, one could argue as well that while women have to *earn* the respect of the men with whom they work, men begin with that respect and must do something to lose it.

REFERENCES

Acker, Joan. 1992. "Gendered Institutions." *Contemporary Sociology* 21(5): 565–69.

Chodorow, Nancy. 1978. *The Reproduction of Mothering: Psychoanalysis and the Sociology of Gender*. Berkeley, CA: University of California Press.

Connell, Robert W. 1985. "Theorizing Gender." *Sociology* 19(2): 260–72.

Dunivin, Karen. 1994. "Military Culture: Change and Continuity." *Armed Forces & Society* 20(4): 531–47.

"Freedom of Press Seen on Trial Now." 1942. *New York Times*, 17 April, 8.

Goffman, Erving. 1977. "The Arrangement Between the Sexes." *Theory and Society* 4(3): 301–31.

Gross, Jane. 1990. "Navy is Urged to Root Out Lesbians Despite Abilities." *New York Times*, 2 September, 24.

Lenskyj, Helen. 1986. *Out of Bounds: Women, Sport and Sexuality*. Toronto: The Women's Press.

The MINERVA Center. Spring, 1994. "Proportion of Women Growing Among New Recruits." *Minerva's Bulletin Board*, 1–2.

———. Fall/Winter, 1994. "Second Woman to Qualify as F-14 Pilot Dies in Crash." *Minerva's Bulletin Board*, 3–4.

Pauley, Jane. 1992. *Dateline NBC*: Interview with MAJ Rhonda L. Cornum. New York.

Shilts, Randy. 1993. *Conduct Unbecoming: Lesbians and Gays in the U. S. Military Vietnam to the Persian Gulf*. New York, NY: St Martin's Press.

Steinberg, Ronnie. 1992. "Gender on the Agenda: Male Advantage in Organizations." *Contemporary Sociology* 21(5): 576–81.

Veterans Administration. 1985. *Survey of Female Veterans: A Study of the Needs, Attitudes, and Experiences of Women Veterans*. Office of Information Management and Statistics, IM & S M 70-85-7.

West, Candace and Sarah Fenstermaker. 1993. "Power, Inequality and the Accomplishment of Gender: An Ethnomethodological View," in *Theory on Gender/Feminism on Theory*, P. England (ed.). Hawthorne, NY: Aldine de Gruyter, 151–74.

West, Candace and Don H. Zimmerman. 1987. "Doing Gender." *Gender & Society* 1(2): 125–51.

6

Sisyphus in a Wheelchair: Men with Physical Disabilities Confront Gender Domination[1]

Thomas J. Gerschick

Sisyphus, the King of Corinth in Greek mythology, has been condemned for all eternity by the Judges of the Dead to roll a large boulder up a mountain. Each time he approaches the summit, after much bitter toil, he inevitably loses control and the rock returns to the plains below. He repeatedly retrieves it and wearily begins the climb anew. The myth of Sisyphus captures the struggle and frustration men with physical disabilities experience as they seek to create and maintain masculine gender identities in a culture that views them as "not men." The cruel irony of this metaphor is that Sisyphus earned his domination; men with physical disabilities have not.

This chapter focuses specifically on the ways in which men with physical disabilities experience gender domination by the temporarily-able-bodied[2] in the United States.[3] This domination depends upon a double-bind: men with physical disabilities are judged according to the standards of hegemonic masculinity which are difficult to achieve due to the limitations of their bodies. Simultaneously, these men are blocked in everyday interactions from opportunities to achieve this form of masculinity. The most significant barriers they face occur in the key domains of hegemonic masculinity: work, the body, athletics, sexuality, and independence and control.[4] Because men with physical disabilities cannot enact hegemonic standards in these realms, they are denied recognition as men. As "failed" men, they are marginalized and occupy a position in the gender order similar to gay men, men of color, and women. Successfully creating and maintaining self-satisfactory masculine gender identities under these circumstances is an almost Sisyphean task. Men with physical disabilities, at times, act complicit in their domination by internalizing the dominant group's stereotypes and images of them. Hence these men's struggle against gender domination occurs not only with others, but also with themselves. The effort to resist gender domination has led some men with physical disabilities to develop counter-hegemonic gender identities.

In order to explore the struggle that men with physical disabilities undergo to create a realistic and positive self-image as men, I address the following three questions. First, how are men with physical disabilities dominated due to their inability to meet the demands of hegemonic masculinity? Second, how do they act complicit with, or resist, hegemonic masculinity? Third, what can be learned from the struggles of men with physical disabilities, especially from the alternative gender identities that some men with physical disabilities develop as a result of these struggles?

Data to address these questions come from two sources. First, an associate and I conducted in-depth, semi-structured interviews with 11 men with physical disabilities.[5] Initial interviews lasted an average of an hour. We provided informants with their transcripts and asked them to read them carefully to ensure that they were accurately represented. We then conducted follow-up interviews with most of these men to clarify statements and to ask questions which were stimulated in the first round of interviews. All of the interviews were tape recorded and transcribed verbatim. Correspondence with several informants continues and has been added, with permission, to the transcripts. Most of the informants had paraplegia and sustained their disabilities through either accidents or disease. None of the men we interviewed had a congenital disability. Their ages ranged from 16 to 72. Nine of these men were white, two were Black. Seven were professionally employed, one was a retired business-owner, two were full-time students, and one was a service-sector worker. The second source of data is ten autobiographies, semi-autobiographies, and collections of essays.[6] None of these books were expressly about masculinity and disability, however, all of them addressed issues related to these topics at least implicitly. Extensive notes were taken from these accounts which were then treated as fieldnotes.[7] I used a semi-structured frame to code the data and utilized analytical induction to analyze them.[8]

The lives of men with physical disabilities provide an instructive arena in which to study gender domination for three reasons. First, men with physical disabilities contravene many of the beliefs associated with being a man. Studying their gender identity struggles provides valuable insight into the struggles that all men experience in this realm. Second, men with physical disabilities occupy a unique subject position in what Patricia Hill Collins (1990: 225–7) calls the matrix of domination and privilege.[9] These men have gender privilege by virtue of being men, yet this privilege is significantly eroded due to their disability, which leaves them subject to domination and marginalization. Their marginal position in the gender order provides access to knowledge that is obscured from those in the mainstream (Beisser 1989; Janeway 1980). One of the goals of this chapter is to elucidate their "fugitive information," as writer Kay Hagan (1993) calls the knowledge of the marginalized, and how it can be used to construct counter-hegemonic masculine gender identities. Third, little has been written about the intersection of disability and gender. Where gender has been explored with reference to disability, the research has primarily focused on women. Consequently, this research addresses a lacuna in the literature.

Life at the Crossroads: Physical Disability and Masculinity

In order to contextualize the gender domination that men with physical disabilities experience, three sets of social dynamics need to be woven together. The first involves the stigma associated with having a physical disability, the second concerns gender as an interactional process, and the third is the hegemonic gender standard to which men with physical disabilities are held.

To have a disability is not only a physical or mental condition, it is also a social and stigmatized one (Goffman 1963; Kriegel 1991; Zola 1982). As anthropologist Robert Murphy (1990: 113) observed:

> Whatever the physically impaired person may think of himself [*sic*], he is attributed a negative identity by society, and much of his social life is a struggle against this imposed image. It is for this

reason that we can say that stigmatization is less a by-product of disability than its substance. The greatest impediment to a person's taking full part in this society are not his physical flaws, but rather the tissue of myths, fears, and misunderstandings that society attaches to them.

This stigma is embodied in the popular stereotypes of people with disabilities; they are perceived to be weak, passive, and dependent (Shapiro 1993). Our language exemplifies this stigmatization: people with disabilities are de-formed, dis-eased, dis-abled, dis-ordered, ab-normal, and in-valid (Zola 1982: 206).

This stigma is also embedded in the daily interactions between people with disabilities and the temporarily-able-bodied. People with disabilities are evaluated in terms of normative expectations and are, because of their disability, frequently found wanting. As a consequence, they experience a range of reactions from those without disabilities from subtle indignities and slights to overt hostility and outright cruelty. More commonly people with disabilities are avoided, ignored, and marginalized (Fine and Asch 1988; Shapiro 1993). This treatment creates formidable physical, economic, psychological, architectural, and social obstacles to their participation in all aspects of social life. Having a disability also becomes a primary identity which overshadows almost all other aspects of one's identity. As a consequence, it influences all interactions with the temporarily-able-bodied, including gendered interactions.

In order to accomplish gender, each person in a social situation needs to be recognized by others as appropriately masculine or feminine. Those with whom we interact continuously assess our gender performance and decide whether we are "doing gender" appropriately in that situation. Our "audience" or interaction partners then hold us accountable and sanction us in a variety of ways in order to encourage compliance (West and Zimmerman 1987). Our need for social approval and validation as gendered beings further encourages conformity. Much is at stake in this process, as one's sense of self rests precariously upon the audience's decision to validate or reject one's gender performance. Successful enactment bestows status and acceptance, failure invites embarrassment and humiliation (West and Zimmerman 1987).

In the contemporary United States, men's gender performance tends to be judged using the standard of hegemonic masculinity which represents the optimal attributes, activities, behaviors, and values expected of men in a culture (Connell 1990). Social scientists have identified career-orientation, activeness, athleticism, sexual desirability and virility, independence, and self-reliance as exalted masculine attributes in the United States (Connell 1995; Gerschick and Miller 1994; Kimmel 1994). Consequently, the body is central to the attainment of hegemonic masculinity. Men whose bodies allow them to evidence the identified characteristics are differentially rewarded in US dominant culture over those who cannot. Despite the fact that attaining these attributes is often unrealistic and more based in fantasy than reality, men continue to internalize them as ideals and strive to demonstrate them as well as judge themselves and other men using them. Women also tend to judge men using these standards.

In the remainder of this chapter, I explore the gender domination that men with physical disabilities endure in everyday interactions in the key arenas of hegemonic masculinity: work, the body, athletics, sexuality, and independence and control and how their responses make them complicit or resistant to this domination.[10]

Arenas of Gender Domination, Complicity and Resistance

Work

The prejudice and discrimination that many men with physical disabilities face in the labor market threaten to undermine an important measure of self-determination and a key component of their masculine gender identity. Despite being qualified, these men report being discriminated against in hiring, workplace accommodations, retention, and promotion. They encounter a particular form of double-bind. Due to the actions of the temporarily-able-bodied, men with physical disabilities are discouraged or prevented from competing for highly remunerated or prestigious jobs and are then devalued as men because they do not have them. Given the importance of work to a masculine identity, this situation reinforces their marginalized status as men.

Many men with physical disabilities have internalized the importance of work to enacting masculinity, realizing that in our culture the type of job a man has and the income he earns contribute significantly to his status and power. For instance, after contracting polio as a teenager, Leo realized "I didn't want to be weak. I wanted to be strong. I wanted to have a regular job, bring in income, be a success." When asked what being a man meant to him, Michael, an Independent Living Skills Specialist who has paraplegia, replied, "being able to work, to pay my own way ... It [having a job] enhances my self image."

Due to ignorance and prejudice, many temporarily-able-bodied people do not perceive men with physical disabilities as valuable employees; instead they are perceived to have high rates of absenteeism, to have low rates of productivity, and to be expensive to accommodate and insure (Shapiro 1993). The extent of this prejudice and discrimination is hard to determine, largely because few data have been collected. However, my informants repeatedly provided examples of it. Brent, an administrator of a university's disability program who has paraplegia, observed that:

> In this culture there is a quite a bit of stereotypical attitudes about people with disabilities, about who we are, what we can do, why we do what we do, and I think that makes it difficult for me to be, to have job flexibility. I don't think that I have the same access to jobs that other people do. I don't think I have the same access to promotions that other people do.

Having tired of being tracked into jobs which lacked recognition and opportunities for advancement, Brent recently took early retirement. Another of my informants, Jerry, a high school junior with Juvenile Rheumatoid Arthritis, lamented, "I know I have had a hard time finding part-time jobs, just because it seems like people are really intimidated and sort of afraid." Attitudes like these on the part of the temporarily-able-bodied contribute significantly to the 41 percent unemployment rate for men with physical disabilities (McNeil 1993, table 24: 62).[11]

Men with physical disabilities are frequently steered into low status, low paying, low prestige white collar or service sector jobs. Generally these involve some type of social service work, most frequently disability-related, which is deemed more culturally appropriate. Harold, for instance, noted that people who are temporarily-able-bodied "want to pigeonhole you. They see a disabled guy and they go, oh, the only thing you can write about is, you know, covering the disability scene. But that's not always true." Harold's example reveals how the temporarily-able-bodied subtly attach conditions to the employment of men with physical disabilities which impede their ability to compete for higher-status jobs, which in turn hinders their ability to be recognized as "real" men. The segregation in the labor force that many of these men face is similar to that experienced by people of color and women (Amott and Matthaei 1991) and gay men (Levine 1992) and demonstrates the similarity of their subject positions.

Several of my informants report cooperating in their labor force segregation. Of the eight informants who held jobs at the time of their interviews, six worked in disability-related occupations. Three noted that they gravitated to their occupations because they "knew it would be easier to find work" or it "seemed appropriate." Perhaps unconsciously they turned to disability-related jobs because they knew they would face less prejudice and discrimination.

Given their generally low status and low power position in society, men with physical disabilities do not control how they are perceived among the temporarily-able-bodied. As a consequence, they face formidable barriers in the labor market. The prejudice and discrimination they face make it difficult for them to achieve economic success, which is a key characteristic of hegemonic masculinity. Consequently, their difficulties in the labor market contribute to their marginalized position within the hegemonic gender order.

The Body

Men with physical disabilities do not meet mainstream notions of what is athletic, physically attractive, or sexually desirable. Instead, because of their bodies, they "contravene all the values of youth, virility, activity, and physical beauty that Americans cherish" (Murphy 1990: 116). As a result, men with physical disabilities are significantly less likely than temporarily-able-bodied men to be publicly recognized as athletes and/or potential sexual partners. These are two of the bedrocks upon which masculine gender identities are built. Consequently, masculinity is threatened when corporeal appearance and performance are discordant with hegemonic expectations, such as in the case of having a physical disability (Connell 1995; Gerschick and Miller 1994).

Bodies are important in contemporary social life. One's body and relationship to it provide a way to apprehend the world and one's place in it (Gerschick and Miller 1994). When one is alienated from one's body, one is alienated from one's sense of self. Psychiatrist Arnold Beisser (1989: 166–7), who had polio, explains:

> I felt as though I were cut off from the elemental functions and activities which had grounded me. I was quite literally separated from the earth, for while I spent my time in an iron lung, in a bed, or in a wheelchair, my feet almost never touched the ground. But more important, I believe, was being separated from so many of the elemental routines that occupy people. Even if I would work, I did not have any experience of physical exertion. I could not, on my own, assume the familiar positions of standing, sitting, and lying down. I was even separated from my breathing, as it was done by a machine. I felt no longer connected with the familiar roles I had known in family, work, and sports. My place in the culture was gone.

Thus having a physical disability compromises men's connection to one of the key sources of their identity: their bodies.

In US culture, bodies are simultaneously symbolic, kinetic, and social (Connell 1995). They are kinetic in that they allow us to move, to accomplish physical tasks, to perform. Bodies are also social; people respond to one another's bodies which initiates social processes such as validation and the assignment of status (Goffman 1963). Finally, bodies are symbolic. They are a form of self-presentation; one's body signifies one's worth. Bodies, then, are essential to the performance and achievement of gender. This becomes clear when one investigates men with physical disabilities' experiences with athletics, sexuality, and independence and control.

Athletics

In our sports-obsessed culture, ability, especially athletic ability, has become a key way for men to embody their masculinity. Sports provides men with an opportunity to exhibit key characteristics of hegemonic masculinity such as endurance, strength, and competitive spirit (Goffman 1977). The institutional organization of sports also embeds social relations such as competition, hierarchy, exclusion, and domination (Connell 1995: 54).

The athletic performances of men with physical disabilities tend not to be socially recognized and validated but instead are trivialized and devalued (Taub and Greer 1997). One of Taub and Greer's (1997: 13–4) informants, a 23-year-old student, described temporarily-able-bodied people's reactions to encountering him in the gym:

> It's people's perceptions [that] kill me…it doesn't seem like it's respect…it's just like a pat on the head type thing… "you're so courageous…you're overcoming all these boundaries…that's so good what you're doing." I wish people would…just look at wheelchair basketball as a sport…instead of just like a human interest story.

Because athletic performance embodies gender performance, not being taken seriously as an athlete symbolizes not being taken seriously as a man.

When men with physical disabilities are recognized as athletes, that recognition is conditional. This is represented by the qualifiers attached to titles such as "Special" Olympics, "wheelchair" basketball, and "disabled" athletes. Scott, a paraplegic, explained:

> Softball, I play it now from a wheelchair. I play in a regular city league, so it's able bodied, everyone else in the league is able-bodied. Um, I find that I do pretty well and everybody seems to think that I'm, the guys I play with now have never seen me play before my disability, and so they are all impressed. For me sometimes, it bothers me because I know I'm not the player that I used to be, but I do still enjoy it, but occasionally I have those frustrated times where I feel like, you know, everybody is impressed that I'm a good player, for a gimp, where I just want to be a good player.

Qualifying men with physical disabilities' athletic performances is condescending and patronizing. The devaluation of these men's efforts reveals that social acceptance and recognition are based both on the ability to perform and on the quality of the performance. Men who cannot perform to the hegemonic standard, due to a disability for instance, are marginalized as feminine or sissies (Messner 1992). The lack of recognition of men with physical disabilities as athletes undermines their ability to establish and maintain self-satisfactory gender identities.

Sexuality

Similar to athletic marginalization, men with physical disabilities tend not to be perceived as sexually attractive. "What bothers me more than anything else is the stereotypes, and, even more so, in terms of sexual desirability," Brent complained in his interview, "because I had a disability, I was less desirable than able bodied people and that I found very frustrating." Men with physical disabilities have a difficult time being recognized as potential life/sexual partners because they do not meet societal standards of beauty. Political scientist Harlan Hahn (1989: 54) explains:

> Much as they would prefer to deny it, the unavoidable reality is that men with disabilities are significantly devalued in modern society. This devaluation occurs not only in the labor force, where disabled men are often prevented from fulfilling the traditional role of "bread-winner," but also in the social marketplace, where they frequently are deprived of romantic partners and lasting companionship. Both forms of exclusion may result as much from aesthetic aversion to a different physical appearance as from limitations on functional capabilities.

One of my informants noted that the emphasis on the body is particularly costly for gay men with physical disabilities like himself because the body is so central to conceptions of beauty and sexuality in gay male culture.

Not only are men with physical disabilities frequently perceived as undesirable, they are also perceived to be asexual (Zola 1982). While there are exceptions, the sex lives of men with physical disabilities symbolize the passivity and dependency that is pervasive in their lives which contravenes what most men strive for: activity, initiative and control (Murphy 1990).

Like in other arenas of domination, men with physical disabilities act complicit in this one. In the following quote, Billy Golfus (1997: 420), who was disabled due to a motorcycle accident, illustrates the insidiousness of internalizing asexual stereotypes about people with disabilities when he discusses a potential relationship:

> Even though she is attractive, I don't really think about her that way partly because the [wheel] chair makes me not even see her and because after so many years of being disabled you quit thinking about it as an option.

The woman in this illustration was as invisible to him as his own sexuality was. This example reveals how deeply some men with physical disabilities internalize hegemonic standards of desirability and sexuality which make them complicit in their own domination.

Similarly, many men with physical disabilities internalize the value associated with hegemonic masculinity that men's sexuality and sexual desirability determine their self-worth as men. Author and cartoonist John Callahan (1990: 121) explained:

> I can remember looking at my body with loathing and thinking, Boy, if I ever get to heaven, I'm not going to ask for a new pair of legs like the average quad does. I'm going to ask for a dick I can feel. The idea promoted in rehab of the socially well-adjusted, happily married quad made me sick. This was the cruelest thing of all. Always, I felt humiliated. Surely a man with any self-respect would pull the plug on himself.

The lack of self-esteem in this crucial masculine arena leads men with physical disabilities to withdraw further into the margins as a form of self-protection, as the late sociologist Irving Zola (1982: 215) described: "We do not express or even show our wishes, because we have learned that in our condition of disablement or disfigurement, no one could (or should) find us sexually attractive."

Yet another strategy to deal with one's compromised sexuality is to enact hyper-sexuality as Michael attests:

> My sexuality and being able to please my partner...is my most masculine, the thing most endearing to my masculinity...It's probably the thing I feel most vulnerable about...I think that my compensation for my feelings of vulnerability is I overcompensate and trying to please my partner and leave little room to allow my partner to please me...Some of my greatest pleasure is exhausting my partner, while having sex.

Through his sexual behavior, Michael seeks validation of himself as a man. This is especially important to him because he has internalized the hegemonic standard and feels vulnerable that he will not be able to meet it. Michael's accordance with hegemonic masculinity in this example comes from sacrificing himself and his pleasure while pursuing an unobtainable ideal.

It is hard to be masculine if people restrict the opportunities to earn the recognition as a man. This is the difficulty that men with physical disabilities face in a culture where bodies are a type of social currency. Men's bodies become validated in two key arenas: athletics and sexuality. Due to temporarily-able-bodied people's stigmatization of men with physical disabilities, these arenas of self-expression and self-validation are largely closed to them. This situation further undermines men with physical disabilities' opportunities to establish and maintain satisfactory gender identities and reveals the pervasiveness of the domination they experience from the temporarily-able-bodied.

Independence and Control

Self-reliance is extremely important in the presentation of self to others in social interaction. As Jerry noted, this is especially true for men:

> If I ever have to ask someone for help, it really makes me, like, feel like less of a man. I don't like asking for help at all. You know, like even if I could use some I'll usually not ask just because I can't, I just hate asking … [A man is] fairly self-sufficient in that you can sort of handle just about any situation, in that you can help other people, and that you don't need a lot of help.

The independence and control that most men take for granted is compromised for men with physical disabilities due to the response of temporarily-able-bodied people. In cultures like the United States where few accommodations are made for people with disabilities, dependency is synonymous with powerlessness and powerlessness is antithetical to masculinity. Arnold Beisser (1989: 21–2), paralyzed from the neck down and forced to rely on an iron lung after a bout of polio, describes how being dependent undermined his masculinity:

> I had been thrust backward in the developmental scale, and my dependence was now as profound as that of a newborn. Once again I had to deal with all of the overwhelming, degrading conditions of dependency that belong with infancy and childhood – at the same time that I considered myself a mature adult. I did not adjust easily to my new dependence, and despised giving up what I had won

years ago in long-forgotten battles. The baby and the man were in conflict.

Through their actions, temporarily-able-bodied people subtly, and at times unconsciously, undermine the independence of men with physical disabilities and replace it with dependency. The following examples illustrate this process and the double-bind in which it places these men. The first example involves Irving Zola (1982: 52) who contracted polio at age 15, which weakened his back and legs. As a consequence, he utilized several braces. He described the change in his status when he took on the role of a wheelchair user in order to do participant observation:

> As soon as I sat in the wheelchair I was no longer seen as a person who could fend for himself. Although Metz had known me for nine months, and had never before done anything physical for me without asking, now he took over without permission. Suddenly in his eyes I was no longer able to carry things, reach for objects, or even push myself around. Though I was perfectly capable of doing all of these things, I was being wheeled around, and things were brought to me – all without my asking. Most frightening was my own compliance, my alienation from myself and from the process.

Metz had worked closely with Zola and was cognizant of his use of braces and a cane. Interacting with Zola in a wheelchair, however, immediately transformed Metz's sense of Zola's capabilities and initiated a profound change in the status of their relationship. Zola was no longer an independent and accomplished man, but rather a dependent child.

One of my informants, Robert, who has paraplegia, helped explain Zola's compliance when he noted that having people do things you can do for yourself "kind of strips you of your independence. But it's a Catch-22 because a lot of times people do it with good intentions, you know, not recognizing that this guy really wants to [do it] by himself." This double-bind was felt most acutely by Jerry who provided the second example. He noted that his friends were "uncomfortable" about his disability and his use of a wheelchair. "They feel like you need to be sort of helped all the time, even when you don't." he said. This led to an unspoken social contract between he and his friends. When together socially, he would allow them to push him in his wheelchair, thereby making them feel more comfortable in the interaction, and they would in turn, hang around with him. Thus Jerry was forced to make a difficult decision: surrender his independence and remain in the group, or retain his autonomy at the expense of his friendships. Jerry acquiesced to his domination, but, given his lack of alternatives, one can clearly understand why.

These examples reveal the domination and complicity inherent in the social relations between the temporarily-able-bodied and men with physical disabilities. By doing something for men with physical disabilities that they could do for themselves, the temporarily-able-bodied deny these men of a sense of agency, independence, and control. Through this treatment, they infantilize men with disabilities.

In a similar way, the actions of the temporarily-able-bodied make it difficult for men with physical disabilities to control their public gender performance. For instance, Michael noted in his interview that:

> I'm confronted with my disability because someone blocks the curb and then I, um, try and get up over the curb and I end up, you know, not doing it very, with very much style. I look pretty awkward at it, and I don't like looking awkward, so I have a hard time.

By not being able to control his immediate physical environment, Michael was not able to control his public gender performance. According to the dictates of hegemonic masculinity, Michael should be in control of himself and his image at all times. But the carelessness of the temporarily-able-bodied can quickly and easily undercut these pretensions (Murphy 1990: 121).

Michael reveals the importance of control to many men with physical disabilities' sense of their masculinity in an additional example:

> If I fall in public, it's difficult, if not virtually impossible, for me to get back into my chair and I find it embarrassing. It makes me feel … if I am laying on the ground because I can't walk, I feel more disabled that way than I do if I'm just up and about in my chair. I feel crippled.

This helpless and dependent position is antithetical to hegemonic masculinity. To be a cripple, is not to be a man.

Philosopher Susan Wendell (1997: 273) has observed that "dependence on the help of others is humiliating in a society which prizes independence." Yet in US culture, dependency and lack of control are thrust upon men with physical disabilities. Temporarily-able-bodied people infantilize these men through their attitudes and actions. This keeps men with physical disabilities marginalized and subordinated within the gender order.

Confronting Sisyphus: The Denial of Masculinity

When one considers the entire set of impediments: the stigmatization, marginalization, limited economic opportunities, rejection of athleticism, barriers to sexual expression and relations, and obstacles to cherished independence and control, it becomes apparent that the primary way that men with physical disabilities are dominated is through not being recognized or validated as men. As Jerry observed, they are figuratively emasculated: "I think you're not looked upon as much as a, you know, like you're, like I might be a really nice person, but not like a guy per se... you're sort of genderless to them." This lack of recognition occurs because the temporarily-able-bodied block access to the crucial arenas of masculine accomplishment.

The lack of recognition makes it difficult for men with physical disabilities to think of themselves as men. Jerry explained:

> I think it [others' definition of what it means to be a man] is very important because if they don't think of you as one, it is hard to think of yourself as one or it really doesn't matter if you think of yourself as one if no one else does ... You're sort of still a boy even if you think of yourself as a man and you would be a man if you weren't disabled ... It's so awful if no one else thinks of you as one, even if it doesn't affect how you think of yourself. It limits you so much to what you can do and how others regard you as opposed to how they regard other people that it makes it hard. It doesn't really matter if you do as much as they do.

Despite Jerry's youth, he had already experienced and clearly understood how others invalidate his masculinity and the masculinity of other men with physical disabilities.

The denial of gender identity leads men with physical disabilities to experience what Robert Murphy (1990) calls embattled identities. They are not perceived as men and they know that they are not women. Yet they inhabit a similar social space, as the following quote illustrates:

> Whoever I was, whatever I had, there was always a sense that I should be grateful to someone for allowing it to happen, for like women, I, a handicapped person, was perceived as dependent on someone else's largesse for my happiness, or on someone else to *let* me achieve it for myself. (Zola 1982: 213)

This gender domination and resulting marginalization make it exceedingly difficult for men with physical disabilities to create and maintain self-satisfactory masculine gender identities. Because of the power of hegemonic masculinity, many men with physical disabilities act as modern day Sisyphi struggling with the social, economic, and physical barriers; the temporarily-able-bodied; and themselves to enact a form of masculinity which is recognized and validated.

Men with physical disabilities respond to their gender domination in a variety of ways. One response is to heed the siren call of hegemonic masculinity and to continually try to prove one's masculinity to oneself and to others. This leads to hyper-masculinity (Gerschick and Miller 1994) as Michael illustrates:

> I had just begun dating again after an eighteen month break while adjusting to being paralyzed. The girl I was dating lived on the second floor of an apartment complex without an elevator. I was so determined to see her and didn't want to ask for help that I tried to wheel myself up the stairs. I knew that it was impossible, but I tried anyway. I had been working out extensively since just after my accident and had good upper body strength. By popping the front wheels of my chair in the air while simultaneously rolling forward. I got up five stairs. It was hard work. By the time I reached the fifth stair, my strength gave out and my chair tipped back and I skidded back down the stairs on the back of my head. My girlfriend heard the noise and found me. I was never so embarrassed in all my life.[12]

By trying to get up the stairs and maintain his independence and control, and thus his masculinity, all the while realizing the futility of it, Michael personified a modern day Sisyphus. As with Sisyphus, he was destined to fail. By taking hegemonic masculinity's demand for independence to an extreme, he resisted the limitations of his disability but he did so in a way that made him complicit with the demands of hegemonic masculinity to a point where he almost killed himself.

Escaping Sisyphus' Fate: Reconstructing Gender Identity

A resistant, and more healthy, response to gender domination comes from distancing oneself from hegemonic masculinity and the expectations of others while redefining masculinity for oneself. Ironically, for men with physical disabilities, being marginalized creates a social space where expectations are reduced, scrutiny is diminished, and there is more latitude for action. In this space counter-hegemonic masculine gender identities can be constructed, performed, and revised with minimum interference from the temporarily-able-bodied. In order for this reconstruction to occur, men with physical disabilities must resist the stigmatization associated with having a disability, change their primary reference group, and reject or redefine the hegemonic standards of career orientation, activeness, physical strength and athleticism, sexual desirability and virility, and independence and control.

Men with physical disabilities tend to internalize the hegemonic standard of career-orientation, however, they resist the labor market and workplace barriers associated with gender dominance. Rather than being governed by the prejudice and discrimination of others, they create work opportunities for themselves. Aaron, for instance, described how he begot his first job after a gunshot accident left him with paraplegia: "[I was] watching television one night and said, Wow! What a great vehicle for educating the public, and changing attitudes. I could do that...I think I will do that." The next day he arranged a meeting with a television station manager and convinced him that he should be hired as a reporter who focused on people's abilities, not their disabilities. Aaron later founded a social service agency dedicated to assisting people with disabilities. Three additional informants demonstrated a similar sense of vocation by working in disability-related positions. By defining their occupation for themselves, these men resisted the domination embodied in the prejudice and discrimination that steers others toward work that they would not otherwise do.

There are a variety of strategies that men with physical disabilities use to resist the activity and athletic ideals embodied in hegemonic masculinity. Some of these men reject temporarily-able-bodied persons' perceptions of them as non-athletes. Taub and Greer (1997), for instance, report that their informants did not internalize temporarily-able-bodied people's negative assessments of them because these men looked to alternative reference groups for their recognition. Other men with physical disabilities counter the hegemonic masculine ideal of physical strength and athleticism by rejecting it. Brent noted:

> I think that I am probably insolent by the cultural norms that say that manhood is, that physical strength and physical well being is [*sic*] important. But, um, to me I don't think that's what makes me a, makes me who I am, as how strong I am or how weak I am phys-ically … So physical strength is not, or ability is low down on the scale for me.

Yet others replace physical strength and athleticism with other forms of strength. For instance, Harold focused on his mental acu-ity: "I think the greatest thing a man can do is to develop his mind and think." Harold's conception of masculinity also privileged mental fortitude:

> Strength is a very vague term … you can lack physical strength in the power sense or the soldier of fortune sense and you can be very strong in other areas … Disabled men can be very, very strong with-out even being able to, you know, do anything physically active, okay? It's the amount of crap that you can tolerate.

Attention to the mind as a place for demonstrating masculine strength leads to more emphasis on emotional connection to others. For some men with physical disabilities, this connection takes precedence over activity and ability. Brent explained:

> Emotionally more than anything else, is the most important. You know, for me that is my measure of who I am as an individual and who I am as a man, is my ability to be able to be honest with my wife, be able to be close with her, to be able to ask for help, provide help, um, to have a commitment, to follow through and to do all those things that I think are important.

The attention to the emotional side of relationships reveals that some men with physical disabilities are incorporating traditional "feminine" characteristics into their counter-hegemonic masculine identities. For instance, Aaron remarked that, "Manhood today means, um, being responsible for one's actions, being considerate of another's feelings, being sensitive to individuals who are more vulnerable than yourself to what their needs would be."

Resistance to hegemonic masculine sexuality is based on rejecting the ideal standards and replacing them with more realistic ones. Alex, a college student with quadriplegia, exemplifies this:

> There is a part of me that, you know, has been conditioned and acculturated and knows those [hegemonic] values, but my practical experience…keeps my common sense in order. You know, …because I may have to do something different or nonstandard or difficult sexually, I don't think makes me less of a man, or even if I couldn't have sex at all, because I've learned that there's definitely a difference between fucking and making love and that even within the range of sexual behavior, there's a lot of different ways to give a partner that you care about pleasure and to receive pleasure.

While Alex demonstrates a willingness to enact his sexuality in a non-traditional way, his resistance is only successful if he can find a partner who shares his approach. This is possible, but difficult due to the cultural devaluation of men with physical disabilities.

In place of the unobtainable hegemonic demand for independence and control, some men with physical disabilities privilege interdependence and cooperation. Brent, for instance, shared that: "One of the values I have for myself, though, is to be more cooperative and to be able to help and to be helped in turn." This reflects a very different understanding of what it means to be a man.

The ramifications of rejecting the unobtainable ideals embodied in hegemonic masculinity and embracing new ways of performing gender are not limited solely to men with physical disabilities. The gender practices of men with physical disabilities who have developed counter-hegemonic identities provide viable models for new forms of masculinity for all men to practice. As a consequence, the struggles that men with physical disabilities experience have implications for all men regarding their masculinity and all people regarding gender relations.

Conclusion: Sisyphus in a Wheelchair

Returning to the metaphor with which I opened this chapter, for men with physical disabilities, Sisyphus' mountain represents hegemonic masculinity and his boulder their domination. The exertion of pushing the boulder to the summit represents the struggle that men with physical disabilities experience as they seek to gain recognition of themselves as men within the hostile hegemonic gender order that is largely controlled by the temporarily-able-bodied. Many men with physical disabilities act complicit with this domination and continue their Sisyphean struggle for acceptance according to the hegemonic standards.

There are limits, however, to this metaphor. While Sisyphus's struggle is futile and eternal, men with physical disabilities' exertions need not be. Despite the pervasive dominance that they face, they have an agency that Sisyphus lacks. They have the power to resist this domination. By rejecting hegemonic masculinity, changing their reference groups, and asserting their agency, it is possible for men with physical disabilities largely to escape their gender domination and to construct counter-hegemonic alternatives. In so doing, these men become models for all men who struggle with their masculinity.

NOTES

1 I would like to thank Bob Broad and Georganne Rundblad for their insights and many suggestions as they read multiple drafts of this chapter. Additionally, I would like to thank the editors for their patience, support, and advice, without which this chapter would not have been completed.
2 Among those who identify with the Disability Rights Movement, the use of this term acknowledges that almost everyone will experience a disability before death. The term underscores the similarities between those who currently have a disability and those who are likely to have one in the future. For more on the importance of language in this context, see Zola 1993.
3 Relatively little research has been done comparing the experiences of men and women with disabilities. While I value such work, it is beyond the scope of this chapter. For accounts of the challenges that women with disabilities face, see Fine and Asch 1988.

4 The type and severity of a person's disability interact with other social characteristics to influence the kind and extent of domination they experience. As a consequence, the domination experienced by men with physical disabilities varies depending on their social class, race and ethnicity, age, and sexual orientation. Space constraints preclude me from exploring this in detail here.

5 I would like to acknowledge the assistance of Adam S. Miller. Under my supervision, he conducted most of the interviews and assisted in transcribing the interview tapes.

6 These are: Beisser 1989; Callahan 1989; Dubus 1992; Fries 1997; Hockenberry 1995; Kovic 1976; Kriegel 1991; Murphy 1990; Puller 1991; and Zola 1982.

7 Sociologist Robert Newby (1992: 508) has noted that "when social scientists are investigating subjects for which there is not a substantial body of social science research, literature can serve as an excellent source of ideas."

8 For an excellent description of this method cf. Denzin 1989: 165–75.

9 The key axes of this matrix are race, social class, gender, ethnicity, sexual orientation, age, and ability/disability.

10 The degree of domination that these men face varies according to the number of realms in which it occurs. Most men with physical disabilities face a combination of threats in the realms of work, the body, athletics, sexuality, and independence and control. The more realms that are threatened, the more difficult it is to establish and maintain a masculine gender identity. Again, space constraints preclude me from exploring this in detail here.

11 Rates of unemployment vary depending on the definition of disability that is used (Altman and Barnartt 1996) and the severity of the disability (McNeil 1993). For the definition of disability used to compile this statistic, see McNeil 1993: 1–3.

12 Michael related this account to me in a private conversation after a visit to my class. I sketched notes of it when I returned to my office and later used those notes to reconstruct his story.

REFERENCES

Altman, Barbara M. and Sharon Barnartt. 1996. "Implications of Variations in Definitions of Disability Used in Policy Analysis: The Case of Labor Force Outcomes." Paper presented at the annual meeting of the Society for Disability Studies, June 13, Washington, DC.

Amott, Teresa and Julie A. Matthaei. 1991. *Race, Gender, and Work: A Multicultural Economic History of Women in the United States*. Boston, MA: Southend.

Beisser, Arnold. 1989. *Flying Without Wings: Personal Reflections on Being Disabled*. New York, NY: Doubleday.

Callahan, John. 1989. *Don't Worry, He Won't Get Far on Foot*. New York, NY: Vintage Books.

Connell, R. W. 1990. "An Iron Man: The Body and Some Contradictions of Hegemonic Masculinity," in *Sport, Men, and the Gender Order*, M. Messner and D. Sabo (eds). Champaign, IL: Human Kinetics, 83–96.

———. 1995. *Masculinities*. Berkeley, CA: University of California Press.

Denzin, Norman. 1989. *The Research Act: A Theoretical Introduction to Sociological Methods*. Englewood Cliffs, NJ: Prentice Hall.

Dubus, Andre. 1992. *Broken Vessels*. Boston, MA: David R. Godine.

Fine, Michelle and Adrienne Asch, (eds). 1988. *Women with Disabilities: Essays in Psychology, Culture, and Politics*. Philadelphia, PA: Temple University Press.

Fries, Kenny. 1997. *Body, Remember*. New York, NY: Dutton.

Gerschick, Thomas J. and Adam S. Miller. 1994. "Gender Identities at the Crossroads of Masculinity and Physical Disability." *Masculinities* 2(1): 32–53.

Goffman, Erving. 1963. *Stigma: Notes on the Management of Spoiled Identity*. New York, NY: Simon and Schuster.

———. 1977. "The Arrangement Between the Sexes." *Theory and Society* 4(3): 301–31.

Golfus, Billy. 1997. "Sex and the Single Gimp," in *The Disability Studies Reader*, L. J. Davis (ed.). New York: Routledge, 419–28.

Hagan, Kay Leigh. 1993. *Fugitive Information: Essays from a Feminist Hothead*. New York, NY: HarperCollins.

Hahn, Harlan. 1989. "Masculinity and Disability." *Disability Studies Quarterly* 9(1): 54–6.

Hill Collins, Patricia. 1990. *Black Feminist Thought*. Boston, MA: Unwin Hyman.

Hockenberry, John. 1995. *Moving Violations: War Zones, Wheelchairs, and Declarations of Independence*. New York, NY: Hyperion.

Janeway, Elizabeth. 1980. *Powers of the Weak*. New York, NY: Alfred A. Knopf.

Kimmel, Michael S. 1994. "Consuming Manhood: The Feminization of American Culture and the Recreation of the Male Body, 1832–1920," in *The Male Body*, L. Goldstein (ed.). Ann Arbor, MI: The University of Michigan Press, 12–41.

Kovic, Ron. 1976. *Born on the Fourth of July*. New York, NY: Pocket Books.

Kriegel, Leonard. 1991. *Falling into Life*. San Francisco, CA: North Point Press.

Levine, Martin P. 1992. "The Status of Gay Men in the Workplace," in *Men's Lives*, 2nd edn, M. S. Kimmel and M. Messner (eds). New York, NY: Macmillan, 251–66.

McNeil, John M. 1993. *Americans with Disabilities 1991–92.* US Bureau of the Census. Current Population Reports, P70–33. Washington, DC: US Government Printing Office.

Messner, Michael A. 1992. *Power at Play: Sports and the Problem of Masculinity.* Boston, MA: Beacon Press.

Murphy, Robert F. 1990. *The Body Silent.* New York, NY: Norton.

Newby, Robert. 1992. "Review Symposium: Black Feminist Thought." *Gender and Society* 6(3): 508–11.

Puller, Lewis B. Jr. 1991. *Fortunate Son.* New York, NY: Bantam.

Shapiro, Joseph P. 1993. *No Pity: People with Disabilities Forging a New Civil Rights Movement.* New York, NY: Random House.

Taub, Diane E. and Kimberly R. Greer. 1997. "Sociology of Acceptance Revisited: Males with Physical Disabilities Participating in Sport and Physical Fitness Activity." Paper presented at the annual meeting of the Midwest Sociological Society, April 4, Des Moines, IA.

Wendell, Susan. 1997. "Toward a Feminist Theory of Disability," in *The Disability Studies Reader,* L. J. Davis (ed.). New York, NY: Routledge, 260–78.

West, Candace and Don H. Zimmerman. 1987. "Doing Gender." *Gender and Society* 1(2): 125–51.

Zola, Irving Kenneth. 1982. *Missing Pieces: A Chronicle of Living with a Disability.* Philadelphia, PA: Temple University Press.

——. 1993. "Self, Identity, and the Naming Question: Reflections on the Language of Disability," in *Perspectives on Disability,* 2nd edn, M. Nagler (ed.). Palo Alto, CA: Health Markets Research, 15–23.

7

Class Dismissed? Quad City Women Doing *The Life*

Martha L. Shockey

The Voices of Prostitution

You'd be surprised if I told you all the names of the guys I've had as clients. Let's see...there's been one judge, a court bailiff, and several doctors...lots of the guys are influential in this town. But, if *you* asked 'em they'd tell you they don't associate with hookers... they wouldn't even admit to it. But, I'll tell you...there was this one bailiff who paid me just to spank him. That's all, just spank him. And then there was this other guy...a big name doctor around here. He paid me a hundred dollars just to have sex with his wife while he watched. It's really kinda funny...all these people that say we ought to get rid of prostitution...they're the ones that are coming to people like me. The thing is, most people just don't know who our clients really are. (Lynn)

As we sat across from each other in the small visitation room of the county jail, a mesh screen preventing us from any personal or physical contact, Lynn candidly described her life as a sex worker. I listened attentively as she, a 40-year-old African American woman, told me what it meant to be a Quad City prostitute. Without a doubt, Lynn, by her own accounts, had aged both physically and emotionally during the eight years that had passed since turning her first trick at the age of 32.

It did not take long in the field for me to realize that Lynn's experiences and self-perceptions were more the rule among local prostitutes than the exception. More than a few Quad City women have grown old living and doing *the life*.

You know, I'm 38 now and this time I drew the line. I knew it was enough for me. I have a lot of health problems... something that runs in the family. I want to raise my grandchildren. I have a grand-daughter that's four months old and I've never seen her. I want to know her. I've got a grandson that's two years old and I want to know him. I want to take my grandchildren and raise them. I want to see the little ones grow. (Christie)

These are the stories of women's lives, private historias if you will. Embedded in each lie the descriptions of an unconventional occupation, one that both mirrors and reinforces the stratified social relationships and arrangements already in place within the larger society. The stories told here are, in many ways, little different from those told by even the most "conventional" of women. These are the stories of women who have, through their personal and professional endeavors, attempted to gain a modicum of control over their own lives.

Prostitution – as an enduring institutional form and as a life – can be usefully understood from this vantage point. The web of circumstances that constitutes the life is complex, dynamic, and contradictory in nature; it is comprised of, and maintained through, a series of everyday encounters, exchanges, and inter-actions that give it life. It is also a resilient social institution main-tained by women who are viewed, and have often come to view themselves, as "America's least wanted." The women who are mired in the complex web of economic, cultural, and interpersonal hierarchies that constitute the life describe long hours, difficult working conditions, and a "road out" beset with many obstacles.

The Sociologist as *Bricoleur*

In telling me her historias so I would put them into a book that would talk in the tongue of the gringos, Esperanza definitely placed both herself and me in a paradoxical position. In the masked tongue of translation, she hopes she'll be invulnerable to the snakes; only in her original tongue would her confessions be dan-gerous. But with the border between the United States and Mexico, like the border between life and death, being so permeable, can I, no matter how hard I will try, keep guard over this book? How can I be sure it won't return to talk where it shouldn't? No doubt about

it, this book is a talking serpent. Too late to cut its tongue now.
(Behar 1993: 20)

Scholars in general, and sociologists in particular, have long been
interested in prostitution. In spite of this scholarly fascination,
little progress has been made toward understanding prostitution
as a social institution in its own right since Kingsley Davis first
addressed the phenomenon in his work, "The Sociology of
Prostitution" (1937). Yet, largely because of this scholarly fascination with prostitution, sex work itself and society's response to
its presence share a rich and well documented history (see Jenness
1993; Posner 1992; Jenness 1990; Bullough and Bullough 1987;
Hoigard and Finstad 1986; Walkowitz 1983; Davis 1937). It is a
history laden with passive acceptance and active denial, a history
of social tolerance and public dogmatism.

Just as prostitution is largely misunderstood, so, too, is the
prostitute. From the scholarly journals to television's more popu-
larized *20/20*, from *Les Misérables* to *Pretty Woman*, society has
been inundated with specific, yet contradictory, images of the sex
worker, her life, and the control she exerts over each. Prostitution
is not merely an unconventional lifestyle, but one that can be
understood and explained by debating the contemporary scholarly issues of free choice versus constrained opportunity. It is
much more than a labor form propelled by forces of supply
and demand; it is more than a deviant activity engaged in by
women lacking opportunity in the conventional labor market or
seeking excitement within an accepting social milieu. Prostitution
is both a *lived experience* and a *social institution* in its own right.

This is a story of and about many women. It is a story told
by the women themselves – women who are Black, white, and
bi-racial; women in their teens, twenties, and middle years;
women raised in poverty and women who claim to have had
every advantage at their disposal. It is a story of lived experiences.
Each account is as unique and compelling as the woman who
originally told it to me. In toto, the stories retold here blend
together into a rich tapestry – one that is, more often than not,
woven together by the common threads of anger, fatigue, and
a loss of personal control. These shared feelings, expressed by
many of the women I interviewed, have emerged over time
as each woman found herself first becoming, and later being, a
prostitute.

The Setting and the Scene

> Well, you know, 99 percent of the people who live in this area have
> no idea there's any prostitution at all. And you sit down with the
> average citizen and say, "I can take the *Quad City Times* and I can
> have a girl at your house in 15 minutes and you don't even have to
> have money – as long as you have plastic, you can have a woman at
> your house." And they won't believe it because they don't think it
> exists. (Lt. Greg West, Rock Island County Sheriff's Department)

As the sun rises over the Mississippi River on a Sunday morning
in mid-June approximately 5,000 bicyclists navigate the streets of
the Quad Cities. They are part of the annual family outing which
has come to be known as Ride the River. On this particular
Father's Day the 20-mile route takes the cyclists east from the river
front train depot in Davenport, Iowa, to a ferry landing in
Bettendorf where the riders, with bicycles in tow, board a barge to
cross the Mississippi River into Illinois. After landing at the Ben
Butterworth Parkway in Moline the riders travel into East Moline
before retracing their westward route back through Moline and
into Rock Island. The journey ends late in the afternoon as the
cyclists travel north across the Centennial Bridge and head back
into the Iowa Quad Cities.

The riders are a diverse group. Many ride as families; training
wheels and family pets are not unusual sights along the route.
A few in the group are serious cyclists. They are the ones who will
ride an additional six miles on scenic Illinois Highway 84 before
joining the rest of the group to cross the Centennial Bridge, eventually ending the day's activities back in Davenport. The order of
the day is fun. Few, if any, of the riders have seriously thought
about the streets they have covered on their ride. Fewer still have
given any thought to the people who work these same streets once
the sun sets over the Mississippi River.

The community of prostitutes I studied exists within the Quad
Cities, a region comprised of four mid-sized communities in eastern Iowa and western Illinois. Two of the cities, Davenport and
Bettendorf, are located in Iowa and the other two, Moline and
Rock Island, are in Illinois. The combined population of the four
cities is slightly over 200,000 persons (US Department of the Census
1992a: 2, 9; US Department of the Census 1992b: 2, 3). The cities
share a rich yet diverse cultural heritage as riverboat communities

that evolved into industrial centers. Following the worst national recession in 50 years and a severe contraction in the farm implement industry during the 1980s, multiple factory shutdowns and rampant unemployment altered the financial and social climates of the communities (Svendsen 1987). The economic focus of the communities shifted at this time. Using its location on the Mississippi River to its advantage, the Quad Cities turned its attention and efforts toward developing the region as a tourist attraction, riverboat gambling site, and convention area (Svendsen 1987).

I modeled my study on the seminal works of Eleanor Miller (1986), Laud Humphreys (1975), and Howard Becker (1963), at all times maintaining an emphasis on process and meaning while viewing myself as the storyteller (Denzin and Lincoln 1994). Although initially guided and informed by existing theory, the scope and outcome of the project benefit from the categories, concepts, and understandings that emerge vis-à-vis the data (see Glaser 1992, 1978 and Glaser and Strauss 1967).

Relying upon a "creative snowball" sampling procedure I initiated contact with the individuals who, eventually, became participants in my study. I then accessed the "story of prostitution" by conducting in-depth, semi-structured interviews with women who either have been or still are prostitutes, members of the local police departments, and helping professionals whose contact with prostitution is more indirect in nature. All in all, 24 interviews were taped during an 11-month period beginning in August 1993 and continuing through June 1994. The completed interviews represent the following: (a) 11 former or currently active prostitutes; (b) eight police and/or local corrections officers; (c) two members of the local jail ministry team; (d) one attorney; (e) one ride-along with the vice commander of the Davenport Police Department to observe prostitution; and (f) one male nightclub owner considered by the local police to be a pimp, a claim he adamantly denies. With the informed consent of the respondents, the interviews were taped whenever possible. When taping was not allowed, such as in the county jails, I took copious and detailed notes which were taped immediately after the interview. A duplicate copy was made of each tape for precautionary purposes. All of the tapes were then transcribed for analysis and saved on hard copy and on floppy disk.

Diversity appears to be the name of the game among Quad City prostitutes. The women I interviewed spanned an age range from

21 to 43 years old. Six of the women began hooking in their teens and one entered prostitution in her twenties. Two others were in their thirties when they entered the life and the two remaining women were servicing men well before their teen years. Six of the women I spoke with are of African American descent and five are white. The remaining interviewee described herself as bi-racial, the offspring of an Italian father and African American mother.

> There is no typical hooker. When you bust them they all claim to have legitimate jobs … and you'd be surprised how many of these girls go to Scott Community College. There was one lady who worked out at John Deere. She'd come down two or three times a week to just drive around looking for some guy that was looking. And she'd get him to pull over and take him to her house for a couple of hours. In fact, she hit on me one time and it was going to cost me 200 dollars. Keep in mind the going rate right now is 15 dollars for going down on some guy. And it's not a lot more for tak-ing your clothes off and having sex with the guy. Anyway, she promised some pretty interesting things, but I sure wouldn't pay 200 dollars. She'd be on the road by eight or nine o'clock at night, to bed by midnight, and at work at John Deere by eight o'clock the next morning … 200 dollars richer. Two or three times a week, that's some good cash … tax-free money. I busted one girl who was 15 at the time … then there's the one that's been around the block more than a few times … she's sixty-five. The majority of them have kids. I would hazard a guess that better than 90 percent of them have kids … now, whether they're trick or not I don't know. Once they have the kids then a sister, a mother, or a grandmother takes care of them while she's on the streets. Sister, mom, grandma. [They] may not even care what she's doing because she's bringing money into the house. It's basic economics. (Lt. George Owens, Davenport Police Department)

Class Dismissed?

> … has led some commentators to proclaim that the factors of race, ethnicity, or gender are now the driving force behind the evolution of stratification systems. (Grusky 1994: 21)

For many the prostitute's life is neither conceivable nor under-standable. She is neither fish nor fowl; she operates at all times with one foot in an unconventional environment and the other firmly planted in mainstream society. The Quad City sex worker is truly marginalized, procuring a living wage from within one social milieu while facing the scrutiny and even soliciting her clients from yet another.

> When I got involved in jail ministry the first woman I met was a prostitute. At the time that I met her, my daughter was 17 and she had decided she was old enough to leave home. It was the summer between her junior and senior years in high school. So, my daughter had moved out and I was sharing that with Kate, the prostitute. She was the first woman with whom I had contact who had any empathy or compassion. She just looked at me through the bars and said, "You weren't ready for her to leave, were you?" And I said, "No, you know, I really wasn't." And then we started into this cycle … a cycle of hospitality that I really believed in firmly … not knowing who's the host and who's the guest. But, what had happened was my friends, middle class women who also had daughters, were afraid of the thing because it might be contagious and … what if their daughter moved out … and they just didn't quite know how to deal with it or me. So, I'll always remember Kate was human enough to know exactly what I was going through. She may have been incarcerated, but she could reach out to me when my typical friends couldn't. She looked me right in the eye … she didn't avoid me. I think we sometimes forget that the prostitutes have a humanity. (Sherry Fine, Churches United of the Quad Cities)

The labor market for prostitution tends to be stratified along many of the same dimensions found in other institutional and organizational settings, as well as in the larger social structure (see Heyl 1979). There exists within the overarching structure of the institution a hierarchy of rewards and statuses that correlate with the type of prostitution one enters. At the lowest end of the occupational ladder is the Quad City street hooker. She ranks only slightly lower than the dancer. Moving up the occupational ladder one encounters either the call girl or escort prostitute. At the pinnacle of the hierarchy is the house prostitute. She is most often encountered in locations where prostitution has been legitimated and legalized, although I have met one woman who established herself as a house madam in the local community.

The cultural capital the novice prostitute brings with her to the profession often determines the type of prostitution into which she is recruited. The more articulate, educated, and attractive the woman, the more likely she is to enjoy recruitment into the better paying, higher status forms of prostitution. However, this is not given nor does it guarantee upward mobility or even the positional security many women expect to find when they enter the occupation. The prostitutes I interviewed indicate they have experienced downward, rather than upward, mobility. The women I met during my time in the field were as diverse as the backgrounds from which they came. Yet they shared one common experience. Regardless of where they began their careers as prostitutes, once in the life, each experienced the downward spiral that led them to the lowest form of hooking available – street prostitution.

Of the 11 women I interviewed for this project only two, Debbie and Amber, consider themselves to be, above all else, high class sex workers who have made it in the world of prostitution. Although Debbie and Amber both described themselves as "high class hookers," they had clearly occupied different strata in the occupational hierarchy of sex work. Throughout her career, Debbie had known only the life and clientele of the Quad City street hooker. As a legalized house prostitute in Carson City, Nevada, Amber had rubbed elbows with society's rich and powerful.

Knowing what I did about the hierarchical ranking of prostitution I found the similar self-perceptions described by Debbie and Amber to be confusing. Given their different occupational experiences, I intuitively assumed their self-assessments and descriptions would also differ. Yet, in reality, Debbie and Amber are little different from those who occupy positions within the conventional labor market.

Scholars have long been interested in the contradictions appearing between the more subjective nature of self-reported class affiliation and objective attempts to assign class membership (see Gilbert and Kahl 1993; Bott 1954; Centers 1949). The apparent discrepancies in the accounts offered by Debbie and Amber cast little doubt on my claim that the social institution of sex work mirrors other, more conventional, institutions in place within society. Rather, their life stories fall directly in line with what has been known about conventional society for a very long time.

> There is no such thing as an *objective* status structure that can be viewed by the completely neutral observer. Prestige is embedded in attitudes about the relationships between persons, positions, and symbols, and it varies according to the perspective from which it is viewed. (Gilbert and Kahl 1993: 45)

Debbie and Amber both report having attained feelings of self-worth and prestige as hookers. Each *perceives* herself as a high class hooker. Hence, it appears the subjective experience of class may well provide more insight into the sex worker's occupational experiences and outcomes than any objective class ranking ever can.

I first met Debbie at the Residential Corrections Facility in Davenport, Iowa, where she was incarcerated on forgery charges. Although Debbie had been placed in the facility as a result of her deviant activities, she was more than candid as she talked about her desire to obtain her release and resume her previous lifestyle. As our conversation unfolded it became exceedingly clear that Debbie considered herself to be a sex worker, even though she had not actively practiced her trade since entering the corrections facility four months prior to our meeting. It was also evident that Debbie will always view herself as a prostitute, regardless of her occupational status in the upcoming years.

> Once you *learn* to be a prostitute you're always a prostitute … you may just prostitute yourself in a variety of ways, but you never really leave the life. Will I ever leave the life? Never. It will always be with me … I tell you I could be in a grocery story and spot a trick, you know. It's like, it's instinct, it's the way they look at you … it's like a sixth sense. Even if I could walk out of here today … if I could earn a decent living at a normal job … No, I wouldn't do it. Because there's one thing the job can't do … it can't give me what hooking has. There's some good points about hooking … there's a lot of wisdom in it. You meet a lot of people that are intelligent and you make a lot of connections. And as long as you're not using you've got all the choices you could ever want. But, there's always this little thing in me and there always will be. I don't care what I was being paid in another job, there's something that would make me prostitute myself in one way or another even if it's only for knowledge.

As I have already indicated, existing scholarly accounts of prostitution describe it as a hierarchically arranged occupation (Luckenbill 1986; Luckenbill 1985; Heyl 1979). As the individual sex worker proceeds through the occupational levels she encounters progressively greater rewards. At least implied in this work is the assumption that the prostitute will seek upward movement in pursuit of increased rewards. Yet Debbie, in her distinct and unabashed manner, was not hesitant in describing her intent to remain a street hooker because of the personal rewards it offers her.

> Oh, it's very exciting. I think fair exchange then there's no robbery. I'm a firm believer in that. You get what you want, I get what I want. You know, I do have choices. I don't have to deal with individuals I don't want to. And there's plenty out there that I like to deal with, you know. The highest-class form of prostitution? The kind where you make your own choices, whatever you want to do as long as you're not carrying a heavy load like an addiction … or an addiction to a person. When you have freedom of choice totally. *You* decide who, when, what, where, and how.

Debbie has clearly, without naïveté, internalized the sex worker identity as part of the central notion of who she is. She is more than capable of acknowledging the difficulties associated with street hooking. Yet for Debbie, the personal benefits she derives from sex work far outweigh the difficulties she encounters while fulfilling the occupational role. Included among these benefits is an enhanced self-concept, one that is both reinforced by and reflected in the appraisals she receives through her chosen work. Debbie fully intends on remaining a sex worker and even voices plans to expand her occupational horizons by mentoring a new generation of novice prostitutes.

Debbie's indomitable spirit permeated the interview session the day I met with her. It became especially apparent when I asked her to describe herself, her occupation, and the posture she would assume if her daughter voiced the desire to become a sex worker.

> I'm good, I'm a good prostitute … And I can teach others how to be just as good. If [my daughter] wants to be a prostitute then I want her to be good at it. And I would want to show her some of the things that I've gone through so maybe she won't have to go through them. If she's doing it then I want to help her so she can be good at it, too. If you don't have a good teacher then there's sometimes a high price for what you want, for the trades you make.

Debbie is the quintessential sex worker, neither naive nor shortsighted when she talks about her occupation and its disadvantages. Debbie clearly enjoys her life as a sex worker and intends on remaining a prostitute. At the same time she admits she is actively honing other unconventional skills she can put to use should the future become her enemy, a time when aging and fatigue impair her abilities to effectively carry out the sex worker's role. A street-smart survivor, Debbie takes little for granted and has assumed personal responsibility for insuring her future survival on the streets.

> I was intelligent enough to know that there's ways to get more money because you burn out. You get burned out, your body gets worn down, and your personal hygiene goes and you're not making as much money hooking, and you've told all the lies you can possibly tell and get paid for it … So, like most girls like me, I turned to check cashing which is a good one. And see all these criminal activities flow through the area where you prostitute so there's no problem. Boostin' … check cashing, stealing and selling the items … these are the main things I got into. Cashing checks works good … especially if you can get a few of them off your johns.

As evidenced by Debbie's accounts, she considers herself to be a "high class" hooker, even though she has spent her entire career walking the streets of Davenport, Iowa. But, Debbie is the exception rather than the rule. The streets are considered the last stop for most sex workers. Yet, the streets are where most Quad City prostitutes find themselves in the latter stages of their careers, regardless of where they began their professional lives.

Lynn was a 40-year-old sex worker I met at the Scott County Jail. At the time I interviewed her Lynn had been hooking for eight years, having been introduced to the life by a gentleman she worked with at a residential care facility for the aged and disabled. The turning point in Lynn's life came the day her co-worker asked about the income she received from her conventional job.

> I told him I made about a 100 dollars a day. And he looked at me and said, "Well, I can pay you that for a lot less work." I had no idea what he meant, but he told me to come to his house later that night. And he paid me a 100 dollars for 15 minutes of work. I learned real fast that there was a quicker way to make money than the way I'd been doing it. I had an eight-year relationship with this guy … there was no one else, just him. When he wanted sex he'd let me know and I'd go to his house and he'd pay me equal to what I was making in a day at the home. Then two years ago I lost my regular job, I'd just bought a house, and I'd just started using cocaine. I didn't know what else to do … I didn't want to go on welfare … and there I was. I had no job, I still had house payments, I wasn't getting any

public aid, and I had a drug habit to support. That's when I came out of the closet and started working the streets.

For Lynn, her introduction to cocaine initiated what I refer to as the prostitute's "downward spiral," an experience that is all too common among local sex workers who also become addicted to drugs.

Only two of the women I interviewed, Amber and Laura, were drug dependent prior to entering the world of prostitution; the others became addicted after entering the life. Amber was introduced to drugs as a part of the seasoning process carried out by her pimp in the early days of her career. Laura moved into sex work of her own accord, viewing the work as a means of supporting her addiction.

> I was 32 years old when I started hooking. You gotta remember that I was an addict. I was hooked on drugs and alcohol and I was out of money. My marriage had broken up because of my addiction... I had nowhere else to turn. And I'm sitting in this bar one night and this guy comes up to me and says, 'Do you date?' And I'd seen a few other girls hooking since I'd been hanging out in the bars and I *knew* what this guy meant when he asked me if I dated. You sit downtown enough you watch it, you see it, you know what they mean when they ask you if you date. I needed the money... that was the night I turned my first trick. Before the drugs I had it all... I'd been married for 15 years and my husband and I both had good jobs. I've got two kids. But the drugs... they were what happened to me. I'd only been hooking for seven months, but I got arrested in December [1993] and it showed up in the paper. My ex-husband showed it to my kids... they've lost all respect for me now.

In Laura's case, her short career as a sex worker was launched by her need to sustain a drug habit and by the informal education she acquired during her time in the local bars. Laura did not receive the benefit of formal training. She had no active mentor who taught her the ropes of the occupation. Perhaps this accounts for Laura's short and unsuccessful stint as a sex worker, a career that lasted only seven months before she was arrested on prostitution charges.

The route Laura's life took after entering sex work is more than reminiscent of the occupational experiences recounted by other local prostitutes, regardless of where or exactly how they entered prostitution. All too often, the local prostitute finds herself trapped in the unending cycle of drug use and hooking, eventually turning tricks on the streets to feed the addiction. At this stage of the game she finds herself, regardless of age, race, or social class origin, caught in the proverbial Catch 22 – supporting a habit she learned in the life; trapped in the life to support her habit.

Girls Wanted: The Myth of Equal Opportunity Employment

INTERNATIONAL
Escorts – All Races. 24Hrs/7days. Credit cards. 326-1274.

EXECUTIVE/326-2708
Ladies Direct To You......HIRING.

MENDEVA
Fantasy rooms, models, dancers. Visa/MC. Now Hiring. 326-5940

OLDER WOMEN
Like fine wine get better w/age. 24/7. Credit cards. 323-9368

SUGAR'S DANCERS
Now Hiring! Private or Parties. 319/324-3710

Selected excerpts from "The Classifieds."
Quad City Times, June 23, 1997, 2M

Liza was 29 years old when I met her. At the time of the interview Liza had not turned a trick in two months, claiming the dangers associated with sex work were no longer worth the risk of being on the streets. Although she had entered sex work as an exotic dancer Liza, like many other local prostitutes, had turned to the streets of the Quad Cities in the later days of her career. Shortly after making it to the streets, Liza realized she was ill prepared for what the life now offered her. Like many others before her, Liza sought help from the one person able to teach her about life on the streets – the veteran who possessed the wisdom that comes from years in the occupation.

> one [teacher] is the mother, the mother whore. A lot of the people call her mom. She's, uh, she has to be at least 52 [years old] and

> she's been down there ever since I've been working the streets and
> that's been at least 12 years. Yeah, she knows the ropes all right ...
> she's really good people. (Debbie)

In downtown Davenport the "mother whore" commands the
respect of the other women working the streets. I first became
aware of the mother whore's presence and influence among the
street hookers through my conversations with Debbie, a 26-year-
old African American woman who has been involved in sex work
since the age of 14. The mother whore's status among the local
hookers became readily apparent as I observed the hustlers at
work on the Quad City streets.

One observational foray, unparalleled by any others, played
itself out on an October night in 1993 when I accompanied
Lt. George Owens of the Davenport Police Department on a three
hour ride-along. I soon realized the encounters I witnessed during
this particular excursion typified a night on the streets as the prostitute, johns, and police officer experience it. As I took advantage
of this and other opportunities to observe the prostitute at work
I came to appreciate sex work for what it is – a series of encounters, exchanges, and interactions among an often times unlikely
cast of diverse characters.

As I watched the hookers at work I was surprised by their
apparent ages. I had made my way to the streets expecting to see
young, attractive women working the turf. What I saw were primarily middle-aged women who appeared fatigued from their
nights on the street. I discovered the Quad City prostitute can be
any age, race, or from any social class background. And yet, in
spite of these differences, their experiences once in the life are
more similar than dissimilar.

The client pays the "market price" for whatever act he solicits,
although the fee varies according to the type of prostitute he seeks
and the personal attributes she brings to the exchange. The young,
white hooker is able to command a higher fee in all areas of the
Quad Cities than her African American or older counterpart. Debbie,
a 26-year-old African American, recalled her early days on the street
when her comparative youth, lighter than normal complexion, and
attractiveness brought top dollar on the streets of Davenport.

> Back then I was new to the block so everyone wanted me. I was
> doing 50 dollar dates in the car ... real quick things. And I would
> turn about 12 to 17 tricks a day. So, back then the money was

good ... I would make like anywhere from 50 dollars on up. These days it's more like 15 or 20 dollars for a blow job. If you're ugly you get a lot less than that.

There can be little doubt that Debbie perceives herself as a high priced hooker, making big money on the streets. And yet, her experiences and perceptions are quite different from those recounted by Liza, the 29-year-old who began her career as an exotic dancer. For the majority of her time in the business, Liza did not walk the streets. Rather, she concentrated on cultivating a cache of steadies, regular clients she established during her days as an exotic dancer. These were the men who were willing to pay a high price for Liza's services. They were also the same men Liza used to her advantage, learning very early in her career how to exploit the relationship with her steadies.

What I was doing ranged anywhere from a 100 to 500 [dollars] ... and sometimes I would lie and say I needed such and such ... things or whatever ... and I could do that. There were some I could call every other day and say I needed 800 dollars for this and whatever. And sometimes I wouldn't even have to have sex with them. That's why they called them steadies ... they're more like a boyfriend type thing.

Both Debbie and Liza came from lower-class backgrounds. Their common experiences prior to entering the life stand in direct contrast to what I know of Pam, the sex worker who came from middle-class roots and sold herself for next to nothing on the streets of Davenport. I am well acquainted with both Pam and her family, having lived next door to them for 15 years. I first became aware of Pam's occupational activities several years ago when her name and address appeared in the local newspaper following her arrest on prostitution charges. That knowledge did not prepare me, however, for the surprise I felt when I discovered Pam's photograph among the police records of women who had been arrested for prostitution. During our interview session Lt Owens described Pam and the circumstances surrounding her arrest.

Yeah, that's Pam all right. I remember the night I busted her. She was 17 at the time and I saw her down walking the row looking for somebody. I happened upon her ... I just saw her walking and I mean she made a deal in 15 seconds flat. She wanted to give me a blow job for ten dollars standing in the alley behind the bus station. She said she needed money for gas for her boyfriend's car so they could get back across the river. It's like, "You sleazy little bitch." Ten dollars to put gas in her boyfriend's car ... and he was sitting half a block away.

During my observations and interviews I gained insight into the attitudes the local police hold about their jobs and the women they encounter in their work. Lt Owens was more than generous in offering his views about the prostitute, her reasons for engaging in sex work, and his feelings about her chosen lifestyle.

Mostly it's the money they're after ... it's money that's unheard of anywhere else. I mean, even a black girl, an ugly black girl can get 20 dollars for ten minutes. And if she rotates guys ... let's just say three an hour, that's 60 dollars an hour. And, however many hours you want to work, it's there. You know for three hours you're clearing almost 200 dollars and it's tax free. Plus you've got your welfare check and anything else you're pulling in scheming ... it's a pretty lucrative racket. And the better looking you are the more money you can make. White girls are premium now. But, every woman has a value ... I guess that sounded pretty sexist. I look at them working the streets and if I can see them away from that street corner ... like at Vander Veer Park the next day with two kids ... that helps me accept why they're down there. I don't understand why they're down there after drugs. I used to give them all kinds of shit about taking 20 dollars and then giving some 65-year-old guy a blow job. I used to get graphic with them trying to give some shock value. But, it's like I said, if I see one on the street corner on Thursday night and then on Friday morning she's in the park with two kids at least you know there's a reason she was down there. Then there's people like Bobbie there, the big mouth of the group. She just pissed everybody off. You can tolerate some ... and some of them are even friendly and you can talk to them. But, she's just a different case. Then there's the ones you really can't understand. Like the one white girl who's down there working when she's nine months pregnant. We sent an ambulance down there to take her up to the hospital to deliver ... she was still working to the day she delivered.

Master of the House: The Myths of Autonomy and Self-Control

Unfortunately, policing seems to be part of the problem these days. How often do we really help? And that's not policing, Andy ... This is not about politics or power or merely rounding up offenders. Policing always has been and always must be about all of us getting along and helping each other. We're one body. (Charlotte, NC, Police Chief Judy Hammer in *Hornet's Nest* by Patricia Cornwell)

Although the nature of Quad City sex work has changed over the years and fewer women are working under the control of pimps, the male's presence has not disappeared from the prostitute's life. Nor has his control.

Contemporary feminist scholars have claimed the disadvantages and constraints found in most occupations reflect the patriarchal nature of the conventional labor market itself (Hartmann 1990; Reskin and Roos 1990). Within this context women have been disadvantaged by males who strive to promote their own self-interests by protecting the economic and social benefits they have historically enjoyed.

There is little doubt that female workers have realized many benefits as a result of the contemporary women's movement of the 1960's. However, it is also true that many women in the conventional labor market continue to be systematically constrained to gender-specific, second-class jobs that offer lower pay, less autonomy, and fewer benefits than traditional male occupations (Hartmann 1990; Reskin and Roos 1990; Bergmann 1986; Chamallas 1986; Smith 1983). The effects of this gender stratification are only intensified for the Black woman whose family is of lower class socio-economic standing.

Given the persistent inequities of the conventional labor market, it makes intuitive sense to assume that prostitution could well serve as an attractive labor form for many women in contemporary society. Sex work appears to be an occupational sphere in which women enjoy autonomy and freedom from male control. The sex worker is presumed to be in control of her occupational activities, decisions, and the income she receives as a result of her activities. Yet, the prostitute's reality is seldom one of autonomy and self-control. Rather, Quad City sex work is patriarchal in nature and the relationships formed within the world of prostitution tend to control, rather than emancipate, the female sex worker.

In many cases the boyfriend has replaced the traditional pimp. Although the boyfriend assumes a place of importance in the prostitute's personal life, he often acts as the sex worker's pimp while also sharing an intimate relationship with her. Even the more elite Quad City call girl is seldom able to remove herself from others' control, more often than not responding to the dictates of a male manager. Typically it is the manager, not the woman herself, who controls the sex worker's activities – supervising her schedule, managing her income, and, in the process, effectively denying her the right to make her own occupational choices and decisions.

The gendered nature of the sex worker's relationships extends well beyond those she encounters on a daily basis. It is obvious the local police officer and sex worker often become more than a little familiar with one another, with unique relationships developing as a result of this mutual familiarity. And it is this relationship that often works to the disadvantage of the female sex worker while benefiting the male agent of social control.

The male police officers I interviewed describe their jobs much like the lay person describes a game of cat-and-mouse. A night on the streets becomes a test of wits to see who will prevail. On any given night the goal for each of the players is success. Will the street hooker successfully walk home with the night's profits in hand or will the police officer return to the station to brag to his comrades about the number of busts he can record at the end of the night?

I asked Lt Owens about his job and the reasons he stayed in undercover work. Had he ever considered changing professions entirely or at least pursuing a different line of police work, one that did not involve the nightly expeditions and encounters that are a routine part of the vice cop's life? Lt Owens' response was short and to the point.

> Well, you see, I did this for eight years. Then I went out for two [years] and now I'm back. [I've been back] for about a year and a half. And, uh, there aren't a lot of new faces [on the street]. Did I leave because I wanted to or because the work disgusted me? No, I enjoy it. I do, I enjoy it. I mean, it's a macho kind of thing that I really enjoy.

The women I interviewed spoke disparagingly about the local cop and the role he plays in the sex worker's life. Yet, they also tend to assess the Illinois and Iowa officials quite differently. According to the women I met, the Illinois police treat the local hooker humanely, employing strategies and tactics considered to be fair and just. In contrast, the Iowa police are seen as using unethical tactics in their dealings with the local prostitute. Lynn talked candidly about her views of the local police and was especially expressive when discussing her opinions of the Davenport vice cops.

> I'm angry, really angry, at how the cops treat us. When you're a hooker you learn real early to ask a guy to show you his dick because a cop can't do that ... it's entrapment. But, in Davenport they'll do anything they want ... they do it so they can entrap you. They get their own kicks *and* they fill the city coffers. You know, they still don't know how to tax prostitution because it's illegal. So, the fines we have to pay when we are entrapped by a police officer becomes a form of taxation. Legalize it and you're going to get rid of all this other garbage.

Liza holds and expresses similar views about the local police and their tactics. But, Liza's concerns center around the treatment afforded the black prostitute by members of the criminal justice community. Liza clearly maintains the perception that a woman's race plays a significant role in determining the actual treatment she receives from social control agents, especially in the Iowa communities. In fact, according to Liza, differential treatment according to both race and gender are the rule rather than the exception.

> I think they're all just a lot of pompous assholes. And I think there's a lot of prejudice, especially in Iowa. In Iowa a white girl and a black girl can get the same charge and one goes up and the other doesn't. You see that all the time. And one gets work release while the other one goes to prison ... no matter what the past record was. This charge is my only prostitution charge, but the first time I got in trouble they told me they would give me a plea bargain. Okay, so as soon as I agreed to it they took it back ... they took it back and sent me to prison. Yeah, I think they're dirty ... they are, you know. I admit that you have to suffer the consequences for what you do, but God's going to take care of it all anyway. If they abuse their authority they're not going to get away with it because there's a higher authority than them.

It is apparent that many of the social relationships and arrangements established and maintained within the institution of sex work mirror the gendered nature of work women have historically encountered in the conventional labor market. Yet, precisely because women have made noteworthy strides within the conventional labor market, a major difference separates the sex worker from the more "traditional" female employee.

Within conventional occupations women are raising their voices to protest the differential treatment that has kept them in disadvantaged positions relative to men. The results have not always been positive. In fact, some have made the claim that women's heightened visibility and their demands for equitable treatment have resulted in a backlash effect that has produced less than desirable outcomes (see Faludi 1991). And yet, within the world of legitimate work, it is at least possible for women to speak out against the kinds of treatment and social arrangements that sustain and reinforce their inferior status. This is not the case for the woman who engages in sex work. Precisely because sex work is viewed as an illegitimate and illegal form of work, the prostitute often feels she has little recourse but to accept whatever treatment she receives from the outside audience.

Class Revisited

the essence of the higher class position is the expectation that one's decisions and actions can be consequential; the essence of lower class position is the belief that one is at the mercy of forces and people beyond one's control, often, beyond one's understanding. (Kohn 1969: 189)

In essence, the accounts I have presented here are the stories of women who have, through their occupational endeavors, attempted to gain control over their own lives. More often than not, the Quad City prostitute knows what it means to *be controlled* long before she knows what it means to be *in control*. Hers is, more often than not, a reality defined not by her own making, but by individuals and factors external to herself.

First, the Quad City prostitute is controlled by her market value, a price often determined by the hooker's race rather than by anything else. During the course of my research I was repeatedly told the white sex worker was more highly valued on the market than the African American prostitute. Similarly, racial differences appeared with regard to the prostitute's treatment by local law enforcement agents. The African American hooker is more likely than the white prostitute to be arrested. Once apprehended she is also more likely to receive harsher penalties than the white sex worker.

Second, the prostitute is disadvantaged by her gender. This appears especially true when considering the treatment she receives from local law enforcement officials, her manager, and even, at times, her significant other. According to prostitutes and police officers alike, the Quad City legal system is inherently biased in nature, enforcing legal mandates against the female sex worker while ignoring the male john although each has officially violated the law. Gender effects also appear when considering the manner in which male vice cops interact with and treat the female prostitute. More than a few of the police officers I interviewed during my time in the field displayed an almost total disregard for the humanity they encountered on the streets, choosing to disparage and demean the sex worker rather than treat her humanely.

Finally, the prostitute is controlled by economic forces as she finds herself assigned to a class status that is both uncompromising and unenviable. America has long embraced the notion that all are afforded equal treatment and respect in its eyes; in reality it recoils from its poor and marginalized. The sex worker knows all too well the feelings of being an outcast, marginalized by her poverty as well as by the unconventional nature of her occupation.

During the past decade important social movements emerging at a national level have endeavored to redefine prostitution as work, hoping these efforts would also change societal perceptions of the sex work trade and all it entails. In essence, these efforts have attempted to remind us all of a basic value that lies at our cultural core – the belief that all within US society have been granted the right to exercise individual control over our lives and employment decisions. While endeavoring to legitimate the prostitute's *work* these efforts have, in many cases, also introduced elements of respectability, self-worth, and self-control into her *life*.

Without a doubt, COYOTE (for a full discussion of COYOTE see Jenness 1993 and 1990) and other organizations of its ilk have been successful in changing the way in which many within US society view sex work and the women working within its ranks. Yet it can and must also be said that, at least according to appearances, these attempts have had the greatest impact on those working within the upper ranks of prostitution in major US cities. These organizations have, in reality, done little to change the lives of those walking the streets and working the trenches of Quad City prostitution. These women have, for all apparent purposes, been ignored by their sisters in sex work while also being maligned by those within conventional society. This reality compels anyone interested in the humanity of sex work to ask some demanding and pointed questions – questions with no easy answers. Yet these are the very questions that must be asked. With the answers to these questions comes the possibility for change – change directed at those in contact with, as well as directly involved in, the day-to-day activities of prostitution as it plays itself out in the Quad Cities and countless other cities across the United States.

Why have organizations like COYOTE failed to appear among and respond to the needs of those occupying the lower ranks of prostitution? Have the sisters working the trenches merely been left behind or have previous attempts to organize these women already proved fruitless? Would organizations like COYOTE help dissolve the barriers of race, class, and gender that advantage some while disadvantaging others in the world and work of prostitution? Would efforts aimed at bringing women together, even unionizing them if you will, fall well short in their attempts to change not only the face and nature of Quad City sex work, but also the way in which the local community perceives and responds to the local prostitute? If COYOTE and organizations like it are unable to change the prostitute's lived experience, then what might? What changes – whether they be individual, organizational, or societal in nature – would contribute to the likelihood that the Quad City prostitute will come to know what it means to live a fully human existence, one that carries with it the promise of self-control, self-respect, and social acceptance so crucial to all our lives?

> We've got to bring humanity back into what we do or there's no hope.
> (Charlotte, NC, Police Chief Judy Hammer in
> *Hornet's Nest* by Patricia Cornwell)

REFERENCES

Becker, H. S. 1963. *Outsiders*. New York, NY: The Free Press.

Behar, R. 1993. *Translated Woman: Crossing the Border with Esperanza's Story*. Boston, MA: Beacon Press.

Bergmann, B. R. 1986. *The Economic Emergence of Women*. New York, NY: Basic Books, Inc.

Bott, E. 1954. "The Concept of Class as a Reference Group." *Human Relations* 7(3): 259–86.

Bullough, V. and B. Bullough. 1987. *Women and Prostitution: A Social History*. Buffalo, NY: Prometheus Books.

Centers, R. 1949. *The Psychology of Social Classes: A Study of Class Consciousness*. Princeton, NJ: Princeton University Press.

Chamallas, M. 1986. "Women and Part-time Work: The Case for Pay Equity and Equal Access." *The North CarolingLaw Review* 64(4): 709–75.

Cornwell, P. 1996. *Hornet's Nest*. New York, NY: G. P. Putnam's Sons.

Davis, K. 1937. "The Sociology of Prostitution." *American Sociological Review* 2(5): 746–55.

Denzin, N. K. and Yvonna S. Lincoln. 1994. "Introduction: Entering the Field of Qualitative Research," in *Handbook of Qualitative Research*. N. K. Denzin and Yvonna S. Lincoln (eds). Thousand Oaks, CA: SAGE Publications, 1–17.

Faludi, S. 1991. *Backlash: The Undeclared War Against American Women*. New York, NY: Anchor Books.

Gilbert, D. and J. A. Kahl. 1993. *The American Class Structure: A New Synthesis*, 4th edn. Belmont, CA: Wadsworth Publishing Company.

Glaser, B. G. 1978. *Advances in the Methodology of Grounded Theory: Theoretical Sensitivity*. Mill Valley, CA: Sociology Press.

———. 1992. *Emergence vs. Forcing: Basics of Grounded Theory Analysis*. Mill Valley, CA: Sociology Press.

Glaser, B. G. and A. L. Strauss. 1967. *The Discovery of Grounded Theory: Strategies for Qualitative Research*. New York, NY: Aldine De Gruyter.

Gordon, D. A. 1995. "Border Work: Feminist Ethnography and the Dissemination of Literacy," in *Women Writing Culture*, Ruth Behar and Deborah A. Gordon (eds). Berkeley, CA: University of California Press.

Grusky, D. B. 1994. "The Contours of Social Stratification," in *Social Stratification: Class, Race, & Gender in Sociological Perspective*, D. Grusky (ed.), Boulder, CO: Westview Press.

Hartmann, H. I. 1990. "Capitalism, Patriarchy, and Job Segregation by Sex," in *Women, Class, and the Feminist Imagination*, K. V. Hansen and Ilene J. Philipson (eds). Philadelphia, PA: Temple University Press.

Heyl, B. S. 1979. "Prostitution – An Extreme Case of Sex Stratification," in *The Criminology of Deviant Women*, F. Adler and R. J. Simon (eds). Boston, MA: Houghton-Mifflin, 196–210.

Hoigard, C. and L. Finstad. 1986. *Backstreets: Prostitution, Money and Love*. University Park, PA: The Pennsylvania State University Press.

Humphreys, L. 1975. *Tearoom Trade: Impersonal Sex in Public Places*. Hawthorne, NY: Aldine de Gruyter.

Jenness, V. 1990. "From Sex as Sin to Sex as Work: COYOTE and the Reorganization of Prostitution as a Social Problem." *Social Problems* 37(3): 403–20.

———. 1993. *Making it Work: The Contemporary Prostitutes' Rights Movement and the Social Problem of Prostitution.* Hawthorne, NY: Aldine de Gruyter.

Kohn, M. L. 1969. *Class and Conformity: A Study in Values.* Homewood, IL: Dorsey Press.

Luckenbill, D. F. 1985. "Entering Male Prostitution." *Urban Life* 14(2): 131–53.

———. 1986. "Deviant Career Mobility: The Case of Male Prostitutes." *Social Problems* 33(4): 283–96.

Miller, E. M. 1986. *Street Woman.* Philadelphia, PA: Temple University Press.

Posner, R. A. 1992. *Sex and Reason.* Cambridge, MA: Harvard University Press.

Quad City Times. June 23, 1997, 3M.

Reskin, B. F. and P. A. Roos. 1990. *Job Queues, Gender Queues: Explaining Women's Inroads into Male Occupations.* Philadelphia, PA: Temple University Press.

Smith, V. 1983. "The Circular Trap: Women and Part-time Work." *Berkeley Journal of Sociology* 28: 1–17.

Svendsen, M. 1987. *Davenport: A Pictorial History.* G. Bradley Publishing, Inc.

US Census Bureau. June 1992a. *1990 Census of Population: General Population Characteristics Illinois.* Washington, DC: US Government Printing Office.

US Census Bureau. June 1992b. *1990 Census of Population: General Population Characteristics Iowa.* Washington, DC: US Government Printing Office.

Walkowitz, J. R. 1983. "Male Vice and Female Virtue: Feminism and the Politics of Prostitution in Nineteenth-Century Britain," in *Powers of Desire: The Politics of Sexuality.* A. Snitow, C. Tansell, and S. Thompson (eds). New York, NY: Monthly Review Press, 419–38.

8

Managing Everyday Racisms: The Anti-Racist Practices of White Mothers of African-Descent Children in Britain

France Winddance Twine

An analysis of the 1990 British census data reveals that "As many as half of British-born Caribbean men, and a third of women, had chosen a white partner and this may be an indication of the likely pattern for future generations... it is striking that, for two out of five children (39 percent) with a Caribbean mother or father, their other parent was white. As expected from the analysis of marriage, this was more often a black father and white mother than the other way around (Modood et al. 1997). These figures suggest that white mothers of children of African-Caribbean ancestry play a pivotal role in everyday anti-racism as parents. The ethnographic literature provides virtually no insights into how these mothers manage and respond to racism.

While motherhood has been a primary arena of theoretical innovation in feminist analyses of the family, little attention has been given to transracial motherhood. In an analysis of white women in interracial families, Carmen Luke (1994: 56) reminds feminist scholars that "Virtually no research exists on white women-mothers in interracial family formations, and there is a near total lack of research on women of color in relationships with white men." While US feminist scholars trained in English have begun to publish autobiographical explorations of their consciousness of racism such as recent works by feminist scholar-mothers Maureen Reddy (1995) and Jane Lazarre (1996), there has been little forthcoming from disciplines in the social sciences.

Stigmatized Motherhood and Stratified Reproduction

A nuanced analysis of contemporary racism and anti-racism must include the experiences of white parents of nonwhite children, particularly those of mothers located in multi-ethnic families. Transracial mothers, that is mothers who self-identify or are socially classified as members of a racial category that is presumed to be distinct from that of their birth children, can disrupt, hierarchies of inequality by challenging ideologies of white supremacy (and of racial differences). By exploring the everyday anti-racist strategies employed by white mothers negotiating the multiple forms of racism within and outside of their families, this study provides an analysis of motherhood that illuminates the complex intersections of racial, gender, and class subordination in contemporary Britain.

In her study of West Indian immigrant childcare workers providing childcare for US white upper class professionals living in New York, Shellee Colen employs the concept of *stratified reproduction*, which she defines as:

> Physical and social reproductive tasks are accomplished differentially according to inequalities that are based on hierarchies, class, race, ethnicity, gender, place in a global economy, and migration status and that are structured by social, economic and political forces. The reproductive labor – physical, mental, and emotional – and of bearing, raising, and socializing children and of creating and maintaining households and people is differentially experienced, valued, and rewarded according to inequalities of access to material and social resources in particular historical and cultural contexts. (Colen 1995: 78)

An analysis of how white mothers accomplish parenting in the context of stratified reproduction may illuminate the ways in which everyday anti-racism operates among women who may not be actively involved in more visible anti-racist political organizations.[1]

Research Methods and Sample

This paper draws on 80 focused life history interviews conducted between April of 1995 and August 1997 with working class and middle class white birth-mothers (and in some cases their black male partners) parenting African-descent children.[2] It is part of an ongoing feminist research project on transracial motherhood and anti-racism in the United Kingdom and the United States. I identified and recruited volunteers to participate in this study with the assistance of Julia O'Connell Davidson, a member of the faculty in the Sociology Department at the University of Leicester. Former students who had previously enrolled in Sociology courses provided the initial point of contact. Additional interviewees were recruited through snowball sampling in which the women interviewed directly contacted the white partners of their husbands' black friends and invited them to participate. No one contacted declined to be interviewed. All of the interviews were tape-recorded with the permission of the interviewee and took place in the homes or workplaces of the women interviewed. I followed an interview guide of topics that I explored with all of the women interviewed. Transcripts of the interviews were mailed to all of the participants for their comments and generated the questions for the second follow-up interview.[3]

Racial Betrayals and Bloodlines:
Minimizing Contact with White Grandparents

One anti-racist parenting strategy described by working class and middle class mothers interviewed involves their negotiation of the racism in their natal family. A frequent theme that emerged in discussions with white mothers is illustrated by the comments of Cassandra, the 45-year-old mother of three daughters. She was expelled from her home at the age of 16 within one hour of informing her parents that she was pregnant by a black man; she also socially isolates herself from whites, particularly her family of origin. She has lived in the same house on a council estate (the UK equivalent of public housing) for the past 20 years. In response to the question "How has your perspective changed as the mother of mixed-race children?," Cassandra describes why she made the decision to discontinue all social contact with her white parents.

When my youngest one was three, four...[1979] my [youngest] brother had grown up and met a white woman. And [my sister] was going through a divorce, but they subsequently married and, of course, the inevitable happened: they had children. They had a little girl, and this little girl was white, and it was overnight...It was as if my children didn't exist and [...] And we were at my brother's house, and he'd got his first child, and she must have been about six months old, and my daughter, Carrie, was tapping her grandmother, saying, "Grandma, I've learned a new song." "Yes, wait a minute. I'm feeding Emily," which was my brother's daughter. And she'd feed, you know, and Carrie was waiting patiently to sing this little song, and then it...As soon as she'd finish, she says, "Grandma, Grandma, I want to tell you this, sing this song." "Yes, yes, wait. I'm playing with Emily now." And it was almost as if I had a, a flash and I thought, "What are you doing here? You've been through all this. You've taken prejudice and, you know, been through so much turmoil in your life," and the one thing that I've always impressed upon my children is that color doesn't matter – it's who you are that matters...You know, saying to them, "Your color is irrelevant." We'd [raised them]...You know, reared them to understand these things and, yet, here were my own parents, who next to your mum and dad, you're supposed to look to your grandparents for support and love and acceptance. And they were being cut off. And I came home that night, and I made a very clear decision that night that was it: I would no longer allow my children to be subjected to racism from their own grandparents because that, that was what it was...And from that day [1979] to this, I've never seen my parents or my brother. My, my brother lives about ten minutes walk from here, and I have never seen them. I've never spoken to my parents [...] so I gave up a lot to have my children. I gave up an entire family. I gave up a way of life that I knew and went into something that was very alien to me, but I gave that up for this child that I was having, and so my three daughters actually mean the world...I couldn't let anybody do that to them because, to me my parents were doing them damage. So I cut myself off, and there's been no effort on either side for reconciliation.

In this excerpt we can see that once Cassandra perceived racism among her parents, who appeared to privilege their putatively "white" grandchildren in the family and neglect her children of African-Caribbean ancestry, she decided that she would not allow this to continue. To protect her children from racism from their white grandparents she cut off all contact with her family of origin. Other white mothers reported having to *threaten* to discontinue social contact with their parents and extended family to alter their parents racist behavior. Erica, a 33-year-old mother, who lives in a multiracial community in East London, describes her mother's family as "very racist." Her comments illustrates the measures that she took to minimize the racism that their children will face by their white grandparents. In the following excerpt Erica describes her conversations with her mother during her seventh month of pregnancy, after her mother exhibited disinterest in the arrival of her first grandchild.

> I remember I said to her, "Your attitude stinks. I always knew you were brought up in a racist family, but I thought you were bigger than that. But I can't change your attitudes. I just don't want to talk to you." And I think I either hung up or the conversation ended. And I was very, very upset. And it was very difficult because my mother had also said that her mother, my nanna, had said about "Oh, bloody niggers in the family." So [the racism] was coming from the whole of my mother's family really. And I was very upset, but I didn't know whether to talk to Alex about it or not. I didn't want to upset him, but anyhow he saw that I was upset when he came home. I did ... I've never to this day told him the whole of it. [What did you tell him?] I just said that mum was having problems with Phoebe being mixed-raced. And I wish then I hadn't told him because then he just went absolutely ape-shit. And, you know, "your bloody mother" and this. So in the end, I ended up with Alex not talking to my mum and hating my mother and her mother and my mother not willing to talk to Alex or accept the fact that I was pregnant. It was very, very difficult time ... I gave it a couple of weeks and then I phoned, I phoned my mother up. And, you know, she sort of started again, and I think I did probably what was the best thing looking back. I just, I just tried to stay calm, and I just ... explained what the situation was. I said to her "Look, Mum, Alex is Black. We're having a mixed-race baby, that's not going to change. I'm having the baby. Alex and I are staying together. We love each other. That's how it's going to be. I understand that you're getting pressures from different sides of the family or friends or whatever and that you're finding it difficult to accept and it's not going to happen overnight, but that's the situation as it is, and you've got a choice now. You either cut yourself off, off from me and your grandchild by your attitude or you try to come to terms with it and become included in the family."

As a Londoner living in the East End, Erica has access to a community of other white mothers in her age cohort, who are parenting young children of African descent. Consequently, feeling less dependent upon her natal family for support, as a member of a group of women connected through her African partners' friendship networks, she was able to constitute an alternative community where she was not stigmatized as a deviant mother.

Working class mothers living outside of London reported having more difficulty coping with the racism of their parents. They also reported having fewer social resources. In several cases women reported suffering from profound depression which led them to seek professional counseling. In her research on depression among mothers, the British sociologist, Ann Oakley, found several factors that predict postnatal depression among (presumably white) British women. A community survey in London of working class women found four vulnerability factors predictive of depression. Ann Oakley also found several factors that predict postnatal depression among presumably white British women:

> In my own study, the occurrence of depression was associated most strongly with four 'vulnerability factors': lack of a job outside the home, housing problems, a segregated role relationship with the baby's father and little previous experience of babies. In the presence of four vulnerability factors the depression rate was 100 per cent, falling to twenty per cent for those with one factor. (Oakley 1993: 87)

Neither Oakley nor the other surveys of British mothers considers race. These surveys seem to assume that the mothers and their children are not racially marked. Furthermore these studies don't address mothers who may not occupy the same racial category as their mother. In my interviews I found that a central predictor of depression was not the number of children that the mother had but whether her parents withheld support and affection for the grandchildren. In those cases where the mothers' parents actively participated in the caring of their grandchildren, regardless of whether they were described as "racist," women reported less depression and seemed to be more optimistic about their children's future. This was true even when the grandparents were described as "very racist." Thus if racism is expressed through the social ostracism of the grandchildren, this can cause even more anxiety for the mother.

Alliances with African and African-Caribbean Women

A second maternal strategy for managing racism and providing support for African-descent children who have been rejected by their white grandparents is to establish close alliances and friendships with African-Caribbean women and with the black extended family. The importance of social and cultural ties to Black British communities and the affirmation that white mothers receive from African-Caribbean women in particular, was a repeated theme in the narratives of these transracial mothers. These social ties are particularly crucial for those mothers who have been rejected by their parents and extended family. Friendships and caretaking alliances with black mothers enable white mothers to compensate for and counter the white supremacist ideologies of their natal family.

When asked to describe how they are preparing their children to cope with racism *working-class* white mothers reported establishing and maintaining long term relationships with black men and women. They framed this as a *conscious* decision to teach their children to learn to deal with racism as "blacks" in Britain. This can be illustrated by the comments of Monique, the single mother of a 6-year-old living in London. Like the other thirty-something mothers interviewed, who had grown up in the East End, she had established close ties and lifelong friendships with African-Caribbeans (Jamaican origin) as a child living on housing estates.

Monique describes her Jamaican-British male and female friends who are helping her to raise her daughter.

> I rely on my friends. [Which friends?] My black friends to give her that part. [Like whom?] Other women? so she has, you know, an understanding of what [West Indian food] is, and now as she gets older then I'll just try and teach her more through the help of my friends: you know, the history of black people ... so that she does have an[black] identity, and it isn't a question of her not wanting to be who she is. And wanting to be white. I don't want her going through where she feels she has to be white and, you know, scrubbing her skin ... And all that comes down to a lot of what she's going through. I'll try and explain to her that she's going to experience racism and she's going to experience stuff ... the sense of, a sense of identity, a sense of feeling comfortable, not estranged around black people, you know? Feeling okay about being with black people, and it's not alien to them, do you know what I mean? Because a lot of [mixed-race] children grow up like that.

Alicia, another Londoner, has a 16-month-old daughter who was fathered by an African doctor. After describing to me some of the differences between her attitudes about child rearing and those of her husband, she argues:

> Because I'm not black ... I can't possibly understand how it's going to feel to be called a black in a sort of insulting way which I'm sure will happen to her at some point. I guess the trouble with being white is that you don't know what it's like [to be targeted for racial violence] so it's never occurred to me. I'm in a white country. I'm not scared of the police.

Mona, a 51-year-old mother of four children who grew up in a rural working class community in the East Midlands during the late 1940s and 1950s, describes why her relationships with the US black armed services community in Britain has been so important to her. Describing her experiences as a young mother in the late 1950s and early 1960s she says:

> I was totally ignorant as to how to prepare my son for racism. There wasn't a black [movement] then. I must have been naive in those days. There was no information [about raising black children]. There was no discussion of [racism] so if you got a [mixed-race] child, you just got on with it.

The US black military community in Britain provided economic, social, and cultural support to Mona. She was integrated into a network that shielded her from some of the racism of her white rural working class neighbors.

All of the mothers interviewed acknowledged that their children would not be perceived as "white" or completely accepted by the white British community. Vivian, the 35-year-old mother of five children, describes why she needs her African-Caribbean friends:

> What I am afraid of is not being able to say the right things to comfort [my daughter]. I don't want to say things that are not going to mean anything to her, you now. But the thing is, you handle [racism] the way you think is best, but [it] isn't not always the right way. You're not always telling them the right thing, and that's what I'm basically afraid of because I can't know how she's feeling because I'm not mixed-race, you know.

Vivian considers her experiences as a *white* woman and her relationship to her black in-laws a daily reminder that she grew up in a *different* world and that motherhood has not magically conferred maternal competence upon her. Like other mothers interviewed, she feared what her whiteness would mean to her daughter later in life. Would it become a barrier? Middle-class women tended to report having few, if any black female friends but they often relied on their African or African-Caribbean mothers-in-law and/or sisters-in-law to provide their children, particularly their daughters, with the cultural information they believed that they themselves were not capable of providing. They expressed their ambivalence about their children becoming too "close" to the black side but all acknowledged that their children would not be seen or treated as white, but as either black or mixed-race.

Choosing Multiethnic Residential Lives: Shifting the Reference Group to Communities of Color

A third anti-racist parenting practice identified by working class women is the explicit rejection of white supremacist ideologies that promote residential segregation between white and nonwhite communities. The working class mothers interviewed typically expressed a strong preference for living in multiracial or black residential neighborhoods. They expressed feeling more comfortable in communities that contained a significant number of African-Caribbeans and/or South Asians (Bangladeshis, Pakistanis, East African Asians). They argued that as the parents of black children, they had more in common with "black" mothers and thus the whites with whom they had grown up no longer constituted their community of reference. Christina, the 33-year-old mother of a teenage daughter, describes an incident that illustrates this practice:

> [Being a mother of a black child] affected me a lot because I feel ostracized from [the white community], and I've ostracized myself from it. I've excluded myself and I have also been excluded by them because I can't sit in a pub or anything and listen to all the crap that they come out with. I can't. So there's a lot of white people that I feel that I have nothing in common with, only color, and color's not enough to bind us because I've got different experiences from [other white mothers of white children]...because I've got a black daughter.

One motivation for living in multiracial communities is to protect their children from the type of routine racial harassment that Patricia, the 51-year-old mother of five children, encountered in the 1950s. She describes herself as "the first woman to have a child for a black man in this city." Patricia who married a US black serviceman stationed in Britain after World War II reported being constantly harassed by her white neighbors, who defined her as morally suspect and unfit because of her marital relationship with a black man.

> If [blacks] came over to our house, [white neighbors] would phone the police up and say that we were having parties and we were dancing naked in the living room [laughter]. I mean the [neighbors] knew that these things weren't true. They phoned the Customs and Excise up and said that we were selling American booze and cigarettes. We were having a children's birthday party at the time. They really made our lives miserable ... there was a family that used to live across the street from us ... and they would, at every opportunity say [racist] things about my son. I can remember when he first started sitting outside in what we call prams (I don't know what you call them in these days) but he was sitting out. And the children would be coming home from school and they'd be saying "Oh, look the little *Wog*[4] is sitting outside in his pram ... And I was really furious. I really was. And went over to their house and I rang the doorbell. And the mother and father [of the children] came to the door. And I said, "I think you should talk to your daughter." I said, "You know she's just called my little boy a wog" and I said, "There's no need to be calling him that." So the father said, "Why, he is a wog." ... They took me to court. I was fined 10 shillings ... they bound me over for twelve months.

The incident that Patricia describes in the above reveals the degree to which she was harassed and ostracized by the white community. In a 1970 study of interracial families living in London, Susan Benson (1981: 76) argued that "it should be noted that it was the white woman, not the black partner, in these relationships who encountered social disapproval. Similarly it was only white women who reported hostility from neighbors."

I have described several of the coping strategies employed by white mothers to protect their children from the racism of the white community. I found that in contrast to the middle class mothers interviewed, working class mothers repeatedly compared their parenting practices to those of black mothers – their reference group, when evaluating their maternal competence. The working class mothers interviewed challenged and sometimes inverted white supremacist hierarchies by choosing the Black British community as their residential and cultural community of choice. They also looked to the Black British communities for their cultural models, coping strategies, and affirmation as mothers of African-descent children.

Conclusion: The Instability of White Supremacist Hierarchies

In the context of British nationalism whiteness has typically signified (for whites) superiority, normalcy, naturalness. The mothers currently living in a domestic partnership with African or African-Caribbean men all reported that their *maternal competence* had been called into question by African or African-Caribbean in-laws. Their *whiteness* symbolically signified cultural *inferiority*, although they were usually ranked by West Africans as culturally superior to West Indians. The women described being routinely humiliated by West African mothers-in-law who demanded control over the child rearing practices and household decisions affecting their children. Thus the women interviewed had to manage the multiple meanings of their whiteness. They learned to see themselves as culturally *inferior* from the perspective of African and/or African-Caribbeans who did not always privilege Anglo-British cultural traits and forms.

The theme of *English* inferiority was echoed by women from both working class and middle class origins as they described their struggle to learn to cook, wash clothes, and manage a household as a "Caribbean" or "African" woman would. White mothers argued that, in the eyes of their African and African-Caribbean in-laws, cultural traits defined as "Anglo-British" were defined as inferior to those of Africans and Caribbean. This constitutes a symbolic inversion of the national hierarchies. Vivian provides an illustration of how her domestic skills, as a white Anglo-British mother, are evaluated by her African-Caribbean family members.

> And it's as if I've had to prove myself worthy of being in their family. Because I do cook black food, and I do cook it very well, and

like they will even eat at my house now, whereas before they wouldn't even eat at my house because as far as they're concerned what do white people know about black people's food...my [mother-in-law] never thought I'd be able to cook for him like a black woman could. Or I think she'd thought I'd sort of take him away from his kind, from his black roots. He's become all Englishified, you know...Because a lot of [the] time it used to be said [by his family] "Well, you white people do things differently," and "You white people bring your children up differently from us," and "Why don't you white people breast feed your children?" And that's a lot of the things I used to get. And like for the first real seven years of our relationship it was pure hell, pure hell really.

We can see how Vivian was perceived as *culturally incompetent* as an Anglo-British. This sense of incompetence also affected her ability to parent, because she was perceived as not being able to teach her children to cope with racism. The theme of maternal incompetence emerged repeatedly, as the mothers described how their experiences as [white] children were different from those of their children. They had eaten different foods, had different cultural expectations regarding discipline. Vivian, like several other mothers, described learning to see herself as inferior and thus had to prove that she was worthy of being in a black family.

Another area of *maternal incompetence* described by white mothers parallels what I found in my US research (Twine et al. 1991). The grooming and care of their children's curly hair was seen as an area where white mothers were disadvantaged. This is of particular importance because if they are ostracized by their natal families because of their marriage to blacks, they are even more vulnerable and more dependent upon support and affirmation from their black in-laws. Ashley describes what she has had to learn as a *white* mother parenting black children and how she feels she is perceived by her black in-laws.

Well, the children's hair, that was another thing. With being white, you never sort of think that their hair is different from yours. With having mixed-race children...Like we [whites] just use shampoo, but you've got all these lotions that they need. Do you know? Jerry's sort of had to help me along with that, saying, "Well, you can't put that, you know into their hair because their scalp's different...He's sort of taught me in that way what's missing...But in conversations, when you talk about everyday things, about your washing and things, it's just things that come out that I think [my mother-in-law] feels that he, you know he could have married a black person at the time. Especially with the children, you know, with things like when they're playing, when they're doing games, and whatever [their black grandmother] likes to show her way of doing it and more or less saying that you know a black person would [be able] to show them how to do different things ... I just can't put it into words. But I just get this feeling that [my mother-in-law] would have preferred [my husband] to have married a black person.

For Patricia the mother of five children mentioned earlier, we can see how her whiteness is a source of anxiety for her. As the mother of African-descent children, she considers how the racism of her parents generates distance between her children and the white community. She has come to define whiteness as a source of shame because of its link to white supremacist ideologies.

> Well, it's not, not to be ashamed to have part of [a] white person in you because like I said, they see themselves more as black because ... but not to be ashamed, you have got some white person in you ... Because [white racism] is what they've seen ... [their white-grandparents] don't associate with blacks ... And I don't want them to feel that because I'm white that [racist] thoughts are going through my mind and I'm their mother [...] I get upset some-times because I feel like. I'm yea, I'm white. I'm not very happy with the way things have served them ... like from my family, and I'm not very happy about the things I can't change, but I wouldn't like them to see me the same way [as racist]. I wouldn't like them to see all, all white people the same sort of way, you know, as my family's been with them.
>
> TWINE: Are you afraid of being rejected in some way by them?
>
> Definitely.

From this excerpt we can see how Patricia has to bear the shame of being a member of a white racist family and of her inability to change her family.

Conclusion

This chapter explores a dilemma that has received little attention from feminist scholars interested in family studies: the burden of white racism for white birth-mothers of African-descent children. My research suggests that transracial mothers bear their whiteness differently from the white mothers of white children, since their cultural experiences as Anglo-British women have not typically prepared them to cope effectively with anti-black racism. Furthermore, for those mothers who see *black* mothers, rather than white mothers as their reference group, their *competence* as mothers is contingent upon their ability to protect and prepare their children to cope with racism.

A nuanced understanding and theoretically useful account of contemporary racism must consider the experiences of white women located in multiracial families. Transracial motherhood and multiracial families are sites where understandings of racism and anti-racism are articulated. If African-descent children are to be prepared to cope with racism, then more information is needed of how white mothers defend their nonwhite children and families from the racism in their own communities.

NOTES

1 I am employing the term "African-descent children," not because I am privileging the "male" heritage of the children of the white mothers interviewed, but rather because I recognize that race is socially constructed. The mothers interviewed are parenting children of multiracial heritage whom they argued, will be classified as "black" by non-black British society and, as in the United States, this reflects a construction of race that relegates multiracial children of any known African ancestry to the "black" socioracial category.

2 All interviews were conducted by the author.

3 The women interviewed included birth mothers who self-identified as white and had raised their children. Their civil status and domestic arrangements included: (1) never married; (2) married and living with the father of her children; (2) not married and living in domestic partnership with the father of some or all of her children; (3) divorced or legally separated and living with no domestic partner; (4) living with men other than the father of their children. None of the women interviewed self-identified as bisexual, lesbian or transgendered and none reported having female domestic partners. The women interviewed had origins in several countries including Germany, Ireland, Scotland, Poland, and England. The interviews ranged from two to four hours.

4 This was considered a very derogatory term which was coined during the war. She defined it as the equivalent of the US term "nigger." British soldiers who went abroad used it, but it originally stood for Western Oriental Gentleman.

REFERENCES

Benson, Susan. 1981. *Ambiguous Ethnicity: Interracial Families in London.* Cambridge/London: Cambridge University Press.

Cashmore, Ellis, and McLaughlin, Eugene (eds). 1991. *Out of Order?: Policing Black People.* New York, NY/London: Routledge.

Colen, Shellee. 1995. " 'Like a Mother to Them': Stratified Reproduction and West Indian Childcare Workers and Employers in New York," in *Conceiving the New World Order: The Global Politics of Reproduction.* Faye Ginsburg and Rayna Rapp. (eds). Los Angeles/Berkeley: University of California Press.

Collins, Patricia Hill. 1994. "Shifting the Center: Race, Class and Feminist Theorizing About Motherhood," in *Mothering: Ideology, Experience and Agency.* Evelyn Nakano Glenn, Grace Chang, and Linda Rennie Forcey (eds). New York, NY/London: Routledge.

Essed, Philomena. 1991. *Understanding Everyday Racism: An Interdisciplinary Theory.* London: Sage Publications.

Felstein, Ruth. 1994. "I Wanted the Whole World to See: Race, Gender and Constructions of Motherhood in the Death of Emmett Till," in *Not June Cleaver: Women and Gender in Postwar America, 1945–1960.* Joanne Meyerwitz (ed.). Philadelphia, PA: Temple University Press.

Frankenberg, Ruth. 1993. *White Women, Race Matters: The Social Construction of Whiteness.* Minneapolis, MN: University of Minnesota Press.

Gilroy, Paul. 1987. *"There Ain't No Black in the Union Jack": The Cultural Politics of Race and Nation.* Chicago, IL.: University of Chicago Press.

Ginsburg, Faye and Rapp, Rayna. 1995. *Conceiving the New World Order: The Global Politics of Reproduction.* Berkeley/Los Angeles, CA: University of California Press.

Hatched, Carol. 1988. *The Interracial Maternal Experience.* PhD dissertation. Union for Experimenting Colleges and Universities, Cincinnati, OH.

Kunzel, Regina. 1994. "White Neurosis, Black Pathology: Constructing Out-of-Wedlock Pregnancy in the Wartime and Postwar United States," in *Not June Cleaver: Women and Gender in PostWar America, 1945–1960.* Joanne Meyerowitz (ed.). Philadelphia, PA: Temple University Press, 304–34.

Lazarre, Jane. 1996. *Beyond the Whiteness of Whiteness: Memoir of a White Mother of Black Sons.* Durham, NC: Duke University Press.

Luke, Carmen. 1994. "White Women in Interracial Families: Reflections on Hybridization, Feminine Identities, and Racialized Othering." *Feminist Issues* 14(2): 49–72.

Modood, Tariq, Berthoud, Richard et al. 1997. *Diversity and Disadvantage: Ethnic Minorites in Britain.* London: Policy Studies Institute.

Oakley, Ann. 1993. *Essays on Women, Medicine and Health*. Edinburgh: Edinburgh University Press.

Reddy, Maureen T. 1994. *Crossing the Color Line: Race, Parenting, and Culture*. New Brunswick, NJ: Rutgers University Press.

Solinger, Rickie. 1992. *Wake Up Little Susie: Single Pregnancy and Race Before Roe v. Wade*. New York, NY/London: Routledge.

Solomos, John. 1993. *Race and Racism in Britain*, 2nd edn. New York, NY: St. Martins Press.

Tizard, Barbara and Phoenix, Ann. 1993. *Black, White or Mixed Race?: Race and Racism in the Lives of Young People of Mixed Parentage*. New York, NY/London: Routledge.

Twine, France Winddance, Jonathan W. Warren, and F. Ferrandiz. 1991. *Just Black?: Multilracial Identity*. New York, NY: Filmmakers Library.

9

Frontlines and Borders: Identity Thresholds for Latinas and Arab American Women[1]

Laura M. Lopez and Frances S. Hasso

Introduction

I would like to say that I longed not to be defined by the gaze of the other, but to look out upon the world through eyes rooted in the boundaries of my own identity. But it is true that for much of my life I thought if I looked long enough I would find someone to tell me who I am. Turning to the world for some reflection of myself, however, I found only distortion. (Majaj 1994: 67)

This essay compares the ways in which Latina and Arab American women students experienced their racial-ethnic and gender identities at "home" and in a university environment.[2] These women's experiences have for the most part been excluded by a black/white dichotomy that is especially dominant in the sociological literatures on race and gender. Comparing the experiences of these two pan-national, racially diverse groups enriches this literature by exploring how multiple sites of difference (race, class, national, cultural, and sexual) interact with systems of domination, and how these interactions, in turn, affect identity construction. Literally and figuratively, dominance and resistance are not black/white issues. Without undercutting the power of material and discursive anti-African American racism, this dichotomy limits analysis of racism against African Americans, excludes other racialized experiences, inhibits comparison across racialized groups, and, perhaps most importantly from our perspective, restricts the possibilities for alliances across racial-ethnic groups for the purpose of making social change.

While racial-ethnic identities in racist societies are defined and constructed by subordinate groups in a context of exclusion and misrepresentation, the process can also be empowering for minorities. In the educational system in particular, power relations are contradictory, producing

> not only oppression but its opposition – and opposition, in turn, avails itself of power's blind spots and loopholes. The educational system's greater or lesser discriminatory and dehumanizing constructions of the "third world"-origin minority "identity" elicit the minority subject's destabilization of dominant ideology's logic, while oppression and discrimination in turn create the oppressed's desire for empowerment, equality, and justice. (Pérez 1993: 269).

In response to racism and the configuration of racial-ethnic identities, both the Arab American women and Latinas interviewed found the university to be an identity threshold – a place where racial-ethnic identity was reconfigured. Both groups of women were excluded and misrepresented in a variety of ways. As underrepresented minorities, the Latinas contended with a myriad of messages that they were unqualified to be university students *because* of their racial-ethnic backgrounds. This was compounded by a dichotomized racial-ethnic discourse that often excluded their experiences as Latinas. The Arab American women grew up in a popular culture that almost uniformly denigrated their Arab and/or Muslim backgrounds, and live in a social environment in which political discourse about the Middle East is generally both uninformed and highly charged. For the Arab Americans, political conflicts related to the Middle East played out on campus in ways that created identity "frontlines."

Whereas racial-ethnic identities were emphasized in the university, both groups of women focused on issues of authenticity when discussing their "homes" – family, community, or nation. Language-knowledge, class mobility, and obedience to racial-ethnic gender and sexual norms affected whether the women felt and/or were treated as "authentic" community members. In addition, both groups discussed physical appearance (skin color, hair texture, and body size) as a focus of discipline and control within and outside their communities. Rather than being mutually exclusive categories, "home" and university experiences interactively defined racial-ethnic and gender identities; at the same time, different identity issues were stressed in the two settings.

Method and Representation

The findings in this report stem from a joint fieldwork project undertaken in the 1993–4 academic year during a graduate qualitative research methods course at the University of Michigan, Ann Arbor. Using the same interview guide, Frances Hasso conducted one- to two-hour semi-structured interviews with eight Arab American women students, and Laura Lopez did the same with eight Latinas; the groups were evenly split between undergraduate and graduate students.[3] Together we conducted two group interviews that included both Arab Americans and Latinas, one of which was designed to share information and get feedback on preliminary analysis.

The eight Arab American women interviewed had parents originally from Egypt, Palestine, Lebanon, Morocco, and combinations of these countries; three of the women had Euro-American mothers, and one (Mona) had a Euro-American father. Seven of the Arab Americans were born in the US and one (Suha) was naturalized as an infant. Three of the women identified as Muslim and five as Christian (although only one in each category was practicing). None of the Arab American women's parents were divorced, although one (Hana) had parents who were separated.

The call for interviews with Latinas drew only Chicanas and Puerto Rican women. Of the four women who identified as being of Puerto Rican descent, three were born and raised in New York and one grew up in Puerto Rico. The birth mother of one Puerto Rican woman (Linda) was of Euro-American descent (her stepmother, however, was Puerto Rican), and the birth father of another Puerto Rican woman (Margaret) was Asian (although she was raised solely by her single mother). The remaining four Latinas were Chicanas/Mexican Americans from Texas and California, one of whom was born in Mexico and naturalized in the US soon thereafter. One Latina gave no religious identification, and the remainder identified as Catholics (five practicing and two non-practicing). Five of the eight Latinas grew up with both birth parents (although not all fathers were consistently present or financially supportive); two had spent their childhoods partly with divorced mothers and partly in blended families; and one was raised by a single mother.

Five of the eight Latinas were from poor or working-class backgrounds. Additionally, one Puerto Rican said she was "low to middle class" (Linda), a Chicana said she was "middle-class" (Emma), and the Puerto Rican from the island said she was "high middle-class" (Lisa). Both parents of two Puerto Rican women (Linda and Lisa) had bachelor degrees (one had an MA); the single mother of another Puerto Rican woman (Margaret) had earned a BA as an adult; and the father of one Chicana (Emma) had attended two years of college after earning a graduate equivalency diploma. The remaining four Latinas came from families in which neither parents nor siblings had ever attended college. Moreover, three of these women came from households in which neither parent had graduated from high school.

In contrast, all eight Arab American women had at least one college-educated parent (and usually both were college-educated). Seven out of the eight (Jamila is the exception) had at least one parent (and usually both) who had an advanced academic or professional degree. With the exception of one middle-class woman (Hana), all the remaining women came from upper middle-class backgrounds. While some of the women had spent parts of their childhoods living in the Arab world, when they lived in the US seven of the eight had grown up in mostly white, upper middle-class neighborhoods and went to schools (public and private) with similar characteristics. While they did not live in Arab neighborhoods, the parents of four women were involved in religious, professional, cultural, and/or political activities in Arab American communities.

It was not possible to compare the socio-economic indicators of the women interviewed with those of other Arab American and Latina/o students at the University of Michigan because of the absence of such data, including a complete lack of any information on Arab Americans as a group. According to university data, during the 1992–3 academic year, approximately 4.1 percent of the student body (undergraduate and graduate) were "Hispanic/ Latino"; included in this category are persons of "Mexican, Puerto Rican, Cuban, Central or South American, or other Spanish culture or origin, regardless of race..." (University of Michigan, June 1993: 35).[4] During the 1992–3 academic year, approximately 76 percent of graduate and undergraduate students were categorized as "white," 8.4 percent as Asian American, 7.9 percent as African American, and 0.65 as Native American (University of Michigan, June 1993: 39, 41).

In this study, we are looking at "segments within segments" of communities intersected by a number of axes of difference, not least of which is that both "Arab American" and "Latina/o" are constructs that include different national, class, and religious backgrounds. In addition, while there are class differences among Arab Americans, US Census Bureau data indicate that they are significantly better off as a group than either Mexican Americans or Puerto Ricans, whose poor class standing has been connected to a long history of US colonization and exploitation of these two groups (Montejano 1987; Moore and Pachon 1993; Munóz, Jr 1989; Rodriguez 1989).[5] While there are many voices (e.g., men, working-class Arab American women, and upper middle-class Latinas) not represented in this study, those who are provide insights with respect to both racial-ethnic groups. Instead of emphasizing the representativeness of the women interviewed, we would prefer to stress the dynamic and context-specific nature of identity and identity formation, in keeping with the goal of "partial, locatable, critical knowledges sustaining the possibility of webs of connections" (Behdad 1993: 45, citing D. Haraway).

Renato Rosaldo (1989) and others have argued that knowledge and theorizing occurs relationally and is always a subjective process involving the researcher and the researched. Our own subjectivities and experiences as an Arab American woman and a Chicana provided critical insights throughout this research project. We undertook the project as two women of color for whom racism has been a tangible part of growing up in the United States and our university experiences. As members of these respective communities, we also had expectations about the types of issues that would resonate with the women we interviewed. At the same time, we approached the project from an inductive perspective, being careful to remain open to differences of subjectivity and experience. Indeed, while our social and class locations and experiences were sometimes similar to those of the women interviewed, they were also different in many respects. Like Laura, three of the Latinas interviewed had been primarily raised by a single or divorced mother and a number of them had struggled economically growing up. Unlike Frances, none of the Arab American women came from working-class backgrounds.

Oppositionality and Identity

According to Chela Sandoval, "oppositional consciousness" is an ideological strategy for subordinated persons confronting domination. It refers to

> the capacity to re-center depending upon the kinds of oppression to be confronted … [and it also] depends upon the ability to read the current situation of power and self-consciously choosing and adopting the ideological form best suited to push against its configurations, a survival skill well-known to oppressed peoples. (Sandoval 1991: 14–15)

This type of consciousness allows "weav[ing] 'between and among' oppositional ideologies," much like the clutch of an automobile allows a driver to "select, engage, and disengage gears in a system for the transmission of power" (Sandoval 1991: 14).

For the Latinas and Arab Americans interviewed, identity was redefined in opposition to the racialized narratives operative on campus. That is, while race, class, and gender identities were bound together, because racial-ethnic identities were emphasized by the dominant culture, they were usually the most salient in the university; gender was not irrelevant, but *less* relevant than racial-ethnic identity. Exclusion and misrepresentation in this setting contributed to a more definitive sense of "Arabness" or "Latinaness," and the women often relayed identity "coming out" stories. It is not that racial-ethnic identity did not exist as an affirming process, but that oppositionality *on campus* redefined it.

Oppositionality operated in different ways for the Arab American women and Latinas. The Latinas redefined their identities in opposition to the university's predominantly white environment, white racism, and a Eurocentric curriculum; they were told that they were "unqualified" and did not "belong" in a myriad of ways in this setting. On another level, however, their experiences were also shaped by tension and exclusion by students of color who had limited definitions of race. For the Arab American women, oppositionality was very much related to the way international events played out on college campuses. The Middle East's political-economic importance, its real frontlines of war and political crises, its ubiquity in the news, and the treatment of such issues in classrooms created "frontlines" in the university that compelled women to make identity decisions.

The "Forced Alienation" of Latinas

[P]eople talk about assimilation in one voice and alienation in another voice and I don't think that they're that separate – not in my life – they're not. If you could take anything from, you know, what I just splurted out, it would be that, that my life has been one of confused assimilation and forced alienation. (Linda)

Upon their entrance to the university, most of the Latinas interviewed found themselves relocated from racially diverse or predominantly Latino/a neighborhoods to a largely white educational institution and city. Latino/a students' relatively low representation at the university defined and exacerbated their sense of oppositionality. One Chicana (Emma) characterized this low representation by saying, "it was a long time before I found another Mexican." A Puerto Rican woman (Janie), who had described the university and surrounding community as "too white-bread," said it took her a long time to find other people of color on campus.

Further, most of the Latinas interviewed left communities where their cultural events, music, and food were more readily accessible and came to study at a university that lacked many of the cultural comforts of "home." As Emma put it, "there's nothing here of what I am used to ... like food, music, you know all these ... I had to bring everything from back home to even have just a little bit."

Teresa, another Chicana observed:

It took me a while to figure out that they didn't have any Spanish radio stations ... or TV stations [at that time] and it took me probably three months to figure out that the tortillas were in the frozen section ... and the minute I opened the package I knew I wasn't going to like them. So that was really depressing.

Their sense of oppositionality to the dominant culture at the university was exacerbated by discriminatory encounters with white students and professors, and an academic discourse and environment that excluded their experiences. Margaret, a Puerto Rican/Chinese American student, related the following:

I've almost always had white professors – white male professors ... here at the university ... I don't know, I have always wondered about that because I go into the classroom and I never felt very comfortable talking to the professor ... and I'm sure a lot of it is just me, but I wonder why it is that some of these other people feel so comfortable doing that, feel so comfortable being ... loud or being whatever kind of way in class, which I wouldn't do because ... maybe because it would attract too much attention, I don't know ... [I] can't really be myself or feel comfortable enough to ask questions in the middle of class. I know that the one time when I did have a Black professor here in one of my hard sciences courses ... I felt so comfortable – even though I rarely talked to the professor at all – but just walking in there, sitting down, I loved going to class because he was Black and I felt like "wow, somebody at least I feel like I can identify with," you know, who might at least be able to identify with me a little bit better.

Janie, also Puerto Rican, discussed feeling "out of place in school":

I was probably the only Latina ... in all of my classes, which was really sad. And I think being from out-of-state, and being Puerto Rican, and being lower-class, I think everything was just very diffi- cult. So when I got here I felt really alienated. I had a tough time with the politics of being in graduate school. I did not get along with my advisor ... I just had a hard time.

A Chicana student encountered racist remarks on two different occasions at the beginning of her tenure in a PhD program. First, a white male literature professor criticized this US-born and edu- cated woman (Anne) for her command of the English language, and she was within earshot on another occasion when another white male professor remarked that the students of color from her entering cohort "were just a joke." Linda, a Puerto Rican/Euro- American student, similarly noted:

I was insulted, I was stepped on, I was criticized, I was questioned [by white students and professors] ... to the point that, even if I thought that they were nice people or they had some particular personality characteristic that I might have wanted to hang out with, it was impossible for me to do that and maintain a sense of self-worth ... When people found out that I had minority fellow- ships, I was no longer a smart kid. You know, it wasn't the kind of research experience I had, it wasn't the college I went to, the classes I had, or the things that I said in class. It was that she's this minor- ity, she has this fellowship ... .

Feeling marginalized, the Latinas sought out other Latina/o students in social and political groups, and the few Latina/o professors on campus for mentorship. They attempted to build cultural spaces and small communities in opposition to an alienating academic community, which further contributed to a sense of "Latina-ness" or "woman of colorness," versus "them" or "whiteness." Some of the lighter-skinned Latinas even reacted negatively to being "mistaken for" or labeled as "white" by whites or other students of color in the university whose race thinking worked from only black/white scripts. Teresa, a light-skinned Chicana, relayed the following story about her first summer at the university:

> I guess, again, coming from California it was OK to mix different groups and nobody ever had any problems with it, you know, and people knew who you were or at least they had been exposed to more groups than just blacks and whites. And when I got here this summer I went to a party and one of the black guys that was there said "Who brought that white bitch?" and who they were talking about was me and I overheard that so it was sort of like "well, do I cuss this motherfucker out...?"

Significantly, her angry response was not because she had been called "bitch" by another man (i.e., he was offending her as a woman), but because she had been called a "*white* bitch" by an African American.

Thus, as a result of racialized-cultural opposition from whites (and sometimes, African Americans), and the lack of the cultural comforts of home, "Latina" became a critical part of these women's identities in the university. Emma summarized this feeling when she said "I've become more conscientious about it [being Latina]...because who thinks about it when you're all the same? ... Being up here makes me more aware and more proud of who I am." In addition to increasingly associating predominantly or even exclusively with other Latinas/os, these Latinas also learned or brushed up on Spanish language skills as necessary, and all but one (a student in the physical sciences) focused on Latino/a issues in their studies.

Arab American "Frontlines"

[Misconceptions about the Middle East on campus] really stir feelings of rage and frustration [in me] and it's like an actual emotion rather than knowledge. And I think, how did it happen to me? What did my parents do to make me so wrapped up in it? ... And my parents never – I almost wish they had – but they never sat me down and said: "This is the history of your [Palestinian] family. First they killed so and so." It just came out gradually, these things that happened, sad things and terrible things, but never explicitly. (Mona)

The racialized campus experiences of the Arab American women differed from those of the Latinas. They did not confront the dislocation experienced by the Latinas interviewed, largely because most of them came from upper middle-class backgrounds, lived in predominantly white neighborhoods, and attended schools with similar characteristics. Even as they remained "Arab" within their homes, as children, most of the Arab American women had assimilated in public contexts as much as they were allowed to until they became university students – avoiding "role conflict" by becoming "Americans by day and [Arabs] by night" (Swanson 1996: 244). When they reached the university, however, almost all were compelled to make identity decisions about their "Arabness" – whether or not to "come out," so to speak – largely in response to the way Middle East-related events played out on campuses.

These international events are highly politically charged and for the most part (mis)represented in both the media (Said 1981; Shaheen 1984; Shaheen 1993) and school and university classrooms. Recent examples include the 1990–1 Gulf War, the 1994 World Trade Center bombing, and the ongoing Arab–Israeli conflict. In university classroom situations, the Arab American women had to either disregard misrepresentations or racist characterizations of Arabs, Muslims, Islam, or Arab culture, or publicly confront their professors, teaching assistants, or fellow students. "Taking a stand" exposed their Arab American identities (if others did not already know), and often subjected them to being labelled a number of things that are assumed by the dominant culture to be inherently Arab or Muslim: "terroristic," anti-Semitic, violent, and unreasonably angry. As a result, confusion and silence were common responses to such misrepresentations.

(Mis)perceptions of the Arab–Israeli conflict in particular were often provocative for the Arab American women. One Palestinian/Euro-American graduate student remembered the following conversation with a white male housemate soon after arriving in Ann Arbor:

> He was seeing a Jewish girlfriend and he just found out I was Palestinian and he said, "well, that puts me in an awkward position. ... I'm going out with a Jewish girlfriend, and you being Palestinian." I said, "Yeah, but I mean we're adults here. Why does that make a difference?" [she laughs slightly] ... And do you know what he said to me? He said, "If you ever did anything to hurt this girl, I will come after you and blow your head off." This is *a week* after I lived with this guy. And I was stuck with him for a whole four months. Can you believe that? (Katy)

This woman, whose hair is blondish and skin light-colored, told few others in her professional program that she is Palestinian American after this incident.

Another Palestinian/Euro-American graduate student discussed her ambivalent silence in classrooms at her "very Ivy League" undergraduate institution:

> I mean, I didn't feel comfortable saying my opinions [about the Middle East] in class or in really any setting, except with close friends, and even then it would be a little hard. I have a lot of Jewish friends and stuff who have an amazing blind spot when it comes to certain things. But definitely not in classes; I would not give my opinion; I always was restraining myself and saying I have to be diplomatic, I have to be understanding, I have to remember this, this, and the other thing, so I never actually brought it to a head by doing something. So, I just avoided it, but I knew I was consciously avoiding something, because I felt that it would cause trouble, but I can't prove that it would because I didn't. I had friends who told me about other incidents and it just scared me and I wasn't up to dealing with it ... . (Mona)

Many women, including this Egyptian American undergraduate, remembered the 1990–1 Gulf War as making life particularly difficult for Arab Americans: "It was difficult because I have a lot of friends who are Jewish ... And so, you know, it was – it was difficult ... I was against the war and I didn't – I felt that most people were really just supporting the war out of blind patriotism and nothing else" (Amy). A Moroccan/Euro-American graduate student who had been politically active during the Gulf War described how she was accused at various points of being unpatriotic, un-American, and anti-Semitic: "I got obscene and pornographic hate mail, threatening me with rape...My classmates spread a rumor...that I had given up my American citizenship" (Hana). Anti-Muslim sentiment was at such heights during the Gulf War, that for the first time she began identifying herself as a *Muslim* Arab American: "I wanted to set myself as much apart [as possible] from this culture and in line with that culture...and I thought that was one way to do it" (Hana).

While these incidents were frightening and alienating for the Arab American women, they also galvanized most of them to study the political debates into which they were inextricably pulled, and to be prepared for intellectual confrontations. All except one (Katy) of the Arab American women interviewed became politically active, took courses on the Arab-Israeli and other regional conflicts, studied the Arab countries from which they originated, and/or focused their studies on the Arab world during college. A Lebanese American woman discussed the effects of a course she took on the Arab-Israeli conflict:

> I became stronger with my identity as an Arab and a Lebanese... Why I did, I'm not sure...[When she was one of the few women and only Arab American to publicly disagree with the professor's and other students' analysis in a class of over 100 students] I don't know how to explain it, but I know I felt cornered [in class]. It's not because I'm anti-Jewish, but I am against what the Israeli government does. I'm against what the US does. Do you know what I'm saying? Um, so I identified more and more and that's where my Arab identity came into larger play. (Jamila)

Similar to the Latinas' responses to racism and exclusion on campus, all but one of the Arab American women learned or relearned Arabic, interrogated their families about their own histories, travelled to the Arab world, and/or socialized with other Arab Americans and Arabs. While many of the women became more comfortable with their "Arab-ness," most could not ignore the intertwining of oppositionality and identity. As one activist noted in relation to being attacked at the university for her political positions: "Isn't it funny how that [people attacking you] makes you feel more Arab, too?...it's sort of like opposition defines you" (Michelle). While oppositionality generally strengthened racial-ethnic identity, for three of the Arab American women (two of whom were bi-racial), "coming out" was a personal, not public, process. As indicated by their narratives, some of these women remained afraid of the reputational and professional consequences of confronting racism and stressing their racial-ethnic identities in the university. In addition, as they became more aware of their histories and backgrounds, the cultural dilemmas became more stark for most of the women, who found themselves in situations where they felt neither "Arab" nor "American," in practice redefining both identities.

"Bordered" Racial/Gender Identities

In the remainder of the paper, we address racial/gender identities by looking at physical appearance, language knowledge, class mobility, and sexuality. These issues were most (but not exclusively) relevant in "home" spaces, and were often tied to whether women were treated as "authentic" community members. Physical appearance, language knowledge, class mobility, and obedience to cultural rules of behavior about gender and sexuality were important both to how others identified the Latinas and Arab American women and how they self-identified. These were interdependent processes: identity was socially constructed in relation to how others defined them.

The concept of "home" has been discussed by a number of feminist scholars (Martin and Mohanty 1986; Pratt 1984). Martin and Mohanty argue that some feminist scholars' "pursuit of safe places and ever-narrower conceptions of community relies on unexamined notions of home, family, and nation, and severely limits the scope of the feminist inquiry and struggle" (1986: 191–2). Even though most needed "home" for comfort, security, and sustenance, the women interviewed problematized these locations as sites of restrictive sexual norms and essentialized definitions of the "authentic" Latina or Arab woman.

The "borders" metaphor captures the conflicts and contradictions that arose for the Latinas and Arab American women as they negotiated within limiting definitions of identity. Over the past decade, the metaphor has characterized the experiences and geopolitical spaces of Latinas/os as a colonized people: they are products of interaction and exchange between different cultures, races, and nations with often diametrically opposed ideologies and cultural practices (Anzaldua 1987; Saldivar-Hull 1991).

Borders, therefore, divide two or more different states of existence that may contradict each other, making conflicts common for those whose identities straddle such borders. The concept is also a metaphor for the histories, experiences, and social spaces of other "hybrid" peoples who are compelled to live in borders because conventional spaces do not accept their multiple identities (Anzaldua 1987). Thus, borders are also margins of safety, spaces in which "hybridity" is allowed.

Appearance Borders

The relationship between physical appearance and "bordered" racial/gender identities was stressed in the individual and group interviews by Latinas and Arab American women. The women varied in terms of their physical features: they were light to dark-skinned; had "kinky," "nappy," "big," or straight hair, ranging from black to blonde; and had differently shaped facial features and body sizes. However they identified themselves, the Arab American women were frequently thought to be Greek, Latina, African American, African/Euro-American, or white, and the Latinas were sometimes assumed to be African American or white.

Women in both groups felt that hair and body size have been significant foci of discipline and control in different contexts. They discussed unsuccessful attempts at feathering, perming, or straightening their hair in order to look like white teenagers, and the gendered implications of some of their mothers' pressures to contain their "big" hair into tight braids, knots, or with hair clips. One Latina believed this pressure was actually about containing girls' sexuality, and an Arab American woman explained such control with a different feminist argument:

> "[Y]our hair is too big, it's like uncontrollable." I think that's the thing about trying to keep women small, too, you know? ... So why do we have to take up this much space [she curves both hands on the table facing each other about a foot apart], you know [everyone laughs]? (Michelle)

Both groups discussed body size standards within their communities as liberating in comparison to those dominant in US culture. Most US men, they believed, want "petite, they all want petite" (Amal). A Chicana joked about the US Southwest as a place "where men really appreciate women," and an Arab American woman joked about her father's Arab country of origin as "the only place in the world where I'm considered too thin." While variations in skin color occasionally came up as disciplinary issues *within* some homes and communities – with lighter skin considered more beautiful than darker skin for women – their discussions largely centered on how "external" groups perceived them based on their skin color.

The light-skinned Chicanas, as mentioned earlier, were often defined as white and ostracized by some students of color on campus. Carol said she "got literally ignored, brushed off by some people in the African American community because they thought I was white because I'm light skinned ... Some of them didn't accept me as a person of color, they had to be told."

Conversely, Janie felt that it was difficult to be both black and Puerto Rican within the African American community:

> Last year I think I identified myself more with the racial aspect of it because I was getting so much – you know, it was like people were identifying me a lot by my race and it was frustrating for me. It was like "How can I explain to them? ... I don't identify myself by my race, but then I don't want to be excluded and that was important for me ... but last year I started ... saying that I was black Puerto Rican.

Another black Puerto Rican woman who had attended a predominantly Black university as an undergraduate found herself in a similar situation when she began applying for graduate schools:

> I put Puerto Rican on the box, or Hispanic, or whatever the box was at that time, my adviser told me "Why am I putting that?" and I said because that's what I am and he said "No, you're black" and I said, "You know, my grandfather is as African as your grandfather, but my experience isn't, my experience is a Puerto Rican experience." (Linda)

Thus, because discussions of race and ethnicity in the university were usually based on a black/white schema, the Latinas were often pigeon-holed into one or the other category, excluding their other identities and experiences.

All the darker-skinned Arab Americans said that as children they frequently wished they were lighter-skinned and lighter-haired, and less identifiably "Arab," especially during Middle East-related crises. Most had childhood memories of being called "niggers," "sand niggers," "Ayrabs," and "camel jockeys":

> [B]ecause my hair's really curly and very tight curls, I got all kinds of – you know, some people would think I was Black so they would call me "nigger." Some people knew that my parents were from Egypt, so they … would say "sand nigger," I got that a lot. (Amy)

In response to constant harassment for her brown skin and kinky hair, Amy admitted: "I felt bad. I mean, when I was eight, I wanted to have blonde, straight hair, this was my ideal. And now I realize how hideous I would look if I had blonde straight hair."

While the less phenotypically "Arab" women were much less likely to have their physical appearances be sources of difference during their childhoods, this physical blending was problematic later in life when they wanted to affirm their "Arabness." The dissonance between their identification as Arab Americans and their physical appearance contributed to feeling "phoney" when using a self-identifier such as "Arab American" or "woman of color." Indeed, three of the four bi-racial Arab American women wished they looked darker. For example, when asked if she considered herself a woman of color, Hana said:

> It's really interesting that you should ask me this question because this for me is one of the most difficult issues … because I look white. I mean, it's very difficult because it's an identification that I feel very strongly about. And again, I think that very much came out of the Gulf War … But I sometimes feel ridiculous saying it ["I am a woman of color"] because for people looking at me it's like: "What's this person talking about?" Which has always been something that is extremely complicated for me because I always wanted to look like my – like I was an Arab.

Six of the eight Latinas strongly identified as women of color, whereas only two of the eight Arab American women did so. The two Latinas and two of the six Arab Americans who did not identify as women of color identified instead as a Chicana, Puerto Rican, Lebanese, and Egyptian, respectively. The generally weaker "women of color" identification among the Arab Americans may be related to the fact that their school and neighborhood interactions have largely been with white people. At the same time, six of the eight Arab Americans strongly believed that they were not white and all eight were ambivalent about being legally categorized as such.

Language Borders

Language knowledge existed as a marker of authenticity in both communities. Four of the eight Latinas interviewed spoke Spanish fluently; two of the four who did not grow up speaking Spanish fluently sought to learn the language as adults. Among the Arab American women, with the exception of one who was fluent in Arabic, five were learning or relearning the language, and two said they wanted to learn it. Latinas and Arab American women who did not speak Spanish or Arabic fluently often felt inadequate as a result in their respective communities. Indeed, some of the Latinas interviewed whose first language was Spanish resented other Latinas/os who did not speak Spanish. As Emma put it: "[I]t really bugs me when some people are Mexican and they don't know Spanish."

Lack of language knowledge created a sense of distance from their racial-ethnic communities for both groups of women. As Margaret stated, "For me, not being fluent in Spanish has always been an insecurity ... it has kind of been one of the things that has kept me apart from certain Latino communities ... [because] there's some expectations on this campus that a Latino should speak Spanish." An Arab American similarly stated:

> I've had long conversations about the significance of feeling at home nowhere. When I'm here [in the US], I'm sure that I belong there [in the Arab world] and when I'm there, I'm sure I don't belong there ... Language has been a big issue simply because a lot of them [my relatives abroad] I can't speak with. (Hana)

Some of the women who were not fluent in Arabic or Spanish attributed "loss" of language to social obstacles. One Chicana (Anne) said that her parents were physically and psychologically sanctioned for speaking Spanish in school and she believed this resulted in her being discouraged from speaking the language as a child. Margaret believed that English was her first language because her Puerto Rican mother was educated in a US convent, where she was punished for speaking Spanish. Linda similarly said, "I minored in Spanish in college ... but it wasn't something that was reinforced in our lives."

Loss of language was relevant for three of the four Arab American women, both of whose parents were of Arab descent; the fourth woman was almost fluent as a result of consistently traveling between the Arab world and the US. Like the Latinas, these Arab American women discussed how US racism and ethnocentrism compelled them to forget their Arabic when they were young and/or resulted in teachers discouraging their parents from using the language with them. An Arab American who was frequently harassed by white children because of her physical appearance also discussed her own resistance to maintaining her Arabic language knowledge when she was younger:

> I had a very bad attitude towards speaking Arabic. My mom would try to teach me periodically. You know, she'd get the books out and say, "Okay, this is *alef*, this is *bey*, this is *tey*" [the first three letters of the Arabic alphabet]. And I really – I mean, I very much did not want any part of Arabic. Like I remember being seven and eight and her trying to teach me, and I remember thinking, "This is America, we have to speak English." ... To speak the [Arabic] language would only make me more a part of something I didn't want to be a part of. (Amy)

Amy, who was relearning the language, regretted this loss of Arabic as an adult and saw a powerful relationship between language knowledge and racial-ethnic identity:

> I really regret their [her parents] not having spoken [Arabic] at home and my not having learned the language when I was much younger, when it would have been easier... And I really feel, too, since having been able to read and write a little bit, there is great power of the language to allow me to identify with that culture more. I just – it makes it so much easier when you get the window into that culture, do you know what I mean? (Amy)

Class Borders

Earlier, we discussed how many of the women interviewed were alienated in the academic setting and how in most cases this strengthened their racial-ethnic identities. A paradox arises for the

Latinas, however, because many simultaneously feel alienated from their home communities as a result of their higher education and impending class mobility. Getting a university education created a distance – physically, economically and socially – between these Latinas and members of their families and communities, most of whom were poor to working-class and far less educated; they felt that their educations were privileging them in relation to their families and communities.

After being at the university for a year or so, a Chicana undergraduate from Texas (Emma) noted being disturbed and offended when she was told by a former teacher back home that she "sounded so different... so white." The interplay between class, race, and education was also apparent in her following statement:

> [W]hen I go back home with my family – because I am the first one to go to college and I was the second one to graduate from high school... now they see me as like "Oh, well Miss College here." I don't know. My whole family is proud of me, but it's like in a sense they're – some of them actually go "Oh, you think you're big shit because you're over there." (Emma)

Linda, a Puerto Rican graduate student, similarly stated:

> Earlier on it was hard to justify being here and wanting the education and ... having my father telling me that I was distancing myself from the community... but society expects education to be that method by which you go about change, so when you go back there you're not part of that community anymore ... [My family told me,] "College was OK, but what's this PhD business?"... I want to go back, but there is still that issue of, first, where do you put a PhD in the middle of East Harlem?

Anne, a Chicana graduate student, was concerned about trying to balance efforts to help her community "without alienating or intimidating them." Another Chicana graduate student remarked that while her parents were proud of what she was accomplishing, they did not really understand what she was doing. When she does go home she is careful not to let her "academic hat" place her above others:

> I think my sister and my brother would be the first ones to slap me in the face – not literally, but you know – and say "You're at home now ... don't impress us ... we know you" ... to them I'm still

the same person [as when] I left ... But I think to my parents it's much more of a big deal that I'm getting [a PhD] than probably to anybody else. Even though I don't think they understand it themselves ... I guess in some sense I am my mother's dream come true, that she never went to school and at least I got that opportunity. (Teresa)

Education and upward mobility did not distance the Arab American women interviewed from their families and communities, for two related reasons: first, none of their families lived in Arab neighborhoods, where class differences are much more salient. And second, the women came from middle- to upper-middle-class backgrounds, in which at least one and usually both parents were highly educated. As one woman noted in response to this issue: "In fact, I feel like they've [her parents] obtained a certain level of education and there's actually great expectation on me to at least equal that or surpass it ... So if anybody is feeling intellectual inferiority, it's me not them" (Amy).

Sexuality Borders[6]

The women interviewed discussed the often repressive aspects of "home" with respect to gender, sexuality, and sexual practices. Both groups believed that being a woman in Latino/a and Arab cultures had its own limitations, especially with respect to controlling their sexuality as unmarried women. In asking women to discuss their formal and informal sexual educations, the major themes that arose were silence, denial, and control. The two groups diverged in a number of ways, however, most importantly in that the Latinas were particularly concerned about not becoming pregnant, whereas the Arab American women were most concerned with the implications of losing their virginity.

Latina scholars have argued that the sexual repression of Latinas begins early, and girls are taught to be "submissive, virtuous, respectful of elders and helpful of our mothers, long suffering, deferring to men, industrious, and devoted" (Ramos 1987: xxvi); the most common strategy has been to deny "young women's imminent sexuality" (Castillo 1991: 32). As one Chicana said, her mother "didn't know" and "didn't want to know" about her sexual development and practices. If sex was discussed in the

Latinas' homes, it was often bluntly discouraged. This angered the Latinas interviewed, and most were taught to be ashamed of sexuality. When asked about her informal sex education, one Puerto Rican woman responded: "I didn't get anything from my mother, absolutely nothing. I think she did such a poor job with that; I'm sorry, but she did [she laughs]. She really dodged it." This silence and denial with respect to sexuality affected her later when she "couldn't look her mother in the face" after her first experience of sexual intercourse. Almost all the Latinas received their sexual educations from peers, in school, and/or from television. According to another Chicana: "[My mom] just once told me 'if you have anything you want to talk to me about, just ask me.' And the first time we talked about menstruation was when I already had it … But as far as sex, never, never a conversation."

The sex education experiences of the Arab American women were more divided. Interestingly, all of the women whose parents are both Arab had very open discussions with one (not always the mother) or both parents about anatomy, sexuality, and even sexually transmitted diseases before the onset of their menstrual cycles. One woman said that she often tried on her older sister's and mother's sanitary napkins for fun before she got her first period, and another woman argued about female anatomy with her Arab father as an 11-year-old. Three of the four bi-racial Arab American women, in contrast, received little to no sexual education from their parents and were generally not encouraged to discuss sexuality issues. One of these women said that her first period was "traumatic – very traumatic … I didn't know how to deal with the irregularity and cramps … [I felt] isolated and abandoned [laughs], and I just survived." This woman, who was a virgin and engaged to be married, asked a number of questions about birth control during her individual interview.

While pre-marital sexual activity was discouraged by the Latinas' families, all the Arab American women received much stronger explicit and implicit messages that they should remain virgins until they married. "Nice Arab girls" were not supposed to lose their virginity before marriage. In order to control the sexuality of unmarried daughters, unchaperoned dating is generally strongly discouraged in Arab cultures, and Arab American girls are punished for violating these cultural norms (Aswad and Gray 1996). The virginity narrative was an especially strong source of internal conflict for the five Arab American women who had engaged in pre-marital sex. One respondent who eventually slept with a partner discussed this ambivalence:

> I went through a phase for a while, because I think a lot of Arabs – in-between women go through – which is that "If I lose my virginity, I can't marry an Arab... It's awful, I mean it's awful... I'm really glad that I didn't have sex earlier because my experiences with men have been on the whole extremely shitty and it seems to me like it would have just made everything worse.

A number of the Arab American women were sexually active with men but tried to abstain from intercourse. One of these women described her first experience of sexual intercourse with her Arab American boyfriend as a rape, which she believed he knew would force her to make a premature commitment to him: "Oh, yeah, I mean, I have slept with him, I wish we never did. I wish – because I know that I became more attached and closer to him. I think maybe, maybe... had I not slept with him, maybe I would not continue seeing him." Her primary concern after this was what would occur if she and her boyfriend did not marry: "What man is going to take me, a non-virgin, in our society?"

When asked if her parents had specifically warned her against having sex, an Arab American who had not engaged in sexual intercourse responded: "[T]hey never came out explicitly and said, you know, 'Don't sleep with anyone.' ... [I]t was implicit in everything else that they said, do you know what I mean?" This Arab American demonstrated that ostracization from family and society was the most effective form of social control:

> [I]t was always very clear in terms of sexual mores what was and wasn't permissible... [I]f I ever got pregnant and I wasn't married, that they would have nothing to do with me. That would be the end of it... And that, you know, instilled enough fear in me that I was never going to put myself in a situation, you know, where I would jeopardize my being related to them or them not having anything to do with me.[7]

The three Arab American women who had not engaged in pre-marital sex said that they were unwilling to do so until they married. One of these women stated that she remained a virgin

> [n]ot because they'd [her parents] forbid me to, but just because I see – you know, sleeping with somebody is such an intimate thing

and it binds you to them in ways that you're not bound to any-body else. And that's not something that … I just want to do with anyone.

Discussions about sex and the loss of virginity often brought up the fear of pregnancy or the consequences of unwanted early motherhood for the Latinas, a phenomenon highly informed by the fact that most of them came from poor to working-class back-grounds. These women had seen many friends and family mem-bers whose lives had been changed by early motherhood. One Puerto Rican woman said her "biggest fear was getting pregnant" at an early age as her mother had done when she was 19. She added, "[in] turning 19 and 20, for me to be able to make it that far and not to have a baby, that was like my goal in life." Fear of unplanned pregnancy also came up when women were asked their views of abortion, a right that all but one Latina strongly supported. The Arab American women, in contrast, were much more ambivalent about abortion. While five of the eight stated they were pro-choice, most believed abortion was morally wrong, and all expressed discomfort with the idea.

Despite the fact that many of the women grew up in households where sex was not discussed and/or sexual expression was dis-couraged, a number of the Latinas and Arab Americans spoke about transgressing some of these cultural norms. Two of the Latinas interviewed disclosed that they had engaged in sexual relationships with women as well as men, and another had exper-imented with a female friend as a pre-adolescent. One Chicana said that she had to "change her thinking" about expressing her sexuality because she grew up in a very "restricted" household. She didn't want to be sexually repressed as she had seen her "father make [her] mother be." This theme is clearly articulated by a Puerto Rican, who said:

> I've had to replace values. In the very beginning, that was part of my value system that "Oh, I can only be with one person"… but now that I've dated and that I've had – that I've been sexually inti-mate with people … it's not part of my value system anymore.

The Arab American women interviewed did not bring up sex-ual experiences with other women, possibly because they were uncomfortable discussing the issue. Five of the eight Arab American women interviewed had engaged in pre-marital sex despite strong messages to the contrary from their families and communities. Three of these women continued to feel ambivalent about their sexual activity, however, while two were more comfortable. According to one in the latter group:

> [A]ll through high school, because my parents were so, like, "You can't date, you can't do this," that when I got to college, I was like, "Oh, let's check it out!" [We both laugh.]...I think that maybe when it all first started happening, I felt a little strange about it because I know that my parents were sort of like, "No pre-marital sex. No pre-marital sex."...But I don't feel like that about it anymore...I just do it because I think it's right and this is what I want to do and if you're not – ...[I]f the person I want to marry does not accept that then that's not the kind of person I need to marry.

Conclusion

Whereas the Arab American women and Latinas interviewed differed along a variety of axes, all found the university to be a threshold for racial-ethnic identity. They discussed the university as a site where racial-ethnic identity was defined oppositionally, and "home" as culturally affirmative *and* a place with its own inflexible racial-ethnic/gender norms. Rather than being mutually exclusive categories, home and university sites emphasized different identity issues that were interactively defined. Although there is a common assumption, especially in non-academic circles, that racial-ethnic identities are natural and fixed, they are always being constructed and redefined in social interaction and through social practices. Anti-Arab and anti-Latina/o racisms were undergirded by different assumptions by the dominant culture, and, like identities, both were "performed" in daily interactions. While oppositional consciousness was governed by both "structural" location and context, subjective experiences ultimately meant that these Latinas and Arab American women practiced a range of identity strategies over time and tailored them for different sites. They responded in a variety of ways to rigid identity categories, providing evidence that racial-ethnic identity is a process of both external social construction and political self-definition.

NOTES

1   The authors share equal responsibility for this article. We thank Judith A. Howard, the anonymous reviewers of *Qualitative Sociology*, Tomás Almaguer, Natalie Bennett, Mark Chesler, Jeff Dillman, Janet Hart, Moon-Kie Jung, Maria Teresa Koreck, Michael Sulieman, Steve Sumida, and Patricia Zavella for reading and commenting on the paper, which we presented at the August 1995 meeting of the American Sociological Association in Washington, DC.

2   We use the term "racial-ethnic" to capture both the racialization of people of color by the dominant culture *and* the idea that people of color can affirmatively define their histories, languages, and customs. We assume that racial-ethnic identities are not stable or unitary, but socially constructed, contingent and historical (Hall 1992; McCarthy and Crichlow 1993; Omi and Winant 1994). Similarly, oppression based on gender, race, class, and sexuality is interlocking and the intersections of these identities are multiple and dynamic (Alarcon 1991; Collins 1990; Crenshaw 1991; Zinn and Dill 1994; Harris 1991; Martin and Mohanty 1986; Mohanty 1991). For women of color, then, multiple hierarchies condition and define their material positions and subjective experiences.

3   The Arab world encompasses 21 Arab countries in North Africa and Southwest Asia and the Occupied Palestinian Territories. The term "Middle East" refers to these Arabic-speaking countries, as well as Turkey, Iran, Israel, and sometimes Pakistan and Afghanistan. "Latina/o" is an umbrella term used to describe peoples of Latin American or Spanish origin, including Chicanos and Puerto Ricans. The students interviewed were recruited through solicitations on the Arab American Student Association and the Latino/a electronic mail networks, personal contact, and word of mouth. Those who agreed to participate in the study were self-selected in that they identified as Arab Americans or Latinas and were willing to discuss identity issues. For convenience, we limited the sample to women who had US citizenship. We use pseudonyms to protect confidentiality.

4   The university does not track the specific racial-ethnic backgrounds of Latino/a students and does not keep records on their family income levels. In addition, it does not maintain separate records on Arab Americans, who are categorized as "white."

5   Based on 1990 census data, while the overall US official poverty rate was 13.1 percent, the rates were 26.3 percent for persons of Mexican origin, 31.7 percent for persons of Puerto Rican origin, and 14.5 percent for persons of Arab ancestry. Arab Americans 25 years or over were significantly more likely than the overall population to have

received a high school diploma (82.4 compared to 75.2 percent), a bachelor's degree (36.3 to 20.3 percent), and a graduate degree (15.2 to 7.2 percent). Among Puerto Ricans, 53.4 percent received a high school diploma, 9.5 percent received a bachelor's degree, and 3.2 percent received a graduate degree. Among Mexican Americans the figures are 44.2 percent, 6.3 percent, and 2.0 percent, respectively (US Bureau of Census 1990).

6 The populations of Chicanas, Puerto Rican, and Arab American women students at the University of Michigan, Ann Arbor, are small. To safeguard confidentiality, which women were particularly concerned about when discussing sexuality, we do not attribute quotes in this section.

7 Aswad and Gray (1996) discuss the oppressive and affirmative functions of patrilineal family membership for Arabs and Arab Americans; Swanson (1996: 245) examines how these functions are used to "psychological[ly] coerce children [so as to] assure compliance with parental expectations."

REFERENCES

Alarcon, N. 1991. "The theoretical subject(s) of this bridge called my back and Anglo American feminism," in *Criticism in the Borderlands: Studies in Chicano Literature, Culture and Ideology*, H. Calderon and J. D. Saldivar (eds). Durham, NC: Duke University Press.

Anzaldua, G. 1987. *Borderlands/La Frontera: The New Mestiza*. San Francisco, CA: Aunt Lute Books.

Aswad, B. C., and N. A. Gray. 1996. "Challenges to the Arab-American family and ACCESS," in *Family and Gender among American Muslims: Issues facing Middle Eastern Immigrants and their Descendants*, B. C. Aswad and B. Bilgé (eds). Philadelphia, PA: Temple University Press.

Behdad, A. 1993. "Traveling to teach: postcolonial critics in the American academy," in *Race, Identity, and Representation in Education*, C. McCarthy and W. Crichlow (eds). New York, NY: Routledge.

Castillo, A. 1991. "La macha: Toward a beautiful whole self," in *Chicana Lesbians: The Girls our Mothers Warned us About*, C. Trujillo (ed.). Berkeley, CA: Third Woman Press.

Collins, P. H. 1990. *Black Feminist Thought: Knowledge, Consciousness, and the Politics of Empowerment*. Boston: Unwin Hyman.

Crenshaw, K. 1991. "Demarginalizing the intersection of race and sex: A Black feminist critique of anti-discrimination doctrine," in *Feminist Legal Theory: Readings in Law and Gender*, K. Bartlett and R. Kennedy (eds). Boulder, CO.: Westview Press.

Hall, S. 1992. "The question of cultural identity," in *Modernity and its Futures*, S. Hall, D. Held, and T. McGrew (eds). Cambridge: Polity Press.

Harris, A. 1991. "Race and essentialism in feminist legal theory," in *Feminist Legal Theory: Readings in Law and Gender*, K. Bartlett and R. Kennedy (eds). Boulder, CO: Westview Press.

Majaj, L. S. 1994. "Boundaries: Arab/American," in *Food for Our Grandmothers: Writings by Arab-American and Arab-Canadian Feminists*, J. Kadi (ed.). Boston, MA: South End Press.

Martin, Biddy and Chandra Talpade Mohanty. 1986. "Feminist Politics: What's home got to do with it?," in *Feminist Studies/Critical Studies*, Teresa de Lauretis (ed.). Bloomington, IN: Indiana University Press, 191–212.

Mohanty, C. 1991. "Under Western eyes: Feminist scholarship and colonial discourses," in *Third World Women and the Politics of Feminism*, C. Mohanty, A. Russo, and L. Torres (eds). Bloomington, IN: Indiana University Press.

Montejano, D. 1987. *Anglos and Mexicans in the Making of Texas, 1836–1986*. Austin, TX: University of Texas Press.

Moore, J. and H. Pachon 1985. *Hispanics in the United States*. Englewood Cliffs, NJ: Prentice-Hall.

Munóz, C., Jr 1989. *Youth, Identity, Power: The Chicano movement*. London: Verso.

Omi, M. and Winant H. 1994. *Racial Formation in the United States: From the 1960s to the 1990s*, 2nd edn. New York, NY: Routledge.

Pérez, L. E. 1993. "Opposition and the education of Chicana/os," in *Race, Identity and Representation in Education*, C. McCarthy and W. Crichlow (eds). New York, NY: Routledge.

Pratt, Minnie Bruce. 1984. "Identity: Skin blood heart," in *Yours in Struggle: Three Feminist Perspectives on Anti-Semitism and Racism*, Elly Bulkin, Minnie Bruce Pratt, and Barbara Smith. Brooklyn, NY: Long Haul Press.

Ramos, J. 1987. Introduction, in *Compañeras: Latina Lesbians (an Anthology)*, J. Ramos, (ed.). New York, NY: Latina Lesbian Project.

Rodriguez, C. E. 1989. *Puerto Ricans: Born in the U.S.A.* Boston, MA: Unwin Hyman.

Rosaldo, R. 1989. *Culture and Truth: The Remaking of Social Analysis*. Boston, MA: Beacon Press.

Said, E. W. 1981. *Covering Islam: How the Media and the Experts Determine How We See the Rest of the World*. New York, NY: Pantheon Books.

Saldivar-Hull, S. 1991. "Feminism on the border: From gender politics to geopolitics," in *Criticism in the Borderlands: Studies in Chicano Literature, Culture and Ideology*, H. Calderon and J. D. Saldivar (eds). Durham, NC: Duke University Press.

Sandoval, C. 1991. "U.S. third world feminism: The theory and method of oppositional consciousness in the postmodern world," *Genders* 10: 1–24.

Shaheen, J. G. 1993. "Aladdin: Animated racism." *Cineaste* 20(1): 49.

Shaheen, J. G. 1984. *The TV Arab*. Bowling Green, OH: Bowling Green State University Popular Press.

Swanson, J. C. 1996. "Ethnicity, marriage, and role conflict: The dilemma of a second-generation Arab-American," in *Family and Gender among American Muslims: Issues Facing Middle Eastern Immigrants and their Descendants*, B. C. Aswad and B. Bilgé (eds). Philadelphia, PA: Temple University Press.

University of Michigan. 1993. *Faculty, Staff and Students of Color: a Statistical Profile for Academic Years 1982–83 through 1992–93*. Ann Arbor, MI: Office of Affirmative Action and Office of Minority Affairs (June).

US Bureau of the Census. 1990. "Persons of Hispanic origin in the U.S.," CP-3-3 (CPH-L-150), and "Ancestry of the population in the United States," CP-3-2 (CPH-L-149), in *1990 Census of Population and Housing*.

Zinn, M. B., and B. T. Dill (eds). 1994. *Women of Color in U.S. Society*. Philadelphia, PA: Temple University Press.

Part III

Institutional Dynamics

10

The Image That Dare Not Speak Its Name: Homoerotics in New Deal Photography

Shelley Kowalski

Congress, spurred by Senator Jesse Helms, bars the National Endowment for the Arts from funding "homoerotic" art, thereby equating art involving gay themes with obscenity. Now, all N.E.A. grant recipients must sign an oath declaring, among other things, that their art is free of homoeroticism.

Gara LaMarche and William Rubenstein,
"The Love that Dare Not Speak"

Nearly a decade later, I find the above statement a still frightening political limitation of self-expression, yet would like to suggest that Helms' amendment[1] against homoerotic art is ultimately impossible, premised as it is on inflexible notions of both cultural meaning and eroticism. In examining the photographs of the Civilian Conservation Corps,[2] a New Deal program designed to train and employ poor and working-class youth at the eve of and during the United States' switch to a war-time economy, I demonstrate that a certain homogenizing into heterosexuality was attempted. Despite the governmental and juridical attempts to control the viewing and performing of sexuality,[3] these images of young, mainly white, American males are not at all readable in absolute terms of gender and sexuality. In re-viewing the visual records of the 1930s and 1940s, I consider how the production of cultural imagery is never final – a specific meaning can never be assigned absolutely to an image, but is in large part determined by the context of viewing (Wolff 1981, 1990; Trachtenberg 1989; Sekula 1983; Solomon-Godeau 1991). While the Civilian Conservation Corps photographs were created with one agenda and meaning, contemporary viewers can see them now quite differently. That one can view these images with a decidedly queer eye, that is, homoerotically,[4] both points to the social construction of masculinity within the relations of social production and offers a de-naturalization of an assumed heterosexual history.

Pictures are Mute

Most of us in the Western world have seen photographs; they are understood to be visual measures of the world around us. But what is *in* a photograph that we see? Anything? everything? nothing? Anything, everything and nothing *can be* in a photograph. Anything can be in a photograph, at least anything real. Despite the current prevalence of doctoring photographs and digital photography, we have every reason to believe that with, for example these images of black male interaction (plates 1 and 2, both from

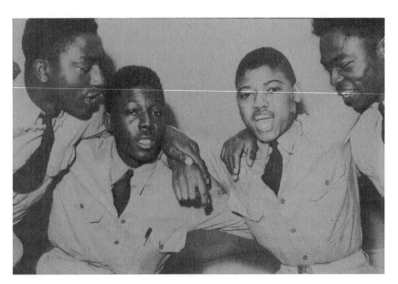

Plate 1   Camp Life. Yanceyville, North Carolina. May 5, 1940. (Wilfred J. Mead)

Plate 2 Camp Life. Yanceyville, North Carolina. May 5, 1940. (Wilfred J. Mead)

Wilfred Mead's *Camp Life*, 1940), there was an occasion when several young African American men wearing uniforms were singing and dancing. This undoubtability of the photograph comes from being grounded in sense certainty and indexicality – we trust what we can see and take as real that which our eyes set upon. If anything real can be in a photograph, then – plausibly – in the sense that more than one thing can be seen in an image – many things real can be in a photograph. If many real things are in an image, then how many more views or opinions of those very real things exist in the photograph when different people look at it? Here the "reality" of real things gives way to interpretation.

Photographs are polysemic texts – they can be of a host of subjects, each holding a myriad of different meanings. In this way, a photograph is a culturally, not just mechanically, produced item. Historical photographs, such as those of the Civilian Conservation Corps, are particularly liable to multiple readings. First, the circumstances under which the historical photographs were taken may no longer be retained in our memory. In essence, historical photographs serve as a proxy for our own recollections; they become our memory, and as such individuals read and interpret them differently based upon how they correspond to other memories. Ironically, historical photographs can in this way transform and rewrite history – my memory and my interpretation of the old photograph may be different from someone else's. Second, we may not have even been present at the initial instance of the photograph's creation. Here, historical photographs become a type of visual folklore. And like folklore, it is open to various accounts and interpretations. The meaning of the same image, like the denouement of the story, will vary depending upon reader and context. Thus, we can say that everything, or many more things than are merely shown, resides in the photograph. And herein lies the crux; we believe that the image is of something real, but we do not always agree amongst ourselves as to what that reality is.

So, what is in a photograph? Everything and nothing may seem a facetious answer, but maybe, by having more than just the "Truth" represented in the photograph, we have something other than everything – maybe it is a case of nothing being in a photograph. Roland Barthes wants to suggest that there is simply nothing in the photograph:

> Photography is unclassifiable because there is no reason to mark this or that of its occurrences; it aspires, perhaps, to become as crude, as certain, as noble as a sign, which would afford it access to the dignity of language: but for there to be a sign there must be a mark; deprived of a principle of marking, photographs are signs which don't take, which turn, as milk does. Whatever it grants to vision and whatever its manner, a photograph is always invisible: it is not it that we see. (1981: 6)

What is seen is a product of individual perspectives. In plate 3, *Boys taking test on softball rules, San Marcos, Texas*, June 30, 1939, you may see just a room of nearly naked boys sitting at desks; a mother may see her beloved son learning the All-American game; a young boy in junior league might view the inspiration for his career; and a gay male may envision a potential romantic fantasy. Just as it is written on the blackboard in the photograph, all readings are both True + and False −. According to Barthes, what we see is what we want to see and what we want. Viewed collectively then, photographs are points of convergence between various desires. Thus, a picture of something can be of anything. That is, a photograph can mean more than one thing, as the meaning is socially constructed. But this is not to say that just any and every

Plate 3 Boys taking test on softball rules. San Marcos, Texas. June 30, 1939. (Wilfred J. Mead)

meaning can be garnered from an image. Photographs carry various and conflicting desires, ideals, and ideologies. In Althusserian terms, photographs and other visual images become both the sites and sources of struggle over meaning. So then, viewed collectively, not all constructions are equally probable. An image can be of anything, but what it will be taken to mean is more or less fixed by our socio-historical conditions – the various desires, ideals, and ideologies circulating in a society. Trachtenberg expands this thought to note that for an image to be of anything meaningful, it must be seen in a specific context (1989: 87–8). What we see, and concomitantly what we desire to see, is part of the social structure. Just as we must learn to see the "hidden image" in the stereoscopic, 3-D images popular not long ago,[5] we are socialized to see things in a particular way. One must learn to see things as the dominant ideology suggests in order to communicate effectively in society.

While there is no inherent, absolute meaning in a photograph, the one that jibes with the prevailing social views will win out, and appear as if natural. Just as it takes a force of will to change our perceptions to see the "hidden image" in the 3-D stereoscope, it takes a shift in political power or at least political consciousness, to see beyond the dominant readings of historical photographs.

Just as the social structure is in constant flux, I consider visual images problematic sites open to different readings, depending on historical conditions and the readers' socialization. To view the world queerly – from outside the dominant ideology, one must first learn to discern the dominant "straight" meaning of an image and then reverse pattern and ground – so that what was hidden becomes visible. Those who view the world queerly then end up developing a double vision. Before going on to explore how this double vision is possible, I will trace the origin and history of the Civilian Conservation Corps (CCC) photographs and explore how changing ideologies are materially produced and socially disseminated through the same photographic practice. From there, I demonstrate how the homoerotic cannot be expunged or even ever completely censored.

All American Images: 1933–45

The Civilian Conservation Corps was created by Franklin D. Roosevelt in 1933 as a way to occupy the unemployed youth during the Great Depression, at first through forest and agricultural conservation, and later through defense-related training. During its nine year life-span, the CCC enlisted more than 2.5 million men between the ages of 17 and 25, most of whom were poor, poorly educated, and unemployed. Also during its time, the activities of the CCC were recorded in nearly ten thousand photographs, most under the direction of Roy Stryker who headed the Farm Security Administration's photographic division and was responsible for the dissemination of such now famous documentary photographs as *Migrant Mother* (*Pea Picker*) by Dorothea Lange.

As the unstated aim of the Corps was to fend off middle class fears of growing youth deviancy and communism by enlisting them, if not in the armed services then at least in the production of war arms and in the maintenance of American agricultural might,[6] the Corps was publicly well-received and needed very little photographic publicity to sell it in comparison to other New Deal programs. In fact, the CCC hired only one professional photographer, Wilfred Mead, who was responsible for 4,000 of the National Archives collection of CCC photographs, and whose photographs form the basis for this discussion. As Maren Stange (1987: 69) noted, Mead's photographs transformed the original agrarian ideal of the CCC into a more modern iconography: "The production of wealth and power, both material and spiritual, is here [in Mead's photographs] removed entirely from traditional, organic rhythms and relationships to an industrial order whose dynamic responds only to the voracious needs of the war economy." Stange analyzed the power that the Corps, and the photographs by which the public saw the program, had to shape the ideology of the American people during the 1930s and 1940s. She remarks that they still continue to be historically important today by "[r]evealing more today than their makers ever meant them to do, they help us grasp more consciously the forces that have shaped American culture" (1987: 70).

I would like to suggest that the photographs reveal even more than Stange had in mind, in that they continue to be a shaping force in American culture. Stange understands that the photographs of the Civilian Conservation Corps carried a certain meaning, one of rational production, domestic betterment, and absolutist heterosexuality when they were taken, but that they can now register very different meanings of that history. But Stange is looking back at and beneath the ideology of 1940s America to register changes in our perceptions of history through the photographs' meanings. Here, l am looking at how the ideals and contested ideologies at play in *today's* society change our reading of the images. Here, I am striving for an understanding of the way ideology operates visually.

Wendy Kozol (1994: 11) notes "ideology is not imposed but produced through material social and cultural practices." Relatedly, Dick Hebdige (1979: 11) explains the less than tacit nature of this ideology, which exists "by definition beneath consciousness. It is here, at the level of 'normal common sense,' that ideological frames of reference are most firmly sedimented and most effective, because it is here that their ideological nature is most effectively concealed." Photography is one such material and social practice that produces ideology without appearing to do so. While proclaiming it's evidentiary value as an "image of reality," the image of reality that is recreated in the photograph will be determined by the most dominant ideology. And when the forces that hold up the ideology change, readings of the images can be transformed as well. The texture of American culture has changed dramatically since the Great Depression. The traditional American ideology of the white male breadwinner in a heterosexual nuclear family no longer resonates with many American's reality. As our culture has changed, our ideals, and the ways we relate to the traditional, and still dominant ideology, have changed. In a sense, the ideological lens which focused the CCC images during the 1940s has cracked.

Reading the All American Today

A seemingly pointless, lost war in Vietnam, a series of civil rights movements by African Americans, women, gays, and lesbians, and the end of the cold war are just some of the events and processes that have created and seized the spaces between the lens's cracks. And it is here, in the fissures of the dominant ideology, that a homoerotic reading of CCC photographs can be found. In examining several CCC photographs below, I excavate the homoerotic elements that lay below the dominant New Deal discourse.

John Paul Ricco (1994: 70) claimed that "Artists are often producers of indexical signs, signatory traces which may in turn assume iconic or symbolic status. Yet indexical signs, like the notorious example of footprints on a sandy beach, are forever under risk of being erased ... Only if recorded, preserved, or frozen will these fragile traces survive, achieving a value or importance which such acts of preservation first assign." In light of the structuring force of cultural discourse and production this insight seems limited. Yes, indexical signs may become iconic or symbolic (the powerful machine in front of the virile man's crotch is a symbol of phallic power as seen in plate 4 – Wilfred J. Mead, *Road Construction*, 1940) but it is impossible to freeze any signification. The iconography in *Road Construction* connotes a manly man, but for whom is this youth being manly?[7] The mainstream American society of the 1940s in all its World War II productive glory, or a more isolated, gay male of today who registers the power of the jack hammer in politico-sexual terms? The youth in the photograph is being manly for both. It is just that what "manly" connotes differs so enormously between the two audiences; they are, for all intents and purposes, looking at two different pictures. Photographic meaning resides in the spaces between the photograph, subject, photographer, and viewer. Michael Camille (1994: 162–3) explains that, "Charting the changes an image undergoes in being viewed and used in different contexts will ... locate

Plate 4 Road construction. CCC enrollee operating pneumatic jack hammer in drilling holes for dynamite "shots." Salem, Virginia. July 28, 1940. (Wilfred J. Mead)

meaning in the various audiences of the image up to and including ourselves." This dual reality – the historical "straight" reading and the contemporary queer one – is possible as the meaning is manufactured in the process of the various audiences' encounters with the image. *Road Construction* is an example of how the meaning of being manly, i.e., the ideology of masculinity, changes within the same photographic image. That one can look at this image with a dominant eye or a subversive eye is very much a matter of how the social forces of production work to shape and construct the audience's vision and desires.

John Tagg noted that photography is a medium which produces both the description of an individual and the inscription of that person's social identity (1988: 37). In looking at this photograph of coal miners (plate 5 – Marion Post Wolcott, *Coal Miners*, 1938) we have both a physical description of the people (i.e., we could later identify them in a different photograph or in a police line-up) and a social identity – miners and a "smart guy." The captions of "The Lady's

Plate 5 Coal Miners. The "lady's man" and "smart guy." Bertha Hill, West Virginia. September 1938. (Marion Post Wolcott)

Man" and "Smart Guy" only reconfirm the look of dandyism we register from the relaxed yet poised posture of the man, his willingness to not merely meet the gaze of the camera, but even slightly entice it by grinning. Yet the caption registers an explicitly heterosexual identity that would be far from unambiguous if no caption were present.[8] Laura Mulvey 1989, Ann Kaplan 1983 and others have shown that "the gaze is male," and that a generic female gaze is logically impossible within a male dominated society. When the image is read then by a presumedly male gaze the nearly "come hither" look of the man can take on an element of homosexual, not heterosexual discourse. The man in the picture may be "the lady's," but it is not for her he is posing. As Allen Ellenzweig explained:

> Whenever men are placed in a sexual or physically admiring context in photographs, the viewer has to play a more active role. Long-established conventions make automatic our responses to pictures of the female nude or to any image that encompasses the socialized "feminine." We accept without question the erotic base, or erotic possibility, of the male response to images of women... No such parallel "automatic" response is built into our viewing of images of men; ... The male nude, and pictures that observe the range of male bondings, are today taken as slightly deviant. (1992: 4–5)

As erotically deviant, the "Smart Guy" is read as queer. His come-hither look is aimed at another man. And his heterosexual history is presumed no more.

In this National Youth Administration[9] photograph (plate 6, Rondal Partridge, *Roadside Repair*, 1940) we have the chance to use our "double vision" again: we see both men and women in what could be termed today "butch" attire – jeans, leather jackets, bandannas. In a queer context, a celebration of both gay leather boys and butch-femme lesbians can be produced. The females in the photograph, as it was originally produced and disseminated, retain their subordinate position only through the use of the caption which reads "On their way to the hill climb, the motorcycle party stopped by the roadside while one of their machines was repaired. *The girls were pillion seat riders* [my italics]." Far from a notion of mutually aggressive same-sex sexualities, in the mainstream, straight reading offered with the caption, the women are not dykes on bikes, but merely go-along girls and by implication, the boys are safely straight. Without an over-determining ideology – without the straightening caption – a play of readings is possible – we can see the image queerly. Clearly the context of

Plate 6   Roadside repair. On their way to the hill climb, this motorcycle party stopped by the roadside while one of their machines was repaired. The girls were pillion seat riders. Santa Clara County, California. April 5, 1940. (Ronal Partridge)

production and consumption matter in the legibility of male imagery and in the reading of social identities.

That sexuality, as well as sexual identity and sexual desire, is not "naturally" but socially constructed is now undoubted, save for amongst the most politically conservative commentators. Photographs form a basis for the representation and creation of sexed bodies. Ruehl noted that "representations do not merely reflect sexuality but play an active role in its production. Sexuality is always mediated and it is through representations that our bodies, and our fantasies, come to be sexually organized" (1991: 10). Yet this analysis, while recognizing the social constructedness of sexuality, is incomplete for it fails to address where, how, and why representations are created. What we are able to see is determined – imprecisely maybe, but determined nonetheless – by the cultural apparatus of our vision. We all wear relatively permanently implanted lenses[10] shaped by the specific historical moment of our viewing. In other words, the libidinal economy of the photographs, the erotic representation or reading given today, contradicts or transgresses the original political, economic purpose of the CCC photographs. But that this is so is not merely a matter of linguistic changes; it is the result of how America is structured today, i.e., by a marketplace capitalism. With this link to the marketplace, the structure of society is shown to be a determinant of sight (Sekula 1983: 194). The modern American landscape is framed on a political horizon where divergent sexuality, as well as non-dominant race and class standing give a multitude of often disparate visions of what "is." The socio-economic arena is a frame in which the photograph takes on meaning. And as well, it is in this arena that the homosexual and the homoerotic exist.

Sex and Gender, American Style

If photographs are culturally produced copies of the material world, the homosexual is structurally produced along with them and in them. Judith Butler recognized the "homosexual as copy" and argued that gender is itself "reproduced by imitation." Camille (1994: 165) places this thinking in direct relation to the photographic arguing, "that the homosexual body could only come 'out' and about in Walter Benjamin's 'age of mechanical reproduction.' " That is, the homosexual as a social identity is manufactured by a modern capitalist culture. What Butler (1991: 20) has referred to as "the culturally intelligible grids of an idealized and compulsory heterosexuality," which in our discussion translates as the manly ideal as exemplified in the CCC photographs, exists only as a product moment and can be broken down by a different, post-industrial, queer structure of relations.

Butler describes the way queer identities expose masculinity as not a naturalized essence, but a socially-constructed performance of gender:

> the parodic or imitation effect of gay identities works neither to copy nor to emulate heterosexuality, but rather, to expose heterosexuality as an incessant and panicked imitation of its own naturalized idealization. That heterosexuality is always in the act of elaborating itself is evidence that it is perpetually at risk, that is, that it 'knows' its own possibility of becoming undone. (1991: 23)

The CCC photographs, out of their original context and in today's world, work in a similar fashion. The manly ideal exemplified in these CCC photographs exposes the very unnatural formation of masculinity and undoes the presumed heterosexuality accrued to them. This is amply demonstrated in Wilfred Mead's *Work Project*, no date (plate 7). Different captions read "Work Project. Husky enrollee wielding sledge hammer in cracking rocks for park retaining walls and gutter bases," and "The slogan of the Civilian Conservation Corps is 'We can take it!' Building strong bodies is the major CCC objective. More than half of the enrollees who entered CCC during the last year were seventeen years of age. Work, calisthenics, marching drill, good food and medical care feature the CCC health program." From the second caption it is obvious that the CCC created and utilized a specific form of manhood in the interests of the capitalist state. Remembering that this New Deal program took in lower- and working-class youth, it is interesting to note how there was an overt glorification of the male body as a source of strength and productivity. The implication is that the working-class male is all body and no mind. It is his brute, brutish body that is of sole importance to the ambitions of the CCC and to America.[11]

Michael Kimmel posits a model of masculinity for whom "identity is based on homosocial competition" (1994: 122). This

Plate 7 Work project. Husky enrollee wielding sledge hammer in cracking rocks for park retaining walls and gutter bases. The slogan of the
Civilian Conservation Corps is "We can take it!" Building strong bodies is
a major CCC objective. More than half of the enrollees who entered CCC
during the last year were seventeen years of age. Work, calisthenics,
marching drill, good food, and medical care feature CCC health program.
(Wilfred J. Mead)

"Marketplace Masculinity" describes the normative definition of
American masculinity. It specifies characteristics – aggression,
competition, anxiety – and the arena in which those characteristics
are deployed – the public sphere, the marketplace (1994: 124).
Marketplace masculinity came about precisely at the same historical moment the CCC photographs were being circulated. Melosh
notes that specifically during the New Deal:

> Images of labor celebrated the transformation of nature, affirming a
> producer ideology of craft and industrial work…Treatments of
> labor were steeped in ideologies of manhood. In sharp contrast to
> the comradely ideal of the farm family, representations of wage
> labor consistently excluded and hence made invisible women's pro-
> ductive work, privileging the male domains of craft and heavy
> industry…More directly than any other subjects of representation,
> constructions of wage work speak to the contemporary crisis of
> masculinity. (1991: 83)

Thus, the iconography of the manly worker included physical strength, pride, heroism, patriotism, and cooperative labor. The masculine ideal of a strong body and adherence to a demanding work ethic was performed in large part, in reaction to the panics of the Great Depression. The classic sociological works of the era recorded men's and women's anguish over unemployment in ways that repeatedly invoked such gender ideology. Ruth Shonle Cavan and Katharine Howland Ranck's *The Family and the Depression* used the loss of male authority as the measure of family disorganization: "A man is not a man without work... Public art bracketed the shame of unemployment by putting it out of sight and replacing it with the enduring ideal of manly labor" (cited in Melosh 1991: 96).

It was also during the New Deal era that scientific and rational procedures for the "management of life" began to epitomize all forms of production (and increasingly reproduction). That there was no discussion of homosexuality in public discourse is a sign of what Foucault calls the "reverse discourse of the body." Silence was a discourse in itself,[12] and homosexuality was addressed obliquely in the numerous and frantic insistences on heterosexual, reproductive sex (Simons 1994: 83). Hollier notes that with increasing modernization:

> the sexual act is rationalized out of existence. It is replaced by sexual transaction which comprises every practice – including social behavior, language, representation... sexual transaction is socially pervasive. It helps regulate desire within a regime of production and consumption, giving it value by finally transforming it into work and exchange. Through this process it confers an identity upon us. (1988: 200)

According to D'Emilio (1996), it was precisely because of capitalism – the modernization of work and exchange – that sexuality became an identity. In order to get over its crises in the Great Depression, capitalism had to modernize itself; entailing a more thorough division of labor and more complete separation of work from home. In creating an economic and social sphere separate from the familial household, a separation of sexuality from procreation occurred, and with it, the "conditions that allow some men and women to organize a personal life around their erotic/ emotional attraction to their own sex" (D'Emilio 1989: 266). "Homosexuality" as an individual's identity thus came into existence during this time in a way that allowed for both it's recognition and it's condemnation. With homosexuality as an identity, a category or class of persons, it becomes open to investigation, surveillance and control. D'Emilio noted that, "as the subculture expanded and grew more visible in the post World War II era, oppression by the state intensified, becoming more systematic and inclusive" (1996: 268).

Kimmel notes that "the fear...that others might perceive us as homosexual propels men to enact all manner of exaggerated masculine behaviors and attitudes to make sure that no one could possibly get the wrong idea about us" (1994: 133). This hypermasculine paranoia was particularly acute during this era. At the time of the New Deal, the nation's strength, it's masculinity, was on the line – it was reinforced to such an extent that we are now able to read it as over-exposed. During the war, capitalist production and economic growth demanded a continued emphasis on the masculine ideal. However with the war came a very large male-only culture – the army. The circumstances of so many men in the armed services living in a perilous world, removed from family and loved ones, released many "deviant" desires. As D'Emilio and Freedman write, "the war created a setting in which to experience same-sex love, affection, and sexuality, and to participate in the life of gay men ... Truly, World War II was something of a nationwide 'coming out' experience" (1988: 289).

Just as "the homosexual" arose as an individual identity because of the socio-economic structure of capitalism, the homoerotic view was allowed to surface. During the 1970s the United States began to realize a crisis in its productive capacity. With this major slump in the economy, jobs migrated to overseas sites and the emphasis on industrial productivity shifted to consumption. Foucault's silent discourse and its incorporation into a hyper-masculine ideal shown in the buffed bodies of the CCC workers, began to be re-articulated. It is in this more recent crisis of capitalism and the focus on homosexual rights that grew with it, that a way to see the CCC images homoerotically has come out of hiding (Sinfield 1994).

The Image is/as Queer

Why can we see these images in a queer light now? The over-exposure of masculinity in these photographs is precisely what allows for a different, queer reading. After a military defeat by the

Viet Cong during the 1970s and a technological and economic usurpation by the Japanese in the 1980s, the American manly image reads false. Ideologies of manhood are circulated on behalf of the ruling interests. As seen above, male authority choreographed the performance of masculinity in the CCC photographs to be viewed by a presumed male gaze. During the 1970s, this ideology was destabilized as the politico-economic relations it was founded on and through crumbled. In term of cultural vision, there occurred what Myers terms "the instability of the male pin-up": a male cannot pose, cannot be the object of a male gaze without losing his very masculinity, as defined by Kimmel's heterosexual, homosocial (yet homophobic) marketplace man. In becoming an image for another, the male cedes his heterosexual masculinity. Thus, through out the 1970s and up to today there has been a gradual queering of the photograph. With a male gaze filtered through a consumer-capitalist lens, these images take on a homoerotic hue.

Richard Meyer noted that once the gaze moves from one of patriarchal production to a more feminized eye of consumption, eroticism replaces out right aggression (1991: 261). CCC photographs were originally made precisely to be looked at with an eye of aggression and production – they were produced on behalf of the war and it's growing military-industrial imperialism (Stange 1989). Further, Stange noted that the CCC photographs were part of the wartime promotion of the American Dream to allies in socialist-infested Europe, and that in America, youths were "highly susceptible to the glamorous fantasies which continue to be churned out by mass media even as production in most sections of the economy stagnated" (1989: 93). These images made impressions on the youthful audiences of the 1940s in a very real way. And they continue to be of consequence today. In our post-production, Western consumer capitalism, the photographs now merge identification with the object in the photograph with desire to consume and have that object in the photograph. What was once possibly role model ("I want to be like that man"), becomes now object of desire as well ("Not only do I want to be like that man, *I want that man*"). Leppert (1996: 248) notes, "to be *looked at sexually* is to be consumed or taken *by sight*. Not for nothing is the gaze – the stare – said to be penetrating."

Additionally both feminism's dismissal of the feminine as "natural" (Brownmiller 1984; hooks 1981; Butler 1990, 1991, 1993; Lorber 1994) and Western gay males' celebration of the body as an area of pleasure, not just production (Barthes 1981; Crimp 1992; D'Emilio 1983; Foucault 1990) have shaped the lens through which we are able now to both laugh at the photograph's past attempts at bravado and appropriate it's glorification of the body through same-sex desire. While a gay and lesbian "sub-culture" has been in existence for quite some time, it has only been in the period of post-industrial capitalism, in the change from a production to consumption economy after World War II (and especially during the past two decades) that the feminine as a false ideal and queer ideas have weighed so on the *public* consciousness (Clark 1991). It is only now that "queer sells," that the over-exposed masculinities in the CCC photographs can become an element of homoerotic consumption and delight. While previously the images may have served to strengthen the American military and productive machine, today the image of the manly man serves libidinal, consumptuary purposes. As Leppert noted in discussing today's body-builders, "the 'strength' they possess is literally for show only. Pumping iron is in part an activity prepatory to one's being looked at by other men ..." (1996: 250). The images, such as Wilfred Mead's *Surveying*, 1941 (plate 8) are out there today to be cruised, and not to crusade for American patriotism.

From Stange's and Melosh's analysis of the normalizing power of the New Deal era photographs we can presume that the photographs *Camp Life* (plates 1 and 2) were not originally intended as signs of homosexual dating during the CCC program (however aptly named), but the fact that we can read them that way points out the economic and material relations that (over)determine our sexual (among other) identities. We are labeled queer, straight, black, and white, in the interest of capitalism and rising conservative power. This power, however, is not simply dispersed everywhere through discourse, but is materially grounded (Morton 1993). At their point of creation, there was no material grounding from which to see these photographs homoerotically. It is not that the content has changed in 40 years, but that our economic and cultural relations have. As Hennessey (1993: 54) states, "What is intelligible or unintelligible in any historical moment – including constructions of the body ... – is so from a given historical position within a symbolic system which is part of an ensemble of mutually determining social practices." Our historical position of mass consumption and individualized pleasure allows us to consume, to take in, the CCC photographs in way only covertly possibly 60 years ago.

Plate 8 Surveying. Enrollee George Steen of Pittsburgh, Pennsylvania, sights through a transit during operations in surveying and laying out a curve on forest road in the George Washington National Forest. George is a member of the champion surveying crew of the George Washington National Forest. Camp Roosevelt, F-I. Edinburg, Virginia. July 19, 1941. (Wilfred J. Mead)

Through an appropriation – and a demonstration as false – of the hyper-masculinity of the "marketplace man" which helped define patriarchy and capitalism, these images now ironically threaten it. The change in the reading of these photographs is part of the late capitalist cultural arena where queer awareness (if not acceptance) is rapidly becoming a commodity, sold and bought like cars and computers. As Freitas in this collection notes, the right to participate in the society becomes synonymous with consumption and from this an identity is formed which in turn is used as a target market for further selling and consumption. In the movement from a production economy to consumer capitalism, the intendments of the CCC photographs shift from one of producing on the same level as the images to consuming these very images; to be desirous of the image – not in emulation but through appropriation.

Although queer awareness has grown, the backlash against it has as well. I do not mean to suggest that simply because we live in a post-industrial economy, we necessarily partake of the homo-erotic pleasures in these photographs. The dominant discourse is still against such viewings. It is only that space is afforded in which such viewings are *possible.* Hennessey (1993) notes that different sensibilities are found in the cracks and gaps of the dominant discourses. And the trajectory of the CCC photographs through history is replete with the space to provide contesting readings. Defining a photograph as erotic – either hetero- or homo – depends upon the photographer, subject matter, audience and socio-economic context in which it was produced and appears. Where we find the erotic is, then, in the social structure and in a changing social structure, it is not possible to "capture" the hetero-or homoerotic elements in a photograph. And hence, Helms will never be able to banish the homoerotic in art.

It seems to be the case that just like beauty, the erotic is in the eye of the beholder. Our eyes however, are not ours alone; they are a set of culturally negotiated and agreed upon practices. That Helms can understand Mapplethorpe's images as homoerotic is because he is able to read the genre – in a way an ironic tribute to growing queer awareness and cultural identity.[13] (To play on the slogan, If you can see us, that must mean, "we *are* everywhere.") At this level in the definition of the visually erotic and homoerotic, Helm's attempt to regulate what is immoral and homoerotic breaks down. Without a timeless, universal sexual and erotic identity, what is heteroerotic and what is homoerotic are no longer mutually exclusive. Beyond the breakage of this binary, what is immoral and what is sexually permitted also becomes a matter of contention.

In the forgoing, I have argued that sexuality is not merely an identity, but a relationship, a series of actions. Photographs cannot capture relationships, but they can be used to foster visibility of divergent, non-heterosexist social forces. However, visibility does not confer meaning, nor does it produce acceptance. Pictures can say almost anything; as such they are subject to the politics of containment. The irony of Helms' agenda is that in searching out and attempting to restrict that which is considered objectionable, the ideals he strove to preserve are exposed as false. The ideological underpinnings that were hidden in the dominant reading of images become visible. With the recognition of these socially constructed optical options, we are no longer forced to view the world in heteronormative terms. Helms, in seeking what is inadmissible, actually highlights the cracks in the dominant hierarchy and a potential way in which to view the deplorable as desirable. The hidden images – the homoerotic elements – are exposed. But they are exposed as being *exactly what was presumed safe*. In looking for subversive images, we find them everywhere. In attempting to ban "the bad" we note the corruption of the entire frame and find the inevitability of alternative viewings.

In re-installing homosexuality in recent American history, we must pay clear attention to the forces that worked to foster both the presumption of heterosexuality and the foregrounding of the masculine ideal. As photographs carry no truth, it is up to queer activists to form erotic relations in the reading of these images. In his history of the male nude photograph, Ellenzweig writes "But if we accept the homoerotic photograph as merely a marginal phenomenon, we will miss a truth of the history of photography. For the homoerotic photograph has been pervasive; it was just called something else" (1992: 5). In examining the photographs of the Civilian Conservation Corps, we see what a wonderful, elegant understatement Ellenzweig's comment is.

NOTES

1 The Helms amendment to the NEA/NEH appropriation bill reads "None of the funds authorized for the National Endowment for the Arts or the National Endowment for the Humanities may be used to promote, disseminate, or produce materials which in the judgment of the National Endowment for the Arts or the National Endowment for the Humanities, may be considered obscene, including but not limited to, depictions of sado-masochism, homo-eroticism, the sexual exploitation of children, or individuals engaged in sex acts and which, when taken as a whole, do not have serious literary, artist, political or scientific value." Congressional Record of the US House of Representatives October 2, 1989, p h 640 7.
2 Abbreviated CCC hereafter.
3 For a detailed explanation of how gender boundaries and sexualities were constructed and reinforced through photographs and public art works, see Melosh, 1991 *Engendering Culture*. For a more general, yet rigorous examination of the use of public photographs to regulate private lives and identities see Kozol, 1994 *Life's America*. Also,

Maren Stange's 1989 *Symbols of Ideal Life* looks at the various normative practices produced in Farm Security Administration and other
depression-era documentary photography.

4 While an admittedly broad term, I am using Ellenzweig's definition
of the homoerotic:

> Of course, the homoerotic is so linked with homosexuality (with good
> reason) that it seemed unnecessary even to acknowledge that there is
> indeed a distinction between the two. The homoerotic engages in
> varying degrees those feelings of desire, intimacy, admiration, or
> affection between members of the same sex, whereas the homosexual
> engages in the physical, or more properly, the sexual – the genital –
> expression of those sentiments. Homoerotic feelings may therefore
> encompass the full range of male or female bondings." (Ellenzweig
> 1992: 2)

For a visual account of the erotic, see the special issue of *American
Photo* December 1993 and for the specifically homoerotic in popular
visual arts, especially photography, see Hooven 1995.

5 It is not without irony that small children can find the hidden picture
with much greater facility than adults. Their vision, both literally and
figuratively, is still in the process of being shaped by society.

6 James Curtis's *Mind's eye, Mind's Truth* (1989), Guimond (1991), Daniel
et al. *Official Images* (1987), especially the contributions by Maren
Stange and Sally Stein, as well as Maren Stange's (1989) *Symbols of
Ideal Life* all explore the reformist, anti-communist thrust of many of
the New Deal programs and photographic efforts.

7 In a way it is the very presence of the jackhammer that forces this
man into this position and makes him manly. This again, quite clearly
shows how the relations, or here the tools, of production create both
gender identities and sexualized bodies.

8 It should be noted that the caption "The Lady's Man" is a trope and
the term "lady's man" is itself a peculiar historic form, part of a specific cultural ideology. Moreover, this term and the ideology it carries
is fading from the cultural linguistic landscape. That we no longer
have a "lady's man" in the sense of a Cary Grant, or better, a Rock
Hudson, may imply that we are losing the ability to know what the
term meant in 1938. Thus, even with accompanying text, the meaning
produced with and through photographs rides on changing cultural
waves.

9 The National Youth Administration was created to incorporate more
young women and urban dwelling youth into the New Deal schematic.
As Sally Stein noted "The rugged conditions of isolated camps for
jobless men under army rule ... limited the number of men willing to
join the CCC and failed altogether to meet the needs of young

women. As the Depression continued, it became evident that a far broader sector of the youthful population needed to be discouraged through relief measures from immediately entering the job market. Thus in the summer of 1935, Roosevelt established by executive order the NYA to administer a diverse set of relief programs designed for youth of both sexes, in and out of school" (Daniel et al. 1987: 94). I justify the inclusion of this photograph as the similarity between the programs was so great and both the NYA and CCC's photographic effort were headed by Roy Stryker.

10 By "relatively permanently implanted" I mean that we are not able to change lenses, to change the meaning of what we see as easily as we are able to don a pair of glasses. Thus this metaphor has the potential to obscure the recalcitrant nature of cultural hegemony in a way I do not want to realize. Through learning and socialization, the programs we are given by which to make sense of the world quickly become "hard-wired."

11 The fact that there are very few men of color in these photographs points to the racist nature of American society at that time as well, and the contradictions it faced in creating racialized and sexed bodies. While the African American male has historically been associated with the purely physical, even the animalistic, they were not given the opportunity to use their bodies in work during the Depression. It was more important to employ white males, even at hard manual labor, in the few jobs available. Further, the general public would not have looked favorably upon a black body in an overtly heroic pose. The few images of African Americans in the CCC show black youth in service-oriented positions and providing entertainment for others.

12 As Biddy Martin notes, "Western culture, far from having repressed sexuality, has actually produced it, multiplied it, spread it out as a particularly privileged means of gaining access to the individual and the social bodies, as a way of 'policing' society through procedures of normalization rather than prohibition" (1988: 8).

13 Peter Plagens (1994: 37) notes that "Mapplethorpe's real transgression, according to Hickey, was not in making public such dungeon deeds as fisting, but in implying that the beholder of the X photographs is complicit in their commission. 'The comfortable role of art beholder is written out of the scenario,' he says, 'as we are cast in roles before the image that we are unaccustomed to acknowledging – at least in public.' "

REFERENCES

Barthes, Roland. 1981. *Camera Lucida*. New York, NY: Hill and Wang.
Brownmiller, Susan. 1984. *Femininity*. New York, NY: Linden Press.

Butler, Judith. 1990. "Gender Trouble, Feminist Theory and Psycho-analytic Discourse," in *Feminism/Postmodernism*, Linda J. Nicholson. (ed.). New York, NY: Routledge.

Butler, Judith. 1991. "Imitation and Gender Insubordination," in *Inside/Out: Lesbian Theories, Gay Theories*, Diana Fuss (ed.). New York, NY: Routledge.

Butler, Judith. 1993. *Bodies that Matter*. New York, NY: Routledge.

Camille, Michael. 1994. "The Abject Gaze and the Homosexual Body." *Journal of Homosexuality* 27(1–2): 161–88.

Clark, Diane. 1995. "Commodity Lesbianism," in *Gender, Race and Class in Media*, Gail Dines and Jean M. Humez (eds). Thousand Oaks, CA: Sage Publications, 142–51.

Cohen, Ed. 1991. "Who Are 'We'? Gay 'Identity' as Political (E)motion (A Theoretical Rumination)," in *Inside/Out: Lesbian Theories, Gay Theories*, Diana Fuss (ed.). New York, NY: Routledge.

Creet, Julia. 1993. "Anxiety and Repetition: Loss and Lesbian Identity." *RFD/DRF* 20(1): 82–7.

Crimp, Douglas. 1992. "Right On, Girlfriend!" *Social Text* 30 (Spring): 78–96.

Curtis, James. 1989. *Mind's Eye, Mind's Truth: FSA Photography Reconsidered*. Philadelphia, PA: Temple University Press.

Daniel, Pete, Merry A. Foresta, Maren Stange, and Sally Stein. 1987. *Official Images: New Deal Photography*. Washington, DC: Smithsonian Institution Press.

D'Emilio, John. 1983. *Sexual Politics, Sexual Communities: The Making of a Homosexual Minority in the United States, 1940-1970*. Chicago, IL: University of Chicago Press.

——. 1989. "Capitalism and Gay Identity." in *Powers of Desire: The Politics of Sexuality*, Ann Snitow, Christine Stansell, and Sharon Thompson (eds). New York, NY: Monthly Review Press.

D'Emilio, John, and Estelle B. Freedman. 1988. *Intimate Matters: A History of Sexuality in America*. New York, NY: Harper & Row.

Edwards, Tim. 1994. *Erotics and Politics: Gay Male Sexuality, Masculinity and Feminism* . New York, NY: Routledge.

Ellenzweig, Allen. 1992. *The Homoerotic Photograph: Male images from Durieu/Delacrois to Mapplethorpe*. New York, NY: Columbia University Press.

Foucault, Michel. 1990. *The History of Sexuality: The Uses of Pleasure*. New York, NY: Vintage.

Fraser, Nancy. 1989. *Unruly Practices*. Minneapolis, MN: University of Minnesota Press.

Guimond, James. 1991. *American Photography and the American Dream*. Chapel Hill, NC: The University of North Carolina Press.

Hebdige, Dick. 1979. *Subculture: the meaning of style*. London: Metheun.

Hennessy, Rosemary. 1993. *Materialist Feminism and the Politics of Discourse*. New York, NY: Routledge.

Hollier, Robert. 1988. "Introduction," in *Guilty*, Georges Bataille (ed.). Venice, CA: Lapis Press.

hooks, Bell. 1981. *Ain't I a Woman: Black Women and Feminism*. Boston, MA: South End Press.

———. 1984. *Feminist Theory from Margin to Center*. Boston, MA: South End Press.

Hooven, Valentine F. 1995. *Beefcake: The Muscle Magazine Of America 1950–1970*. Cologne: Taschen.

Kaplan, E. Ann. 1983. "Is The Gaze Male?," in *Powers of Desire: The Politics of Sexuality*, Ann Snitow, Christine Stansell, and Sharon Thompson (eds). New York, NY: Monthly Review Press.

Kimmel, Michael S. 1994. "Masculinity as Homophobia," in *Theorizing Masculinities*, Harry Brod and Michael Kaufmann (eds). Thousand Oaks, CA: Sage Publications.

Kozol, Wendy. 1994. *"Life's" America*. Philadelphia, PA: Temple University Press.

LaMarche, Gara, and William B. Rubenstein. 1990. "The Love That Dare Not Speak." *The Nation*, November 5, 524–6.

Leppert, Richard. 1996. *Art and the Committed Eye*. Boulder, Colo.: Westview Press.

Lorber, Judith. 1994. *Paradoxes of Gender*. New Haven, CT: Yale University Press.

Martin, Biddy. 1988. "Feminism, Criticism, and Foucault," in *Feminism and Foucault*, Irene Diamond and Lee Quinby (eds). Boston, MA: Northeastern University Press.

Melosh, Barbara. 1991. *Engendering Culture: Manhood and Womanhood in New Deal Public Art and Theater*. Washington, DC: Smithsonian Institution Press.

Merck, Mandy. 1991. " 'Transforming the Suit': A Century of Lesbian Self-Portraits," in *Stolen Glances: Lesbians Take Photographs*, Tessa Boffin and Jean Fraser (eds). London: Harper Collins.

Meyer, Richard. 1991. "Rock Hudson's Body," in *Inside/Out: Lesbian Theories, Gay Theories*, Diana Fuss (ed.). New York, NY: Routledge.

Morton, Donald. 1993. "The Politics of Queer Theory in the (Post)Modern Moment." *Genders* 17(Fall): 121–50.

Mulvey, Laura. 1989. *Visual and Other Pleasures*. Bloomington: Indiana University Press.

Plagens, Peter. 1994. "Unruly Images." *Art In America* 11: 35– 6.

Rand, Erica. 1994. "Lesbian Sightings: Scoping for Dykes in Boucher and Cosmo." *Journal of Homosexuality* 27(1–2): 123–39.

Ricco, John Paul. 1994. "Queering Boundaries: Semen and Visual Representation from the Middle Ages and in the Era of the AIDS Crisis." *Journal of Homosexuality* 27(1–2): 57–80.

Ruehl, Sonja. 1991. "Developing Identities," in *Stolen Glances: Lesbians Take Photographs*, Tessa Boffin and Jean Fraser (eds). London: Harper Collins.

Sekula, Allan. 1983. "Photography Between Labor and Capital," in *Mining Photographs and Other Pictures, 1848–1968*, Benjamin H. D. Buchloh and Robert Wilkie (eds). Halifax: Nova Scotia Press.

Simons, Patricia. 1994. "Lesbian (In)Visibility in Italian Renaissance Culture: Diana and Other Cases of donna con donna." *Journal of Homosexuality* 27(1–2): 81–122.

Sinfield, Alan. 1994. "Sexuality and Subcultures in the Wake of Welfare Capitalism." *Radical Philosophy* 66: 40–43.

Solomon-Godeau, Abigail. 1991. *Photography at the Dock: Essays on Photographic History, Institutions, and Practices*. Minneapolis, MN: University of Minnesota Press.

Stange, Maren. 1989. *Symbols of Ideal Life: Social Documentary Photography in America 1890–1950*. Cambridge: Cambridge University Press.

Tagg, John. 1988. *The Burden of Representation*. Amherst, MA: University of Massachusetts Press.

Trachtenberg, Alan. 1989. *Reading American Photographs: Images as History*. New York, NY: Hill and Wang.

Tyler, Carole-Anne. 1991. "Boys Will Be Girls: The Politics of Gay Drag," in *Inside/Out: Lesbian Theories, Gay Theories*, Diana Fuss (ed.). New York, NY: Routledge.

(various). 1993. "What Is Erotic? A Photographic Survey." in *American Photo* 4.

Wolff, Janet. 1981. *The Social Production of Art*. London: Macmillan.

——. 1990. *Feminine Sentences: essays on women and culture*. Berkeley, CA: University of California Press.

Zita Grover, Jan. 1990. "Dykes in Context: Some Problems in Minority Representation," in *The Contest of Meaning*, Richard Bolton (ed.). Cambridge, MA: MIT Press.

11

Reproducing Racial and Class Inequality: Multiculturalism in the Arts[1]

Jennifer L. Eichstedt

Introduction

October 14, 1992 was the quincentennial of Columbus's arrival in "the New World." It was an event celebrated, mourned, and ignored in the Americas. In Santa Cruz County California, different groups considered varying responses to the quincentennial. One of those groups, the Santa Cruz Ethnic Arts Network (SCEAN), was headed by Ms Door, a white working-class woman involved with African drumming and dance. She wanted to organize an "America Discovers Columbus" event to "celebrate a New World Order based on Social Responsibility and Collective Self-Esteem." Through a flyer distributed to publicize the event, SCEAN portrayed their intentions in the following manner:

> Working with Tony Hill (a local African-American activist) we want to promote the release and healing of tensions still manifesting based on historical inequities – in a totally positive way – through INCLUSION of affected groups (such as Native Americans and African-Americans, etc.) presenting their own creative "display" of satire and mockery that all carnival worldwide is rooted in. (Since Carnival has its roots in pagan Europe, it can also be "owned" by the "European descendants" so prevalent in American Culture.) (Santa Cruz Ethnic Arts Network 1992)

Through an "inclusive" event, SCEAN hoped to bring together people from different racial/ethnic groups and use theater and other forms of cultural production to mediate a variety of racial tensions. The event did not take place. According to people involved, there was no widespread support for the event among those whom SCEAN envisioned participating. Additionally, the Indigenous Council of the Central Coast questioned the legitimacy of Ms Door's work. Door believed that the Indigenous Council felt that they "owned Columbus day" and it wasn't up to her, as a white woman, to put together such an event. She also was told by other people of color (some of whom attended the Central Coast Indigenous Council meeting with her) that she should cease pursuing the event, because it was a "people of color thing." Door persisted in trying to organize the event – she had faith in her good intentions, faith in her effort to reach out and help people heal. Others perceived her efforts as intrusive and an attempt to direct the responses of people of color, rather than letting them apply for, and use, scarce resources in a manner they developed. It was a local struggle over resources, racialized meaning, control of cultural production, and identity. It was, therefore, a struggle over multiculturalism.

In the 1980s and 1990s multiculturalism, as a set of discourses and practices, came to represent struggles over racialized meanings and inequalities that exist in social, cultural, political and economic domains (Bourdieu 1984; Lippard 1990; Gans 1983). Multiculturalism, however, is not a uniform set of practices, or discourses (Goldberg 1994). What it is, or what it should be, is continuously contested. In the above anecdote, Door believed that her efforts at inclusion and healing should be recognized as valid attempts at multiculturalism. Other whites, both in the local community I have explored and in the larger artistic and social world, make similar attempts at cross-racial interaction and networking. Their involvement is not always welcome; at times they are seen by peoples of color as interlopers and cultural cannibals. In contrast, these whites almost always perceive themselves to be non-racist, well intentioned, supporters of multiculturalism. What I will argue is that white and elite involvement in multiculturalism, while potentially useful, is likely to further the dominance of whites and elites if white-centric and elitist assumptions, frameworks, and practices are left unchanged.

Clearly the assertions I make draw on larger understandings of how systems of oppression operate. For instance, I am convinced by the research (Wellman 1993; Feagin and Hernan 1995) which demonstrates that whites (Euro-descendant peoples in the US) receive material and ideological advantage from the "white-centric" ways our economic, political, social, and ideological systems are organized. However, whites generally deny that we receive undue advantage from the ways our society is structured (McIntosh 1988; Wellman 1993; Frankenberg 1993). Indeed whites generally do not see ourselves as white; we deny we have any social location and instead see ourselves as the universal "individual." Hence, we believe individualism and meritocracy explain our group and individual location in a system of advantages and disadvantages (Wellman 1993). We often, even when we are "well intentioned," end up recapitulating systems of oppression because we do not recognize how routinized white-centric behavior and decision making excludes peoples of color or incorporates them only if they fit our presumably race neutral standards. Therefore, even when we are ostensively working to "incorporate" people of color we often end up containing and limiting their presence and contributions.

Some of the most powerful "processes of containment" are those which rest on discourses of meritocracy in education, business, and the arts, and discourses of neutrality and objectivity in culture and in the natural and social sciences (Harding 1993; Gould 1981). What these discourses have in common is a denial that the social location of the producer, observer, or consumer of a product or phenomenon has any effect on that phenomenon. Indeed, the process of sorting, choosing (in hiring, funding) and producing "knowledge," is assumed to be neutral – to enact no underlying set of political, social, economic, racial, gendered interests. In a parallel fashion, those with no "identifiable" interests, i.e. those who occupy the unmarked, invisible (denied) center (see Lorde 1984), are presumed to be the most capable of producing work which is universal in theme, concerns, and content. Conversely, those whose difference from this norm is visible (white women, peoples of color) are assumed to have interests and concerns which taint their objectivity and profoundly limit their potential contributions.[2] They are therefore less likely to be included in many spheres unless they can demonstrate that their interests are in line with the "disinterested" gatekeepers (Alvarez 1994; Raven, Langer, and Frueh 1988). That is, people must assimilate the visions, desires, and beliefs of dominant groups to even hope to be "accepted." However for peoples of color such assimilation is no guarantee that their presence will be tolerated or their contributions valued.

Contrary to an assumption that those who occupy the unmarked "centers" are neutral in their approaches to the world, or that their products (including artistic) are devoid of all racial, economic, and political influences, I believe that all production and consumption of social knowledge (including art) is affected by the social location of those who produce, police, and consume cultural production. More specifically, research clearly demonstrates that art is socially produced (Becker 1982) and that processes which determine which forms of art are funded, validated, produced, etc., are affected by issues of class (DiMaggio and Useem 1978), race (Lippard 1990; Failing 1989), and gender (Raven, Langer, and Frueh 1988). That is, art is firmly located within, and contained by systems of racism, sexism, and class inequality. Ultimately, the politics/processes of containment that operate through art/culture, parallel the forms they take in other spheres.

The claims that I make about white involvement in multiculturalism are based on 50 focused interviews and two and a half years (1992–5) of participant observation and participatory research in arts organizations located in Santa Cruz County, California. The interviews were with arts administrators, patrons, and artists. Of those I interviewed more than three-quarters were predominately middle-to upper-class Euro-Americans. The remaining interviewees were primarily middle-class Latinos (six) and African Americans (three). My decision to interview Euro-Americans as my chief source of information grows out of the importance of understanding not only those who are the targets of oppression, but also those in dominant positions as well. This focus on researching up the power ladder means that much of what I have to say is based on my analysis of the practices and discourses of individuals who are privileged by race, and often by class. Additionally, my choice to conduct participatory research means that I am fully implicated in the field I present. Throughout my time in the community I was an active participant in many of the discussions that I analyze and in the groups that I investigate. In these sites I acted from my multiple social locations – as a white woman, as an activist committed to anti-racist politics, and as an artist. Finally, it should be noted that though I talk of whites employing strategies and processes of containment, I am not imputing *motives* to these individuals. In fact, I am willing to accept that these people are concerned, as they say, with inequality. However, all US whites are enmeshed in systems from which we benefit. These benefits/privileges and the discourses and practices that sustain them are part of the taken-for-granted world around us; they are, in essence, the air that we breathe. Without some sort of intervening experience, it is very unlikely that we would identify these systems (including explanations for these systems) as unjust and challenge them. Therefore, my comments should not be understood as a condemnation of these particular whites, or their particular organizations; instead, these processes, strategies, discourses are ones that almost all whites employ to some degree.

Competing Versions of Multiculturalism

My research and analysis suggests that race and class strongly influence how individuals and groups construct multiculturalism as both discourses and practices. I identified three ideal types of multiculturalism operating in the community – each was affected by the racial and class position of those through whom it was articulated.

Economically privileged whites were more likely to articulate the first form of multiculturalism, what I call a neo-liberal/conservative multiculturalism which asserts that equality in the art world can only be achieved by adhering to a neutral set of aesthetic, and organizational, standards. They believe that these aesthetic standards are universal and allow "everyone" to recognize quality cultural production. They generally believe that difference in prestige reflects difference in effort, or that inequality in outcome reflects inequality in talents, work effort, and ability. This discursive repertoire of neo-liberal conservative multiculturalism clearly aligns with an emphasis on meritocracy and transcendence (or more accurately absence) of social location that I noted earlier. Its effect in the local art world is similar to its effect elsewhere – it often works to maintain the status quo of funding and access to resources and gallery space.

The second discursive repertoire of multiculturalism, liberal color/power evasive multiculturalism (Frankenberg 1993), is articulated primarily by wealthy and middle-class whites, as well as a number of middle-class people of color; it is the dominant approach to multiculturalism in the County. A common assumption in this discursive repertoire is that while there may be a neutral standard for determining the quality of art, past barriers have made adherence to these standards impossible for artists of color. Therefore, proponents of this model generally recognize the need for *some* intervention to "assist" minorities in becoming better qualified to compete in the larger, seemingly neutral arena.

Finally, the author, and approximately 40 percent of the artists and administrators of color that I interviewed and observed hold to a radical race-cognizant multiculturalism which is underwritten by a sense that inequality is ingrained in the very fabric and institutions of the United States. Instead of arguing that minorities need to be let into an already existing canon, race-cognizant multiculturalists are more likely to point out the race and class biases embedded in current artistic parameters and call for redefinition. Clearly this repertoire of multiculturalism is critical of the politics and processes of containment that are employed throughout the community. Since such containment tactics are seen by the majority of white participants as race, class, gender neutral enactments of "universal" norms, those arguing for a recognition of these *as containment strategies* are often dismissed as hysterical, angry, and/or "separatist."

These different models of multiculturalism are articulated through whites and peoples of color who work and volunteer in a variety of capacities for local arts agencies. In the community, however, it is generally assumed that it is only people of color's racial/ethnic "difference" that matters; whites tend to see themselves as occupying a neutral racial location. For example, when asked to discuss issues of race and ethnicity in the arts, whites rarely discussed the position of whites *as whites* in the community. In only two cases did whites reference "white culture" as something that "oppressed" racialized others. When asked what "white culture" was, however, both interviewees laughed and then said that there is no whiteness – it is at its core, empty. Most whites, however, did not mention whites, or white culture, as salient to issues of race or ethnicity. Similarly, class differences are often an unspoken but an important mediating category. While often unacknowledged in the community, I argue that the positions that whites and elites occupy in these organizations are mediated by race, class and gender – and these positions provide us with opportunities to either reinforce, or subvert, systems of dominance.

In this chapter I suggest that the involvement of whites (and economic elites) in multiculturalism, though generally explained by reference to concern with, and interest in,[3] "diversity," is potentially fraught with peril. More specifically, while it is not *necessarily* the case, the practices that whites engage in, and the frameworks that guide white and elite actions, often work to produce types of multiculturalism which end up enforcing (elite) white privilege in the art world(s). Additionally, race and class intersect so that the community definitions of quality, appropriate organizational structure, and "good art" often rest upon elitist and white-centric approaches to the social world. In this short piece, I will explore a handful of practices and discursive repertoires that whites (and economic elites) employ that reconstitute white and elite advantage while appearing to work for the benefit of racialized Others. The material and ideological practices that I present here include: the ways that certain constructions of "quality," "merit," "art," and "aesthetics" favor works produced by whites; attempts to recruit peoples of color on to the Boards of Directors of white-centric and Euro-descendant focused arts organizations, and white involvement in the production of "ethnic art" and the arguments used to legitimate such production. It is to a consideration of these practices that I now turn.

(White) "Art" as Transcendence – "Ethnic Art" as Education

The dominant belief about art and creativity in the community is that they transcend cultural, racial, gender boundaries. This is a position articulated by relatively economically poor people of color as well as economically affluent whites. However, only relatively affluent whites argued that since art is based on socially unlocated (i.e., racially empty) "pure creativity," it can and should be judged solely on the presumably race, gender, and class neutral expression of that impulse. If in fact it is about pure creativity, then universal, neutral standards and gatekeeping behaviors can and should be used to judge art. Further, such standards should not be seen as racist, sexist or elitist in their conception or employment.

The notion that "neutral standards" for art exist is fairly common in the arts community among neo-liberal/conservative multiculturalists. While most of these people felt that racialized minorities should be included in the local art world (which means receiving funding, access to space, etc.) they are clear that "universal standards" should be applied to police the borders, and that one's artwork must transcend social/personal "difference" and thus speak through "universal" aesthetics to a universal audience.

This position was clearly demonstrated in the following example. In 1993 a prominent national artist served as consultant to a public sculpture "competition" held by Santa Cruz City. Approximately 56 pieces of sculpture were submitted by local artists for review. Of these pieces nine were picked by the City Arts Commission, with consultation from two local sculptors (who also are art professors at the university). From these nine sculptures, members of the public voted for their top choices. These public votes were tallied and the sculptures that received the most votes were bought by the City Arts Commission for permanent installation in downtown Santa Cruz. During the initial screening of the sculptures, one member of the Commission (a white "radical" lesbian) was concerned about the absence of "ethnic images" in the sculptures present. This member suggested this situation be taken into account for the final vote. In response, the artist/professor/consultant suggested that while the "ethnic thing is correct in a way, it also can lead to the worst sort of patronage, since it supports work that really is inferior in the name of diversity." He also noted that "by all means ethnics should be expected to participate, but they also should be held to a certain standard." When I asked what the standard was, he said it had to do with certain formal qualities (which were linked to education) in the art work. Or as an administrator from the McPherson Center for Art and History said in another context, there are "certain formal standards" and "certain formal rules that some pieces come closer to than others." Clearly the assumption is that these formal rules are universal – not marked by race or class. Here both discourses of assimilation and assumptions of white and elite neutrality work to constrain and limit the participation and evaluation of peoples of color.

While this is only one event, I witnessed other reviews and decisions where the notion of universal "standards" and aesthetics were employed to police cultural boundaries and contain the intrusion of racial Others. Sometimes this strategy was used by "experts" from the academy and at other times it was used by wealthy patrons and commissioners who have been trained in university art programs. What was consistently lacking in the use of such standards was any discussion of, and reflection about, the elite quality of the process. Additionally, in neither the art consultant's, nor the staff from the Art Museum's statement, is there acknowledgment that such standards, and the training that provide people with a sense of formal qualities, originate within a Western European elite art tradition. Non-Western forms and visions have been expropriated (Root 1996) and reworked into this (evolving) tradition, but their inclusion has largely been via Western artists (Cubists, etc.). This silence about the elite European-descendant nature of the standards and processes is, of course, socially, politically, and economically useful because it reaffirms the belief that the "best art" is that which has risen to the top of the art world. That is, it would not have achieved this status if we weren't all able to see it's universal quality and worth. Such discourses of merit and universality are effective precisely because they mask their class, race, gendered location, and hence their status as processes of containment.

Most whites I interviewed and observed did not employ this model in its purer form; instead, they articulated a liberal power-evasive multiculturalism to argue that while all art must be "good," multiculturalism should be supported for its educational potential and as a way of preserving authentic ethnic arts. This, in some ways, is the flip side of valorizing and funding arts which meet some neutral standards. Here, arts produced by peoples of color are romanticized if they can be interpreted as authentic displays of racial/ethnic difference; this also provides room for whites to show support for multiculturalism while rejecting art seen as "culturally exclusive" or "separatist." As Trinh Minh-ha (1989: 89) so eloquently states:

> Today, planned authenticity is rife; as a product of hegemony and a remarkable counterpart of universal standardization, it constitutes an efficacious means of silencing the cry of racial oppression. We no longer wish to erase your difference, We demand, on the contrary, that you remember and assert it. At least to a certain extent.

In the County as a whole, the ethnic art form which receives the most funding is Folklorico dance. It is an art form which I understand to have different meanings for Chicanos involved in it, and for the majority of non-Chicanos who either fund it, or consume it as entertainment. For whites Folklorico is full of beautiful costumes, dancing, smiling people – it is essentially non-confrontational. It also is a form of Latino culture which harkens to a past – it does not appear on the surface to be about present concerns, politics, inter-ethnic tension, or the future. Ethnicity and race are re-inscribed (for whites) as part of the mythic past, and divorced from current and future struggles. On the other hand, according to some Chicanos, it instills a sense of cultural/ethnic pride in the community, and it also allows people to gather and through gathering to engage in political discussions and organization. There is nothing, from within the culture, that insists that Folklorico dance is apolitical. But from the outside it appears (to non-Latinos) safe, happy, and "soft": an appearance which reinforces the idea that art is, or should be, non-confrontational and pleasing – an appearance favored by white donors and some white administrators. As one white upper-middle class participant said of all ethnic arts: "it's important to support because it provides a comfortable way for people to learn about people who are different."

In addition to favoring cultural production which allows the (white) viewer to focus on costumes, dancing, and history, whites also appear to value "ethnic art" because of what it will teach "us" about cultures of which we are ignorant. In this conception, multiculturalism and ethnic art should be supported because it bridges differences and provides educational opportunities. While the educational component of art can't be denied, it is useful to consider the difference between focusing on the aesthetic qualities of (racially unmarked) art versus focusing on the historical, authentic, or educational uses of multiculturalism.[4]

While not as blatant as past practices of racial and cultural Othering, seeing ethnic arts organizations as educational resources, rather than as representations of art forms that are as aesthetically valuable as the symphony or local Shakespeare company, is a form of devaluation – a devaluation that allows white definitions of aesthetics and quality of art to remain firmly intact. Here, containment discourses of merit and universalism are employed in ways which protect white privileging because these discourses rest on a larger erasure/denial/silence about whiteness (for discourses and gaps see Foucault 1970, 1976; Said 1978). The very discourses upon which art and culture rest – merit, talent, transcendence, aesthetics – demands racial emptiness/neutrality.

Racial emptiness (presumed to equal racial neutrality), however, is a condition only really grantable to those who (presumably) have no racial location, i.e., whites. Whiteness exists as an unmarked, invisible, and central place in art and multiculturalism; whites then produce "art," while people of color produce (racially marked) educationally useful, "ethnic art."

Additional arguments that whites presented to explain their support of multiculturalism included: (1) multiculturalism promotes the assimilation and integration of peoples of color. In specific instances where participants (always white) used the language of assimilation, they suggested that funding ethnic arts/cultural organizations was important because it would "speed up the assimilation of minorities." The greatest anxieties seemed to be about Latinos, particularly recent immigrants. White patrons made comments such as: "this work is important because it teaches them how to do things the American way," and "we (X arts organization) really want to have events that integrate Hispanics, but that's not happening. We need to do more work to integrate and assimilate them to the larger culture." This last comment is particularly interesting, given that in the particular city in question over 60 percent of the population is Latino. The assumption that underlies assimilationist discourses is that "they" will be better off when they do things like "us" (presumably white). Such language was also often coupled with a concern over separatism (see discussion below, page 325) and the presumed "self-segregation" of peoples of color. (2) A second type of argument made by whites for supporting multiculturalism is that it allows for the education of board members of color who then can move up to "better" organizations. That is, we can train them in their "own" organizations and then recruit them to serve on the boards of directors for larger, generally white-centric, agencies. This will fulfill these agencies' need to have a "diverse" board of directors when they apply for state funding (see discussion in next section). (3) Finally, the third additional argument for multiculturalism made by whites is that it can empower racial/ethnic minorities. This last category, however, even for the most "well-intentioned" liberal whites, was problematic since they worried about the "separatism" of people of color (and didn't worry about the de facto segregation of whites).

In addition to the advantages maintained by "fostering" multiculturalism within a white-centric and elitist discursive framework, race(ist) and class advantage or dominance may be reinforced through a variety of white-centric practices. These include the attempted recruitment of people of color as members of local Boards of Directors, and the involvement of whites in the production of "ethnic arts."

Incorporating Racial Minorities on
Arts Agencies' Boards of Directors

One of the primary ways that federal, state and local agencies determine if a group is becoming multicultural or is "furthering multiculturalism," is whether it has people of color serving as board members or staff. However, a few Euro-American arts administrators dismiss the effort to increase the presence of people of color on local Boards as a fad that will soon blow over – allowing arts organizations to go on with producing and promoting presumably universal art. Other Euro-American artists and arts administrators note the problem of wanting to increase the involvement of people of color but of not knowing *how* to create such an increase. This dilemma reflects the history (and presence) of segregation in our country and in the local community. Euro-Americans, particularly upper-class Euro-Americans by and large *don't know* people of color. Through housing policies, economic strategies, and cultural patterns (education, marriage, etc.) whites have historically remained largely segregated from people of color (Massey and Denton 1993). This lack of meaningful connection with people of color, and its conflation with economic disparities, makes their recruitment on to largely white boards difficult.

In Santa Cruz County there is a definite sense that boards are constructed along class lines – though "class" was a term used only by a few of the interviewees – other interviewees consistently referred to issues such as access to money, pull or influence in the community, and prestige as reasons that board members are recruited.[5] This observation is in line with much sociological literature which suggests that the Boards of Directors for "elite" or "benchmark" arts, are constructed along class lines (DiMaggio and Useem 1978) and that elites construct, control, and consume culture in ways designed to enhance their own class position (Bourdieu 1984). While public arts agencies (such as the local County Cultural Council) spend a great deal of time considering

how well potential board members fulfill representational requirements of geography, business, education, politics, community
leadership, gender, and race/ethnicity; for most large, private, non-
profit organizations (with correspondingly large budgets), access
to money is an overriding category of concern. Given that class,
race and ethnicity are conflated, the likelihood of minority incorporation on the larger organization's Board of Directors is slim.

A high ranking white administrator for one of the local art
museums clearly articulated the vision that class, or access to
money, is the pivotal consideration when constructing a Board of
Directors. When discussing the issue of bringing minorities onto
Boards of Directors, he said:

> We struggle with that too, because if you take a look at our board
> and it's a very white board, we sit and struggle with it and struggle
> with it, but sit there, and say, well being a private non-profit, we
> can justify it otherwise, and say, well, you know, but there are only
> four Hispanics in great positions, or x number who are in great
> positions who can help us out, they're already serving on every
> damn board in town. We've had them here once, and a farm worker
> is not going to do us any good, which is true, you know.
>
> Q: Good in terms of having contacts in the community, around
> funding?
>
> Yea, mainly around funding and serving a purpose for, every fully
> private non-profit the Board is responsible to raise all the money
> that we do every year. Each museum trustee is responsible for a cer-
> tain amount of money, give, gets or facilitate. Well, if you've got
> someone there who can't do that, then they're not sharing, not to say
> that they can't do it in some other way, but sometimes you can get
> so overboard on the other side that you get diminished in that then
> you've lost your whole purpose because you don't have enough
> money to even do anything with. Even though you're PC correct,
> you know, you could die and have a little gravestone R.I.P. over
> here, you know. So, sometimes there's some things that weigh about
> that. Again, you know, politics to a degree, but it's quiet politics.

His comments reflect an understanding, shared by others I interviewed, that the function of Board members, at least for "major"
organizations (such as the Museum, Symphony and Shakespeare
Santa Cruz) is to bring in money – either through personal donations or through networking in the community. From the Museum
Center's point of view – farm workers (who are presumably the

only other choices among Latinos if you can't recruit the "four or so" wealthy Latinos) can't help the Museum. Wealth then, is held up as the race-neutral standard which operates to exclude peoples of color. What should also be noted in this discourse is its assimilationist assumptions. The message is: if you give according to our definition of giving then you fit in, but if you don't/can't then you are useless. This, of course, is one of the paradoxes of assimilationist efforts undertaken by (economic and racial) elites. The official push for incorporating people of color rests on the idea that bringing people of color into an organization will enrich a group; they can bring perspectives and ways of doing things that stem from a different tradition. On the other hand, it is only those who fit the pre-existing definitions and categories of contribution who are considered to be worthwhile. Constructions of contribution which emphasize wealth, then, may appropriately be understood as working to maintain a particular cultural and political milieu in the organization. So, just how do organizations, such as the Museum, attempt to meet the mandate of diversity and keep the structure and ambience of their board relatively unchanged?

Most evidence suggests that when local Boards of Directors do recruit a minority Board member they not only attempt to find someone of the same class background, but also someone who may be more conservative politically and socially than their (almost always) white counterparts. In this way, whites assure themselves that they are getting someone unlikely to "rock the boat." Mary Kay Hubbard, a white, wealthy, woman who has sat on the Board of Directors for virtually every large arts/cultural agency in the County, notes that one of the effects of recruiting people to be a "figurehead" is that "you run out and find someone with a Latino last name and stick them on the Board." She says that usually such recruitment is a problem because "most people who are picked to do that are ineffective, kind of lost – haven't had any training. Kind of out of the social orbit, it's a difficult position for them. It doesn't work."[6] Hubbard then went on to praise one Latina staffer for the Cultural Council who also briefly served as a County Arts Commissioner. Of G. Hernandez, Hubbard says:

> Now in cases like (Hernandez) who's just as bright as a button – perfect – I wish we could clone her and put her on every Board. She's someone who is learned, and is *interested and curious,* and just couldn't have been better. And that's the kind of ... [Three second

pause]. And I'm sure there's billions of people out there like that, but how do we find them. ...

This is an interesting situation: on the one hand, Hubbard is a supporter of "diversity" and she recognizes that the behavior of Boards can subvert the potential of bringing in people who may have different perspectives to offer the organization. Further, she criticizes groups who only attempt to incorporate peoples of color in order to alleviate pressure from the State, and not because they are seen as potential valuable contributors. On the other hand, Hubbard (who is representative of a sentiment articulated by other affluent whites) engages in a common elite (and white) practice of placing the responsibility for lack of representation and preparation on people of color. Therein lies the contradiction. First, responsibility seems to lie with the Boards who attempt to respond to the need for multiculturalism in very facile ways. However, when she starts to talk about Hernandez she talks about how she is *interested and curious* and she learns, and "she couldn't be better." The explanation for Hernandez's success is her own abilities and interest. By extension, the onus for fitting in is put on the Latino community and its members. Hubbard lamented that if we could only clone Hernandez and her attributes, we would solve the problem of minority Board members who "don't fit in." "Fit" here is conceived in very assimilationist and individualist terms. Like the art museum administrator, she is cognizant that "networks" work to exclude people, that if you are not part of the elite network you won't fit in, you won't be able to network in the community to raise money. However, when it comes down to it, the responsibility for these issues is placed back onto peoples of color who are expected to assimilate into existing networks and adopt white-centric ways of "belonging in a community."

In the cases above, the maintenance of white and class hegemony is not too difficult to detect – whites and economic elites maintain control of organizations and attempt to incorporate people of color because they feel they must to remain competitive for funding. At the same time, most of these whites say they are staunchly in support of multicultural art, and diversifying existing white art organizations. They don't consider, however, how their organizational and personal practices may in fact exclude people of color from meaningful consideration to be board members or from meaningful involvement once they've been recruited.

Instead, "failure" to be an "involved" board member is attributed to lack of interested or ability on the part of people of color. They fall back on presumably neutral categories of interest, hard work, and visibility, to explain how, on a personal level, such incorporation has not taken place. These discourses of personal responsibility and assimilation allow donors and administrators to distance themselves from the maintenance of racial hierarchy and segregation while fully employing strategies of containment. Of course, the mechanisms that work in this community to maintain race and class inequalities are not always so straightforward. In the case of white involvement in the production of art forms embedded in traditional and living communities of peoples of color (also referred to as "ethnic arts") the effects, and the arguments about such involvement, are more complex.

White Involvement in the Production of "Ethnic Art"

Whites are involved with the production of a variety of ethnic arts in the community. For instance, they participate in and teach "African-inspired" drumming and dancing, Taiko drumming, Folklorico dancing, and a multitude of other "ethnic" arts forms. Such involvement, not surprisingly, is contested by some people of color who argue that white involvement represents cultural appropriation and cannibalism. In response to these claims, explanatory models have developed to explain the conditions under which white (non-indigenous) involvement might be acceptable.

There are three primary models presented in the community under which white involvement *may be* legitimate. They are: first, that what legitimizes cultural production is not the producer's race/ethnicity, but whether they produce high quality work. Pure aesthetics, ability, and a sense of universal connection are called into play to legitimate white involvement. This model was only presented in my research by whites – particularly middle-class and affluent whites. Second, the majority of the people in the community (both whites and peoples of color) argue that white involvement is unproblematic if the Euro-American has "good intentions." The third category of responses, which was only made by peoples of color, is more complex. Adherents believe that white involvement (or any non-indigenous involvement) is only justifiable if it is done in collaboration with an indigenous producer of a given cultural form. Each of these categories has adherents in the local community, and in some cases individuals use multiple justifications to explain their own, or others', involvement. Since my emphasis in this chapter is on the ways that white and economically elite domination is reconfigured in the art world, I will only discuss the first two legitimizing frameworks; for a complete discussion, please see Eichstedt (1995).

Quality is the Key

The first response to critiques of white involvement in ethnic art is: "*If you do it well, you have the right to do it.*" As I mentioned above, this response is rooted in a sense of universality. Those artists and arts administrators who make this response claim that it's not the color of someone's skin, nor their heritage, that determines their ability to communicate through art but their artistic *ability*. Clearly ability and race/ethnicity are uncoupled in this configuration. Once again, this construction aligns easily with discourses of universalism and meritocracy – discourses which in most instances presume the socially uninterested location of whites. Interestingly, this particular response and the legitimation it offered was only raised by whites who participate in the production of ethnic arts – it was not made by any of the African Americans or Latinos whom I interviewed.

For instance, Patricia Ackby, a white theater producer, wrote and produced a play in the early 1990s, based on the story of Huck Finn, but told from a slave's point of view. Ms Ackby spoke passionately about the legitimacy of whites "crossing borders," and with disdain of those she sees as promoting separatism and censorship. She linked this move toward censorship and separatism not only to certain local people of color in town, but to a group of leftist whites. When Ackby started looking for funding for the play, she both anticipated, and found, that the legitimacy of her doing such work was questioned. In response to the questions "who are your co-writers" and "what makes you think you can do this?," she said:

> I've always researched everything I do, that's what I do as an artist, as a writer, as a person who looks at life. That's what I do and

> I think I'm valid, I believe that if that's what you do and you do it
> well, that you have every right to do it. That's what Hemingway
> did, he wrote *The Old Man and the Sea* as a Cuban fisherman, and
> yes, you have the right to do this.

Throughout her interview Ms Ackby reiterated her belief that
one should have the right to "do something" if one does it well.
Questioning this "right" represents, in her mind, separatism and
censorship, which she finds "quite troubling." While Ms Ackby
acknowledges a history of oppression and racism, she also feels
that attempting to build up your own power by excluding others
is limited and, that multiculturalism, by the very way it is defined,
is, to some extent, anti-white.

Ackby most clearly articulated her sense that excluding whites
from ethnic cultural production is censorship, when discussing
the January 1994 Ethnofete.[7] She says:

> Well, it felt very anti-Anglo … as soon as they talked, when they go
> through that big thing about false representation of culture, it
> comes out a lot. Because that's really, in an atmosphere like that, it's
> like censorship, and … the atmosphere is so charged that a reason-
> able person couldn't, it would be hard to work inter-racially or
> interculturally. Working interculturally is not an issue for them,
> or it's not what they're after, I mean, every person [louder/higher
> voice] seemed to be for their cultural identity, as though it were the
> whole universe. I mean, that's what I got, and, and they wanted to
> support others who felt likewise.

Part of the way Ackby knows something is separatist is because of
the emotions it is built upon (from her perspective) and it's *effect*
on whites. She repeatedly referred to separatism as "coming from
a place of a lot of anger … and it's intimidating, alienating, and
noninclusive." In her opinion, anger (or rage) is not something
a "reasonable person" should have to be exposed to. While she
understands that people may draw together amongst themselves
and exclude others, because "they're trying to build up their own
identity after being squashed," she ultimately just "doesn't believe
in it because it's 'limiting.' " While it may be that many people feel
that long-term separatism is less politically efficacious than multiracial alliances, it is important to note that white(s') ability to deny
a salient white identity, coupled with our proclivity to see ourselves as representative of all human experience, means that it's

comforting to dismiss anti-racism efforts by people of color as "too narrow" or as "limiting." Such a dismissal rests on the fact that whites generally aren't compelled to be ever-cognizant of how race operates in our daily lives, such a dismissal, therefore, can be analyzed as an exercise in racial (and class) privilege.

Further analysis suggests that the move to label critiques of white involvement as censorship and separatism is predicated on a certain logic and has a number of effects. The logic is interesting because the exclusion of people of color is explained in terms of merit and ability, while the exclusion of Euro-Americans is explained by censorship. In both cases culturally sanctioned explanations are being used to explain issues of inclusion and exclusion in ways that get Euro-Americans off the hook of racism and maintain their racial privilege. That they contradict each other, or that different explanations are applied to different groups, does not appear to be a consideration.

These arguments parallel those at the national level – for instance the 1990 furor over the selection of (white) British actor Jonathan Pryce to play the lead role of a Eurasian pimp in the Broadway production of *Miss Saigon*. The Actor's Equity Union voted to bar Pryce from reprising the role he had played in London because the union said it "could not appear to condone the casting of a Caucasian in the role of a Eurasian" (*New York Times*, August 26, 1990: H7). After the show was canceled, and the producer argued the right of artistic freedom, the Actor's Equity Union reversed its decision. Asian American actors who had criticized Pryce's hiring were accused of self – interest and prominent white actors and white conservative pundits claimed that excluding whites from portraying people of color was reverse discrimination, racism, and an affront to "artistic freedom." In this scenario, as in local ones, critics argued that it is morally wrong to limit who can play a role on racial grounds – the grounds should be those of creativity and ability. Claims of "artistic freedom" and "ability" have been used in the art world to justify, or explain why certain people receive sponsorship, recognition, and prestige and others have not. Following this logic, they got there because they were the best – not because they were unduly advantaged in any way. According to Ellen Holly of the *New York Times* this ignores:

> a long and profoundly frustrating history in America in which … the ideal world we all long for has functioned so that whites are

free to play everything under the sun while black, Hispanic and Asian actors are not only restricted to their own category, but forced to surrender roles *in their own category* that a white desires."(August 26, 1990: H7)

This one-way street, while recognized as racist by many people of color, has been defended by most whites on the basis of the duplicitous nature of acting, and on the foundation of talent, creativity, and "stardom." In other words, white advantage is hidden (and maintained) through the use of culturally sanctioned explanations which do not implicate those making them as racist (see Wellman 1993). Again, processes of containment work here to ensure that the presumption of white disinterestedness is preserved, while the exclusion of people of color is justified through "racially neutral" discourses and practices.

The second, and most common, way of explaining white involvement is to reference the "good intentions" and "interests" of whites. These claims of good intentions rest on power/color evasive theories of race, and on dreams of art as providing a bridge across racial difference.

Good Intentions

The good intentions explanation for white involvement basically asserts that if whites are involved because they are truly interested in, and (hopefully) respectful of the art form they wish to study, their involvement is legitimate and non-problematic. This was a discursive formation employed repeatedly in the community, and the subject position it worked to construct for whites was one of concerned, well meaning, participants.

Ms Door, who is represented in this chapter's opening vignette, is representative of whites who articulated this vision. As a self-defined white, working-class, hippie involved with African Dance, and former head of the Santa Cruz Ethnic Arts Network (SCEAN), Ms Door, was compelled to construct and draw upon an explanatory model for her involvement that could successfully counter claims that she was not only an interloper, but a cultural imperialist.

Door legitimizes white people studying African dance/drumming by arguing that social change (loss of tribal ways) is going to happen in all cultures, and preservation of traditional ways is important. According to her, traditions, in all cultures, fall apart as young people seek to be more westernized. If there are people "on the other side" who have the resources and want to learn traditional customs through Master sources, then they should be welcomed. For her, information *will be* "transferred"; it's primarily a matter of the manner in which that transference takes place.

In her estimation, it is the willingness of white people to learn a culture respectfully that legitimizes their entry into a given field. This is underwritten by an understanding of racism as attitudes and individual acts of meanness – not as a systematic disadvantaging (or pillaging of the cultures) of peoples of color. This blends seamlessly with a belief that whites' "respectfulness" is more important than structural arrangements of power. It is also interesting to note the way that the *inevitability* of "information transfer" and social change, is called upon to legitimize the involvement of whites. The assumption that information transfer is inevitable and that the desire of "young people to be more westernized" is a natural fact, allows her to feel that her own involvement, and that of other well-intentioned whites is unproblematically beneficial to minority cultures. They are "saving" those cultures from unscrupulous others, and working to better the world.

Many of the points that Door makes are important and perhaps "correct" in a way; what is problematic in her explanation, however, is the essentialist underpinning and somewhat exoticizing framework from which she operates. For instance, Door argues that there is an affinity between hippies and ethnic arts because hippies are "tribal people" and therefore connect with "tribal arts." This use of the notion of "tribal" is important because it draws on exoticizing notions of tribal and native people; tribal people are seen as close-knit, local, in touch with nature, spiritual, innocent, and as inherently opposed to capitalism and/or imperialism. This is coupled with her belief that white hippies are drawn to ethnic arts because "dominant culture" is "empty" and "unsatisfying." Ultimately, then, for Door (and for other whites in the community) whiteness is largely empty and lifeless – blackness (or any racial/ethnic "otherness") becomes the sign of authenticity and cultural richness. All one needs to access this rich authenticity are good intentions and an open heart.

This faith in good intentions was shared by a number of participants in the local art world; good intentions could open doors and get people inside the culture they wished to either be part of, or represent. This model, it should be noted, is largely underwritten by an understanding of racism as a collection of attitudes and individual acts of meanness – not as a systematic disadvantaging of peoples of color. As I noted, both whites and peoples of color in the community expressed this ideal. However, people of color tended to shade this ideal slightly differently – as interviews progressed, people of color were more likely to mix talk of good intentions with talk of the need for collaboration. Others in the community take it farther and argue that to legitimately produce in a culture that is not one's own, one must be involved with peoples from that group/culture (in a sustained way) and collaborate in the production of the cultural form. This approach seems to me to be much more cognizant of racial inequality stemming from differential access to resources and issues of group dynamics as opposed to individual good will.

Conclusions

The above assertion of good intentions works so successfully because one of the most powerful discourses in the US is that of individualism. Individualism is not merely an assertion of individual responsibility, rather it can be more rightly understood as a denial of systemic forces and of our own complicity with systems of oppression. When individualism is coupled with systemic refusal to acknowledge whiteness (as a system of beliefs, attitudes, behaviors, institutions, privileges) then whites become *individuals* par excellence. As individuals, what matters more than anything are our own "intentions," desires, and personal attitudes (Scheurich 1993).

The ethic of individuality and opportunity that underwrites many elite and white discourses and practices clearly allows the reproduction of systems of domination that benefit whites/elites. This is true in discourses of art which favor "neutral standards" with absolutely no regard to where those standards came from, nor how they evolved, nor who has the educational access to learn about them. As Paula Rothenberg (1990: 47) asserts:

> In a context where wealthy, white, males set the standard, race and gender paradigms that assert either "separate" or "different"

but "equal" will always perform the dual function of implicitly evaluating as "inferior" what they purport to be describing as "different."

This is also true in recruiting practices which equate "contribution" solely with money. That is, when money is uncritically accepted as the only legitimate form of contribution and the class and racial *effects* of such a definition are denied, then any other contribution is seen as inferior and undesirable. Finally, such discourses of individualism and universal opportunity firmly underwrite arguments that white involvement is okay as long as individual participants mean well – to even raise the issue of exploitation or appropriation becomes an attack on an individual – and is not perceived as a critique of historical and contemporary structural circumstances that individuals, perhaps unwittingly, reproduce through their individual practices.

In these examples, individualism, the denial/erasure of the salience of whiteness, and beliefs in racism as primarily an issue of attitudes all intersect in ways which significantly limit the effectiveness of white support for (or constructions of) multiculturalism. In fact, in each of the three areas I have explored in this paper whites (and elites) draw upon culturally sanctioned discourses to explain why it is legitimate that business as usual continues and how the perpetuation of racial and class inequality is therefore out of their hands. *That is, they employ process/strategies of containment that work to their material and ideological advantage.*

What is striking is that these things all occur in a community where almost every white person I spoke with asserted their interest in, and commitment to, doing away with racial/ethnic injustice. (Not surprisingly, not one affluent or middle-class person whom I interviewed ever mentioned doing away with class inequality.) But our desire to do away with injustice is clearly not enough.

If local groups staffed predominately by whites really want to make a dent in racial inequality, or build bridges across racial divides, they need to look at how their own practices marginalize the contributions of non-white, non-elite people; that is, they need to understand their practices and frameworks *as processes of containment.* They also need to understand themselves as actors located in specific historical conditions – that is, we have to understand how discourses of individualism, merit, and universality speak through us. Whites are constructed through these discourses as particular kinds of privileged subjects but we are not passive in this. For instance, while I cannot shed my white/elite privileges I can develop a different consciousness about my location. I, and other whites, can also use those privileges to work for racial and economic justice. However, we cannot work for real racial and economic justice if we do it in isolation from people of color (and those who are economically poor). If participants continue to apply frameworks and criteria that on the surface ignore both power and race, whites (and economic elites) can continue to both feel good about themselves (as non-racists) and maintain their racial and class advantage. As Ms Door discovered, when whites construct visions for "healing" that aren't constructed *in concert with* peoples of color we strongly risk engaging in politics which are paternalistic and which continue to privilege white ways of organizing and building community. If local (and national) groups are serious about addressing cultural inequities, we must engage in a radical positionality that challenges assumptions and practices of normality and neutrality, assumptions and practices which maintain elite/white privilege and racial inequality. We must develop and enact a race and power cognizant multiculturalism that recognizes and challenges containment processes that derail efforts at constructing a just world.

NOTES

1 I would like to thank Carole Corcoran, Judy Howard, and Jodi O'Brien for their thoughtful comments on this essay.
2 For instance, in a study of diversity at UC Berkeley, African American students reported white students acting surprised when they encountered them outside the natural science buildings (Diversity Project 1989). Also see Alvarez (1994) for a discussion of the assumptions in academics that Chicanos all bring the same knowledge, outlook, and contributions to academics – so that to hire more than one Chicano would be "redundant."
3 Though I don't elaborate on it here, it is important to consider the ways in which white "concern" and "interest" may be problematic. While on the surface these things are benign, when located in a racist structure, concern and interest can be paternalistic, can rest on a desire to assimilate those whose difference is seen as threatening, or grow from a desire to consume that which is imagined as exotic and

exciting. Conversely, such involvement can also signal genuine concern with structural inequality and a willingness to be a solid ally. My work suggests that this last option is not very common.

4 These ways of conceiving of the cultural/art production of non-European descendant peoples are not new – there is a long history of valuing such production for what it can do for whites. For instance, the discourse and practice of Primitivism extended the practice of colonization to the pillaging of artistic and cultural form. Likewise the collecting and displaying practices of most Western museums served to justify Western expansion on the grounds that other cultures were primitive. (see Foster 1985; Fusco 1995; Harrison and Wood 1992; Rydell 1984).

5 In many ways this emphasis on status, influence and access, parallels both Weber's and Domhoff's conceptualization of class. However, few of the local participants will label themselves as being of a certain class – instead references to what sociologists consider "class" are much more oblique.

6 What is left largely unexplored is the experience of those people of color who have participated in dominant arts organizations. Unfortunately, there are only a few people of color who have participated as members on these more prestigious Boards of Directors, and I did not interview all of them. Those few I have interviewed, however, indicated a shared awareness that they were being chosen as "tokens." However, one Latino who has served on various Boards spoke of doing what he wanted on the Board "regardless of the tokenistic intent" of those who recruited him. Another spoke of pursuing programs in which they were interested, regardless of the original intentions of other Board members. I do not have the data to speculate whether this is a sentiment shared by other people of color who serve as Board members to prestigious groups. While I recognize the limitations such an exclusion places on my work, I think it is worthwhile to consider the ways that arts administrators and patrons that I did speak with understand local efforts to incorporate people of color.

7 Ethnofetes were gatherings, sponsored by the County's Cultural Council, of peoples involved in the multicultural or ethnic arts communities.

REFERENCES

Alvarez, Robert R. 1994. "Un Chilero en la Academia: Sifting, Shifting, and the Recruitment of Minorities in Anthropology," in *Race*, Steven Gregory and Roger Sanjek, (eds). New Brunswick, NJ: Rutgers University Press.

Becker, Howard. 1982. *Art Worlds*. Berkeley, CA: University of California Press.

Bourdieu, Pierre. 1984. *Distinction: A Social Critique of the Judgement of Taste*, trans. Richard Nice. Cambridge, MA: Harvard University Press.

DiMaggio, Paul and Michael Useem. 1978. "Cultural Property and Public Policy: Emerging Tensions in Government Support for the Arts." *Social Research* 45(2): 357–87.

Eichstedt, Jennifer L. 1995. *Challenging and Maintaining Racial Inequality: Multiculturalism in a Local Arts Community*. Unpublished Dissertation. University of California, Santa Cruz.

Failing, Patricia. 1989. "Black Artists Today: A Case of Exclusion." *ARTnews* 88(3): 124–31.

Feagin, Joe R. and Vera Hernan. 1995. *White Racism: The Basics*. New York, NY: Routedge.

Foster, Hal. 1985. *Recodings: Art, Spectacle, and Cultural Politics*. Port Townsend, WA: Bay Press.

Foucault, Michel. 1970. *The Order of Things: An Archeology of the Human Sciences*. New York, NY: Random House.

———. 1978. *History of Sexuality*, Vol. I. New York, NY: Pantheon Books.

Frankenberg, Ruth. 1993. *White Women, Race Matters: The Social Construction of Whiteness*. Minneapolis, MN: University of Minnesota Press.

Fusco, Coco. 1995. *English is Broken Here: Notes on Cultural Fusion in the Americas*. New York, NY: W. W. Norton and Company.

Gans, Herbert. 1983. "American Popular Culture and High Culture in a Changing Class Structure," in *Art, Ideology, and Politics*. J. Balfe and M. Wyszomirski. New York, NY: Praeger.

Goldberg, David (ed.). 1994. *Multiculturalism: A Critical Reader*. Cambridge, MA: Basil Blackwell.

Gould, Stephen J. 1981. *The Mismeasure of Man*. New York, NY: W. W. Norton and company.

Harding, Sandra. 1993. *The "Racial" Economy of Science: Toward a Democratic Future*. Bloomington, IN: Indiana University Press.

Harrison, C. and Paul Wood. 1992. *Art in Theory: 1900–1990*. Oxford: Blackwell Publishers.

Holly, Ellen. 1990. *New York Times*. August 26, Section H7.

Lippard, Lucy R. 1990. *Mixed Blessings, New Art in Multicultural America*. New York, NY: Pantheon Books.

Lorde, Audre. 1984. *Sister Outsider*. Trumansburg, NY: The Crossing Press.

Massey, Douglas S. and Nancy A. Denton. 1993. *American Apartheid: Segregation and the Making of the Underclass*. Cambridge, MA: Harvard University Press.

McIntosh, Peggy. 1992. "White Privilege and Male Privilege: A Personal Account of Coming to See Correspondences," in *Race, Class and Gender*,

Margaret Anderson and Patricia Hill Collins, (eds). Belmont, CA: Wadsworth.

Minh-ha, Trinh. 1989. *Woman, Native, Other*. Bloomington, IN: Indiana University Press.

Morrison, Toni. 1992. *Playing in the Dark: Whiteness and the Literary Imagination*. New York, NY: Vintage Books.

Raven, Arlene, Cassandra Langer, and Joanna Frueh. 1988. *Feminist Art Criticism*. Ann Arbor, MI: UMI Research Press.

Root, Deborah. 1996. *Cannibal Culture: Art, Appropriation, and the Commodification of Difference*. Boulder, CO: Westview.

Rothenberg, Paula. 1990. "The Construction, Deconstruction, and Reconstruction of Difference." *Hypatia*, 5(1): 42–55.

Rydell, Robert. 1984. *All the World's a Fair: Visions of Empire at American International Exhibitions, 1876–1916*. Chicago, IL: University of Chicago Press.

Said, Edward. 1978. *Orientalism*. New York, NY: Pantheon.

Santa Cruz Ethnic Arts Network. 1992. Flyer: "America Discovers Columbus: A Call to Participate." September.

Scheurich, James J. 1993. "Towards a White Discourse on White Racism." *Educational Researcher* 22(8): 5–16.

Ware, Vron. 1991. *Beyond the Pale: White Women, Racism, and History*. New York, NY: Verso.

Wellman, David T. 1977, 1993. *Portraits of White Racism*. New York, NY: Cambridge University Press.

12

The Politics of Race and Sport: Resistance and Domination in the 1968 African American Olympic Protest Movement[1]

Douglas Hartmann

Introduction: The Paradox of Cultural Politics

Somewhere in *Race Matters* Cornel West (1993) comments: "One irony of our present moment is that just as young black men are murdered, maimed and imprisoned in record numbers, their styles have become disproportionately influential in shaping popular culture." Then, there is the parable Pierre Bourdieu (1990: 156) told about black athletes in prestigious American universities in the 1970s: despite their seeming prominence and importance, these student-athletes found themselves in "golden ghettos" of isolation where conservatives were reluctant to talk with them because they were black, while liberals were hesitant to converse with them because they were athletes. These two anecdotes, I think, call our attention to the ambiguities, paradoxes, and contradictions of the relationships between culture (especially in its more "popular" forms), political power, and social change in liberal democratic societies. On the one hand, cultural arenas provide racial and ethnic peoples with their most tangible and direct access to, and influence in, mainstream society; and yet, on the other, this cultural capital seems to produce very little in the way of concrete social change, and may, ultimately, reinforce the very injustices and inequalities these disempowered groups mean to confront and contest in the first place.

One response to these observations is to argue that the mere fact of ethnic group dependence upon such non-traditional and seemingly less-than-important social spaces simply symbolizes the powerlessness, marginalization, and inequality of these groups, and the ultimate futility of their efforts to effect meaningful social change. One might conclude, furthermore, that if these cultural and symbolic forms are political at all, they are simply truncated, even sophomoric versions of the usual politics and results of grassroots resistance.

My own approach, however, is somewhat different. While I acknowledge that the politics and political results of such cultural practices typically reproduce a dialectic of resistance and domination that is by now all too familiar and discouraging for disenfranchised groups; I would also suggest that they are not the same old politics as usual, but the working-out of a more complicated, complex form of the resistance and domination dialectic. More specifically, I would argue that in an age when power and capital have developed sophisticated techniques to insulate themselves against traditional, materialist forms of protest and challenge, cultural arenas provide one of the few public spaces in which otherwise marginalized and disempowered groups can express social grievances and begin to fashion some sort of mobilization on their behalf. This is not to say that cultural resistance necessarily "succeeds"; indeed, more often than not, it falls rather short of its mark. But it is to advance the claim that the terrain of social struggle has shifted to a profoundly cultural or ideological level; it is also to pose the question of what this development implies about the structure and operation of domination more generally speaking. It is with these issues in mind that I will explore the history of a clear and self-conscious attempt to use sport as a forum for racial protest: the 1968 African American Olympic protest movement.

To the extent that they know about this "movement" at all, most Americans probably associate it with a single and singularly powerful image: that of two African American athletes poised on the victory stand, Olympic medals hanging around their necks and black-gloved fists raised high above lowered eyes and bowed heads. The image itself was the performative work of Tommie Smith and John Carlos, two American sprinters who had finished first and third respectively in a world-record setting 200-meter dash at the 1968 Mexico City Olympic Games. At the traditional awards ceremony, the two victorious athletes mounted the award podium shoeless, clad in sweat suits and black stockinged feet. Smith wore a black scarf around his neck, Carlos a string of Mardi Gras beads. Both men displayed buttons reading "The Olympic Project for Human Rights." In the conventional ritual of the Olympic victory ceremony, the Star Spangled Banner was played as the stars and stripes of the United States flag were lifted upward to honor the nation of the Olympic champion Smith. In a stark break with convention, however, Smith and Carlos thrust black-gloved fists – Smith his right, Carlos his left – above lowered eyes and bowed heads. In what would remain his only public comment on the demonstration for over 20 years, Smith described the significance of these actions to ABC's Howard Cosell:

> My raised right hand stood for the power in black America. Carlos' raised left hand stood for the unity of black America. Together they formed an arch of unity and power. The black scarf around my neck stood for black pride. The black socks with no shoes stood for black poverty in racist America. The totality of our effort was the regaining of black dignity (Matthews 1974: 197).

Within two days, Smith and Carlos's gesture was pictured on the front page (not the sports page, the front page) of newspapers across the United States and around the world, and still today, over a quarter of a century later, references to this image appear – a paragraph here, a sentence or two there, or more often than not, just the photograph itself – with a surprising degree of regularity in a wide variety of contexts.

In a series of works on the socio-logics of Olympic symbology, anthropologist John MacAloon (1982, 1984; forthcoming) has suggested that the power, prominence, and intrigue of this image can be traced to Smith and Carlos's ability to interject or force blackness into a ceremonial system that quite literally had no place for representing non-national collective identities such as race, class, religion, or ethnicity. Not coincidentally, I would add, the limitations of Olympic symbology mirror those of liberal democratic theory and practice especially in their American manifestations. Missing from the ideal-typical understanding of both are the communities of socialization and solidarity that mediate the relationship between individual and society as well as constitute the core identities of many individuals. And it is only in this context – that is, in the context of how liberal democratic ideologies deal with (or, to be even more precise, avoid dealing with) collective identity *and* cultural phenomena – that it is really possible to appreciate the deeper social significance of, and concrete political struggle embodied in this image and this demonstration, as well as in culturally-oriented movements and politics on the whole. But, as is so often the case in sociological analysis, there is a good deal of historical ground that must first be covered before this argument can be properly defended.

This is, after all, an image with a history behind it. Despite what is often implied or assumed, this gesture was not the free-willed or spontaneous act of two isolated and autonomous individuals. Quite the contrary, Smith and Carlos were actually members of a small cadre of world-class athletes and activists led by a young sociologist named Harry Edwaris who tried to engineer an African American boycott of the 1968 Mexico City Games under the official title of the Olympic Project for Human Rights. Though the boycott never did materialize, those associated with the OPHR initiative (who, at one time or another, included: UCLA basketball star Lew Alcindor, aka Kareem Abdul Jabaar, Martin Luther King, Jr, SNCC's H. Rap Brown and Stokely Carmichael, and Muhammad Ali) participated in a series of athletically-based racial protests which attracted a good deal of national attention and provoked a surprising degree of national outrage. The most prominent and outspoken critics were then-governor of California Ronald Reagan, the International Olympic Committee president, an American named Avery Brundage, and US Olympic hero Jesse Owens. At one point, Vice President and presidential candidate Hubert Humphrey even stepped in to try to moderate the dispute.

Since the basic story of this movement has been told numerous times and in numerous places (Olsen 1968; Edwards 1969, 1970, 1979; Grundman 1979; Spivey 1984; Wiggens 1988, 1991; Ashe 1988), many of these details are actually quite familiar to scholars in the field of sport studies. It is not my purpose in this paper either to elaborate upon the cast of characters and incidents that make up this movement (as interesting as many of them are), nor to craft a new or revisionist account of these events. Rather, what I want to do here is synthesize the basic details of this history in a fashion that will formulate and illustrate some more general points about the dynamics of resistance and domination in such culturally-oriented racial movements.[2]

The 1968 African American Olympic Protest Movement

The Olympic Project for Human Rights was formally called into being on November 23, 1967 when a group of approximately 200 athletes and supporters assembled at the Second Baptist Church in Los Angeles and "unanimously voted to fully endorse and participate in a boycott of the Olympic Games of 1968" (Edwards 1969: 55). The boycott idea came most directly from a general resolution passed by the first-ever national black power conference held in riot-torn Newark, New Jersey in the summer of 1967, which urged that black athletes should refuse to take part in the 1968 Olympics or professional boxing matches until Muhammad Ali was restored to his former title as world heavy-weight boxing champion. Early that fall, Edwards along with Tommie Smith (a fifth-year senior and world-class track star) and Kenneth Noel (a former athlete doing graduate work in sociology) seized the idea and took it upon themselves to organize an athletically based racial protest movement around the idea of an Olympic boycott.

Edwards and his colleagues, many of whom were African American athletes or former athletes who attended college on athletic scholarship, had come to recognize the possibilities of using sport as a forum for racial protest during the course of a more general black student protest they had engineered at San Jose State at the beginning of the fall semester. Two events in particular were foundational in helping sensitize them to sport's potential as a protest tool. One was the threat of a boycott of a San Jose State football game they used to focus attention on, and put force behind their demands for racial changes at the institution. The other was Smith's speculation (at an important international track meet in Tokyo, Japan) about the possibility of some concerted form of protest among black American athletes. The national publicity – or, more accurately, national outrage – these events generated convinced the San Jose group that their involvement in sport provided them with a way to continue and advance the movement for racial justice in the United States. With this in mind they chose to pursue an all-out black Olympic boycott.

Their proposal for an Olympic boycott needs to be characterized and contextualized properly, however. Quite unlike their predecessors at the Black Power conference (who seem to have been motivated primarily by Ali's unjust treatment), the OPHR initiative did not specifically define any particular object(s) of protest, nor make any concrete demands at this initial meeting. Nor was it intended to target racism and discrimination within the world of sport. Rather, the idea of an Olympic boycott was aimed against what Tommie Smith described as "racial ostracism" in society at large (*Track and Field News*, November 1967: 3).

What is important to keep in mind here is how difficult and controversial the struggle against racism in the United States had become by this time in the post-Civil Rights period.[3] At least two sets of tensions might be mentioned. The first was whether additional racial change was even necessary. There were those who believed that the Civil Rights movement, having guaranteed individual freedom from segregation and discrimination as well as legal and political equality of opportunity (symbolized and embodied most dramatically in the Civil Rights and Voting Rights Acts of 1964 and 1965), had "solved" the problem of racism in the United States. Yet large portions of the black community found that these procedural changes mattered very little in terms of their daily lives. In spite of all of the "victories" of the civil rights era, they still found themselves in a world of hegemonic racial stereotypes and socio-economic structures of inequality. Clearly, OPHR activists were among those convinced of the need to move beyond civil rights toward more structuralist, collectivist understandings of (and solutions to) the problems of race. But this did not answer the question about how to go about confronting these persistent inequalities and injustices. Unlike voting rights abuses, outright segregation, or overt physical violence, the structural and institutional forms of racism that remained could not be easily pointed out and challenged given American liberal democratic understandings of property rights and individualism. The ambiguities and tensions this difficult situation created, as Doug McAdam (1982: 183) put it, illustrated a "growing disagreement within insurgent ranks over the proper goals of the movement and the most effective means of attaining them." The question, in short, was whether American institutions and practices could be reformed according to basic civil rights logic or whether more radical, fundamental changes had to be carried out. OPHR activists were much less clear on where they stood in terms of this second tension. On the one hand, they were thoroughly implicated with the more progressive, "black-power" forces in the movement; at the same time, Smith and his associates vehemently resisted anyone who attempted to label them as "militants," "radicals," or "revolutionaries."[4]

None of this is necessarily to criticize OPHR activists for being vague or evasive. In many ways these athlete-activists were, like their advisor and mentor Dr King, trying to synthesize the more moderate, mainstream branches of the movement with the more radical, militant ones. Rather, it is to point out the difficult, even impossible structural situation they, like King and all the other activists in the Black freedom struggle, found themselves in at this point in time. This challenge was reflected quite early in the initiative when it became clear that no more than a handful of Olympic-caliber athletes would even consider the boycott idea. Even so, the mere proposal of an Olympic boycott drew press coverage and comment – and almost unanimous condemnation – from all across the country. Edwards and his colleagues took this as an indication that they had "touched a nerve" (*New York Times*, December 18, 1967) and therefore should proceed in trying to build a movement around the idea of an Olympic boycott.

Edwards and his fellow organizers and newfound advisors (including nationally syndicated columnist Louie Lomax) spent the two weeks after their November meeting composing a list of "demands" and "strategies" to justify, consolidate, and organize the OPHR itself. Presented at a press conference on December 14 in New York City, in which Edwards was flanked by Lomax, Martin Luther King, Jr, and CORE's Floyd McKissick, this list included: the removal of the American Avery Brundage (who was considered to be anti-Semitic and racist) from his office as the president of the International Olympic Committee; the exclusion of apartheid nations South Africa and Southern Rhodesia from all international sporting events; the addition of black coaches and administrators to the United States Olympic Committee (USOC); the complete desegregation of the New York Athletic Club (the NYAC annually hosted one of the two most prestigious indoor track and field meets in the country); and the restoration of Muhammad Ali's title and right to box in the United States (*New York Times*, December 15, 1967).

Few of these specific proposals were ever actually carried out, much less even feasible. Nevertheless, in the months that followed Edwards and the OPHR were associated with a broad, if haphazard set of protest activities that included: an extremely successful boycott of the New York Athletic Club's famous February indoor track meet; protests and meetings on some 35 college and university campuses across the nation; demands for the expulsion of South Africa (which did come about, though for reasons much broader than the OPHR); and an aborted effort to organize an alternative "Third World" Olympics. Clearly, the OPHR was helping to mobilize significant numbers of variously discontented athletes and, in the process, attracting a great deal of national publicity and attention to racial problems in sport and society in general.

But whatever the tactical successes of these activities, a series of meetings and discussions near the end of June revealed that they had still not generated enough support among prospective African American Olympians to make the boycott itself actually happen (Matthews and Amdur 1974). While an overwhelming majority of the 30 or 40 prospective Olympians active in the movement were interested in engineering some kind of a statement about the racial situation in the United States, they simply couldn't agree on what that statement might entail or what form it would assume. For all intents and purposes, the boycott movement had ended. Edwards and his colleagues tried to hide this development from the media, suggesting that the OPHR was in the process of shifting its plans for Mexico City but, at the same time, refusing to comment on what this shift might involve. Later when many confused accounts of these meetings began to surface, Edwards cleverly insisted it was a part of a "strategy of chaos," saying, "There is only one thing more confusing than a rumor and that's a million rumors" (*Chicago Tribune*, July 31, 1968). It wasn't until August 29 at the 1968 National Black Power Conference in Philadelphia that Edwards finally admitted (via mailed correspondence) that an all-out boycott would not occur, though he promised some "lesser forms" of protest would be carried out (*New York Times*, September 1, 1968).

Despite extreme precautions, warnings, and threats from the USOC during the whole of the summer trials and training period leading up to the Games, it was clear to many of their teammates that Smith and his black teammates were in fact still searching for some appropriate way to express their feelings (Matthews and Amdur 1974; Moore 1991). Specifically, they were considering losing races intentionally, refusing to participate in Olympic ceremonies, and wearing black socks or arm bands. During the early days of the track and field competition at the Games, a number of athletes wore black socks and berets in their preliminary heats, and after winning the 100-meter dash, a heretofore moderate Jimmy Hines refused to shake hands with Avery Brundage when the latter appeared to present Hines his medal. But these were conveniently overlooked by coaches and officials, and downplayed by the media. Track coach Stan Wright, for example, was quoted as saying, "I was not informed of any demonstration. As far as I know, they wore high stockings because it was cold, but they may have intended it to be a demonstration. If they did, it is their business. We are here to win medals" (*New York Times*, October 16, 1968).

But when Smith and Carlos's dramatic victory-stand gesture finally came the next day, it could not be so ignored. All of the tensions and forces that had surrounded Edwards, Smith, and the others in the months leading up to the Games came to a climactic head, and then exploded outwards. According to IOC President Brundage, Smith and Carlos's actions had been "an insult to their Mexican hosts and a disgrace to the United States," requiring immediate and decisive measures (Avery Brundage Collection, Department of Special Collections, University of Illinois). Within two short days Smith and Carlos were expelled from the Olympic village (by the USOC, acting under immediate and intensive pressure from the IOC), permanently suspended from Olympic competition, and sent back home to the United States.

These actions (or re-actions, really) were deemed appropriate and fitting by most Americans. Newspapers were overflowing with emotional letters to the editor, heated editorials and reports. In a commentary located on its main editorial page, the *Chicago Tribune* called the demonstration "an embarrassment visited upon the country," an "act contemptuous of the United States," and "an insult to their countrymen." *Time* magazine saw it as an "unpleasant controversy [which] dulled the luster of a superlative track and field meet" and *Sports Illustrated* relegated what it called the "Carlos–Smith affair" to four pejorative paragraphs buried on the fifth page of an otherwise verbose 12-page story. ABC's official 35-minute highlight film of the Games (which emphasized American performances almost exclusively and in fact concluded with the playing of the national anthem behind images of American flags and Olympic victors in competition and on the victory stand) made absolutely no mention of the events surrounding

Smith and Carlos despite the fact that the network (using its star reporter Howard Cosell, the "white reporter who could talk to blacks") had milked the incident for all it was worth during its live coverage. Finally, the 1968 American Olympic team itself was the only one before or since not invited by the President to visit the White House.

One of the harshest indictments against Smith and Carlos was issued by a young staff writer for the *Chicago American* named Brent Musburger. Writing from Mexico City, Musburger began:

> One gets a little tired of having the United States run down by ath-
> letes who are enjoying themselves at the expense of their country.
> Protesting and working constructively against racism in the United
> States is one thing, but airing ones dirty clothing before the entire
> world during a fun-and-games tournament was no more than a
> juvenile gesture by a couple of athletes who should have known
> better (*Chicago American*, October 19, 1968).

Calling their demonstration an "ignoble performance" that "completely overshadowed" a magnificent athletic one, Musberger likened Smith and Carlos to "a pair of dark-skinned storm troopers" and concluded that "they should have avoided the award ceremony altogether" (ibid.). All of this came at the same time that Musburger and others celebrated another black athlete, George Foreman, for waving a small American flag in the ring after his gold medal victory in heavyweight boxing.

Not everyone, of course, was so critical of Smith and Carlos's gesture (or so supportive of Foreman's). For example, Robert Clarke, the president of San Jose State, Smith and Carlos's alma mater, predicted that they "would not be received as outcasts in America, but as honorable men" (*Spartan Daily*, October 24, 1968). A few months later Harry Edwards (1969: 107–8) took pains to show that back home Smith and Carlos were treated as "heroes to black Americans," citing receptions accorded them by (unnamed) black African countries at the United Nations and by black Americans in Washington, DC, tributes paid by black leaders such as H. Rap Brown, Stokely Carmichael, Adam Clayton Powell, and Elijah Muhammad and letters and telegrams sent by whites and blacks from around the world. Within months, posters of the two athletes poised on the victory stand appeared in every head shop, radical church, and student-movement headquarters around the country and pictures of those teammates who supported Smith and Carlos by wearing black tams and showing fists after their ceremonies appeared on radical postcards and in Black Panther newspapers.

But this was not the company of mainstream America, white America, the America which dominated the society. When they returned to the States, Smith and Carlos found themselves the center of a controversy that would linger for many years. In a 1973 public opinion survey on issues of politics and race in the United States, Richard Lapchick (1975: 215) asked blacks and whites from six different cities nationwide if they felt that the gestures made by black US athletes in the 1968 Olympic Games were justifiable in terms of the Olympic ideals of politics playing no part in sports: 57 percent of the blacks surveyed thought Smith and Carlos were justified in their actions, while only 32 percent of whites felt the same way (8 percent were undecided in both cases).[5] As with all public opinion research, it is hard to say exactly what these figures indicate (obviously the racial cleavages stand out most prominently and I shall return to them shortly); but at the very least, especially when combined with all the other sources that comprise the historical record, I think it is fair to say that public opinion was polarized and ran strongly against Smith and Carlos's demonstration.

There is perhaps no better indication of this than the fact that, for better or for worse, Smith and Carlos's identity as Olympic protesters had a determining impact upon their personal lives. When Smith returned for his final semester of college and tried to register for his ROTC classes in 1969, for example, he was quietly advised that if he turned in his uniform all would be forgotten. Then Jim Brown, who before the Games had lent Smith money against the football contract the sprinter planned to sign with the Los Angeles Rams, informed Smith that the Rams were no longer interested because they saw Smith as "too eager." (To add insult to injury, Brown demanded his money back as well.) Carlos's ride would be even rockier, as he must have sensed immediately upon his return to the States: "Doing 'my thing' made me feel the freest I ever felt in my whole life. But I came home to hate" (*Sport*, September 1969: 70–2). For a while, there was talk of he and his OPHR lawyers suing the USOC or even the United States government for an infringement of his constitutional rights and misuse of public funds. When this fell through, he went to the Olympics in 1972 only as an employee of a shoe company and as his athletic stock began to wane, Carlos, who never finished his college degree, was forced to take odd jobs to survive. Then in 1977 his wife committed suicide, a tragedy he still blames on the pressures resulting from his role in the 1968 protest.

How do we make sense of all of this? Perhaps more to the point of the larger issues raised in the introduction, what does it tell us about the political significance and broader consequence of cultural protest? To put it concretely: Was Smith and Carlos's resistance as futile and ineffective as these immediate indicators would suggest? The answers to these questions require a closer examination of the social roots and structural limitations of racial resistance in and through sport.

Making Sense of the Controversy: Social Context and Cultural Structures

In many ways, of course, it is not at all surprising that Smith and Carlos's demonstration drew the antagonistic, critical response from mainstream America that it did. In a country already wracked by the fragmentation of the civil rights coalition, urban violence, militant 'black power' protest, and white backlash – in the context, that is, of the polarized racial politics of the era – there was little sympathy or political support for those dramatizing the problems of race once again, much less those who did so on the international stage of the Olympic Games. What is more surprising and revealing, perhaps, was the intensity and ferocity of mainstream American opposition to the demonstration, especially given its silent, fundamentally non-violent and politically ambiguous nature. European commentators, in particular, registered this impression almost immediately. As the official magazine of the British Olympic Association put it, "If this was to be the full measure of Black Power protest on the victory rostrum, then it was a well conceived plan involving the most effective of gestures without, it seemed, giving direct offense to anyone" (*World Sports*, December 1968: 13).

A closer look into the actual charges leveled against the OPHR, their initial boycott proposal, and Smith and Carlos's eventual victory-stand demonstration reveals that what was at stake in these events was much more complicated than any straightforward reading of the racial context would suggest. If and when matters of race were invoked by critics, it was only briefly – to preface their reprehension about the boycott with some vague declaration of support for "civil rights," to argue that things were getting better racially, or to assert that however bad the racial situation in the United States was, it was still much better than in South Africa. Otherwise, the argument that the protest had transgressed the boundaries of acceptable, civil-rights protest was almost unthinkable, perhaps even taboo. In other words, none of these critiques (except, perhaps, in their very most extreme versions) were formulated along explicit racial-political lines. Alternatively, the vast majority put forward some version of the thesis that sport was simply not the proper place for such a protest. Somehow, athletes, coaches, writers, and spectators seemed to believe that there was something special or even sacred about sport that precluded it from serving as a site for racial protest. Indeed, many went so far as to portray these demonstrations as an attack upon sport itself.

This is *not* to imply that the specter of race was *not* involved in the judgments pronounced against Olympic protest. Given that those in the sporting establishment who criticized and condemned this activism were often the very same officials, reporters, and athletes who had congratulated and celebrated sport for its contributions to the advancement of the black race for so many years prior, it only stands to reason that, no matter what these critics said or did not say, there was something about the racial politics they associated with Smith, Carlos, and Edwards that was deeply and directly connected with their objections to them. On the other hand, neither is my point that this sport-as-special, anti-protest rhetoric represented some kind of unholy, racist conspiracy between anti-protest sport idealists and racial conservatives (though it certainly made it possible for Edwards and his colleagues to accuse their detractors of being racists, anti-Semites or "Uncle Toms"). If there was some sort of connivance involved in this controversy, then, I believe it was not a conspiracy of deliberate human agents, but a much deeper, more diffuse collusion of the racialized interests and ideals legitimated in and through the idealization of sport itself.

Even in an era when no aspect of American culture seemed beyond repute, when virtually nothing was sacrosanct, virtually all those who took sport seriously were unified in their commitment to preserving and protecting it from influences that were perceived to be corrupting – and, according to the implicit logic of anti-protest arguments, race-based protest simply happened to fall into this category. No matter how illusory, unrealistic, deceptive, simplistic, or mythologized this sport-as-special, anti-protest rhetoric may seem in retrospect, the fact of the matter is that it ultimately worked – which is to say, it drew otherwise disparate ideological and social commitments into common cause against Olympic racial protest. Indeed, a great deal of its power and effectiveness derived directly from the fact that it involved so little subtlety, nuance, or refinement.

The reason critics of Olympic protest were able to focus only on the sanctity of the sportsworld (and did not feel it necessary to delve into the connections – and contradictions – between racial politics and sport culture), in my view, has to do with the remarkable convergence or mutual interdependence in American society between the culture (one might say "cult") of sport and liberal democratic understandings of political legitimacy and social justice. Though the relationships between these two sets of discursive practice are much more complicated that I can fully elaborate here, they hold at least two fundamental tenets in common: first, the idea of fair play within established, abstracted rules of conduct, and second, the notion that the freely acting individual is the fount and source of all creativity, process and order. Moreover, an appropriate synthesis of these two ideals is considered essential for social progress, ethnic harmony and the greatest possible "good society." Despite their timeless and universal appearances, the ideals expressed in this synthesis are very, very particular. In terms of the case we are concerned with here, they yield a standard of racial justice and civil rights that is thoroughly individualistic and assimilationist and, therefore, diametrically at odds with the kind of collectivist, structuralist racial critique implied by the Olympic protesters. The fact that sport culture and liberal democratic ideology were so closely and unquestionably intertwined made it impossible for outsiders to racial injustice and discontent to even begin to understand, much less sympathize with the protesters' collectivist grievances and concerns. For critics of athletic protest, to put it another way, sport was inherently about racial justice and civil rights; or, to put it even more starkly, sport *was* just and right for everyone, no matter what their particular standing in the larger social order.[6]

Situated in the context of these cultural structures (or strictures), in fact, what may be most surprising about this entire episode is not that Smith and Carlos were so widely criticized and condemned, but that they and their associates even dared to undertake racial protest in an athletic arena at all. And this is where the difficult, paradoxical situation the larger movement found itself in – the dissolving (or dissolved) civil rights coalition, on the one hand, and the increasing commitment of many black activists to the need for further social and economic change, on the other – becomes most directly relevant to our broader theoretical concerns. It was *only* in this context of searching for new and more forceful means of activism – even as support for such activism was waning both inside the movement and out – that some African Americans began to consider engaging in acts of social resistance in a cultural arena (sport) they had long considered one of the few in which they were actually afforded a relatively full, fair, and free opportunity to participate in American society.

Sport-oriented protest became an attractive option for a variety of reasons. For one, sports had long constituted an important, if under-appreciated set of activities and institutions in the black community, providing many of its leaders and one of its most established spaces for collective action (second only perhaps to the Church itself). Second, and connected with this, sport was one of the few social arenas where blacks as a group had actually achieved some measure of success and representation, and thus enjoyed some amount of cultural capital that could be used as a lever against the persistent problems of race in the United States. It is important to formulate this carefully because it was probably the factor that most directly motivated the most activist athletes. Because sport had been relatively open to black Americans for so many years (as those in the media repeatedly emphasized), a number of black Americans – a few "star" athletes like Tommie Smith and Lew Alcindor in particular – were now engaged in activities that mattered a great deal to many other Americans thus marking them, their actions, and their opinions as somehow interesting, important, and even essential. And precisely because they were so valued, the thinking went, black athletes might be able to press social change in much the same way that boycotts and other non-violent forms of protest had done all throughout the civil rights movement. They were simply using, as Lew Alcindor put it, "what they had" (Edwards 1969: 53).

Third, a critical mass of athletes was beginning to recognize and resist forms of racism and exploitation that persisted in the sports-world, as well as to connect their personal experiences with the

condition of black Americans in the society at large (Olsen 1968).
What is more, sport provided a protest forum that did not require
participants to take concrete (and potentially conflicting) ideological or political positions; instead they could simply express a sense
of discontent and need for change. Sport protest – and culturally-
based activism more generally – was, in this sense, usefully
ambiguous. Finally, sport itself had long been held up as a realm
untainted by discrimination, racism, and inequality and, moreover, an arena that had been crucial to pushing integration and
mobility for black Americans in society at large. As many activists
saw it, if this seemingly sacred realm of sport was corrupted by
racism and inequality, this would carry important implications for
the rest of society as well.

Of course, it worked out in quite the opposite fashion. From
its very first splash in the national media to the Smith/Carlos
demonstration, athletically-based racial protest was unambigu-
ously condemned and rejected by an overwhelming and powerful
segment of American society not so much for its racial politics, as
for simply saying something political in the realm of sport. To put
it more precisely, the 1968 Olympic protest movement met the fate
that it did because mainstream Americans perceived that it was
interjecting "dirty" political agendas into the "sacred," pure-play
realm of the sportsworld. This language of the sacred and formulation of the political is, in my view, the key to the possibilities and
ultimate limits of resistance to the American racial order. In a certain
sense, it is also one of the issues where blacks and whites agreed
completely in Lapchick's survey conducted in 1973: 77 percent of
whites and 78 percent of blacks thought that politics should have
no influence in sport (though only one-third – 33 percent – in both
groups felt this was the case in national competition). It turns out,
in fact, that the questionnaire items that exhibited significant racial
cleavages in responses (such as the Smith/Carlos item I mentioned above) are those that touched on explicitly racial issues.
Given that both groups equally expressed the view that politics
should be kept out of sport, the explanation for this otherwise
anamolous result must be that many black respondents simply
did not see racial issues as "political" (and thus inappropriate)
but instead viewed them as legitimate, morally justified social
grievances. In short, the very same factors that made sport such
an attractive protest arena were also those which dictated its
ultimate rejection.

It is at this point – in the struggle over what counts as "political," as opposed to what is considered "legitimate" or just social protest – where the otherwise seamless connections between sport culture, racial progress, and the ideology of individual meritocracy break down, and the deep cultural and ideological foundations of domination begin to emerge more clearly formed. The 1968 African American Olympic protest movement was shocking and controversial (and thus required such intensive condemnation) because by forcing race into the equation it exposed – or at least threatened to expose – the ways in which sport culture and American liberal democratic ideology usually served (and serve) to legitimate a very particular, very interested, and very individualistic vision of racial justice and civil rights.

And yet, it seems one can only say "exposed" or "dramatized," because ultimately, as we have seen, it seems as if the boycott movement failed: the forces of power and authority lined up to condemn the movement and then expel Smith and Carlos and everything they stood for. There seems to have been no tangible social progress to see, no material or social gains that were made. Is this reading accurate? Are there resources to structural power contained in cultural arenas? How valuable is cultural or symbolic capital? Can sport – or any cultural form for that matter – be used to actually force concrete social change? In terms of the questions I posed at the outset, this analysis would seem to have raised more questions than it answered.

Conclusions

The problem with these questions and impressions, as I have just posed them, is that they buy into overly materialistic, short-term, and uniform, one-dimensional standards of evaluating resistance and social change.

In the first place, given the rigid and unrelenting structure of racial formations in the United States in the late 1960s, the challenge for activists was not to push for additional institutional change in the realm of race relations, but simply to keep the issues and injustice of race on the table for future consideration and debate. In many ways, I think that the protesters actually sensed this very early on. As Jackie Robinson, an exceptional black personality and the man who integrated major league baseball, explained when he offered his controversial support for the boycott:

> I know very well this is not going to work. However, I have to admire these youngsters. I feel we've got to use whatever means, except violence, we can to get our rights in this country. When, for 300 years, Negroes have been denied equal opportunity, some attention must be focused on it (*New York Times*, November 27, 1967).

Though it took an act of striking originality and sheer brilliance to do it, Smith and Carlos were, in fact, able to force the issue of race into a public sphere that had otherwise refused to have anything to do with it. As Lew Alcindor put it in the formative days of the Olympic Project for Human Rights, these black athletes were "simply using what they had" – their own black bodies – to try to combat a social situation they considered unjust.

Second, it is crucial to remember that, by the late 1960s at least, the struggle over race and racism was as much about ideologies of racial justice and expectations of citizenship as it was about interests, resources and institutions. Here, I would follow Hall (1981), Gilroy (1991), and Lipsitz (1990, esp. 133–60) in stressing that the struggle over popular cultural legitimations and identities (as opposed to rights and resources) becomes particularly crucial in a socio-historical era – or, as Harvey (1990) might put it, a post-modern condition – in which capital and power have discovered techniques to insulate themselves against traditional forms of protest, challenge, and change. In a culture that privileged and celebrated sports excellence, especially in the charged international realm of Olympic competition, the fact that these athlete-activists "had" only their bodies and their athletic performances to work with was as much a strength as a weakness, for in this arena it was precisely bodies and performances that were symbolically significant and powerful. And there is no better indication that this struggle over culture constitutes real political struggle than the drastic attempts of authorities to intervene in these proceedings, discipline Smith and Carlos after they carried out their demonstration, and then erase the memory of the image altogether. (Here we are also reminded of the complex, sometimes ironic relationship between racial ideologies and social change: It was, after all, only because of the sporting establishment's commitment to individual meritocracy that Black athletes like Smith and Carlos were in a position to carry out such a collectivist demonstration in the first place.)

And it is precisely the fact that the Smith/Carlos demonstration has not only survived these efforts, but become an icon of popular culture and an object of collective memory which brings up the third and final point: that struggles for hegemony are never simply won or lost, but always continue often in and through popular culture itself. That is not to say that the memories of popular cultural protests necessarily always serve the interests of those in resistance. During the 1984 Los Angeles Olympics, for instance, the story of the Smith/Carlos demonstration was transformed into a celebration of an open and racially tolerant melting-pot society. Indeed, the ability of capital to co-opt cultural images and make them over to its own political purpose cannot be over-emphasized. This is particularly true with regard to sport. As bell hooks (1994) has argued, the cultural fetish surrounding black bodies and blackness in general that emerged with their commercialization and commodification in the late 1970s has made it so that African American athletic images today can be subversive only with a great deal of struggle and in the most unusual of circumstances. What I do mean to suggest, however, is that cultural memories and images do tend to persist as sites of social consciousness and thus as potential sites of contestation. This in mind, I would suggest that it is our task to evaluate how cultural practices and ideologies contribute to the production, reproduction, and transformation of the social order in liberal democratic societies and thus to understand the possibilities for resistance and opposition contained therein. If the study of cultures and identities – which has exploded in recent years – is to be of true political consequence, these issues, I believe, must be taken up.

NOTES

1   This paper is a slightly revised and expanded version of a paper published in *Ethnic and Racial Studies* 19(3): 548–66. I thank the editors of *ERS* for allowing it to be reprinted here in this format. I also want to acknowledge Jodi O'Brien, Judith Howard, and Chandra Mukerji and the members of her writing group at the University of California, San Diego for their support and helpful comments as I was working on these revisions.
2   I should state that in the larger project on which the present analysis is based (Hartmann 1997) I use my own theoretical approach and rather substantial research to subject the story of the 1968 African

American Olympic protest movement to fairly extensive recon-struction. Because this work frames and informs the analysis pre-sented in this paper, I will list some of my main criticisms of the existing literature. The first is that there is simply too much emphasis on the Olympic Project for Human Rights (OPHR) as a social move-ment organization (SMO) and not enough attention is paid to the movement as a complex whole. Second, even for those aspects of the movement that were significantly engineered by the OPHR, there is an overemphasis on Harry Edwards's personal role (stemming, almost certainly, from his own participation in writing and shaping the history of this movement). The third problem with the existing literature is that it is either unaware of, or unconcerned with, the fundamental ambiguities, tensions, and contradictions that composed the movement, the two most important being whether they were using protest to "force" change or simply to "call attention to" injus-tice and the nature of what was targeted as unjust in the first place. The fourth and final limitation of this literature – and the one that speaks most directly to the concerns of this paper – is that it has not explored the broader socio-cultural context within which this movement was situated, much less drawn out its deeper theoretical implications.

3   This sketch of the structural tensions composing the racial politics of the post-Civil Rights period is informed by a large body of literature. Some of the works I have found most useful include: Carson 1981; Colburn and Pozzetta 1994; Matusow 1984; McAdam 1982; Omi and Winant 1994; Piven and Cloward 1977; and Weisbrot 1990.

4   It is difficult at any moment to isolate what the athletic protesters were after programmatically or ideologically and, in fact, there was a great deal of division and debate among the athletes themselves. Even their leader, Harry Edwards himself, appears in the historical record as a liminal figure, torn – both in terms of his politics and his personal style – between mainstream, civil rights appeals and far more radical calls for separation and black nationalism. Even Smith and Carlos's victory stand gesture itself was almost completely ambiguous in terms of concrete politics or programs: while they seemed to be saying that blackness was somehow important, it wasn't at all clear exactly what else – if anything – they were saying about it. The important point in the context of this study, however, is that despite these subtleties and ambiguities, the OPHR was widely condemned as an example of illegitimate black-power extremism.

5   Lapchick's poll surveyed 233 people in New York, Philadelphia, Washington, Norfolk, Denver, Los Angeles on a series of questions regarding the relationship between sport and politics. Respondents were broken down by race, age and gender (77/34 percent black;

155/66 percent white; 87/37 percent women; 146/63 percent men; 58 percent over 30; 42 percent under) but responses were broken down only by race.

6   Given the broader analytic foci of this volume, I should point out that sport is often described – quite appropriately – as a masculine preserve or an arena of "hegemonic masculinity" (Trujillo 1991; see also Messner 1992). There are at least two reasons for this in my view. One is that institutions and practices of sport are dominated by men. The other, suggested by the present analysis, has to do with its affinities with the abstract, universalizing ideology of individualist meritocracy. This is a worldview which is typically understood and described as culturally "masculine" and which stands in contrast to more "feminine" understandings of social life which emphasize caring, commitment, responsibilities, and concrete relationships between peoples (see, for a well-known example, Gilligan 1982; see also Connell 1995). In this context, it is also interesting to note that Harry Edwards, speaking for the OPHR in the year leading up to the Olympics, often described the boycott initiative as an attempt to "reassert the basic masculinity of the black people" (*New York Times*, December 21, 1967). What is so interesting about this formulation is that Edwards inverts the usual cultural assumptions about masculine and feminine traits; here, the masculine comes to be associated with grounded, collective interests and commitments. While I cannot provide a full analysis of it here, I want to make the point, first of all, that Edwards's description mirrors the hypermasculinity exhibited by many Black Power activists during this period as described, for example, by Sara Evans (1979). What I can also say (and what bears directly upon Evans's analysis of how the Women's Liberation struggle grew out of the Civil Rights movement) is that this masculine bias did prevent Edwards and his colleagues from allowing African American women athletes to participate in the OPHR even though several of them – most notably sprinter Wyomia Tyus – wanted to do so. I should also note that despite being snubbed by the OPHR, Tyus publically dedicated the gold and silver medals she won in Mexico City to Smith and Carlos in the aftermath of their expulsion.

REFERENCES

Ashe, Arthur. 1988. *A Hard Road to Glory: A History of the African American Athlete*, Vol. 3. New York, NY: Warner Books.

Bourdieu, Pierre. 1990. "Programme for a Sociology of Sport," in Bourdieu, *In Other Words: Essays Towards a Reflexive Sociology*. Stanford, CT: Stanford University Press, 156–67.

Carson, Clayborne. 1981. *In Struggle: SNCC and the Black Awakening of the 1960s*. Cambridge, MA: Harvard University Press.

Colburn, David R. and George E. Pozzetta. 1994. "Race, Ethnicity and the Evolution of Political Legitimacy," in *The Sixties: From Memory to History*. David Farber (ed.) Chapel Hill, NC: University of North Carolina Press, 119–48.

Connell, R. W. 1995. *Masculinities*. Berkeley, CA: University of California Press.

Edwards, Harry. 1969. *The Revolt of the Black Athlete*. New York, NY: The Free Press.

——. 1970. *Black Students*. New York, NY: The Free Press.

——. 1979. "The Olympic Project for Human Rights: An Assessment Ten Years Later." *The Black Scholar* 10(6,7): 2–8.

Evans, Sara. 1979. *Personal Politics: The Roots of Women's Liberation in the Civil Rights Movement and the New Left*. New York, NY: Vintage.

Gilligan, Carol. 1982. *In a Different Voice*. Cambridge, MA: Harvard University Press.

Gilroy, Paul. 1991. *"There Ain't No Black in the Union Jack:" The Cultural Politics of Race and Nation*. Chicago, IL: University of Chicago Press.

Grundman, Adolph H. 1979. "Image of Collegiate Protest and the Civil Rights Movement: A Historian's View." *Arena Review* 3(3): 17–24.

Hall, Stuart. 1981. "Notes on Deconstructing 'the Popular,'" in *People's History and Socialist Theory*, R. Samuel (ed.). London: Routledge and Kegan Paul, 227–40.

Hartmann, Douglas. 1997. "Golden Ghettos: The Cultural Politics of Race, Sport, and Civil Rights in the United States, 1968 and Beyond." Unpublished PhD dissertation. University of California, San Diego.

Harvey, David. 1990. *The Condition of Postmodernity: An Enquiry into the Origins of Cultural Change*. Cambridge, MA: Blackwell.

hooks, bell. 1994. "Feminism Inside: Toward a Black Body Politic," in *Black Male: Representations of Masculinity in Contemporary America*, T. Golden (ed.). New York: Whitney Museum of Art, 127–40.

Lapchick, Richard. 1975. *The Politics of Race and International Sport*. Westport, CN: Greenwood Press.

Lipsitz, George. 1990. *Time Passages: Collective Memory and American Popular Culture*. Minneapolis, MN: University of Minnesota Press.

MacAloon, John J. 1982. "Double Visions: Olympic Games and American Culture." *Kenyon Review* 4(1): 98–112.

——. 1984. "Olympic Games and the Theory of Spectacle in Modern Societies," in *Rite, Drama, Festival, Spectacle: Rehearsals Toward a Theory of Cultural Performance*, J. MacAloon (ed.). Philadelphia: Institute for the Study of Human Issues Press, 241–80.

——. Forthcoming. *Brides of Victory: Gender and Nationalism in Ritual*. London: Berg.

Matthews, Vincent and Neil Amdur. 1974. *My Race Be Won*. New York, NY: Charter House.

Matusow, Allen J. 1984. *The Unraveling of America: A History of Liberalism in the 1960s*. New York, NY: Harper Torchbooks.

McAdam, Doug. 1982. *Political Process and the Development of Black Insurgency, 1930–1970*. Chicago, IL: University of Chicago Press.

Messner, Michael. 1992. *Power at Play: Sports and the Problem of Masculinity*. Boston, MA: Beacon Press.

Moore, Kenny. 1991. "A Courageous Stand," and "The Eye of the Storm." *Sports Illustrated* 75(6): 61–77 and (7): 60–73.

Olsen, Jack. 1968. *The Black Athlete: A Shameful Story*. New York, NY: Time-Life Books.

Omi, Michael and Winant, Howard. 1994. *Racial Formation in the United States: From the 1960s to the 1990s*, 2nd edn. New York, NY: Routledge.

Piven, Frances Fox and Cloward, Richard A. 1977. *Poor People's Movements: Why They Succeed, How They Fail*. New York, NY: Pantheon Books.

Spivey, Donald. 1984. "Black Consciousness and Olympic Protest Movement," in *Sport in America: New Historical Perspectives*, D. Spivey (ed.). Westpoint, CT: Greenwood Press, 239–62.

Trujillo, Nick. 1991. "Hegemonic Masculinity on the Mound: Media Representations of Nolan Ryan and American Sports Culture." *Critical Studies in Mass Communication* 8(3): 290–308.

Weisbrot, Robert. 1990. *Freedom Bound: A History of America's Civil Rights Movement*. New York, NY: Plume.

West, Cornel. 1993. *Race Matters*. Boston, MA: Beacon Press.

Wiggens, David D. 1988. "The Future of College Athletics is at Stake: Black Athletes and Racial Turmoil on Three Predominately White University Campuses, 1968–1972." *Journal of Sport History* 15(Winter): 304–33.

——. 1991. "Prized Performers, but Frequently Overlooked Students: The Involvement of Black Athletes in Intercollegiate Sports on Predominately White University Campuses, 1890–1972." *Research Quarterly for Exercise and Sport* 6(2): 164–77.

13

Belongings: Citizenship, Sexuality, and the Market[1]

Anthony J. Freitas

General classes of Aliens ineligible to receive visas and excluded from admission: (1) Aliens who are feeble-minded... (4) Aliens afflicted with psychopathic, or sexual deviation, or mental defect... (13) Aliens coming to the United States to engage in any immoral sexual act.

United States public law 212(a)4[2]

From 1953 until 1991, acknowledging your homosexuality to an immigration agent upon entering the United States would have meant being refused entry at the border. If later the Immigration and Naturalization Service found that you had lied about previous homosexual experience you could face denial of citizenship and possibly deportation. The exclusion of homosexuals[3] as a class illustrates the point that gay men and lesbians, like Asians earlier in this century and communists, have been seen by the state as not only inadmissible and unnatural, but unnaturalizeable within white, heterosexual capitalism.[4] While the legal proscriptions on communists remain, as of 1991 homosexuals are no longer denied entry or citizenship (Foss, 1994).[5] This change in immigration policy and practice both coincides with and reflects a larger shift in the naturalization of homosexuality throughout US culture. I offer the recent opening up of legal immigration and naturalization to particular sexual subjects as an analogy for the extension of a different meaning of citizenship to gays and lesbians in the United States. In the discussion that follows, while keeping the act of becoming a legal citizen always in mind, I turn to some of the processes through which gays and lesbians, native and foreign born, are positioning themselves and being positioned as full or naturalized citizens of the society.

By naturalization I am referring to the cultural practices that make once deviant sexual practices normal within a capitalist state. This naturalization is partial and contested, as is evidenced by the "Don't ask, don't tell, don't pursue" policy, efforts such as Colorado's overturned Amendment 2 that would have limited gays' and lesbians' participation in political process, and legislation that prohibits the "positive portrayal of homosexuality." This naturalization of sexual aliens is occurring in a rather unexpected place: the market. A different concept of citizenship forms when issues of national membership meet up with capitalism. I will address this conception of citizenship and the inclusion of lesbians and gays in US culture by looking at a series of sexological and marketing surveys. These surveys operate to quantify and qualify, that is enumerate and describe, homosexuality and homosexuals in particular ways. I use these surveys not as evidence for the number of homosexuals nor for an accounting of the income and consumer behavior of the gay and lesbian communities. Instead I examine the deployment of the statistics garnered from the surveys to simultaneously measure and create a community. This process of constitution is complex and occurs from many sites. It occurs from "within," by self-identifying gays or lesbians and from "outside," by those who position themselves in opposition to the community, conservative politicians and the Religious Right. Additionally, this construction is facilitated by those who conduct the surveys and claim objective interests, scientists and marketers and lesbian and gay market researchers as well. As with censuses, these surveys illustrate how the technologies of demography and the statistics they produce are mobilized to constitute the very communities they are measuring (Foucault 1991; Anderson 1995).

In this paper I will be addressing citizenship in terms of membership: membership within sexual categories, within communities, the larger culture, and the market. In particular, I will examine the historical shifts that have created citizens of a capitalist state from performers of particular sexual acts. In the analysis below, I draw on Jeffrey Weeks's (1987) and Michel Foucault's (1980a) discussions of the social construction of sexuality. I begin with the Kinsey reports on male and female sexuality

(1948 and 1953) and trace some of the processes through which a series of practices by the individual (same-sex sexual acts) are translated into properties of the individual (the homosexual). I follow this turn as "the homosexual" is subsequently naturalized as a category and measured for the purposes of marketing. Turned around by both researchers and the lesbian and gay communities, the results of the marketing research are used to verify both the economic importance and the occupation of the categories gay and lesbian. This "discovery" of a new and powerful market niche, I argue, signals the coming to citizenship of those previously considered alien. While the purported wealth of the gay and lesbian community has laid the grounds for both acceptance and resentment within the larger community, it also brings up a series of issues regarding assimilation, diversity, and community. I conclude this chapter by discussing some of the consequences of figuring gays and lesbians as a powerful consumer block and the impact this has on expanding notions of citizenship and inclusion. However, before I turn to the surveys I will briefly describe other means of understanding citizenship, both to set the stage for my discussion of membership and to understand alternatives to an understanding of citizenship as participation in the market.

Conceptualizing Citizenship

Rooted in a history that pre-dates Aristole, the Western conception of citizenship is a term with multiple and contested meanings. Among these meanings are loyalty, obligation, participation, and membership. These meanings overlap and are interspersed with many cultural, psychological and legal understandings of belonging. This chapter is part of a larger project that examines how economic, psychological, social, and legal issues impinge on ideas of national membership and belonging for sexual aliens. While this chapter focuses on the market's role in lesbian and gay membership in the nation, my point is not that market relations wholly determine the grounds of citizenship. Nor am I trying to argue that homosexuals, as is especially evident in the case of white men, were disenfranchised prior to this historical moment. Instead, I seek to better understand how the market serves as a port of entry into national belonging.[6] Additionally, entry through the market is not entirely iniquitous; as Foucault (1980a) argues, within a capitalist society market relations are not only unavoidable, but constitutive. Further, as I will discuss later, this route has its benefits. However, we must be aware of how market bestowed membership operates and its possibilities and limitations for expanding and strengthening democratic citizenship.

T. H. Marshall is perhaps the best known and influential Post-War theorist to address the issue of citizenship in capitalist societies. Marshall (1964) conceives of citizenship as an historically expanding series of rights. He organizes these rights into three classes: *civil rights*, the "natural" rights of life, liberty, property, free expression, free association, and justice; *political rights*, the rights to participate in governing; and *social rights*, those substantive rights allowing one to participate fully in the society (access to education, economic and physical welfare and security). He traces these rights from their emergence in eighteenth-century England to their culmination in the British welfare state of the mid-twentieth century. Marshall's framework has been criticized by the New Right for its focus on "passive" or "private" citizenship, that is, an emphasis on entitlements rather than obligations, and by the Left for failing to account for the cultural differences and pluralism within modern democracies (Kymlicka and Norman, 1994). However, Marshall's outline still shapes the discussion of citizenship 50 years later.

Judith Shklar (1991) offers an alternative organization of citizenship. Shklar suggests four distinct meanings for citizenship. First, citizenship as nationality, as used in my opening paragraph. Second, ideal republican citizenship, characterized by a life lived in and for the public forum and the good of the community: the mythical citizenship of ancient Athens. Third, the good citizen, the person who participates in his or her community and upholds or betters community standards. Attending PTA and city council meetings, helping with the local youth or charity organization, or keeping a clean and well-kept yard can all come under the rubric of the good citizen. Shklar's fourth meaning, and her focus, is standing. Standing as a citizen means the right to participate in both the political and economic life of the country.

In this chapter, I use citizenship to refer to membership within the political and cultural community of the nation. This idea of citizenship as membership has many similarities to Shklar's (1991) concept of citizenship as standing. For Shklar, standing is represented by the legal and substantive rights to work and vote.

Citizenship as membership refers to the ability to enjoy participation in the political and cultural life of the nation as well as access to jobs and voting rights. I also draw on Bryan Turner (1992) who locates the emergence of membership in the revolutionary struggles against absolutism of the seventeenth and eighteenth century. These struggles sought to change subjects into citizens and define those who had the right and means to rule themselves.

A more recent articulation of citizenship reframes political participation in terms of access to market choices. Stemming from the New Right policies of the Reagan-Bush era and continuing under Clinton, this conception of citizenship is based on the "belief in the superiority of market forces as the basis of the production and allocation of goods and services in society" (King 1987: 17). In this formation access to and representation in the market signifies political representation and electoral clout. However, the citizen-as-consumer model of citizenship works to erode the social rights that Marshall (1964) first articulated half a century ago. By replacing the state with the market as provider of the basic necessities that enable full participation in the political and cultural life of the nation, New Right policies undermine the social rights that Marshall argues are crucial for a democracy. This erosion of social rights (e.g., the roll-back of social welfare programs) reshuffles the citizenship deck with the wealthiest emerging on top while the poor become further under-represented. If the market is the primary site of political participation, those most able to participate in the market are those most able to participate politically. This reshuffling raises a series of opportunities for an advancement in civil rights for some, in this case wealthy gays and lesbians, and a set of questions regarding assimilation, diversity, and community as certain sexual subjects acquire the status of citizens-as-members through market mechanisms.

Lesbians and gays are not the only groups for whom identity and membership are constructed in part through market mechanisms. The notion of Hispanic or Asian American markets are other examples of this constitution. Like gay and lesbian communities, these communities are incredibly diverse. National origin, religion, income, geographical distribution, class position, education levels, and moment of immigration are some of the historically and socially produced differences that constitute the diversity within these groups. Subsuming these differences under the mantle of pan-ethnicity has been politically useful in organizing resistance. However, the use of these terms, gay, lesbian, Hispanic, Asian American, and others, by marketers places these groups in an interesting, and I want to suggest, perilous position. While never having been void of a consuming element, marketers transform these terms of community into terms of consumption. These terms are not only descriptive of the historical relations between these groups and the dominant culture, but they are markers of the consumption patterns of some of the people within these groups. The differences and diversity, already difficult to fully appreciate within the political use of the pan-ethnic terms, become further eschewed by their use as a marketing category. The saliency of these terms as sites for organizing resistant or oppositional identities is challenged in the erasure of the diversity within the terms and the historical specificity to which the terms refers. However, these links between identities and the market are also available for resisting and contesting dominant or oppressive practices. Resistance through the market and commodities can be seen in the boycotts of lunch counters and buses in the Civil Rights movement, in the protests over drug prices by ACT UP and in Queer Nation's field trips to malls. Commodities can also operate as sites of stylistic opposition. Camp, for example, does this through simultaneously mocking and embracing dominant cultural symbols. Again the point is that subjectivity under systems of capital is always fraught because the market is simultaneously constitutive and destructive of identities and communities.

As John D'Emilio (1983) points out, connections between gays and lesbians and the market are not new. Twentieth-century capitalism, with its need for a mobile labor force, its undermining of the material necessity of the nuclear family, and its concentration of workers and warriors in urban areas, provided the circumstances under which gay communities could form. Gathering in urban areas throughout the country, but especially in major ports, homosexuals could meet, socialize, and form networks of relationships away from the expectations and watchful eyes of those back home. This was a luxury especially available to white middle-class males who had a greater degree of social and public mobility than women of all races, all people of color, and the poor. If, as D'Emilio argues, capitalism produced the relative freedoms and concentration of like desiring people that enabled lesbians and gays to perceive themselves as a community in the first place, then sexuality (as with race and gender) and capitalism in America are more deeply intertwined than is frequently acknowledged. The rise of lesbians and gays as target markets marks a new turn in this relationship that has important implications for the politics of sexuality.

Marx said, "a commodity...is in reality a very queer thing," (1995: 42) but I would like to point out that the queer has become a very commodified thing. Lesbians and gay men have become increasingly positioned within the popular imagination as affluent, white, childless, and well educated. Within the past few years, as lesbian and gay communities have been packaged by marketers and sold to advertisers, corporations, and others, gay and lesbian communities have become commodities or target markets. This is not to suggest that we should view target markets and communities as binary opposites (Freitas, Kaiser, and Hammidi 1996). Attempts to separate target markets and communities erase the links between community identity and economic factors. Further, obscuring the role of capitalism in the formation of the community positions target markets as groupings wholly manufactured and imposed from outside the community. As D'Emilio argues, the gay and lesbian community in the United States is in part a product of the organization of sexuality and labor under commodity capitalism. Just as the habits of capitalism shape gay and lesbian communities, the habits and recognition of lesbians and gays shape their representation as target markets. These representations work not only in economic terms but in cultural and political terms as well. In the current system of capitalism we are represented, or rather we come to matter, as citizens because we can consume.[7] Evans (1994) argues that markets are defined by their incorporation of "the norms and practices of advantaged groups" and by their devaluation of "the products and enterprises of identifiable minorities" (39–40). Does being targeted as a market by large companies move gays and lesbians from the status of sexual aliens, an "identifiable minority," to citizens in the capitalist state?

We must address the consequences of the conflation of the concepts of the consumer and the citizen and what it means for those who were once sexual aliens. Access to citizenship through the market means more and more positive portrayals of lesbians and gays in the media, more media outlets,[8] more representation in the political arena, greater recognition of needs and demands in the work place, and a continuing discussion of lesbian and gay families. Most lesbians and gays see these as positive steps towards the integration of gays and lesbians into the larger cultural and political system. Additionally, discrimination against gays and lesbians within the market would appear to be bad for business, thus our role as consumers may ensure us the same precarious job security as our heterosexual counterparts. Despite these gains on the fields of rights and access, we must also question the losses that occur in the discursive transformation of a community into a target market. What does it mean that the struggle for equal access to laws has come to mean equal access to consumer goods and services? While the new found clout and status that gay and lesbian communities appear to have gained are exhilarating, acceptance into the mainstream through market mechanisms comes at a cost.

Survey Says!

In this section, I examine the historical shifts that have created citizens of a capitalist state from performers of particular sexual acts. In the analysis below, I draw on Weeks's (1987), and Foucault's (1980a) discussions of the social construction of sexuality. Both Weeks (1989) and Foucault (1980a) argue that the "homosexual" is a construction of nineteenth-century medicine and law. Although coined in the late nineteenth century to define same-sex sexual acts, the term homosexual became fixed to an unchanging identity only in the early part of the twentieth century (Weeks 1989). Once this category was created, sexuality became not what you did, but who you were (Weeks 1987). In addition, Weeks (1987) and Foucault (1980a) describe how the link between behavior and identity came about through the pathologization and criminalization – the denaturalization – of certain acts. Acts deemed outside the norm performed the work of shoring up the periphery and establishing a better defined center. This pathologization and criminalization bolstered the "necessity" for the study and classification of deviancy. Even studies sympathetic to homosexual behavior couched their analyses in the language of deviancy, criminality, and pathology.[9] This in turn set the stage for studies such as Alfred Kinsey's ground breaking work of 1948 and 1953. While several sexologists had preceded him in the study of deviant sexuality, none had done so on such a large scope and scale.

In his research on sexuality, Kinsey (1948 and 1953) reported that roughly 13 percent of adult males and six percent of adult females engaged in or fantasized about sex with a member of the same sex more than half of the time they engaged in or fantasized about sex. These figures, based on extensive research with over 5,300 males and 5,490 females, are emblematic of the contestation over the meanings of such numbers. Kinsey went to pains in his original texts to point out that these numbers were demonstrative of behaviors rather than identities. Despite these efforts to keep identities and behaviors separate, the findings for men and women are frequently combined to give an overall rate of homosexual acts of ten percent. This ten percent figure quickly and tenaciously became a measure of how many homosexuals there are in a given population. Used for nearly 50 years by gay movements such as the homophile movement of the early 1960s, the Gay Liberation Front of the 1970s, and ACT UP and Queer Nation in the 1980s and 1990s, as an argument for political and cultural recognition, the ten percent figure has also been deployed by the McCarthyites of the 1950s, the Moral Majority of the 1970s and 1980s and the Religious Right of the 1990s.[10] Despite Kinsey's insistence that his findings be regarded in context, the ten percent figure has been bandied about as an unchanging fact for half a century in an attempt to both defend gays and lesbians as a sizable minority deserving of rights, or alternatively to bolster a sense of crisis relating to morality (e.g., homosexuals as child molesters, communists, and spies) by those trying to restrict sexual freedoms and impose particular moral standards on the nation.

The Kinsey Report remained the definitive accounting of homosexuality until 1993, when a survey of 3,321 men by the Battelle Human Affairs Research Center of Seattle, (Painton 1993) threw the results of the earlier study into question. In this survey, only 1 percent of men reported exclusive homosexual activity. This study, called rigorous by reporters, was announced in the press with titles such as *Time's* "The Shrinking Ten Percent" (Painton 1993). Heavily disputed by gay and lesbian rights advocates and much touted by the Religious Right the study came on the heels of the "Don't ask, don't tell, don't pursue" policy and in the midst of the biologization of sexuality (i.e., the "discovery" of the "gay" brain and "gay gene"). Unlike Kinsey, the authors of this study are less careful in distinguishing between sexual acts and sexual identities. In this study, as in the larger public discussions of sexuality, the sexual acts one performs define one's identity. This study takes as given the category gay and assumes that men who have sex with other men will self-identify as gay. However, the elision of sexual acts with identity is problematic. As several authors have pointed out, sex with a member of the same sex in many cultures, including cultures within the United States does not translate into identifying as a homosexual (Almaguer 1991; Magaña and Carrier 1991; Shapiro 1991).

This slippage between act and identity is evident in the ways in which gay and lesbian groups have formed a community of identity around what was once a category of deviant behavior, homosexuality. Once used to mark groups as deviant and then measure the extent of this deviancy, these surveys now define these groups' identities. Furthermore "gay" and "lesbian" have shifted from categories of perversity to an alternative social grouping, a means of measuring social and market demographics. The terms "gay" and "lesbian" decreasingly signify the sexual and instead indicate a certain lifestyle: where you live, shop, and vacation and what you read, eat, drink, and buy. An example of this is a 1993 study by the gay and lesbian market research group Overlooked Opinions (Gallagher 1993). This organization collected information from gays and lesbians by placing survey response cards in lesbian and gay newspapers and at community festivals. Among other findings, Overlooked Opinions reported that gays and lesbians make more than the average American ($42,689 for gay men, $36,072 for lesbians, $29,943 national median), are more likely to have a graduate degree (25 percent as compared to five percent), and vote overwhelmingly Democratic. Overlooked Opinions' results "depict gays and lesbians as yuppies, socially aware, highly educated, and financially well-off" (Gallagher 1993: 43). On the basis of the Overlooked Opinions and subsequent studies, newspapers and magazines have been touting the strength of a highly educated, wealthy, and brand loyal group with large amounts of disposable income and leisure time.

While this study may serve the purposes of the marketing firm in reaching those people most likely to buy, studies such as this are widely circulated, often by the researchers themselves (Gallagher 1993), as unbiased scientific surveys. However, the samples are rarely representative of the wider lesbian and gay population. For example, a recent survey that acknowledges not being representative, had findings similar to those of Overlooked Opinions. In this survey by Simmons Market Research Bureau for Mulryan/Nash, a gay-based advertising agency, respondents were recruited through a political organization, a credit card company, and a mail order company. Twenty-eight percent of respondents reported making over $50,000 and nearly 20 percent over $100,000 a year. This study, like earlier ones, was touted by the press as demonstrating the wealth of the gay community. However, this angle of coverage effectively obscures the diversity within the community. For example, the high incomes reported can in part be traced to the preponderance of men answering the survey: 71 percent. Men still make more money than women for the same job and professional and upper level managerial jobs are more likely to be held by men. The skewed gender representation of the survey is likely to be due to the sources from which the sample was drawn. While the race of respondents is not reported (and presumably it was not asked), it is likely that the sample was overwhelmingly white for reasons similar to why it was overwhelmingly male. Sexuality, like race, drops out of the survey. Rather, sexual identity, like whiteness, is assumed to be self-evident and uncontested. In both of these surveys we see a cementing of "gays" and "lesbians" as groups whose main attribute is not their desire for members of the same sex, but their habits of working, voting, and especially spending. In these surveys, sexual identity was not explicitly linked to questions of sexual behavior or desire. The sexual act drops almost entirely out of the picture.

In 1994, a survey by Yankelovich Partners Inc. (Elliot 1994; Tuller 1994), a highly reputable marketing research firm, found lesbian and gay incomes to be statistically insignificantly different from the incomes of the general population.[11] Additionally, the results from this survey reaffirm some of the consumption patterns described in earlier surveys while calling others into question. Most important, however, is the finding that nearly six percent of the sample identified as "gay/homosexual/lesbian." This figure's importance lies less in its position midway between the Kinsey and Battelle Human Affairs figures than in both its untroubled use of the social markers "gay/homosexual/lesbian" and its assumed veracity because it comes from a marketing research firm rather than a sexology study. As Watts Wader, a partner at Yankelovich, explained in the *New York Times*, "the company wanted to explore

the consumer behavior rather than the sexual behavior of homosexuals because 'this is a very viable market that many clients have
expressed an interest in knowing more about'" (Elliot 1994: D1).
Thus gay and lesbian communities, or rather certain depictions of
the communities, have become appealing market opportunities
for large and small corporations. The appeal of this market translates into attempts to attract gay and lesbian consumers through
advertisements in community publications and sponsorship of
community events. In turn, gays and lesbians respond to this
targeting with support for these corporations, seeing them as
allies in a struggle for equality.

For Love or Money

As discussed above, classification and survey techniques function
not only to quantify the deviant, but also qualify him/her; in other
words, to both enumerate and explain. Through these techniques,
homosexuals, and later lesbians and gays, are produced as marginal groups by institutional classification and measurement.
Importantly, these surveys work to organize desire into particular
identities. At the same time, they naturalize particular ways of
desiring both others and commodities. Surveys and other demographic techniques create norms that operate to contain and structure identity in knowable and understandable patterns. As I have
explained, gays and lesbians living within a capitalist system form
a sense of (deviant) identity around these categories and then are
drawn back into the mainstream culture, through capitalism, as
target markets. These target markets are culturally constructed
identities containing both market and community value. In the
process, the concepts of consumer and citizen merge (Evans 1994),
and access to markets and consumer goods begins to mean not
only visibility but also political and economic clout. Hence, it
becomes important to look at how the cultural, political and economic representations are mobilized into struggles over identity.

Drawing on these surveys, market researchers have determined
recently that gay and lesbian communities, and gay males specifically, have more discretionary income[12] than the population in
general (Schwartz 1992). Moreover, common estimates (using the
Kinsey figure) number this community at roughly 25 million
people. This is seen as a population that "consists of many

consumers who are affluent, highly educated, and brand loyal" (Solomon 1994: 309). Described as DINKs (double income, no kids), gay and lesbian households are seen as lucrative market resources. Accordingly, corporations have begun to develop products and advertising campaigns to attract these consumers. Some of these campaigns have explicitly gay or lesbian themes, such as advertisements depicting two men or two women embracing. Others employ what Danae Clark (1991) calls gay window advertising, using ambiguous images to attract gay and lesbian consumers without coding the advertisement in such a way as to exclude heterosexual readings as well. Famous for this strategy are Calvin Klein ads. For their part, firms such as Absolut and Stolichnaya vodkas, early advertisers in the gay press, run the same seemingly sexuality-neutral ads in both straight and gay venues (Solomon 1994; Kraft 1994). These latter two types of advertising tap into the economic capital of the market by using gay and lesbian cultural media as a conduit, without "labeling" the product through advertising imagery as being specific to the gay and lesbian market.

A 1994 Ikea advertisement represents a different version of these advertising strategies. Ikea, a Swedish furniture firm with stores in the United States, developed what is believed to be the first television commercial featuring a gay male couple as one of many diverse "lifestyle[s] and life-stages" (Gallagher 1994: 25) The commercial shows two affluent white – straight acting, straight appearing, but presumably gay – males shopping for a dining room table and, simultaneously, suggesting their gayness through expressions of commitment to one another. Ikea's advertising firm claims to have developed their inclusive campaign to appeal to consumers dubbed yuppie "wannabes": consumers who are moving up the economic ladder and have a sense of style, and live in double-income households with either no children or one child (Gallagher 1994; Span 1994). An ad like this works not only to include homosexuals within the buying public, but to domesticate and desexualize homosexuality in several ways: first, and most clearly, by having these men set up a home; second, by having them purchasing a table rather than a bed; and third, by making homosexuality not an historically shaped and socially organized identity, but a matter of one consumer style among many. In this ad, homosexuality becomes just another lifestyle with a matching dinette set. What is peculiar to gays and lesbians, specifically our sexuality and the history and social positions interlinked with it, disappears within these representations.[13] In these ads we are simultaneously different from and the same as everyone else.[14]

This loss of difference can also be seen in the numerous magazines now directed at gays and lesbians. There is a plethora of "lifestyle" magazines giving fashion, travel, and relationship tips but almost all of these have either never had or jettisoned any openly sexual content. For example, in an effort to both broaden readership and appeal to mainstream advertisers *The Advocate*, the oldest and most widely circulated gay magazine, removed its personals section and spun it off into another publication. Similarly, *Girlfriends*, a lesbian monthly started in 1993, now sends its centerfold only to subscribers and under separate cover. This loss of the difference that makes a difference registers not only in the media and products we consume, but as a melancholia or nostalgia for a gay culture perceived as more radical and distinctive. This is evident in the recent tenth anniversary celebrations for ACT UP and in Daniel Mendelsohn's (1996) article in *New York* magazine where he asks: "If you look straight, act straight and think straight, why bother being gay?" (25).[15]

The discussion of these advertisements brings us back to issues of representation in the market as a mark of citizenship. As Evans (1994) notes, the right to participate in the society and the right to consume are indistinguishable in contemporary life. The presence of advertisements is read as support for the community, resulting in the impulse to "cast a ballot" in the marketplace through a "pro-gay" product choice. Indeed, some corporations manage to create a space for themselves within gay and lesbian communities and, in some instances, gain reputations as supporters, based on sponsorship of events or charitable donations (e.g., Apple Computer and Visa sponsorship of the 1994 Gay Games). As the profit potential associated with the lesbian and gay communities' economic and political capital becomes more evident to marketers, these communities become more receptive to marketing advances. Yet, as happens in other minority communities, there is no guarantee that the money earned from the community will stay in the community. While all firms prioritize profits, those companies attracted to gay and lesbian consumers because of reportedly high incomes may have less of a stake in the community's viability than those emerging from or based in the community.

If the ultimate mark of citizenship in the 1980s was being a consumer, by the early 1990s it would seem the lesbian and gay communities had arrived. After cutting their teeth on the political and cultural struggles around the AIDS crisis and the conservative backlash of the 1980s, the reported large incomes and voting statistics for gays and lesbians gave a boost to the communities at a time when they were beginning to flex more political and economic muscle. Although the Yankelovich survey would appear to undermine the claims of the studies that found gays and lesbians to be extremely affluent, most marketers, newspapers and many lesbian and gay leaders used the Overlooked Opinions figures to tout the viability of the community as a market segment. At the same time, widely disseminated recent studies called into question the long-held belief that gays and lesbians make up ten percent of the population. This seeming decrease in numbers, combined with the reluctance of both marketers and many of the gay and lesbian community to refute gays and lesbians as the "the last billion dollar niche market" (Span 1994), provides ammunition for the Religious Right's characterization of lesbians and gays as moneyed elites in search of "special rights."[16]

There are ramifications of constructing gay and lesbian identity in "elite" terms. Increasingly it seems lesbians and gays are being likened to the Elders of Zion, or as Sarah Schulman, founder of Lesbian Avengers, has put it "God, we're starting to sound like Jews" (1995). Drawing here on the history of anti-Semitic vilification of Jews as a moneyed elite in control of cultural resources, yet demanding "special rights," Schulman is pointing to the precarious position in which the gay and lesbian movement is placing itself and being placed. The embracing of these market studies has the effect of eroding the ground from which the gay and lesbian rights movement can launch a struggle against structural discrimination.

According to the Religious Right, lesbians and gays have been doing better than the average American all along. Following this logic, rather than gays and lesbians meriting protection, it is heterosexual America that needs to be given additional means to compete with this "powerful minority." The danger in the construction of a homosexual "moneyed class" lies in its precarious positioning of gay and lesbian communities within the path of an ever-strengthening political backlash. Justice Scalia's use of this argument in his dissent to *Romer v. Evans* (1996), which struck down Colorado's Amendment 2, demonstrates how widely this logic circulates. In becoming a target market gays and lesbians as a group become a target of the anger of other disadvantaged groups, such as working- and lower middle-class heterosexuals. The elimination of secure life opportunities (e.g., education, work, home ownership, prestige) that have been perceived by much of white heterosexual America as a matter of course may lead to heterosexuals perceiving their position within the social hierarchy as slipping.

Because the organization of capitalism in our society has naturalized particular social relations and social privileges, it is likely to be difficult for anyone to recognize or effectively challenge the cause of this slippage. As Foucault (1979) and Harris (1993) point out, identities in general are so deeply organized and produced through structures of capital, that when these privileges are disrupted, those who had benefited see not the reorganization of a society formulated as a zero sum system, but rather an assault on their "natural rights." In other words, it is difficult to recognize this insecurity as stemming from advanced capitalism's search for cheaper sources of production and wealthier markets. Locating these origins within a system that is so naturalized disrupts notions of what is fair. Further, it undermines the naturalness of natural rights – liberty, equality, and justice – and threatens the individual's identity as the embodiment of opportunity. Capitalism and the social organization of identities produced through it are so thoroughly naturalized that any serious interrogation of these identities may threaten the challenger with, as Bartky (1988) says, "annihilation."[17] One of the manifestations of this anxiety is the accusation of "special rights." This accusation gives voice to the ideology that our culture is inherently fair and just and when those considered social inferiors begin to succeed and appear to displace those who historically have succeeded or become more visible, then the most available explanation is that the "inferiors" have been granted some sort of special privilege. This understanding can be seen in arguments against welfare, immigration, and affirmative action as well as in the charge of special rights.

Unfortunately, the characterization of gays and lesbians as a "moneyed elite" in search of special rights by conservatives is due in part to the dominant language of rights available to and used by gays and lesbians. By attempting to work within a more tradition civil rights model, the lesbian and gay movement has worked for inclusion into the mainstream. This inclusion takes many forms: domestic partner and marriage rights, custody and adoption rights, and the right to enlist in the military, among other demands. These demands, based on the liberal notion of the individual in a meritocracy, locate and resist state-held power. This political trajectory, however, is increasingly problematic and in need of critical reappraisal. In a post-Civil Rights era, when liberal protest is called into question by people on the right and the left, we need to reframe citizenship and belonging. We need to rethink what we mean by community. The representation of the gay and lesbian community, both in surveys of us and attacks on us, as white, childless, well educated, (upper) middle-class, (and male), quietly and economically erases the range of subject positions within these communities. While the characterization of gays as affluent and well educated may appear to some as a step in the direction of integration into the larger culture, it also works to deny the diversity existing within these communities. With this denial, certain modes of gayness become acceptable to the mainstream while other, less marketable, modes are (re-)marginalized.

The civil rights model that gays and lesbians have wielded for inclusion is based on the liberal notion of the individual as an autonomous, self-actualizing maker of rational choices. This formulation assumes an underlying core being and does not question the social production of identities (sexual, racial, national, class, and gendered). Identities are seen as layers imposed upon an essential core rather than as being fundamentally constitutive of the individual. This conception locates power outside the individual as something that operates on her or him. An example of this is the restrictive power of the state. Foucault (1980a, 1980b) points out that while the state is one site of power, it is the more subtle disciplinary power, with its ability to naturalize, that plays the primary role in the organization of social institutions and representations as well as personal identities and desires. Accepting a liberal argument for inclusion, while enabling some to get jobs and health care, does not allow for a critique of the extra-legal processes that produce these particular identities and social hierarchies in the first place. The discourse of the liberal individual forestalls a critique of the naturalizing forces that produce that very individual. As Marx points out in "On the Jewish Question" (1975), entry into the liberal political sphere requires the relinquishing of certain particularities. Wendy Brown (1995) in her explication of Marx addresses "the irony that rights sought by a politically defined *group* are conferred upon depoliticized *individuals*; at the moment a particular 'we' succeeds in obtaining rights, it loses its 'we-ness' and dissolves into individuals" (98, emphasis original). For both Marx and Brown, it is not the loss of "we-ness" that is at issue, for political emancipation is always partial and conflicting; rather, it is the "loss of a language to describe the character of domination, violation, or exploitation" (Brown 1995: 126) that is detrimental. The rootedness of citizenship in capitalism cuts short any examination of the market as a major force behind the organization of sexual identity.[18] Entry into the citizenry of capital comes at the price of being able to critique it. While this granting of citizenship may soothe the hurt of some, it only works to further exclude (and denaturalize) others who cannot consume as gays and lesbians do, or whose sexuality is not as easily marketable to the culture at large.

Finally, appeals to rights within a liberal framework truncate any notion of community and convert sexual identity from an economic, social, and historic formation to a matter of individual choice. The language of individual choice decontextualizes and trivializes socially produced desires (turning one's sexual desires into a rational choice) and links particular consumer choices with sexual desire. The language of individual choice narrows the possibilities for radical democratic alternatives such as those called for by Chantal Mouffe (1992, 1993) and Brown (1995). For the focus on the individual turns not only desire into an individual decision, but it also erases the structural elements of discrimination. Perceived as violations against or perpetrated by individuals, discriminatory acts are unlinked from their economic and social institutions and the state and cultural privileges granted to particular social and sexual arrangements.

Conclusion

As I have emphasized, sexual minorities must be very wary of the grounds upon which they are granted citizenship. As members of, and in alliance with other marginalized groups, gays and lesbians must interrogate available means and new possibilities for citizenship in American society. We cannot afford to totally eschew the language of liberalism, for this is the dominant discourse of rights today. As Brown (1995) points out, framing lesbian and gay appeals to universalism in the assertions of personhood against the Religious Right's charge of "special rights" positions these claims within a history of radical claims to personhood in the United States by white women and African Americans of both genders. In fighting for rights of inclusion however, we must, as Mouffe (1993) states, "reassert the view of citizenship as a system of rights constitutionally guaranteed for all members of a political community, and to affirm that these rights should not only be political but also social" (4). With this in mind, Mouffe is calling for a more radical and plural formulation of democratic citizenship than that posed by Marshall or the communitarians. Mouffe's conception of citizenship lies not only in the expansion of rights to those previously excluded, for ending here ignores the fact that existing rights have been and continue to be constituted on these very exclusions. Instead, she suggests that we need to reframe citizenship to encompass both the communitarian ideals of civic republicanism, working for what is good, and the liberal notions of liberty and freedom, what is right.

This combination, which she calls radical democratic citizenship, works by recognizing the integral links between our notions of right and our notions of the good; the individual who strives for freedom and liberty is only possible within the context of a society that has valued, worked, and been organized for this as a common goal (Taylor 1985). This form of citizenship represents a "common political identity of persons who might be engaged in many different purposive enterprises and with differing conceptions of the good, but who accept submission to the [commonly agreed upon rules] in seeking their satisfaction and in performing their actions. What binds them together is their common recognition of a set of ethico-political values" (Mouffe 1992: 235). This citizenship is not the primary identity of civic republicanism nor one identity among many as in liberalism. Rather, "it is an articulating principle that affects the different subject positions of the social agent ... while allowing for a plurality of specific allegiances and for the respect of individual liberty" (235).

We must push for an articulation of citizenship that accepts the social agent as an accumulation of subjectivities, discursively produced and always already at the intersections of those accumulations. Likewise, there must be a recognition of the social forces constituting these communities. A notion of citizenship has to enable gays and lesbians to struggle for membership within the national body without denying the social and material forces that constitute them as a group. Additionally, we need this citizenship to recognize the overlapping and intersecting subjectivities that we all embody while allowing a language of common struggle. Brown (1995) suggests replacing the identity fixing formulation "I am," with a recollection of the desire for collective good, "what I want for us" (75).[19] In calling for gays and lesbians to consider this formulation of citizenship, I do not intend to suggest that the enmity, rancor, hurt, and antagonism fostered between various groups in the zero-sum game between liberty and equality in liberal capitalism is easily wiped away, but rather to offer a means to begin challenging those relations of dominance and work for a common understanding of democratic participation.

NOTES

1   This work, like all single-authored works, would not have been possible without the insights, input and help from a number of people. I am especially indebted to Susan Kaiser and Tania Hammidi with whom I collaborated on an earlier paper (Freitas, Kaiser, and Hammidi 1996) that spawned many of the ideas for this paper. Additionally, I wish to express my gratitude to Elizabeth Crocker, Dione Espinoza, Valerie Hartouni, Corynne McSherry, and Alison Schapker who have helped me to think through the issues and arguments raised in this paper.

2   Ch. 447, 66 Stat. 163 (1952) (codified at 8 U.S.C. §§ 1101–1503 (1976 and Supp. II 1978)).

3   I use the term homosexual when referring to acts and identities formed around same-sex sex. I will use lesbian and gay when referring to individuals and communities of homosexuals who self-identify around issues of sexuality.

4   These sentiments can he seen in Bergler's 1956 book *Homosexuality: Disease or a Way of Life*, where he vilifies homosexuals as a threat to national security.

5   In fact, several homosexuals have heen granted political asylum in the US since the late 1980s (Burr 1996).

6   However, citizenship as membership is certainly more than purchasing power. The membership of gays and lesbians in the nation is predicated on a series of mutual recognitions between the gay and lesbian community and the larger culture. The campaign for military service

by gays and lesbians represents one site of struggle over membership in the nation. In addition to being a job training program and a means of escape from restrictive neighborhoods and families, the military is also an important location for the struggle of what it means to be a citizen. The soldier marks his or her citizenship in his or her willingness to die for the nation. Being willing to die for the nation is simultaneously a very selfless and a very selfish act. For in dying (or being willing to die) for your country, you are selflessly giving your life for the preservation of the nation and its aims. At the same time, however, you are also selfishly ensuring your place in the history of that nation. The demands by lesbians and gays for the right to serve symbolizes a struggle for inclusion or membership within the body and the history of the nation as homosexuals. I am indebted to Vicente Rafael for this insight.

7   Here I use "come to matter," drawing on Butler (1993), to mean both to become important (as in "it matters to me") and to come into being, to materialize or make real particular discourses or constructions.

8   One can't help but think of the enormous amount of media attention generated for and by the coming out of Ellen DeGeneres and her televison character Ellen Morgan.

9   For an overview of the history of scientific studies of homosexuality and homosexuals see Terry (1995)

10   Again, see Bergler (1956)

11   According to the findings, lesbians' mean household income was $34,800 while heterosexual women's was $34,400 and gay men's mean household income was $37,400 while heterosexual men's was $39,300 (Elliot 1994).

12   Although the studies found a wide disparity on gross incomes, both the Overlooked Opinions and Yankelovich surveys reported gays and lesbians to have higher discretionary incomes than heterosexuals (Gallagher 1994; Tuller 1994).

13   It is important to note that sexuality and desire are not being totally erased here. They are displaced from the couple onto the product as the commodity becomes fetishized – an object of desire.

14   This idea of "different but the same" is one of the underlying tenets of liberalism. Under liberal notions of rights, we are all distinctly individual but have equal rights. This has important ramifications in terms of law and the market. In anti-discrimination policies, as Brown (1995) points out, differences get piled together and divorced from their historical or social contexts. In the corporate world, as Gordon (1995) comments, difference is something employees bring with them as a skill to be tapped – a new market to access. In both cases the initial struggles for recognition of difference and protecting

those who are different from discrimination are washed away by equating all differences. Difference alone is not the reason for discrimination, rather, it is the social organization of and distribution of privileges based on particular differences. We are all different, but we are neither equally different nor different equally.

15 My chapter too is laced with a sense of nostalgia for what Mendelsohn calls "a once edgy subculture" (1996: 25).

16 This increase in attention from marketers also includes lesbian and gay marketers and market researchers. See, for example, Grant Lukenbill's *Untold Millions* (1995), Wardlow's *Gays, Lesbians, and Consumer Behavior* (1996) or publications such as *Victory! The National Gay Entrepreneur Magazine*.

17 This idea is drawn from Bartky's (1988) argument regarding the social production of femininity. "[A]ny potitical project that aims to dismantle the machinery that turns a female body into a feminine one may well be apprehended by a woman as something that threatens her with desexualization if not out right annihilation" (78).

18 This examination is not necessarily positioned between capitalism and socialism (although there are those aspects, notably in some segments of the lesbian-separatist movement and of ACT UP). Rather the interrogation extends to notions of hedonism and nonproductive expenditure and consumption. The goal in consumption may be tied more to the pleasure of consuming than a recuperation of labor (not that this is an either/or proposition). See Dyer "In Defense of Disco" (1990).

19 Brown is careful to point out that this is not the self-interested "I" of liberalism but an "I" desirous of an identity linked to a community.

REFERENCES

Almaguer, T. 1991. "Chicano men: A cartography of homosexual identity and behavior." *differences* 3, (2): 75–100.

Anderson, B. 1995. *Imagined Communities: Reflections on the Origin and Spread of Nationalism*. London: Verso.

Bartky, S. 1988. "Foucault, femininity, and the modernization of patriarchal power," in *Feminism and Foucault: Reflections on resistance*, I. Diamond and L. Quinby (eds) Boston, MA: North Eastern University Press, 61–86.

Bergler, E. 1956. *Homosexuality: Disease or Way of Life*. New York, NY: Wang Hill.

Brown, W. 1995. *States of Injury: Power and Freedom in Late Modernity*. Princeton, NJ: Princeton University Press.

Burr, C. 1996. "Gimme Shelter." *The Advocate*, July 23: 37–8.

Butler, J. 1993. *Bodies that Matter: On the Discursive Limits of "Sex."* New York, NY: Routledge.

Clark, D. 1991. "Commodity lesbianism." *Camera Obscura*, 25–6: 180–201.

D'Emilio, J. 1983. "Capitalism and gay identity," in *Powers of Desire: The Politics of Sexuality*, A. Snitow, C. Stansell, and S. Thompson (eds), Newyork, NY: Monthly Review Press, 100–13.

Dyer, R. 1990. "In defense of disco," in *On the Record: Rock, Pop and the Written Word*, S. Firth and A. Goodwin (eds), New York, NY: Pantheon Books, 410–18.

Elliot, S. 1994. "A sharper view of gay consumers." *New York Times*, June 9: D1.

Evans, D. 1994. *Sexual Citizenship: The Material Construction of Sexualities.* London: Routledge.

Foss, R. 1994. "The demise of the homosexual exclusion: new possibilities for gay and lesbian immigration." *Harvard Civil Rights and Civil Liberties Law Review* 29(2): 434–75.

Foucault, M. 1979. *Discipline and Punish: The Birth of the Prison*, trans. A. Sheridan. New York, NY: Vintage.

——. 1980a. *The History of Sexuality*, trans. R. Hurley. New York, NY: Vintage.

——. 1980b. "Two lectures," in *Power/Knowledge: Selected Interviews and Other Writings, 1972–1977*, C. Gordon (ed.) New York, NY: Pantheon, 78–108.

——. 1991. "Governmentality," in *The Foucault effect: Studies in governmentality*, G. Burchell, C. Gordon and P. Miller (eds), Chicago: University of Chicago Press, 87–104.

Freitas, A., S., Kaiser, and T. Hammidi. 1996. "Communities, commodities, space and style." *Journal of Homosexuality* 31(1/2): 83–107.

Gallagher, J. 1993. "Margin of error." *The Advocate*, April 20: 42–4.

——. 1994. "Ikea's gay gamble," *The Advocate*, May 3: 24–7.

Gordon, A. 1995. "The work of corporate culture: Diversity management." *Social Text* 44 13(3): 3–30.

Harris, C. 1993. "Whiteness as property." *Havard Law Review* 106(8): 1707–91.

King, D. 1987. *The New Right: Politics, Markets and Citizenship.* London: Macmillan Education.

Kinsey, A., W. Pomeroy, and C. Martin, 1948. *Sexual Behavior in the Human Male.* Philadelphia, PA: W. B. Saunders.

Kinsey, A., P. Gebhard, W. Pomeroy, and C. Martin. 1953. *Sexual Behavior in the Human Female.* Philadelphia, PA: W. B. Saunders.

Kraft, R. 1994. "Absolutely gay-friendly." *The Advocate*, April 5: 48–52.

Kymlicka, W. and W. Norman. 1994. "Return of the citizen: A survey of recent work on citizenship theory." *Ethics* 104, 352–81.

Lukenbill, G. 1995. *Untold Millions.* New York, NY: HarperCollins.

Magaña, J. and J. Carrier. 1991. "Mexican and Mexican American male sexual behavior and the spread of AIDS in California." *Journal of Sex Research* 28(3): 425–41.

Marshall, T. 1964. *Class, Citizenship, and Social Development.* New York, NY: Doubleday.

Marx, K. [1843] 1978. "On the Jewish question," in *The Marx-Engels Reader*, 2nd edn, New York, NY: Norton, 24–51.

——. [1867] 1995. *Capital: A New Abridgment.* Oxford: Oxford University Press.

Mendelsohn, D. 1996. "We're here! we're queer! let's go to coffee!" *New York*, Sept. 30: 25–31.

Mouffe, C. 1992. "Democratic politics today," in *Radical Democracy.* C. Mouffe (ed.). London: Verso, 1–16.

—— 1993. *Return of the Political.* London: Verso.

Painton, P. 1993. "The shrinking ten percent." *Time*, April 26: 27–9.

Romer v. Evans, USSC No. 94–1039.

Schulman, S. 1995. "Now for a word from our sponsor: The emergence of a gay management class and its impact on the print media." Lesbian/Gay/Queer Theory conference. La Jolla, CA, January 21.

Schwartz, J. 1992. "Gay consumers come out spending." *American Demographics*, April: 10–11.

Shapiro, J. 1991. "Transsexualism: Reflections on the persistence of gender and the mutability of sex," in *Body Guards*, J. Epstein and K. Straub (eds) New York, NY: Routledge, 248–79.

Shklar, J. 1991. *American Citizenship: The Quest for Inclusion.* Cambridge, MA: Harvard University Press.

Solomon, M. 1994. *Consumer Behavior: Buying, Having and Being.* Boston, MA: Ally & Bacon.

Span, P. 1994. "ISO the gay consumer." *Washington Post*, May 19: D1.

Taylor, C. 1985. *Philosophy and the Human Sciences.* Cambridge: Cambridge University Press.

Terry, J. 1995. "The seductive power of science in the making of deviant subjectivity," in *The Post Human body.* J. Halberstam and I. Livingston (eds), Bloomington, IN: Indiana University Press, 135–61.

Tuller, D. 1994. "Gays, lesbians listed as 6% of population." *San Francisco Chronicle*, June 10: A3.

Turner, B. 1992. "Outline of a theory of citizenship," in *Radical Democracy*, London: Verso, 33–62.

Wardlow, D. (ed.) 1996. *Gays, Lesbians, and Consumer Behavior: Theory, Practice, and Research Issues in Marketing.* New York, NY: Hawthorn Press.

Weeks, J. 1989. " Inverts, perverts, and Mary-Annes: Male prostitution and the regulation of homosexuality in England in the nineteenth and early twentieth centuries," in *Hidden from History: Reclaiming the Gay and Lesbian Past.* Vicinus and G. Chauncery Jr (eds), New York, NY: Meridian, 195–211.

——. 1987. "Questions of identity," in P. Caplan (ed.), *The Cultural Construction of Sexuality*, London: Tavistock, 31–51.

14

Afterthoughts

Judith A. Howard

There is a formula to the conclusion of an academic book. A conclusion, Webster's Thesaurus says, is supposed to "terminate, bring to an end, complete." It does so by "resolving, confirming, settling." Thus, often a conclusion summarizes the key arguments of a volume, at a minimum repeating the key themes. Preferably, a conclusion also highlights what valuable lessons have been learned. A conclusion might evaluate what goals were accomplished, and how, and which goals were not accomplished. In short, a conclusion is the final word. Such practices reflect the penchant for uniform conclusions, univocal positions.

Because these practices are anathema to our goals for this volume, writing a conclusion poses a particular challenge. Our emphasis on the multivocality and contextual embeddedness of interaction implies that different readers will have different observations of these chapters, taking away different lessons and forming different critiques. We hesitate to impose our particular readings of what one might learn from this volume, while at the same time feeling the need for some statement that encourages our readers to think back on each of these chapters and consider them in light of broader themes that transcend particular chapters. Conclusions do require the writer/editor to assume some responsibility for what has been delivered; in this spirit we offer these final remarks. We adopt the model of a conference discussant; as discussants do, we take some space here to revisit those questions we hoped to address with this volume and how we think these several chapters do and don't address these questions. We do not claim that any of the questions addressed here have been resolved or settled. Indeed, we are not sure resolution would ever be possible in the complex muddiness of human interaction.

What Did We Want to Do?

Exploration of the dynamics, maintenance, and subversion of patterns of domination and subordination is a vital contemporary social scientific agenda. In their much-cited 1987 article, "Doing Gender," Candace West and Donald Zimmerman argue that gender is a routine, methodical, recurring accomplishment; to be perceived as a competent member of society, they maintain, requires the successful performance of gender. In a more recent update, "Doing Difference," Candace West and Sarah Fenstermaker (1995) extend the logic of the earlier article to systems of race and class, developing an analysis of the accomplishment of difference through everyday interaction. This article was timely, appearing at a moment when many scholars were calling for recognition of multiple systems of oppression – consider the number of recent books and articles whose titles include the phrase "gender, race, and class." (The failure of most to mention sexuality was not an anomaly, but a persistent omission.)

Their analysis, however, did not go far enough. West and Fenstermaker themselves noted some needed next steps: (1) to specify precisely how the accomplishment of gender, race, and class link the institutional and the interactional; (2) to address more fully the dynamics of class inequality; (3) to translate these theoretical ideas into empirical research. We would add at least two more points. Although West and Fenstermaker argued for the need to analyze these systems simultaneously, as they are experienced, the very structure of their article belies this goal. Separate sections are titled "Gender," "Race," "Class." Distinctions between systems of hierarchy, in other words, are privileged over the dynamics of hierarchy themselves, in organizing the central themes of this piece.

Moreover, the article is titled "Doing Difference." Difference is posed as if it were a neutral concept. The social psychological literature (not to mention popular culture) demonstrates that it is rare, indeed perhaps nonexistent, to find differences – whether among individuals, groups, or societies – that are not also accompanied by differential evaluation. When we add power to the equation, as we must in any human system, we are dealing with intergroup domination and subordination. The semantic distinction between "difference" and "dominance" is not trivial. The doing of difference maintains the interactional supports for structures of domination.

In varying ways, the chapters we have collected in this volume each address these next steps. As a whole, they reveal the performance of gender, race, ethnicity, class, and sexuality in relationship to space, cultural and material resources, and the everyday dynamics of interaction. Each chapter offers empirical cases that foreground the ways in which these social positions intersect and are played out in everyday interactions; they gather together racialized, classed, sexualized, gendered moments and dynamics, necessarily complicating theorizing about such experiences. The arenas for these explorations range from the micro-level interactions of everyday social greetings through meso-level settings of television and marketing media, to the macro-level institution of the military. Forms of interaction vary from the face-to-face, to print, to televised, to virtual. Some of the chapters are presented from the perspective of those occupying primarily dominant social positions, others from the perspective of those occupying primarily subordinate social positions. Some recognize that given individuals enact both dominant and subordinate positions in their social relationships and situations. What all of these chapters share is an emphasis on how dominance and subordination are accomplished, sustained, and undermined through human interaction.

Thus our goals were to:

- Demonstrate empirically the performance of domination and subordination.
- Conceptualize experiences of domination and subordination across a range of significant dimensions of domination – gender, race, ethnicity, class, sexuality. The papers move toward explorations of the simultaneity of these experiences, rather than rely on a simple additive model.
- Reveal the workings of hierarchy, not just difference, in these empirical instances.
- Consider positions of both domination and subordination. Incorporating multiple perspectives on hierarchy allows these authors to reveal ruptures, subversions, subtle reorderings, as well as reinscriptions of already entrenched dynamics. They

also reveal how dynamics of domination and subordination work both across and within familiar group boundaries.

• Feature work that is itself often eclipsed by methodological hierarchies in the social and natural sciences. Neither social interaction nor social inequalities can be fully analyzed or understood with solely quantitative summaries, or without experiential, observational methods. Whereas much of the theoretical material in this area talks against a positivist tradition, the studies we include here are more in the line of the Chicago urban studies tradition, generating fine-grained grounded research and analyses of situated patterns of relationships.

What Are We Learning?

The Empirical

Every chapter in this volume offers empirical instances of the enactment of hierarchy and subordination. The televised exaggerations of heterosexual dating analyzed by Hollander reveal male privilege in defining the terms of sexual attraction and performance, in using physical space, in verbal sparring; they reveal heterosexual privilege in the very set-up of the show, *Studs*, as well as in the assumptions of all participants about who is and is not available as a sexual partner. The observations offered by the Latina and Arab American women interviewed by Lopez and Hasso reveal both white ethnic and US national privileges in the daily campus negotiations about class content, both white ethnic and male privilege in dating possibilities. Gerschick's interviews and other sources offer searing instances of the privileges of the able-bodied. Shockey's interviews reveal how economic and gender privilege shape the working conditions for women who do sex work. Eichstedt's analyses show how white artists are advantaged over ethnic artists in shaping what kinds of art projects are funded and who has access to the organizational sources of such funding. Both Freitas and Hartmann offer analyses that show how even intentionally subversive actions can be co-opted to perform and reinscribe domination, albeit in transformed ways. Freitas's analysis of queer communities suggests that they have become a marketing niche, attesting to an implicit recognition of citizenship, through commodification processes, among this highly stigmatized community. Hartmann analyzes the 1968 African American Olympic protest to show that sport can serve as a vehicle for racial–ethnic concerns, but also to shape such actions to conform with the highly individualized political agenda of US society, turning such protests away from more materialist forms of resistance. Kendall's participant observations of cyberspace interactions reveal not only male privilege, but also the apparent dependence of social interaction on gender; the mostly young white men with whom she virtually interacted insisted on gendering interactants, and often in more stereotypic ways than occur in face-to-face interaction. In taking up a situation in which actors do not see each other, a situation in which visual markers of hierarchy are invisible, Kendall offers a natural experiment. Can interaction be free of hierarchy? Her analysis suggests it can not.

Back to Webster: one definition of "empirical" reads "relying solely on practical experience and without regard for system or theory." Webster notwithstanding, we do not consider these contributions without regard to system or theory. Rather, we develop theories based upon these empirical instances, rather than the deductive opposite. Each of these, as well as the many other empirical instances of domination, subordination, and resistance found in these chapters, tells us that power is not simply imposed. Power is performed; it is *enacted*, in arenas ranging from everyday encounters to the organization of societal institutions such as the US military. Consistent with the methodological rationale of grounded theory, we theorize from examples, from the enactment of structural, personal positions. Through what routines of interaction are inequalities performed and potentially undermined? In varied ways through these diverse chapters, we provide many concrete examples of just how structural outcomes are socially constructed, and the political force of these processes of construction. Much of the social scientific research on social inequality has minimized the importance of everyday action. Here we articulate the importance of human agency in the construction, maintenance and subversion of inequalities.

Mutual/Simultaneous Constitutions

The social organizations of race, of gender, of class, of sexuality are closely interwoven in both structures and processes. These connections are embodied in individual experiences; each of us experiences our gendered, raced, classed, and sexual positions at one and the same time. Different positions are more or less salient in varying situations, but all are nonetheless present and part of the backdrop or foreground of everyday life. Indeed, the persistence of these systems of domination cannot be fully understood when these are addressed only as separate, distinct, institutions of domination and oppression.

How can we best conceptualize the experience of racial, gendered, classed, sexualized oppressions simultaneously, as they are experienced in material bodies and actual places? Each of these chapters illustrates a common methodological strategy: understanding the simultaneity of positions in these hierarchical systems is advanced by analyzing everyday action and experience, in other words, by looking at how people "do" dominance and subordination. These chapters communicate how all human actors, in one way or another, everyday, perform social relations of dominance and subordination. Because the simultaneity of actors' locations in different systems of domination may not be obvious, we offer several examples from these chapters. Gender hierarchy is prominent in the selections from Hollander and from Herbert. In "Doing *Studs*," however, Hollander also articulates dynamics of sexuality, of race, and of class, some more blatant, some only implicit, in the interactions that take place on this late-night game show. Contestants are marked not only by their gender – in this case, which locates them as studs or dates – but also by their race, evident in that there are virtually no multiple-race pairs, and in the few exceptions, the performer of the more powerful role, the stud, is a white male. They are marked also by their heterosexuality, or at least, by their heterosexual performance. Same-sex desire is not precisely invisible, however; jokes and asides reveal much anxiety about this unacknowledged sexual alternative.

Herbert's exploration of the struggles of military women to be both women and soldiers also traces how doing gender requires doing a particular sexuality. The complication in this context is that a competent gender performance directly contradicts a competent soldierly performance, and a competent soldierly performance raises questions about stigmatized sexuality. Pate's observations of the rituals of interactional acknowledgment reveal not only intricate balances of racial and gender positions, but also cross-racial contrasts in these rituals. African American men are far more likely to enact acknowledgments with each other than are those of other configurations of race/gender categories. Pate speculates that this behavior is a way of doing solidarity among these racially subordinated men. That this is much less true for African American women (and for men or women of other racial categories) may reflect women's generally greater wariness in public space, a sign again that race and gender hierarchies work together. Kowalski's analysis of interpretations of New Deal government-sponsored photography reveals yet other mutual constitutions among class, gender, and sexuality. Kowalski shows that the New Deal photographs, mostly of working-class men, can be seen as homoerotic in our current cultural and political milieux, a reading clearly not intended at the time of their production and initial interpretation.

Systems of Dominance

For several years there have been efforts to institutionalize a curriculum transformation program at the University of Washington, as at many college campuses over the past decade. Recent efforts have been directed toward promoting initiatives within departments. Accordingly, I proposed to the chair of the sociology department that we establish a curriculum transformation committee which would review courses and prepare packets of resources and information that would be available to all instructors for use as they see fit. The curriculum transformation committee viewed this as one step toward a more comprehensive goal of increasing recognition of the ways in which structural power inflects cultural differences. The chair's reaction was: "But we already do this. We don't need a program like that in sociology." This departmental chair, not unlike many other contemporary sociologists, sees curriculum transformation as being about cultural pluralism, that is, about the recognition of differences across different cultures both within and, more often, outside, the United States. Because he sees the curriculum as already pluralistic, he does not see the need for transformation. We and the other authors in this volume work instead with a model of structural hierarchy, of inequalities of power. Courses that teach about difference do not necessarily go on to reveal and analyze the hierarchies that underlie difference.

Each of these chapters underscores the fact that difference is not neutral, but instead marks boundaries of power. Consider the following:

- Filipina and Chicano students cannot get assistance from (even) a Nordstrom's clerk.
- To obtain funding, a woman has to publish three times as many papers in prestigious journals as a man, when applying for Swedish medical research grants.
- a male contestant on *Studs* says he prefers "airheaded" women.
- Carla (who works at Valley Vista Optical) says that her client, the married father of a young woman Carla also helps, has just attempted to french kiss her.
- A black woman student: "I do believe that the black community is the lowest person on the pyramid. And us acknowledging one another is rising us up. I acknowledge men more than women cos I believe that the black man has been brought down so low, that he needs to be pumped up."
- A male mud user says (on screen): "if you're nasty looking, CH [a woman], i'll just hand ya sperm in a petri dish."
- One military woman reports that "women were discouraged from being aggressive, displaying leadership skills, being self-assured and independent."
- A physically disabled man says "If I ever have to ask someone for help, it really makes me feel like less of a man. I don't like asking for help at all."
- A sex worker reports: "They'll [cops] do anything they want. They get their own kicks *and* they fill the city coffers. The fines we have to pay when we are entrapped by a police officer become a form of taxation."
- An Arab American woman, commenting on the fact that she has sex with her boyfriend: "Had I not slept with him, maybe I would not continue with him." Her major worry: "What man is going to take me, a non-virgin, in our society?"
- Analysis of a National Youth Administration photo: "In the mainstream, straight reading offered with the caption, the women are not dykes on bikes, but merely go-along girls and by implication, the boys safely straight."
- A high ranking white administrator for an art museum: "it's a very white board ... we've had them [Hispanics] here once and a farm worker is not going to do us any good, which is true, you know."

- Freitas, commenting on a survey of gay men and lesbians: "Sexuality, like race, drops out of the survey. Rather, sexual identity, like whiteness, is assumed to be self-evident and uncontested."
- Commentary by a staff writer in the *Chicago American*: "Protesting and working constructively against racism in the US is one thing, but airing one's dirty clothing before the entire world during a fun-and-games tournament was no more than a juvenile gesture by a couple of athletes who should have known better."

These voices speak eloquently of power, of inequality. It is not that women are constructed as different from men, that some people are constructed as having color, others as without color, that same-sex and opposite-sex desire have different targets; it is that being male, being white, having money and "class", desiring people of the opposite sex, are constructed as normal, are associated with every possible form of privilege. Indeed, even the ways in which one's differences are marked or not marked is a manifestation of privilege. These privileges are enacted in all social interactional arenas.

Dominance, Subordination, and Resistance

A few of the chapters in this volume reveal the often complicated inconsistencies of power – that many people enact both privilege and subordination. Lopez and Hasso offer some examples of these complexities. They note that the Arab American women they interviewed did not feel distanced from their families and communities on the basis of their education or upward mobility, as the Chicanas did. Indeed, one Arab American woman observed: "In fact, I feel like there's actually great expectation on me to at least equal or surpass it [her parents' education] ... if anybody is feeling intellectual inferiority, it's me not them." At the same time, these same women express feelings of rejection on the basis of their national origins, their ethnicity, and their gender.

Twine identifies ways in which white women negotiate the intricacies of mothering their children of color. Vivian describes how as a white woman, her domestic skills are perceived as inadequate by her Afro-Caribbean extended family. Valerie describes how she relies on her Afro-Caribbean friends to help her daughter deal with experiences of racism. Ashley notes that her in-laws treat her as if she doesn't know how to do a number of domestic and parenting tasks correctly; for these women, to cite Twine, their whiteness is a source of anxiety, not only, as most whites experience it (albeit often not consciously), a source of privilege. Both pieces raise important questions: under what circumstances does the simultaneous experience of both the privileges of domination and the costs of subordination enlighten and under what circumstances does it blind? When does this promote and when does this hinder socially progressive agendas?

When positions are dominant and when they are subordinate is sometimes a complicated question. Shockey reveals conflicts between hegemonic definitions of status and the perceptions of some of the sex workers she interviews: Debbie says "I do have choices ... the highest-class form of prostitution. The kind where you make your own choices ... *You* decide who, when, what, where, and how." Shockey writes of this woman: "Included among these benefits [Debbie derives from sex work] is an enhanced self-concept, one that is both reinforced by and reflected in the appraisals she receives through her chosen work." Van Leuven observes that the women who work at Valley Vista Optical, while in one sense captive audiences for their clients' sexual innuendos, also earn commissions on sales; they use their sexuality to secure those commissions. Comparing their sexy outfits one day, Terri says: "Looks like we're gonna sell a lot today girls." Both the workers at this optical shop and these Quad City sex workers clearly feel power in their use of sexuality.

Given that the hegemonic values of US society reject the exchange of sexuality for money as immoral and generally stigmatize those who engage in these practices, the power these women feel in their sexuality points to the seeds of resistance. When Erica, a white woman pregnant with the child of her black male lover, tells her mother she must either cut herself off from her daughter and her grandchild, or come to terms with her own prejudice, Erica resists the prevailing systems of power. The studies presented in this volume demonstrate the merits of studying social inequalities so that we can better comprehend the systematic character of injustices. Many of these studies point beyond understanding to include possibilities for subversion, for social change. As we end this commentary, we turn our political lens on the practice in which most readers of this volume are engaged: the production of knowledge through education. How can we apply these lessons to perform our own resistances, our own subversions? Different readers will answer this question in different ways, but we propose that one vital strategy is through our teaching. Through our own careful observations, through asking our own questions, through teaching about our processes of inquiry, we can encourage others to ask their own questions, to explore their own ways of further plumbing the depths of social inequalities and injustices, and to develop their own means of effective resistance.

REFERENCES

West, Candace and Don H. Zimmerman. 1987. "Doing gender." *Gender & Society* 1(2): 125–51.
West, Candace and Sarah Fenstermaker. 1995. "Doing difference." *Gender & Society* 9(1): 8–37.

Index

Page references in italics indicate plates.